Presented to:

_____

Presented by:

_____

Date:

_____

From home to home and heart to heart, from one place to another,
the warmth and joy of Christmas brings us closer to each other.

The Greatest Christmas Stories of All Time:
Timeless Christmas Classics That Celebrate the Season

Copyright © 2006 Bordon Books
Published by Standard Publishing, Cincinnati, Ohio. A division of Standex International
Corporation. All rights reserved under International Copyright Law. Contents and/or
cover may not be reproduced in whole or in part in any form without the express written
consent of the Publisher.

Printed in China.

Product developed by Bordon Books, Tulsa, Oklahoma.
Manuscript compiled by Patricia Lutherbeck and Sheila Seifert in association with
SnapdragonGroup^sm Editorial Services, Tulsa, Oklahoma.
Cover Design by Greg Jackson, Thinkpen Design.

All Scripture quotations, unless otherwise indicated, are taken from the *Holy Bible, New
International Version®*. Copyright© 1973, 1978, 1984 by International Bible Society. Used
by permission of Zondervan. All rights reserved.

Scripture quotations marked MSG are taken from *The Message*. Copyright © by Eugene
H. Peterson, 1993, 1994, 1995, 1996, 2000, 2001, 2002. Used by permission of NavPress
Publishing Group.

Joseph's Letter Home. Dr. Ralph F. Wilson. Used by permission of the author.

The Quiet Little Woman © 2002 by Stephen W. Hines. *Louisa May Alcott's Christmas Treasury*. Used with permission by Cook Communications Ministries. To order,
www.cookministries.com <http://www.cookministries.com/>. All rights reserved.

The compiler has sought to locate and secure permission for the inclusion of all copy-
righted material in this book. If any such acknowledgments have been inadvertently
omitted, the compiler and publisher would appreciate receiving the information so that
proper credit may be given in future editions.

ISBN: 0-7847-1953-5

13 12 11 10 09 08 07   9 8 7 6 5 4 3 2 1

THE
GREATEST
CHRISTMAS
STORIES
OF ALL TIME

TIMELESS CHRISTMAS CLASSICS
THAT CELEBRATE THE SEASON

PUBLISHING
Bringing The Word to Life™

Cincinnati, Ohio

God grant you the light in Christmas, which is faith;
the warmth of Christmas, which is love;
the radiance of Christmas, which is purity;
the righteousness of Christmas, which is justice;
the belief in Christmas, which is truth;
and all of Christmas, which is Christ.

WILDA ENGLISH

INTRODUCTION

Christmas is like no other time of the year. Families gather for joyous reunions. Tall, green fir trees grace the windows of almost every home; lights twinkle from rooftops and front yards; and excited shoppers fill every store looking for the perfect gift. It's a time when traditions are honored and stories are told. No wonder so many call it "the most wonderful time of the year."

The Greatest Christmas Stories of All Time is a Christmas wonder. It brings together those familiar tales—the ones we have heard for as long as we can remember and some less familiar stories—also able to tickle your funny bone and tug at your heart strings. First and foremost, it presents the amazing story of the events surrounding Christ's birth, for it is Bethlehem's Child who has given us reason for our celebration.

We hope that these stories will create tender moments, the sound of laughter, and even more treasured memories as you read them together this Christmas season.

CONTENTS

The simple shepherds heard the voice of an angel
and found their Lamb;
the wise men saw the light of a star
and found their Wisdom.

ARCHBISHOP FULTON J. SHEEN

The Greatest Story Ever Told

Perhaps the hardest thing to remember about Christmas is this. "It celebrates the incarnation, not just the nativity. The incarnation is an on-going process of salvation, while the nativity is the once-and-for-all historical event of Bethlehem. We do not really celebrate Christ's "birthday," remembering something that happened long ago. We celebrate the amazing fact of the incarnation—God entering our world so thoroughly that nothing has been the same since. And God continues to become flesh in our midst, in the men and women who make up His body—the church. The birth we celebrate is not just an historical event, but Christ's continuing birth in the members of His body.

These are words to remember as the story of that remarkable event is told. As you read, imagine how His story—His coming—has touched all the corners of your life!

THE BIRTH OF THE CHRIST CHILD
Luke 1:1–2:40 MSG

So many others have tried their hand at putting together a story of the wonderful harvest of Scripture and history that took place among us, using reports handed down by the original eyewitnesses who served this Word with their very lives. Since I have investigated all the reports in close detail, starting from the story's beginning, I decided to write it all out for you, most honorable Theophilus, so you can know beyond the shadow of a doubt the reliability of what you were taught.

A Childless Couple Conceives

During the rule of Herod, King of Judea, there was a priest assigned service in the regiment of Abijah. His name was Zachariah. His wife was descended from the daughters of Aaron. Her name was Elizabeth. Together they lived honorably before God, careful in keeping to the ways of the commandments and enjoying a clear conscience before God. But they were childless because Elizabeth could never conceive, and now they were quite old.

It so happened that as Zachariah was carrying out his priestly duties before God, working the shift assigned to his regiment, it came his one turn in life to enter the sanctuary of God and burn incense. The congregation was gathered and praying outside the Temple at the hour of the incense offering. Unannounced, an angel of God appeared just to the right of the altar of incense. Zachariah was paralyzed in fear.

But the angel reassured him, "Don't fear, Zachariah. Your prayer has been heard. Elizabeth, your wife, will bear a son by you. You are to name him John. You're going to leap like a gazelle for joy, and not only you—many will delight in his birth. He'll achieve great stature with God.

"He'll drink neither wine nor beer. He'll be filled with the Holy Spirit from the moment he leaves his mother's womb. He will turn many sons and daughters of Israel back to their God. He will herald God's arrival in the style and strength of Elijah, soften the hearts of parents to children, and kindle devout understanding among hardened skeptics—he'll get the people ready for God."

Zachariah said to the angel, "Do you expect me to believe this? I'm an old man and my wife is an old woman."

But the angel said, "I am Gabriel, the sentinel of God, sent especially to bring you this glad news. But because you won't believe me, you'll be unable to say a word until the day of your son's birth. Every word I've spoken to you will come true on time—God's time."

Meanwhile, the congregation waiting for Zachariah was getting restless, wondering what was keeping him so long in the sanctuary. When he came out and couldn't speak, they knew he had seen a vision. He continued speechless and had to use sign language with the people.

When the course of his priestly assignment was completed, he went back home. It wasn't long before his wife, Elizabeth, conceived. She went off by herself for five months, relishing her pregnancy. "So, this is how God acts to remedy my unfortunate condition!" she said.

A Virgin Conceives

In the sixth month of Elizabeth's pregnancy, God sent the angel Gabriel to the Galilean village of Nazareth to a virgin engaged to be married to a man descended from David. His name was Joseph, and the virgin's name, Mary. Upon entering, Gabriel greeted her:

> "Good morning!
> You're beautiful with God's beauty,
> Beautiful inside and out!
> God be with you."

She was thoroughly shaken, wondering what was behind a greeting like that. But the angel assured her, "Mary, you have nothing to fear. God has a surprise for you: You will become pregnant and give birth to a son and call his name Jesus.

He will be great,
be called 'Son of the Highest.'
The Lord God will give him
the throne of his father David;
He will rule Jacob's house forever—
no end, ever, to his kingdom."

Mary said to the angel, "But how? I've never slept with a man."
The angel answered,

"The Holy Spirit will come upon you,
the power of the Highest hover over you;
Therefore, the child you bring to birth
will be called Holy, Son of God.

"And did you know that your cousin Elizabeth conceived a son, old as she is?
Everyone called her barren, and here she is six months pregnant! Nothing, you
see, is impossible with God."

And Mary said,

"Yes, I see it all now:
I'm the Lord's maid, ready to serve.
Let it be with me
just as you say."

Then the angel left her.

Blessed Among Women

Mary didn't waste a minute. She got up and traveled to a town in Judah
in the hill country, straight to Zachariah's house, and greeted Elizabeth. When
Elizabeth heard Mary's greeting, the baby in her womb leaped. She was filled
with the Holy Spirit, and sang out exuberantly,

"You're so blessed among women,
and the babe in your womb, also blessed!
And why am I so blessed that
the mother of my Lord visits me?
The moment the sound of your
greeting entered my ears,

> The babe in my womb
> sskipped like a lamb for sheer joy.
> Blessed woman, who believed what God said,
> believed every word would come true!"

And Mary said,

> "I'm bursting with God-news;
> I'm dancing the song of my Savior God.
> God took one good look at me, and look what happened—
> I'm the most fortunate woman on earth!
> What God has done for me will never be forgotten,
> the God whose very name is holy, set apart from all others.
> His mercy flows in wave after wave
> on those who are in awe before him.
> He bared his arm and showed his strength,
> scattered the bluffing braggarts.
> He knocked tyrants off their high horses,
> pulled victims out of the mud.
> The starving poor sat down to a banquet;
> the callous rich were left out in the cold.
> He embraced his chosen child, Israel;
> he remembered and piled on the mercies, piled them high.
> It's exactly what he promised,
> beginning with Abraham and right up to now."

Mary stayed with Elizabeth for three months and then went back to her own home.

The Birth of John

When Elizabeth was full-term in her pregnancy, she bore a son. Her neighbors and relatives, seeing that God had overwhelmed her with mercy, celebrated with her.

On the eighth day, they came to circumcise the child and were calling him Zachariah after his father. But his mother intervened: "No. He is to be called John."

"But," they said, "no one in your family is named that." They used sign language to ask Zachariah what he wanted him named.

Asking for a tablet, Zachariah wrote, "His name is to be John." That took everyone by surprise. Surprise followed surprise—Zachariah's mouth was now open, his tongue loose, and he was talking, praising God!

A deep, reverential fear settled over the neighborhood, and in all that Judean hill country people talked about nothing else. Everyone who heard about it took it to heart, wondering, "What will become of this child? Clearly, God has his hand in this."

Then Zachariah was filled with the Holy Spirit and prophesied,

> "Blessed be the Lord, the God of Israel;
>   he came and set his people free.
> He set the power of salvation in the center of our lives,
>   and in the very house of David his servant,
>   Just as he promised long ago
>   through the preaching of his holy prophets:
>   Deliverance from our enemies
>   and every hateful hand;
>   Mercy to our fathers,
>   as he remembers to do what he said he'd do,
>   What he swore to our father Abraham—
>   a clean rescue from the enemy camp,
> So we can worship him without a care in the world,
>   made holy before him as long as we live.

> "And you, my child, 'Prophet of the Highest,'
>   will go ahead of the Master to prepare his ways,
>   Present the offer of salvation to his people,
>   the forgiveness of their sins.
>   Through the heartfelt mercies of our God,
>   God's Sunrise will break in upon us,
>   Shining on those in the darkness,
>   those sitting in the shadow of death,
>   Then showing us the way, one foot at a time,
>   down the path of peace."

The child grew up, healthy and spirited. He lived out in the desert until the day he made his prophetic debut in Israel.

The Birth of Jesus

About that time Caesar Augustus ordered a census to be taken throughout the Empire. This was the first census when Quirinius was governor of Syria. Everyone had to travel to his own ancestral hometown to be accounted for. So Joseph went from the Galilean town of Nazareth up to Bethlehem in Judah, David's town, for the census. As a descendant of David, he had to go there. He went with Mary, his fiancée, who was pregnant.

While they were there, the time came for her to give birth. She gave birth to a son, her firstborn. She wrapped him in a blanket and laid him in a manger, because there was no room in the hostel.

An Event for Everyone

There were sheepherders camping in the neighborhood. They had set night watches over their sheep. Suddenly, God's angel stood among them and God's glory blazed around them. They were terrified. The angel said, "Don't be afraid. I'm here to announce a great and joyful event that is meant for everybody, worldwide: A Savior has just been born in David's town, a Savior who is Messiah and Master. This is what you're to look for: a baby wrapped in a blanket and lying in a manger."

At once the angel was joined by a huge angelic choir singing God's praises:

"Glory to God in the heavenly heights,
Peace to all men and women on earth who please him."

As the angel choir withdrew into heaven, the sheepherders talked it over. "Let's get over to Bethlehem as fast as we can and see for ourselves what God has revealed to us." They left, running, and found Mary and Joseph, and the baby lying in the manger. Seeing was believing. They told everyone they met what the angels had said about this child. All who heard the sheepherders were impressed.

Mary kept all these things to herself, holding them dear, deep within herself. The sheepherders returned and let loose, glorifying and praising God for everything they had heard and seen. It turned out exactly the way they'd been told!

Blessings

When the eighth day arrived, the day of circumcision, the child was named Jesus, the name given by the angel before he was conceived.

Then when the days stipulated by Moses for purification were complete, they took him up to Jerusalem to offer him to God as commanded in God's Law: "Every male who opens the womb shall be a holy offering to God," and also to sacrifice the "pair of doves or two young pigeons" prescribed in God's Law.

In Jerusalem at the time, there was a man, Simeon by name, a good man, a man who lived in the prayerful expectancy of help for Israel. And the Holy Spirit was on him. The Holy Spirit had shown him that he would see the Messiah of God before he died. Led by the Spirit, he entered the Temple. As the parents of the child Jesus brought him in to carry out the rituals of the Law, Simeon took him into his arms and blessed God:

> "God, you can now release your servant;
> release me in peace as you promised.
> With my own eyes I've seen your salvation;
> it's now out in the open for everyone to see:
> A God-revealing light to the non-Jewish nations,
> and of glory for your people Israel."

Jesus' father and mother were speechless with surprise at these words. Simeon went on to bless them, and said to Mary his mother,

> "This child marks both the failure and
> the recovery of many in Israel,
> A figure misunderstood and contradicted—
> the pain of a sword-thrust through you—
> But the rejection will force honesty,
> as God reveals who they really are."

Anna the prophetess was also there, a daughter of Phanuel from the tribe of Asher. She was by now a very old woman. She had been married seven years and a widow for eighty-four. She never left the Temple area, worshiping night and day with her fastings and prayers. At the very time Simeon was praying, she showed up, broke into an anthem of praise to God, and talked about the child to all who were waiting expectantly for the freeing of Jerusalem.

When they finished everything required by God in the Law, they returned to Galilee and their own town, Nazareth. There the child grew strong in body and wise in spirit. And the grace of God was on him.

The Gift of the Magi

O. Henry

One dollar and eighty-seven cents. That was all. And sixty cents of it was in pennies. Pennies saved one and two at a time by bulldozing the grocer and the vegetable man and the butcher until one's cheeks burned with the silent imputation of parsimony that such close dealing implied. Three times Della counted it. One dollar and eighty-seven cents. And the next day would be Christmas.

There was clearly nothing to do but flop down on the shabby little couch and howl. So Della did it. Which instigates the moral reflection that life is made up of sobs, sniffles, and smiles, with sniffles predominating.

While the mistress of the home is gradually subsiding from the first stage to the second, take a look at the home. A furnished flat at $8 per week. It did not exactly beggar description, but it certainly had that word on the lookout for the mendicancy squad.

In the vestibule below was a letter box into which no letter would go, and an electric button from which no mortal finger could coax a ring. Also appertaining thereunto was a card bearing the name "Mr. James Dillingham Young."

The "Dillingham" had been flung to the breeze during a former period of prosperity when its possessor was being paid $30 per week. Now, when the income was shrunk to $20, though, they were thinking seriously of contracting to a modest and unassuming D. But whenever Mr. James Dillingham Young came home and reached his flat above, he was called "Jim" and greatly hugged by Mrs. James Dillingham Young, already introduced to you as Della. Which is all very good.

Della finished her cry and attended to her cheeks with the powder rag. She stood by the window and looked out dully at a gray cat walking a gray fence in a gray backyard. Tomorrow would be Christmas Day, and she had only $1.87 with which to buy Jim a present. She had been saving every penny she could for months, with this result. Twenty dollars a week doesn't go far. Expenses had been greater than she had calculated. They always are. Only $1.87 to buy a present for Jim. Her Jim. Many a happy hour she had spent planning for something nice for him. Something fine and rare and sterling—something just a little bit near to being worthy of the honor of being owned by Jim.

There was a pier glass between the windows of the room. Perhaps you have seen a pier glass in an $8 flat. A very thin and very agile person may, by observing his reflection in a rapid sequence of longitudinal strips, obtain a fairly accurate conception of his looks. Della, being slender, had mastered the art.

Suddenly she whirled from the window and stood before the glass. Her eyes were shining brilliantly, but her face had lost its color within twenty seconds. Rapidly she pulled down her hair and let it fall to its full length.

Now, there were two possessions of the James Dillingham Youngs in which they both took a mighty pride. One was Jim's gold watch that had been his father's and his grandfather's. The other was Della's hair. Had the queen of Sheba lived in the flat across the airshaft, Della would have let her hair hang out the window some day to dry just to depreciate Her Majesty's jewels and gifts. Had King Solomon been the janitor, with all his treasures piled up in the basement, Jim would have pulled out his watch every time he passed, just to see him pluck at his beard from envy.

So now Della's beautiful hair fell about her rippling and shining like a cascade of brown waters. It reached below her knee and made itself almost a garment for her. And then she did it up again nervously and quickly. Once she faltered for a minute and stood still while a tear or two splashed on the worn red carpet.

On went her old brown jacket; on went her old brown hat. With a whirl of skirts and with the brilliant sparkle still in her eyes, she fluttered out the door and down the stairs to the street.

Where she stopped the sign read: "Mme. Sofronie. Hair Goods of All Kinds." One flight up Della ran, and collected herself, panting. Madame, large, too white, chilly, hardly looked the "Sofronie."

"Will you buy my hair?" asked Della.

"I buy hair," said Madame. "Take yer hat off and let's have a sight at the looks of it."

Down rippled the brown cascade.

"Twenty dollars," said Madame, lifting the mass with a practiced hand.

"Give it to me quick," said Della.

Oh, and the next two hours tripped by on rosy wings. Forget the hashed metaphor. She was ransacking the stores for Jim's present.

She found it at last. It surely had been made for Jim and no one else. There was no other like it in any of the stores, and she had turned all of them inside out. It was a platinum fob chain simple and chaste in design, properly proclaiming its value by substance alone and not by meretricious ornamentation—as all good things should do. It was even worthy of The Watch. As soon as she saw it she knew that it must be Jim's. It was like him. Quietness and value—the description applied to both. Twenty-one dollars they took from her for it, and she hurried home with the 87 cents. With that chain on his watch Jim might be properly anxious about the time in any company. Grand as the watch was, he sometimes looked at it on the sly on account of the old leather strap that he used in place of a chain.

When Della reached home her intoxication gave way a little to prudence and reason. She got out her curling irons and lighted the gas and went to work repairing the ravages made by generosity added to love. Which is always a tremendous task, dear friends—a mammoth task.

Within forty minutes her head was covered with tiny, close-lying curls that made her look wonderfully like a truant schoolboy. She looked at her reflection in the mirror long, carefully, and critically.

"If Jim doesn't kill me," she said to herself, "before he takes a second look at me, he'll say I look like a Coney Island chorus girl. But what could I do-oh! what could I do with a dollar and eighty-seven cents?"

At seven o'clock the coffee was made and the frying pan was on the back of the stove hot and ready to cook the chops.

Jim was never late. Della doubled the fob chain in her hand and sat on the corner of the table near the door that he always entered. Then she heard his step on the stair away down on the first flight, and she turned white for just a moment. She had a habit for saying little silent prayers about the simplest everyday things, and now she whispered: "Please God, make him think I am still pretty."

The door opened and Jim stepped in and closed it. He looked thin and very serious. Poor fellow, he was only twenty-two—and to be burdened with a family! He needed a new overcoat and he was without gloves.

Jim stopped inside the door, as immovable as a setter at the scent of quail. His eyes were fixed upon Della, and there was an expression in them that she could not read, and it terrified her. It was not anger, nor surprise, nor disapproval, nor horror, nor any of the sentiments that she had been prepared for. He simply stared at her fixedly with that peculiar expression on his face.

Della wriggled off the table and went for him.

"Jim, darling," she cried, "don't look at me that way. I had my hair cut off and sold because I couldn't have lived through Christmas without giving you a present. It'll grow out again—you won't mind, will you? I just had to do it. My hair grows awfully fast. Say 'Merry Christmas!' Jim, and let's be happy. You don't know what a nice—what a beautiful, nice gift I've got for you."

"You've cut off your hair?" asked Jim, laboriously, as if he had not arrived at that patent fact yet even after the hardest mental labor.

"Cut it off and sold it," said Della. "Don't you like me just as well, anyhow? I'm me without my hair, ain't I?"

Jim looked about the room curiously.

"You say your hair is gone?" he said, with an air almost of idiocy.

"You needn't look for it," said Della. "It's sold, I tell you—sold and gone, too. It's Christmas Eve, boy. Be good to me, for it went for you. Maybe the hairs of my head were numbered," she went on with sudden serious sweetness, "but nobody could ever count my love for you. Shall I put the chops on, Jim?"

Out of his trance Jim seemed quickly to wake. He enfolded his Della. For ten seconds let us regard with discreet scrutiny some inconsequential object in the other direction. Eight dollars a week or a million a year—what is the difference? A mathematician or a wit would give you the wrong answer. The magi brought valuable gifts, but that was not among them. This dark assertion will be illuminated later on.

Jim drew a package from his overcoat pocket and threw it upon the table.

"Don't make any mistake, Dell," he said, "about me. I don't think there's anything in the way of a haircut or a shave or a shampoo that could make me like my girl any less. But if you'll unwrap that package you may see why you had me going a while at first."

White fingers and nimble tore at the string and paper. And then an ecstatic scream of joy; and then, alas! a quick feminine change to hysterical tears and wails, necessitating the immediate employment of all the comforting powers of the lord of the flat.

For there lay The Combs—the set of combs, side and back, that Della had worshipped long in a Broadway window. Beautiful combs, pure tortoise shell, with jewelled rims—just the shade to wear in the beautiful vanished hair. They were expensive combs, she knew, and her heart had simply craved and yearned over them without the least hope of possession. And now, they were hers, but the tresses that should have adorned the coveted adornments were gone.

But she hugged them to her bosom, and at length she was able to look up with dim eyes and a smile and say: "My hair grows so fast, Jim!"

And then Della leaped up like a little singed cat and cried, "Oh, oh!"

Jim had not yet seen his beautiful present. She held it out to him eagerly upon her open palm. The dull precious metal seemed to flash with a reflection of her bright and ardent spirit.

"Isn't it a dandy, Jim? I hunted all over town to find it. You'll have to look at the time a hundred times a day now. Give me your watch. I want to see how it looks on it."

Instead of obeying, Jim tumbled down on the couch and put his hands under the back of his head and smiled.

"Dell," said he, "let's put our Christmas presents away and keep 'em a while. They're too nice to use just at present. I sold the watch to get the money to buy your combs. And now suppose you put the chops on."

The magi, as you know, were wise men—wonderfully wise men—who brought gifts to the Babe in the manger. They invented the art of giving Christmas presents. Being wise, their gifts were no doubt wise ones, possibly bearing the privilege of exchange in case of duplication. And here I have lamely related to you the uneventful chronicle of two foolish children in a flat who most unwisely sacrificed for each other the greatest treasures of their house. But in a last word to the wise of these days let it be said that of all who give gifts these two were the wisest. O all who give and receive gifts, such as they are wisest. Everywhere they are wisest. They are the magi.

The Little Match Girl

Hans Christian Andersen

Most terribly cold it was; it snowed, and was nearly quite dark, and evening—the last evening of the year. In this cold and darkness there went along the street a poor little girl, bareheaded, and with naked feet. When she left home she had slippers on, it is true; but what was the good of that? They were very large slippers, which her mother had hitherto worn; so large were they; and the poor little thing lost them as she scuffled away across the street, because of two carriages that rolled by dreadfully fast.

One slipper was nowhere to be found; the other had been laid hold of by an urchin, and off he ran with it; he thought it would do capitally for a cradle when he some day or other should have children himself. So the little maiden walked on with her tiny naked feet, that were quite red and blue from cold. She carried a quantity of matches in an old apron, and she held a bundle of them in her hand. Nobody had bought anything of her the whole livelong day; no one had given her a single farthing.

She crept along trembling with cold and hunger—a very picture of sorrow, the poor little thing!

The flakes of snow covered her long fair hair, which fell in beautiful curls around her neck; but of that, of course, she never once now thought. From all the windows the candles were gleaming, and it smelt so deliciously of roast goose, for you know it was New Year's Eve; yes, of that she thought.

In a corner formed by two houses, of which one advanced more than the other, she seated herself down and cowered together. Her little feet she had drawn close up to her, but she grew colder and colder, and to go home she did not venture, for she had not sold any matches and could not bring a farthing of money: from her father she would certainly get blows, and at home it was cold too, for above her she had only the roof, through which the wind whistled, even though the largest cracks were stopped up with straw and rags.

Her little hands were almost numbed with cold. Oh! a match might afford her a world of comfort, if she only dared take a single one out of the bundle, draw it against the wall, and warm her fingers by it. She drew one out. "Rischt!" how it blazed, how it burnt! It was a warm, bright flame, like a candle, as she held her hands over it: it was a wonderful light. It seemed really to the little maiden as though she were sitting before a large iron stove, with burnished brass feet and a brass ornament at top. The fire burned with such blessed influence; it warmed so delightfully. The little girl had already stretched out her feet to warm them too; but the small flame went out, the stove vanished: she had only the remains of the burnt-out match in her hand.

She rubbed another against the wall: it burned brightly, and where the light fell on the wall, there the wall became transparent like a veil, so that she could see into the room. On the table was spread a snow-white tablecloth; upon it was a splendid porcelain service, and the roast goose was steaming famously with its stuffing of apple and dried plums. And what was still more capital to behold was, the goose hopped down from the dish, reeled about on the floor with knife and fork in its breast, till it came up to the poor little girl; when—the match went out and nothing but the thick, cold, damp wall was left behind. She lighted another match. Now there she was sitting under the most magnificent Christmas tree; it was still larger, and more decorated than the one which she had seen through the glass door in the rich merchant's house.

Thousands of lights were burning on the green branches, and gaily-colored pictures, such as she had seen in the shop-windows, looked down upon her. The little maiden stretched out her hands towards them when—the match went out. The lights of the Christmas tree rose higher and higher, she saw them now as stars in heaven; one fell down and formed a long trail of fire.

"Someone is just dead!" said the little girl; for her old grandmother, the only person who had loved her, and who was now no more, had told her, that when a star falls, a soul ascends to God.

She drew another match against the wall: it was again light, and in the lustre there stood the old grandmother, so bright and radiant, so mild, and with such an expression of love.

"Grandmother!" cried the little one. "Oh, take me with you! You go away when the match burns out; you vanish like the warm stove, like the delicious roast goose, and like the magnificent Christmas tree!" And she rubbed the whole bundle of matches quickly against the wall, for she wanted to be quite sure of keeping her grandmother near her. And the matches gave such a brilliant light that it was brighter than at noon-day: never formerly had the grandmother been so beautiful and so tall. She took the little maiden, on her arm, and both flew in brightness and in joy so high, so very high, and then above was neither cold, nor hunger, nor anxiety—they were with God.

But in the corner, at the cold hour of dawn, sat the poor girl, with rosy cheeks and with a smiling mouth, leaning against the wall—frozen to death on the last evening of the old year. Stiff and stark sat the child there with her matches, of which one bundle had been burnt. "She wanted to warm herself," people said. No one had the slightest suspicion of what beautiful things she had seen; no one even dreamed of the splendor in which, with her grandmother she had entered on the joys of a new year.

The Cobbler's Guest

LEO TOLSTOY

There once lived in the city of Marseilles an old shoemaker, loved and honored by his neighbors, who affectionately called him "Father Martin."

One Christmas Eve, as he sat alone in his little shop reading of the visit of the wise men to the infant Jesus, and of the gifts they brought, he said to himself, "If tomorrow were the first Christmas, and if Jesus were to be born in Marseilles this night, I know what I would give Him!" He rose from his stool and took from a shelf overhead two tiny shoes of softest snow-white leather, with bright silver buckles. "I would give Him those, my finest work."

Replacing the shoes, he blew out the candle and retired to rest. Hardly had he closed his eyes, it seemed, when he heard a voice call his name . . . "Martin! Martin!"

Intuitively he felt a presence. Then the voice spoke again . . . "Martin, you have wished to see Me. Tomorrow I shall pass by your window. If you see Me, and bid Me enter, I shall be your guest at your table."

Father Martin did not sleep that night for joy. And before it was yet dawn he rose and swept and tidied up his little shop. He spread fresh sand upon the floor, and wreathed green boughs of fir along the rafters. On the spotless linen-covered table he placed a loaf of white bread, a jar of honey, and a pitcher of milk, and over the fire he hung a pot of tea. Then he took up his patient vigil at the window.

Presently he saw an old street-sweeper pass by, blowing upon his thin, gnarled hands to warm them. *Poor fellow, he must be half frozen,* thought Martin. Opening the door he called out to him, "Come in, my friend, and warm, and drink a cup of hot tea." And the man gratefully accepted the invitation.

An hour passed, and Martin saw a young, miserably clothed woman carrying a baby. She paused wearily to rest in the shelter of his doorway. The heart of the old cobbler was touched. Quickly he flung open the door.

"Come in and warm while you rest," he said to her. "You do not look well," he remarked.

"I am going to the hospital. I hope they will take me in, and my baby boy," she explained. "My husband is at sea, and I am ill, without a soul."

"Poor child!" cried Father Martin. "You must eat something while you are getting warm. No. Then let me give a cup of milk to the little one. Ah! What a bright, pretty fellow he is! Why, you have put no shoes on him!"

"I have no shoes for him," sighed the mother sadly. "Then he shall have this lovely pair I finished yesterday." And Father Martin took down from the shelf the soft little snow-white shoes he had admired the evening before. He slipped them on the child's feet . . . they fit perfectly. And shortly the young mother left, two shoes in her hand and tearful with gratitude.

And Father Martin resumed his post at the window. Hour after hour went by, and although many people passed his window, and many needy souls shared his hospitality, the expected Guest did not appear.

"It was only a dream," he sighed, with a heavy heart. "I did believe; but He has not come."

Suddenly, so it seemed to his weary eyes, the room was flooded with a strange light. And to the cobbler's astonished vision there appeared before him, one by one, the poor street-sweeper, the sick mother and her child, and all the people whom he had aided during the day. And each smiled at him and said, "Have you not seen me? Did I not sit at your table?" Then they vanished.

At last, out of the silence, Father Martin heard again the gentle voice repeating the old familiar words, "Whoever welcomes one of these little children in My name welcomes Me; and whoever welcomes Me does not welcome Me but the one who sent me Me." . . . "I was hungry and you gave Me something to eat, I was thirsty and you gave Me something to drink, I was a stranger and you invited Me in, I needed clothes and you clothed Me, I was sick and you looked after Me, I was in prison and you came to visit Me."

The Other Wise Man

Henry van Dyke

In the days when Augustus Caesar was master of many kings and Herod reigned in Jerusalem, there lived in the city of Ecbatana, among the mountains of Persia, a certain man named Artaban. His house stood close to the outermost of the walls which encircled the royal treasury. From his roof he could look over the sevenfold battlements of black and white and crimson and blue and red and silver and gold, to the hill where the summer palace of the Parthian emperors glittered like a jewel in a crown.

Around the dwelling of Artaban spread a fair garden, a tangle of flowers and fruit trees, watered by a score of streams descending from the slopes of Mount Orontes, and made musical by innumerable birds. But all color was lost in the soft and odorous darkness of the late September night, and all sounds were hushed in the deep charm of its silence, save the splashing of the water, like a voice half sobbing and half laughing under the shadows. High above the trees a dim glow of light shone through the curtained arches of the upper chamber, where the master of the house was holding council with his friends.

He stood by the doorway to greet his guests—a tall, dark man of about forty years, with brilliant eyes set near together under his broad brow, and firm lines graven around his fine, thin lips; the brow of a dreamer and the mouth of a soldier, a man of sensitive feeling but inflexible will—one of those who, in whatever age they may live, are born for inward conflict and a life of quest.

His robe was of pure white wool, thrown over a tunic of silk; and a white, pointed cap, with long lapels at the sides, rested on his flowing black hair. It was the dress of the Magi.

"Welcome!" he said, in his low, pleasant voice, as one after another entered the room.

"You have come tonight," said he, looking around the circle, "at my call to renew your worship and rekindle your faith in the God of Purity. We worship not the fire, but Him of whom it is the chosen symbol, because it is the purest of all created things. It speaks to us of one who is Light and Truth.

"It was the Hebrew Daniel, the mighty searcher of dreams, the counselor of kings, the wise Belteshazzar, who was most honored and beloved of our great

King Cyrus. A prophet of sure things and a reader of the thoughts of the Eternal, Daniel proved himself to our people. And these are the words that he wrote:"

(Artaban read from [a scroll]:) "'Know, therefore, and understand that from the going forth of the commandment to restore Jerusalem, unto the Anointed One, the Prince, the time shall be seven and threescore and two weeks.'"

"But my son," said Abgarus, doubtfully, "these numbers . . . who can interpret them, or who can find the key that shall unlock their meaning?"

Artaban answered: "It has been shown to me and to my three companions among the Magi—Caspar, Melchior, and Balthasar. We have searched the ancient tablets of Chaldea and computed the time. It falls in this year. We saw a new star, which shone for one night and then vanished. If the star shines again, they will wait ten days for me at the temple, and then we will set out together for Jerusalem, to see and worship the promised one who shall be born King of Israel. I believe the sign will come. I have made ready for the journey. I have sold my possessions, and bought these three jewels—a sapphire, a ruby and a pearl—to carry them as tribute to the King. And I ask you to go with me on the pilgrimage, that we may have joy together in finding the Prince who is worthy to be served."

While he was speaking he thrust his hand into the inmost fold of his girdle and drew out three great gems—one blue as a fragment of the night sky, one redder than a ray of sunrise, and one as pure as the peak of a snow mountain at twilight—and laid them on the outspread scrolls before him.

But his friends looked on with strange and alien eyes. A veil of doubt and mistrust came over their faces, like a fog creeping up from the marshes to hide the hills. They glanced at each other with looks of wonder and pity, as those who have listened to incredible sayings, the story of a wild vision, or the proposal of an impossible enterprise.

At last Tigranes, said: "Artaban, this is a vain dream. It comes from too much looking upon the stars and the cherishing of lofty thoughts. It would be wiser to spend the time in gathering money. No king will ever rise from the broken race of Israel, and no end will ever come to the eternal strife of light and darkness. He who looks for it is a chaser of shadows. Farewell."

So, one by one, they left the house of Artaban. But Abgarus, the oldest and the one who loved him the best, lingered after the others had gone, and said, gravely: "My son, it may be that the light of truth is in this sign that has appeared in the skies, and then it will surely lead to the Prince and the mighty brightness. Or it may be that it is only a shadow of the light, as Tigranes has said, and then he who follows it will have a long pilgrimage and a fruitless search. But it is better to follow even the shadow of the best than to remain content with the worst. And those who would see wonderful things must often be ready to travel alone. I am too old for this journey, but my heart shall be a companion of thy pilgrimage day and night, and I shall know the end of thy quest. Go in peace."

Then Abgarus went out of the azure chamber with its silver stars, and Artaban was left in solitude.

He gathered up the jewels and replaced them in his girdle. For a long time he stood and watched the flame that flickered and sank. Then he crossed the hall, lifted the heavy curtain, and passed out between the pillars of porphyry to the terrace on the roof.

Far over the eastern plain a white mist stretched like a lake. But where the distant peaks of Zagros serrated the western horizon the sky was clear. Jupiter and Saturn rolled together like drops of lambent flame about to blend into one.

As Artaban watched them, a steel-blue spark was born out of the darkness beneath, rounding itself with purple splendors to a crimson sphere, and spring upward through rays of saffron and orange into a point of white radiance. Tiny and infinitely remote, yet perfect in every part, it pulsated in the enormous vault as if the three jewels in the Magian's girdle had mingled and been transformed into a living heart of light.

He bowed his head. He covered his brow with is hands.

"It is the sign," he said. "The King is coming, and I will go to meet him."

II

All night long, Vasda, the swiftest of Artaban's horses, had been waiting, saddled and bridled, in her stall, pawing the ground impatiently and shaking her bit as if she shared the eagerness of her master's purpose, though she knew not its meaning.

Before the birds had fully roused to their strong, high, joyful chant of morning song, before the white mist had begun to lift lazily from the plain, the Other Wise Man was in the saddle, riding swiftly along the high road, which skirted the base of Mount Orontes, westward.

Artaban must indeed ride wisely and well if he would keep the appointed hour with the other Magi; for the route was a hundred and fifty parasangs, and fifteen was the utmost that he could travel in a day. But he knew Vasda's strength, and pushed forward without anxiety, making the fixed distance every day, though he must travel late into the night, and in the morning long before sunrise.

Artaban pressed onward until he arrived, at nightfall on the tenth day, beneath the shattered walls of populous Babylon.

Vasda was almost spent, and Artaban would gladly have turned into the city to find rest and refreshment for himself and for her. But he knew that it was three hours' journey yet, and he must reach the place by midnight if he would find his comrades waiting. So he did not halt, but rose steadily across the stubble fields. A grove of date palms made an island of gloom in the pale yellow sea. As she passed into the shadow Vasda slackened her pace, and began to pick her way more carefully.

Near the farther end of the darkness an access of caution seemed to fall upon her. She scented some danger or difficulty; it was not in her heart to fly from it—only to be prepared for it, and to meet it wisely, as a good horse should do. The grove was close and silent as the tomb; not a leaf rustled, not a bird sang.

She felt her steps before her delicately carrying her head low, and sighing now and then with apprehension. At last she gave a quick breath of anxiety and dismay, and stood stock-still, quivering in every muscle, before a dark object in the shadow of the last palm tree.

Artaban dismounted. The dim starlight revealed the form of a man lying across the road. His humble dress and the outline of his haggard face showed that he was probably one of the Hebrews who still dwelt in great numbers around the city. His pallid skin, dry and yellow as parchment, bore the mark of the deadly fever which ravaged the marshlands in autumn. The chill of death was in his lean hand, and, as Artaban released it, the arm fell back inertly upon the motionless breast.

He turned away with a thought of pity, leaving the body to that strange burial which the Magians deemed most fitting—the funeral of the desert, from which the kites and vultures rise on dark wings, and the beasts of prey slink furtively away. When they are gone there is only a heap of white bones on the sand.

But, as he turned, a long, faint, ghostly sigh came from the man's lips. The bony fingers gripped the hem of the Magian's robe and held him fast.

Artaban's heart leaped to his throat, not with fear, but with a dumb resentment at the importunity of this blind delay.

How could he stay here in the darkness to minister to a dying stranger? What claim had this unknown fragment of human life upon his compassion or his service? If he lingered but for an hour he could hardly reach Borsippa at the appointed time. His companions would think he had given up the journey. They would go without him. He would lose his quest.

But if he went on now, the man would surely die. If Artaban stayed, life might be restored. His spirit throbbed and fluttered with the urgency of the crisis. Should he risk the great reward of his faith for the sake of a single deed of charity? Should he turn aside, if only for a moment, from the following of the star, to give a cup of cold water to a poor, perishing Hebrew?

"God of truth and purity," he prayed, "direct me in the holy path, the way of wisdom which Thou only knowest."

Then he turned back to the sick man. Loosening the grasp of his hand, he carried him to a little mound at the foot of the palm tree.

He unbound the thick folds of the turban and opened the garment above the sunken breast. He brought water from one of the small canals nearby, and moistened the sufferer's brow and mouth. He mingled a draught of one of those simple but potent remedies which he carried always in his girdle—for the Magians were physicians too—and poured it slowly between the colorless lips. Hour after hour he labored as only a skillful healer of disease can do. At last the man's strength returned; he sat up and looked about him.

"Who art thou?" he said, in the rude dialect of the county, "and why hast thou sought me here to bring back my life?"

"I am Artaban the Magian, of the city of Ecbatana and I am going to Jerusalem in search of one who is to be born King of the Jews, a great Prince and Deliverer of all men. I dare not delay any longer upon my journey, for the caravan that has waited for me may depart without me. But see, here is all that I have left of bread and wine, and here is a potion of healing herbs. When thy strength is restored thou canst find the dwellings of the Hebrews among the houses of Babylon."

The Jew raised his trembling hand solemnly to heaven.

"Now may the God of Abraham and Isaac and Jacob bless and prosper the journey of the merciful, and bring him in peace to his desired haven. Stay! I have nothing to give thee in return—only this: that I can tell thee where the Messiah must be sought. For our prophets have said that he should be born not in Jerusalem, but in Bethlehem of Judah. May the Lord bring thee in safety to that place, because thou hast had pity upon the sick."

It was already long past midnight. Artaban rode in haste, and Vasda, restored by the brief rest, ran eagerly through the silent plain and swam the channels of the river. She put forth the remnant of her strength and fled over the ground like a gazelle.

But the first beam of the rising sun sent a long shadow before her as she entered upon the final stadium of the journey, and the eyes of Artaban, anxiously scanning, could discern no trace of his friends.

The many-colored terraces of black and orange and red and yellow and green and blue and white, shattered by the convulsions of nature, and crumbling under the repeated blows of human violence, still glittered like a ruined rainbow in the morning light.

Artaban rode swiftly around the hill. He dismounted and climbed to the highest terrace, looking out toward the west. But there was no sign of the caravan of the Wise Men, far or near.

At the edge of the terrace was a little cairn of broken bricks, and under them a piece of papyrus. He caught it up and read: "We have waited past midnight, and can delay no longer. We go to find the King. Follow us across the desert."

Artaban sat down upon the ground and covered his head in despair.

"How can I cross the desert," said he, "with no food and a spent horse? I must return to Babylon, sell my sapphire, and buy a train of camels, and provision for the journey. I may never overtake my friends. Only God the merciful knows whether I shall not lose the sight of the King because I tarried to show mercy."

III

Through the heat and cold, the Magian moved steadily onward until he arrived at Bethlehem. And it was the third day after the three Wise Men had come to the place and had found Mary and Joseph with the young child, Jesus, and had laid their gifts of gold and frankincense and myrrh at His feet.

Then the Other Wise Man drew near, weary, but full of hope, bearing his ruby and his pearl to offer to the King. "For now at last," he said, "I shall surely find Him, though I be alone, and later than my brethren. This is the place of which the Hebrew exile told me that the prophets had spoken, and here I shall behold the rising of the great light. But I must inquire about the visit of my brethren, and to what house the star directed them, and to whom they presented their tribute."

The streets of the village seemed to be deserted, and Artaban wondered whether the men had all gone up to the hill pastures to bring down their sheep. From the open door of a cottage he heard the sound of a woman's voice singing softly. He entered and found a young mother hushing her baby to rest. She told him of the strangers from the far East who had appeared in the village three days ago, and how they said that a star had guided them to the place where Joseph of Nazareth was lodging with his wife and her newborn child, and how they had paid reverence to the child and given Him many rich gifts.

"But the travelers disappeared again," she continued, "as suddenly as they had come. We were afraid at the strangeness of their visit. We could not understand it. The man of Nazareth took the child and his mother, and fled away that same night secretly, and it was whispered that they were going to Egypt. Ever since, there has been a spell upon the village; something evil hangs over it. They say that the Roman soldiers are coming from Jerusalem to force a new tax from us, and the men have driven flocks and herds far back among the hills, and hidden themselves to escape it."

Artaban listened to her gentle, timid speech, and the child in her arms looked up into his face and smiled, stretching out its rosy hands to grasp at the winged circle of gold on his breast. His heart warmed to the touch. It seemed like a greeting of love and trust to one who had journeyed long in loneliness and perplexity, fighting with his own doubts and fears, and following a light that was veiled in clouds.

"Why might not this child have been the promised Prince?" he asked within himself, as he touched its soft cheek. "Kings have been born ere now in lowlier houses than this, and the favorite of the stars may rise even from a cottage. But it has not seemed good to the God of wisdom to reward my search so soon and so easily. The one whom I seek has gone before me; and now I must follow the King to Egypt."

The young mother laid the baby in its cradle, and rose to minister to the wants of the strange guest that fate had brought into her house. She set food before him, the plain fare of peasants, but willingly offered, and therefore full of refreshment for the soul as well as for the body. Artaban accepted it gratefully; and, as he ate, the child fell into a happy slumber, and murmured sweetly in its dreams, and a great peace filled the room.

But suddenly there came the noise of a wild confusion in the streets of the village, a shrieking and wailing of women's voices, a clangor of brazen trumpets and a clashing of swords, and a desperate cry: "The soldiers! The soldiers of Herod! They are killing our children."

The young mother's face grew white with terror. She clasped her child to her bosom, and crouched motionless in the darkest corner of the room, covering him with the folds of her robe, lest he should wake and cry.

But Artaban went quickly and stood in the doorway of the house. His broad shoulders filled the portal from side to side, and the peak of his white cap all but touched the lintel.

The soldiers came hurrying down the street with bloody hands and dripping swords. At the sight of the stranger in his imposing dress they hesitated with surprise. The captain of the band approached the threshold to thrust him aside. But Artaban did not stir. His face was as calm as though he were watching the stars, and in his eyes there burned that steady radiance before which even the half-tamed hunting leopard shrinks, and the bloodhound pauses in his leap. He held the soldier silently for an instant, and then said in a low voice:

"I am all alone in this place, and I am waiting to give this jewel to the prudent captain who will leave me in peace."

He showed the ruby, glistening in the hollow of his hands like a great drop of blood.

The captain was amazed at the splendor of the gem. The pupils of his eyes expanded with desire, and the hard lines of greed wrinkled around his lips. He stretched out his hand and took the ruby.

"March on!" he cried to his men; "there is no child here. The house is empty."

The clamor and the clang of arms passed down the street. Artaban re-entered the cottage. He turned his face to the east and prayed:

"God of truth, forgive my sin! I have said the thing that is not, to save the life of a child. And two of my gifts are gone. I have spent for man that which was meant for God. Shall I ever be worthy to see the face of the King?"

But the voice of the woman, weeping for joy in the shadow behind him, said very gently:

"Because thou hast saved the life of my little one, may the Lord bless thee and keep thee; the Lord make His face to shine upon thee and be gracious unto thee; the Lord lift up His countenance upon thee and give thee peace."

IV

The years of Artaban were flowing very swiftly as he searched for the King. He was seen among the throngs of men in populous Egypt, seeking everywhere for traces of the household that had come down from Bethlehem, and finding them under the spreading sycamore trees of Heliopolis, and beneath the walls of the Roman fortress of New Babylon beside the Nile—traces so faint and dim that they vanished before him continually, as footprints on the wet river sand glisten for a moment with moisture and then disappear. He searched through Egypt. In Alexandria he took counsel with a Hebrew rabbi. The venerable man, bending over the rolls of parchment on which the prophecies of Israel were written, read aloud the pathetic words which foretold the sufferings of the promised

Messiah—the despised and rejected of men, the man of sorrows and acquainted with grief.

"And remember, my son," said he, fixing his eyes upon the face of Artaban, "the King whom thou seekest is not to be found in a palace, nor among the rich and powerful. But the light for which the world is waiting is a new light, the glory that shall rise out of patient and triumphant suffering. And the kingdom which is to be established forever is a new kingdom, the royalty of unconquerable love.

"I do not know how this shall come to pass, nor how the turbulent kings and peoples of earth shall be brought to acknowledge the Messiah and pay homage to him. But this I know. Those who seek him will do well to look among the poor and the lowly, the sorrowful and the oppressed."

So the Other Wise Man traveled from place to place, searching among the people of the Dispersion, with whom the little family from Bethlehem might, perhaps, have found a refuge. He passed through countries where famine lay heavy upon the land, and the poor were crying for bread. He made his dwelling in plague-stricken cities where the sick were languishing in the bitter companionship of helpless misery. He visited the oppressed and the afflicted in the gloom of subterranean prisons, and the crowded wretchedness of slave markets, and the weary toil of galley ships. In all this populous and intricate world of anguish, though he found none to worship, he found many to help. He fed the hungry, and clothed the naked, and healed the sick, and comforted the captive; and his years passed more swiftly than the weaver's shuttle that flashed back and forth through the loom while the web grows and the pattern is completed.

It seemed almost as if he had gotten his quest.

V

Three-and-thirty years of the life of Artaban had passed away, and he was still a pilgrim and a seeker after light. His hair, once darker than the cliffs of Zagros, was now white as the wintry snow that covered them. His eyes, that once flashed like flames of fire, were dull as embers smoldering among the ashes.

Worn and weary and ready to die, but still looking for the King, he had come for the last time to Jerusalem. He had often visited the Holy City before, and had searched all its lanes and crowded hovels and black prisons without finding any trace of the family of Nazarenes who had fled from Bethlehem long ago. But now it seemed as if he must make one more effort, and something whispered in his heart that, at last, he might succeed.

It was the season of the Passover. The city was thronged with strangers.

The children of Israel, scattered in far lands, had returned to the Temple for the great feast, and there had been a confusion of tongues in the narrow streets for many days.

But on this day a singular agitation was visible in the multitude. The sky was veiled with a portentous gloom. Currents of excitement seemed to flash through the crowd. A secret tide was sweeping them all one way. The clatter of sandals and the soft, thick sound of thousands of bare feet shuffling over the stones, flowed unceasingly along the street that leads to the Damascus gate.

Artaban joined a group of people from his own country, Parthian Jews who had come up to keep the Passover, and inquired of them the cause of the tumult, and where they were going.

"We are going," they answered, "to the place called Golgotha, outside the city walls, where there is to be an execution. Have you not heard what has happened? Two famous robbers are to be crucified, and with them another, called Jesus of Nazareth, a man who has done many wonderful works among the people, so that they love Him greatly. But the priests and elders have said that He must die, because He gave Himself out to be the Son of God. And Pilate has sent Him to the cross because He said that He was the 'King of the Jews.'"

How strangely these familiar words fell upon the tired heart of Artaban! They had led him for a lifetime over land and sea. And now they came to him mysteriously, like a message of despair. The King had arisen, but He had been denied and cast out. He was about to perish. Perhaps He was already dying. Could it be the same who had been born in Bethlehem thirty-three years ago, at whose birth the star had appeared in heaven, and of whose coming the prophets had spoken?

Artaban's heart beat unsteadily with that troubled, doubtful apprehension which is the excitement of old age. But he said within himself: "The ways of God are stranger than the thoughts of men, and it may be that I shall find the King, at last, in the hands of his enemies, and shall come in time to offer my pearl for His ransom before He dies."

So the old man followed the multitude with slow and painful steps toward the Damascus gate of the city. Just beyond the entrance of the guardhouse a troop of Macedonian soldiers came down the street, dragging a young girl with torn dress and disheveled hair. As the Magian paused to look at her with compassion, she broke suddenly from the hands of her tormentors, and threw herself at his feet, clasping him around the knees. She had seen his white cap and winged circle on his breast.

"Have pity on me," she cried, "and save me, for the sake of the God of Purity! My father was a merchant of Parthia, but he is dead, and I am seized for his debts to be sold as a slave. Save me from worse than death!"

Artaban trembled.

It was the old conflict in his soul, which had come to him in the palm grove of Babylon and in the cottage at Bethlehem—the conflict between the expectation of faith and the impulse of love. Twice the gift which he had consecrated to the worship of religion had been drawn to the service of humanity. This was the third trial, the ultimate probation, the final and irrevocable choice.

Was it his great opportunity, or his last temptation? He could not tell. One thing only was clear in the darkness of his mind—it was inevitable. And does not the inevitable come from God?

One thing only was sure to his divided heart—to rescue this helpless girl would be a true deed of love. And is not love the light of the soul?

He took the pearl from his bosom. Never had it seemed so luminous, so radiant, so full of tender, living luster. He laid it in the hand of the slave.

"This is thy ransom, daughter! It is the last of my treasures which I kept for the King."

While he spoke, the darkness of the sky deepened, and shuddering tremors ran through the earth heaving convulsively like the breast of one who struggles with mighty grief.

The walls of the houses rocked to and fro. Stones were loosened and crashed into the street. Dust clouds filled the air. The soldiers fled in terror, reeling like drunken men. But Artaban and the girl whom he had ransomed crouched helpless beneath the wall of the Praetorium.

What had he to fear? What had he to hope? He had given away the last remnant of his tribute for the King. He had parted with the last hope of finding Him. The quest was over, and it had failed. But even in that thought, accepted and embraced, there was peace. It was not resignation. It was not submission. It was something more profound and searching. He knew that all was well, because he had done the best that he could from day to day. He had been true to the light that had been given to him. He had looked for more. And if he had not found it, if a failure was all that came out of his life, doubtless that was the best that was possible. He had not seen the revelation of "life everlasting, incorruptible and immortal." But he knew that even if he could live his earthly life over again, it could not be otherwise than it had been.

One more lingering pulsation of the earthquake quivered through the ground. A heavy tile, shaken from the roof, fell and struck the old man on the temple. He lay breathless and pale, with his gray head resting on the young girl's shoulder, and the blood trickling from the wound. As she bent over him, fearing that he was dead, there came a voice through the twilight, very small and still, like music sounding from a distance, in which the notes are clear but the words are lost. The girl turned to see if someone had spoken from the window above them, but she saw no one.

Then the old man's lips began to move, as if in answer, and she heard him say in the Parthian tongue:

"Not so, my Lord! for when saw I Thee an hungered and fed Thee? Or thirsty, and gave Thee drink? When saw I Thee a stranger, and took Thee in? Or naked, and clothed Thee? When saw I Thee sick or in prison, and came unto Thee? Three-and-thirty years have I looked for Thee; but I have never seen Thy face, nor ministered to Thee, my King."

He ceased, and the sweet voice came again. And again the maid heard it, very faint and far away. But now it seemed as though she understood the words:

"Verily I say unto thee, Inasmuch as thou hast done it unto one of the least of these my brethren, thou hast done it unto Me."

A calm radiance of wonder and joy lighted the pale face of Artaban like the first ray of dawn on a snowy mountain peak. A long breath of relief exhaled gently from his lips.

His journey was ended. His treasures were accepted. The Other Wise Man had found the King.

The Holy Night

Selma Lagerlöf

There was a man who went out in the dark night to borrow live coals to kindle a fire. He went from hut to hut and knocked. "Dear friends, help me!" said he. "My wife has just given birth to a child, and I must make a fire to warm her and the little one."

But it was way in the night, and all the people were asleep. No one replied.

The man walked and walked. At last he saw the gleam of a fire a long way off. Then he went in that direction, and saw that the fire was burning in the open. A lot of sheep were sleeping around the fire, and an old shepherd sat and watched over the flock.

When the man who wanted to borrow fire came up to the sheep, he saw that three big dogs lay asleep at the shepherd's feet. All three awoke when the man approached and opened their great jaws, as though they wanted to bark; but not a sound was heard. The man noticed that the hair on their backs stood up and that their sharp, white teeth glistened in the firelight. They dashed toward him.

He felt that one of them bit at his leg and one at his hand and that one clung to his throat. But their jaws and teeth wouldn't obey them, and the man didn't suffer the least harm.

Now the man wished to go farther, to get what he needed. But the sheep lay back to back and so close to one another that he couldn't pass them. Then the man stepped upon their backs and walked over them and up to the fire. And not one of the animals awoke or moved.

When the man had almost reached the fire, the shepherd looked up. He was a surly old man, who was unfriendly and harsh toward human beings. And when he saw the strange man coming, he seized the long, spiked staff, which he always held in his hand when he tended his flock, and threw it at him. The staff came right toward the man, but, before it reached him, it turned off to one side and whizzed past him, far out to the meadow.

Now the man came up to the shepherd and said to him: "Good man, help me, and lend me a little fire! My wife has just given birth to a child, and I must make a fire to warm her and the little one."

The shepherd would rather have said no, but when he pondered that the dogs couldn't hurt the man, and the sheep had not run from him, and that the staff had not wished to strike him, he was a little afraid, and dared not deny the man that which he asked.

"Take as much as you need!" he said to the man.

But then the fire was nearly burnt out. There were no logs or branches left, only a big heap of live coals; and the stranger had neither spade nor shovel wherein he could carry the red-hot coals.

When the shepherd saw this, he said again: "Take as much as you need!"

But the man stooped and picked coals from the ashes with his bare hands, and laid them in his mantle. And he didn't burn his hands when he touched them, nor did the coals scorch his mantle; but he carried them away as if they had been nuts or apples.

And when the shepherd, who was such a cruel and hardhearted man, saw all this, he began to wonder to himself: *What kind of a night is this, when the dogs do not bite, the sheep are not scared, the staff does not kill, or the fire scorch?* He called the stranger back and said to him: "What kind of a night is this? And how does it happen that all things show you compassion?"

Then said the man: "I cannot tell you if you yourself do not see it." And he wished to go his way, that he might soon make a fire and warm his wife and child.

But the shepherd did not wish to lose sight of the man before he had found out what all this might portend. He got up and followed the man till they came to the place where he lived.

Then the shepherd saw that the man didn't have so much as a hut to dwell in, but that his wife and babe were lying in a mountain grotto, where there was nothing except the cold and naked stone walls.

But the shepherd thought that perhaps the poor innocent child might freeze to death there in the grotto; and, although he was a hard man, he was touched, and thought he would like to help it. And he loosened his knapsack from his shoulder, took from it a soft white sheepskin, gave it to the strange man, and said that he should let the child sleep on it.

But just as soon as he showed that he, too, could be merciful, his eyes were opened and he saw what he had not been able to see before, and heard what he could not have heard before.

He saw that all around him stood a ring of little silver-winged angels, and each held a stringed instrument, and all sang in loud tones that tonight the Savior was born who should redeem the world from its sins.

Then he understood how all things were so happy this night that they didn't want to do anything wrong.

And it was not only around the shepherd that there were angels, but he saw them everywhere. They sat inside the grotto, they sat outside on the mountain, and they flew under the heavens. They came marching in great companies, and as they passed, they paused and cast a glance at the child.

There were such jubilation and such gladness and songs and play! And all this he saw in the dark night, whereas before he could not have made out anything. He was so happy because his eyes had been opened that he fell upon his knees and thanked God.

What that shepherd saw, we might also see, for the angels fly down from heaven every Christmas Eve, if we could only see them.

You must remember this, for it is as true, as true as that I see you and you see me. It is not revealed by the light of lamps or candles, and it does not depend upon sun and moon; but that which is needful is that we have such eyes as can see God's glory.

Harry the Singing Angel

ROBERT PENGOLD

Harry wasn't all that upset at the beginning. After all, he had been a singing angel last year, as opposed to a "hovering" angel. The hovering angels were only two and three years old. They didn't say a word. They just stood at the front and looked good. Singing angels were four, five, and six, and Harry was five years old—"mature for his age," he had heard people say.

It was far better to be a singing angel, Harry had concluded last year, since singing angels didn't have to wear those weird halos or fancy wings—the wings of the singing angels were part of the collar of the costume. And . . . the song was pretty simple to sing—not a bad song as songs go. "Hark, the herald angels sing, glory to the newborn king, peace on earth and mercy mild, God and sinner reconciled." He had the words down cold, although he still had a little question about just exactly what "mercy mild" was all about.

Harry's older brother, Billy, was eight years old, and he was going to be a shepherd—also for the second time. Both Harry and Billy had their costumes, which only needed to be lengthened a little at the sleeves and hem. Grandma had finished hemming them even before the first rehearsal.

Yep, it was looking like a pretty routine Christmas program. "No big deal," Harry told himself.

That is, until the announcement came—the announcement about who was going to play the part of Baby Jesus.

Harry was not amused. Somebody—somebody totally out of their minds, he concluded—had decided that Baby Jesus was going to be played by Baby Tommy. His Baby Tommy. Not an anonymous new baby in the church . . . or a new kid on the block . . . but the new kid in the crib in the room next to his room at his house. Baby Tommy, Harry's little brother.

It wasn't that Harry didn't like Baby Tommy, or even love him. At least he never could have admitted it. Mom would have had a fit.

Harry wasn't sure exactly *what* he felt. He knew that in the beginning he had been very excited about having a baby in the house. It was all he had talked about for months. Everybody had said he was taking Mom's pregnancy all in stride. A baby had been welcome news.

Harry had been sure that with the arrival of a new baby, he would no longer have to bear the title of "little brother." He finally was going to be somebody's "big brother"—and that had a pretty cool ring to it. Mom had assured him that he didn't have to give up his bed or his room—he didn't even have to share his room, at least for a while, she said.

Dad had talked about how much fun it would be to have three kids instead of just two, and Harry could see some advantages in that, too. Maybe with a baby brother or sister around, he wouldn't always be blamed when something broke or something went wrong. He was certain he could out-run, out-argue, and out-yell any baby. It might be nice to have somebody to boss around . . . just like Billy bossed him around.

All in all, it was no-o-o-o problem. Harry was excited about having a baby in the family. That is . . . until Baby Tommy actually showed up.

From the best Harry could tell, Baby Tommy appeared to have taken over.

When Baby Tommy cried . . . both Mom and Dad jumped. Mom didn't seem very patient with Billy or Harry these days . . . but when Baby Tommy needed a diaper change or to be fed, Mom was all smiles and lovey-dovey. Dad didn't seem to have as much time to play ball as he did before Baby Tommy arrived . . . but he always seemed to find time when he got home to pick up Baby Tommy and cuddle him.

And . . . it was pretty amazing all the things Mom and Dad both expected Harry to do now. Why, they expected him to be able to dress himself completely, even to tying real shoelaces, and to put his own dirty clothes in the hamper, and to smooth out his bed before kindergarten started. He had never had to do any of those things before Baby Tommy arrived. And not only that, but he had to carry his own dishes to the kitchen sink from the table and worst of all, he had to sit in the MIDDLE of the backseat. There went the window view.

To top it all off, neither Mom or Dad had been very amused when Harry had suggested that maybe—just maybe—they might be able to trade in Baby Tommy on a baby that cried a little less. It was only a suggestion—he didn't see why everybody got that upset. It certainly didn't seem to be worth a time out and no dessert.

No, all in all, Baby Tommy had been a much better "idea" than a reality. And now . . . to have Baby Tommy as the star of the Christmas program . . . to have Baby Tommy playing Baby Jesus . . . well that was just too much to ask, even of a singing angel.

Mom had insisted that Harry go to practices and walk through the motions. Dad had backed up her order with that "look" of his. But, Harry decided all on his own, nobody could make him sing.

"Glory to the newborn king?" Yeah, right. He wasn't about to call Baby Tommy a newborn king—Dad was already calling him a "little prince" and that was far enough in the line of royalty.

Nope . . . Harry may not be able to boycott the entire Christmas program, but he certainly didn't have to sing. Of that he was not only certain, but determined. It would be his little secret, and that was that. No singing for Harry this year.

He almost gave in when Miss Martin came to talk to him about singing. Miss Martin was his kindergarten Sunday school teacher, and besides Mom and Aunt Carla, she was the prettiest and nicest woman Harry had ever met. He had even thought that he might like to marry her someday, maybe after first grade. Miss Martin told great Bible stories—why, she even made some of those people in the Bible seem real. He liked Daniel a lot. It would have been scary to be thrown into a lion's den. Miss Martin seemed to understand that. And it would have been pretty gross to be in the belly of a whale like Jonah—Miss Martin sometimes used words like gross. And he especially like what Miss Martin had to say about Jesus, and about how He healed people and did miracles and all.

Perhaps the very best thing about Miss Martin, though, was that she treated Harry—why, as if he was at least six years old, maybe even seven. She always called him "Harold," which had a very grown-up ring to it as far as Harry was concerned. That was his real name, of course, Harold Reginald Loveless. (But don't tell anybody about that name Reginald.) His older brother was William Samuel Loveless . . . Billy for short. And Baby Tommy was really named Thomas—well, Thomas something Loveless. Harry didn't like it when most people called him Harold, but with Miss Martin it was OK.

Miss Martin had come to him, asking in a very nice voice, "Harold, do you have a sore throat?"

"No, Miss Martin," he had replied.

"Well, I've noticed you aren't singing. You have such a nice, strong voice for a boy, and you always sing in tune and know all the words. We really need you to sing out strong, Harold. We can't do this very well without you!"

Harry had just looked down. He really didn't want to give Miss Martin any reason to dislike him, but he was determined not to sing if Baby Tommy was going to be Baby Jesus.

"Is something the matter?" Miss Martin had asked.

"No, Ma'am," Harry had said.

"Well," Miss Martin said, "I know you know the words and you know the tune, so I believe that when the time comes, you'll be the best singing angel up there."

Harry really was pretty sorry that Miss Martin was going to be disappointed. But this year, it just couldn't be helped. He had one more year of being a singing angel ahead of him, and she would just have to wait until then. He had no doubt he could be the best singing angel . . . but not this year.

The days passed. Rehearsals came and went. Harry hoped against hope that another baby would be born or somebody else would be chosen to be Baby Jesus. He had even hoped in secret that Baby Tommy would get sick so they'd have to find another Baby Jesus. No such luck.

If anything, as the days went by, Tommy just got more and more attention, and became more and more demanding. Why, they even had a party for Baby Tommy and he got all kinds of gifts—it wasn't even Christmas or his birthday or anything. And it seemed everybody in the whole world had been by the house to oooh and aaah over Baby Tommy. They didn't even seem to notice Harry most of the time. It wasn't fair.

Certainly nothing had happened to change Harry's mind. He was deter-mined more than ever to carry out his plan, even if nobody ever knew about it. He'd know, and that's all that mattered. There would be no singing from Harry Loveless' lips this year.

The evening of the Christmas program finally showed up, and so did Baby Tommy bundled in a soft white blanket. Mom helped Billy with the headdress he had to wear as a shepherd and she helped Harry into his singing-angel costume, but mostly she fussed over Baby Tommy, trying to put him to sleep before the show. Harry had to agree that he'd be a lot less trouble asleep than awake.

Miss Martin got everybody lined up in the right order. Then, Reverend Brown showed up to say a prayer and to tell all the angels, "Be sure to sing your best!" Harry pretended not to hear him, which wasn't really all that hard since Clarence Fosdick kept punching him in the ribs. (Even though he was also five years old, it was Clarence's first year as a singing angel, and he seemed pretty ner-vous about it as best Harry could tell.)

Harry walked in like the pro that he was, and when he got up into the choir area, he took his place near the manger. All the kids did pretty good jobs in their speaking parts, he thought—the narrators telling the first part of the story while Mary and Joseph made their way to the choir from the back of the church. Mary was riding a REAL donkey this year! That was a new twist. Harry was pretty im-pressed and everybody else seemed to feel the same way. Yeah, this was turning out to be a pretty awesome Christmas program.

The innkeeper did his part and then Mary and Joseph sang a song and while the spotlight was just on them, a lady dressed all in black brought in Baby Tommy and put him in the manger.

"Baby Jesus, yeah right," Harry said under his breath. He was glad Baby Tommy seemed sound asleep. "He'll never even know he was Baby Jesus," Harry whispered to himself. "And maybe nobody else will."

Then the spotlight went away and the lights came up and Mary and Joseph went over and stood by the manger and Mary kneeled down and started to sing a little lullaby. To Harry's surprise, she reached over and picked up Baby Jesus—that is, Baby Tommy. *Big mistake,* Harry thought to himself. *She's gonna wake him up!*

And sure enough, Baby Tommy started to whimper. Just a little at first. And then a little more.

Oh no! thought Harry. *He's going to spoil the whole thing.*

Harry glanced out at Mom and Dad on the second row and he could tell Mom was getting nervous. Dad, too. Billy was at the back of the church waiting to walk in with the shepherds. Harry could tell Baby Tommy was getting ready to wind up with one of his walloping cries—his face was scrunching up for that moment by moment. What should he do?

Then Baby Tommy really let loose with a cry. It was huge. In fact, it may have been the biggest baby cry that anybody had every heard in that church. Harry could see the lady dressed in black start toward the back entrance to the choir area. *No!* Harry thought. *You can't have a Christmas program without a Baby Jesus in the manger. It just wouldn't be right. She can't come and take Baby Jesus away.*

Harry had known all along that Baby Tommy wasn't going to be a very good Baby Jesus, but Harry couldn't let Baby Tommy ruin the whole program. He stepped out of line without a glance at Miss Martin—he figured she'd probably be upset with him but it couldn't be helped. He quickly walked over and knelt down by the manger and stuck out his hand to take Baby Tommy's little fingers.

"It's OK," he said in a very low little voice while Mary went right on with her song. Baby Tommy seemed surprised at another touch and opened his eyes and Harry leaned over and patted him on the head and whispered, "It's OK. It's OK."

For a few seconds, Baby Tommy stopped whimpering as he seemed to stare up at Harry. Then Harry could see a cry starting to brew again.

Behind him, Harry heard the introduction from the organ for the singing angels song. *Maybe the music will keep him quiet,* Harry thought. But that cry still seemed on the way. What could he do? He had to do something! It wasn't at all what he had planned. But out of Harry's own mouth, he heard a song, "Hark, the herald angels sing"—Baby Tommy seemed to be listening!

Was that a smile? Harry wondered. He wasn't sure he'd ever seen Baby Tommy smile before. "Glory to the newborn king." Yep. Baby Tommy definitely seemed to be listening. "Peace on earth and mercy mild"—Now Baby Tommy was staring all around . . . "God and sinner reconciled."

Baby Tommy was closing his eyes! *Yeah, that's it,* Harry thought. And Mary, smart woman at last, put Baby Jesus—Baby Tommy, that is—back in the manger. Harry still held onto his hand, though, just in case. "Joyful all ye nations rise. Join the triumph in the skies" . . . Sure enough, Baby Tommy seemed to be going back to sleep. "With angelic hosts proclaim, Christ is born in Bethlehem." Harry could feel Baby Tommy's fingers loosening their grip so he let go and stood up to rejoin the choir for the last line. After all he'd sung this much—"Hark, the herald angels sing, glory to the newborn king."

Harry wasn't sure how the rest of the program turned out. He was too busy watching Baby Jesus—that is, Baby Tommy. He guessed that the shepherds did their part OK. Billy didn't say anything later and neither did Mom or Dad so it must have gone alright. The wise men were a big hit. They didn't come in riding on live camels, but they did have humongous trains on their robes that had the entire audience whispering. All Harry cared about was that Baby Tommy was asleep and that he stayed asleep. Pretty soon it was over.

Backstage, everybody was in a jumble trying to get out of their costumes and find their coats.

Harry was feeling very relieved, and then he saw Miss Martin coming his way. How could he tell her that he just had to get out of line? . . . but before he could get much further in his thinking, Miss Martin gave him a big hug and then got down on his level so she could look him right in the eye.

All she said was, "Hark! The angel Harold sang!"

Yeah, he guessed he had. "Well," Harry said to Miss Martin, "sometimes you just have to help other people act like Jesus."

Why the Chimes Rang

RAYMOND MACDONALD ALDEN

✳

There was once, in a far-away country where few people have ever traveled, a wonderful church. It stood on a high hill in the midst of a great city; and every Sunday, as well as on sacred days like Christmas, thousands of people climbed the hill to its great archways, looking like lines of ants all moving in the same direction.

When you came to the building itself, you found stone columns and dark passages, and a grand entrance leading to the main room of the church. This room was so long that one standing at the doorway could scarcely see to the other end, where the choir stood by the marble altar. In the farthest corner was the organ; and this organ was so loud that sometimes when it played, the people for miles around would close their shutters and prepare for a great thunderstorm. Altogether, no such church as this was ever seen before, especially when it was lighted up for some festival, and crowded with people, young and old.

But the strangest thing about the whole building was the wonderful chime of bells. At one corner of the church was a great gray tower, with ivy growing over it as far up as one could see. I say as far as one could see, because the tower was quite great enough to fit the great church, and it rose so far into the sky that it was only in very fair weather that any one claimed to be able to see the top. Even then one could not be certain that it was in sight. Up, and up, and up climbed the stones and the ivy; and, as the men who built the church had been dead for hundreds of years, every one had forgotten how high the tower was supposed to be.

Now all the people knew that at the top of the tower was a chime of Christmas bells. They had hung there ever since the church had been built, and were the most beautiful bells in the world. Some thought it was because a great musician had cast them and arranged them in their place; others said it was because of the great height, which reached up where the air was clearest and purest: however that might be, no one who had ever heard the chimes denied that they were the sweetest in the world. Some described them as sounding like angels far up in the sky; others, as sounding like strange winds singing through the trees.

But the fact was that no one had heard them for years and years. There was an old man living not far from the church, who said that his mother had spoken of hearing them when she was a little girl, and he was the only one who was sure of as much as that. They were Christmas chimes, you see, and were not meant to be played by men or on common days. It was the custom on Christmas Eve for all the people to bring to the church their offerings to the Christ-child; and when the greatest and best offering was laid on the altar, there used to come sounding through the music of the choir the Christmas chimes far up in the tower. Some said that the wind rang them, and others that they were so high that the angels could set them swinging. But for many long years they had never been heard.

It was said that people had been growing less careful of their gifts for the Christ-child, and that no offering was brought, great enough to deserve the music of the chimes. Every Christmas Eve the rich people still crowded to the altar, each one trying to bring some better gift than any other, without giving anything that he wanted for himself, and the church was crowded with those who thought that perhaps the wonderful bells might be heard again. But although the service was splendid, and the offerings plenty, only the roar of the wind could be heard, far up in the stone tower.

Now, a number of miles from the city, in a little country village, where nothing could be seen of the great church but glimpses of the tower when the weather was fine, lived a boy named Pedro, and his little brother. They knew very little about the Christmas chimes, but they had heard of the service in the church on Christmas Eve, and had a secret plan, which they had often talked over when by themselves they would go to see the beautiful celebration.

"Nobody can guess, Little Brother," Pedro would say, "all the fine things there are to see and hear; and I have even heard it said that the Christ-child sometimes comes down to bless the service. What if we could see Him?"

The day before Christmas was bitterly cold, with a few lonely snowflakes flying in the air, and a hard white crust on the ground. Sure enough, Pedro and Little Brother were able to slip quietly away early in the afternoon; and although the walking was hard in the frosty air, before nightfall they had trudged so far, hand in hand, that they saw the lights of the big city just ahead of them. Indeed, they were about to enter one of the great gates in the wall that surrounded it, when they saw something dark on the snow near their path, and stepped aside to look at it.

It was a poor woman, who had fallen just outside the city, too sick and tired to get in where she might have found shelter. The soft snow made of a drift a sort of pillow for her, and she would soon be so sound asleep, in the wintry air, that no one could ever waken her again. All this Pedro saw in a moment, and he knelt down beside her and tried to rouse her, even tugging at her arm a little, as though he would have tried to carry her away. He turned her face toward him, so that he could rub some of the snow on it, and when he had looked at her silently a moment he stood up again, and said:

"It's no use, Little Brother. You will have to go on alone."

"Alone?" cried Little Brother. "And you not see the Christmas festival?"

"No," said Pedro, and he could not keep back a bit of a choking sound in his throat. "See this poor woman. Her face looks like the Madonna in the chapel window, and she will freeze to death if nobody cares for her. Everyone has gone to the church now, but when you come back you can bring someone to help her. I will rub her to keep her from freezing, and perhaps get her to eat the bun that is left in my pocket."

"But I cannot bear to leave you, and go on alone," said Little Brother.

"Both of us need not miss the service," said Pedro, "and it had better be I than you. You can easily find your way to the church; and you must see and hear everything twice, Little Brother—once for you and once for me. I am sure the Christ-child must know how I should love to come with you and worship Him; and oh! if you get a chance, Little Brother, to slip up to the altar without getting in anyone's way, take this little silver piece of mine, and lay it down for my offering, when no one is looking. Do not forget where you have left me, and forgive me for not going with you."

In this way he hurried Little Brother off to the city, and winked hard to keep back the tears, as he heard the crunching footsteps sounding farther and farther away in the twilight. It was pretty hard to lose the music and splendor of the Christmas celebration that he had been planning for so long, and spend the time instead in that lonely place in the snow.

The great church was a wonderful place that night. Everyone said that it had never looked so bright and beautiful before. When the organ played and the thousands of people sang, the walls shook with the sound, and little Pedro, away outside the city wall, felt the earth tremble around him.

At the close of the service came the procession with the offerings to be laid on the altar. Rich men and great men marched proudly up to lay down their gifts to the Christ-child. Some brought wonderful jewels, some baskets of gold so heavy that they could scarcely carry them down the aisle. A great writer laid down a book that he had been making for years and years. And last of all walked the king of the country, hoping with all the rest to win for himself the chime of the Christmas bells. There went a great murmur through the church, as the people saw the king take from his head the royal crown, all set with precious stones, and lay it gleaming on the altar, as his offering to the holy Child. "Surely," everyone said, "we shall hear the bells now, for nothing like this has ever happened before."

But still only the cold old wind was heard in the tower, and the people shook their heads; and some of them said, as they had before, that they never really believed the story of the chimes, and doubted if they ever rang at all.

The procession was over, and the choir began the closing hymn. Suddenly the organist stopped playing as though he had been shot, and everyone looked at the old minister, who was standing by the altar, holding up his hand for silence. Not a sound could be heard from anyone in the church, but as all the people strained their ears to listen, there came softly, but distinctly, swinging through the air, the sound of the chimes in the tower. So far away, and yet so clear the music seemed—so much sweeter were the notes than anything that had been heard before, rising and falling away up there in the sky, that the people in the church sat for a moment as still as though something held each of them by the shoulders. Then they all stood up together and stared straight at the altar, to see what great gift had awakened the long-silent bells.

But all that the nearest of them saw was the childish figure of Little Brother, who had crept softly down the aisle when no one was looking, and had laid Pedro's little piece of silver on the altar.

The Philanthropist's Christmas

James Weber Linn

Did you see this committee yesterday, Mr. Mathews?" asked the philanthropist. His secretary looked up.

"Yes, sir."

"You recommend them then?"

"Yes, sir."

"For fifty thousand?"

"For fifty thousand—yes, sir."

"Their corresponding subscriptions are guaranteed?"

"I went over the list carefully, Mr. Carter. The money is promised, and by responsible people."

"Very well," said the philanthropist. "You may notify them, Mr. Mathews, that my fifty thousand will be available as the bills come in."

"Yes, sir."

Old Mr. Carter laid down the letter he had been reading, and took up another. As he perused it his white eyebrows rose in irritation.

"Mr. Mathews!" he snapped.

"Yes, sir?"

"You are careless, sir!"

"I beg your pardon, Mr. Carter?" questioned the secretary, his face flushing. The old gentleman tapped impatiently the letter he held in his hand.

"Do you pay no attention, Mr. Mathews, to my rule that no personal letters containing appeals for aid are to reach me? How do you account for this, may I ask?"

"I beg your pardon," said the secretary again. "You will see, Mr. Carter, that that letter is dated three weeks ago. I have had the woman's case carefully investigated. She is undoubtedly of good reputation, and undoubtedly in need; and as she speaks of her father as having associated with you, I thought perhaps you would care to see her letter."

"A thousand worthless fellows associated with me," said the old man, harshly. "In a great factory, Mr. Mathews, a boy works alongside of the men he is put with; he does not pick and choose. I dare say this woman is telling the truth. What of it? You know that I regard my money as a public trust. Were my energy, my concentration, to be wasted by innumerable individual assaults, what would become of them? My fortune would slip through my fingers as unprofitably as sand. You understand, Mr. Mathews? Let me see no more individual letters. You know that Mr. Whittemore has full authority to deal with them. May I trouble you to ring? I am going out."

A man appeared very promptly in answer to the bell.

"Sniffen, my overcoat," said the philanthropist.

"It is 'ere, sir," answered Sniffen, helping the thin old man into the great fur folds.

"There is no word of the dog, I suppose, Sniffen?"

"None, sir. The police was here again yesterday sir, but they said as 'ow—'

"The police!" The words were fierce with scorn. "Eight thousand incompetents!" He turned abruptly and went toward the door, where he halted a moment.

"Mr. Mathews, since that woman's letter did reach me, I suppose I must pay for my carelessness—or yours. Send her—what does she say—-four children?—send her a hundred dollars. But, for my sake, send it anonymously. Write her that I pay no attention to such claims." He went out, and Sniffen closed the door behind him.

"Takes losin' the little dog 'ard, don't he?" remarked Sniffen, sadly, to the secretary. "I'm afraid there ain't a chance of findin' 'im now. 'E ain't been stole, nor 'e ain't been found, or they'd 'ave brung him back for the reward. 'E's been knocked on the 'ead, like as not. 'E wasn't much of a dog to look at, you see—just a pup, I'd call 'im. An' after 'e learned that trick of slippin' 'is collar off—well, I fancy Mr. Carter's seen the last of 'im. I do, indeed."

Mr. Carter meanwhile was making his way slowly down the snowy avenue, upon his accustomed walk. The walk, however, was dull today, for Skiddles, his little terrier, was not with him to add interest and excitement. Mr. Carter had found Skiddles in the country a year and a half before. Skiddles, then a puppy, was at the time in a most undignified and undesirable position, stuck in a drain tile, and unable either to advance or to retreat. Mr. Carter had shoved him forward, after a heroic struggle, whereupon Skiddles had licked his hand. Some thing in the little dog's eye, or his action, had induced the rich philanthropist to bargain for him and buy him at a cost of half a dollar. Thereafter Skiddles became his daily companion, his chief distraction, and finally the apple of his eye.

Skiddles was of no known parentage, hardly of any known breed, but he suited Mr. Carter. What, the millionaire reflected with a proud cynicism, were his own antecedents, if it came to that? But now Skiddles had disappeared.

As Sniffen said, he had learned the trick of slipping free from his collar. One morning the great front doors had been left open for two minutes while the hallway was aired. Skiddles must have slipped down the marble steps unseen, and dodged round the corner. At all events, he had vanished, and although the whole police force of the city had been roused to secure his return, it was aroused in vain. And for three weeks, therefore, a small, straight, white bearded man in a fur overcoat had walked in mournful irritation alone.

He stood upon a corner uncertainly. One way led to the park, and this he usually took; but today he did not want to go to the park—it was too reminiscent of Skiddles. He looked the other way. Down there, if one went far enough, lay "slums," and Mr. Carter hated the sight of slums; they always made him miserable and discontented. With all his money and his philanthropy, was there still necessity for such misery in the world? Worse still came the intrusive question at times: Had all his money anything to do with the creation of this misery? He owned no tenements; he paid good wages in every factory; he had given sums such as few men have given in the history of philanthropy. Still—there were the slums. However, the worst slums lay some distance off, and he finally turned his back on the park and walked on.

It was the day before Christmas. You saw it in people's faces; you saw it in the holly wreaths that hung in windows; you saw it, even as you passed the splendid, forbidding houses on the avenue, in the green that here and there banked massive doors; but most of all, you saw it in the shops. Up here the shops were smallish, and chiefly of the provision variety, so there was no bewildering display of gifts; but there were Christmas trees everywhere, of all sizes. It was astonishing how many people in that neighborhood seemed to favor the old-fashioned idea of a tree.

Mr. Carter looked at them with his irritation softening. If they made him feel a trifle more lonely, they allowed him to feel also a trifle less responsible—for, after all, it was a fairly happy world.

At this moment he perceived a curious phenomenon a short distance before him—another Christmas tree, but one which moved, apparently of its own volition, along the sidewalk. As Mr. Carter overtook it, he saw that it was borne, or dragged, rather by a small boy who wore a bright red flannel cap and mittens of the same peculiar material. As Mr. Carter looked down at him, he looked up at Mr. Carter, and spoke cheerfully:

"Goin' my way, mister?"

"Why," said the philanthropist, somewhat taken back, "I was!"

"Mind draggin' this a little way?" asked the boy, confidently, "my hands is cold."

"Won't you enjoy it more if you manage to take it home by yourself?"

"Oh, it ain't for me!" said the boy.

"Your employer," said the philanthropist, severely, "is certainly careless if he allows his trees to be delivered in this fashion."

"I ain't deliverin' it, either," said the boy. "This is Bill's tree."

"Who is Bill?"

"He's a feller with a back that's no good."

"Is he your brother?"

"No. Take the tree a little way, will you, while I warm myself?"

The philanthropist accepted the burden—he did not know why. The boy, released, ran forward, jumped up and down, slapped his red flannel mittens on his legs, and then ran back again. After repeating these maneuvers two or three times, he returned to where the old gentleman stood holding the tree.

"Thanks," he said. "Say, mister, you look like Santa Claus yourself, standin' by the tree, with your fur cap and your coat. I bet you don't have to run to keep warm, hey?" There was high admiration in his look. Suddenly his eyes sparkled with an inspiration.

"Say, mister," he cried, "will you do something for me? Come in to Bill's—he lives only a block from here—and just let him see you. He's only a kid, and he'll think he's seen Santa Claus, sure. We can tell him you're so busy tomorrow you have to go to lots of places today. You won't have to give him anything. We're looking out for all that. Bill got hurt in the summer, and he's been in bed ever since. So we are giving him a Christmas tree and all. He gets a bunch of things—an air gun, and a train that goes around when you wind her up. They're great!"

"You boys are doing this?"

"Well, it's our club at the settlement, and of course Miss Gray thought of it, and she's givin' Bill the train. Come along, mister."

But Mr. Carter declined.

"All right," said the boy. "I guess, what with Pete and all, Bill will have Christmas enough."

"Who is Pete?"

"Bill's dog. He's had him three weeks now—best little pup you ever saw!"

A dog which Bill had had three weeks—and in a neighborhood not a quarter of a mile from the avenue. It was three weeks since Skiddles had disappeared. That this dog was Skiddles was of course most improbable, and yet the philanthropist was ready to grasp at any clue which might lead to the lost terrier.

"How did Bill get this dog?" he demanded.

"I found him myself. Some kids had tin-canned him, and he came into our entry. He licked my hand, and then sat up on his hind legs. Somebody'd taught him that, you know. I thought right away, 'Here's a dog for Bill!' And I took him over there and fed him, and they kept him in Bill's room two or three days, so he shouldn't get scared again and run off; and now he wouldn't leave Bill for anybody. Of course, he ain't much of a dog, Pete ain't," he added "he's just a pup, but he's mighty friendly!"

"Boy," said Mr. Carter, "I guess I'll just go round and"—he was about to add, "have a look at that dog," but fearful of raising suspicion, he ended—"and see Bill."

The tenements to which the boy led him were of brick, and reasonably clean. Nearly every window showed some sign of Christmas.

The tree-bearer led the way into a dark hall, up one flight—Mr. Carter assisting with the tree—and down another dark hall, to a door, on which he knocked. A woman opened it.

"Here's the tree!" said the boy, in a loud whisper. "Is Bill's door shut?"

Mr. Carter stepped forward out of the darkness. "I beg your pardon, madam," he said. "I met this young man in the street, and he asked me to come here and see a playmate of his who is, I understand, an invalid. But if I am intruding—"

"Come in," said the woman, heartily, throwing the door open. "Bill will be glad to see you, sir."

The philanthropist stepped inside.

The room was decently furnished and clean. There was a sewing machine in the corner, and in both the windows hung wreaths of holly. Between the windows was a cleared space, where evidently the tree, when decorated, was to stand.

"Are all the things here?" eagerly demanded the tree-bearer.

"They're all here, Jimmy," answered Mrs. Bailey. "The candy just came."

"Say," cried the boy, pulling off his red flannel mittens to blow on his fingers, "won't it be great? But now Bill's got to see Santa Claus. I'll just go in and tell him, an' then, when I holler, mister, you come on, and pretend you're Santa Claus." And with incredible celerity the boy opened the door at the opposite end of the room and disappeared.

"Madam," said Mr. Carter, in considerable embarrassment, "I must say one word. I am Mr. Carter, Mr. Allan Carter. You may have heard my name?"

She shook her head. "No, sir."

"I live not far from here on the avenue. Three weeks ago I lost a little dog that I valued very much. I have had all the city searched since then, in vain. To-day I met the boy who has just left us. He informed me that three weeks ago he found a dog, which is at present in the possession of your son. I wonder—is it not just possible that this dog may be mine?"

Mrs. Bailey smiled. "I guess not, Mr. Carter. The dog Jimmy found hadn't come off the avenue—not from the look of him. You know there's hundreds and hundreds of dogs without homes, sir. But I will say for this one, he has a kind of a way with him."

"Hark!" said Mr. Carter.

There was a rustling and a snuffing at the door at the far end of the room, a quick scratching of feet.

Then: "Woof! woof! woof!" sharp and clear came happy impatient little barks. The philanthropist's eyes brightened. "Yes," he said, "that is the dog."

"I doubt if it can be, sir," said Mrs. Bailey, deprecatingly.

"Open the door, please," commanded the philanthropist, "and let us see." Mrs. Bailey complied. There was a quick jump, a tumbling rush, and Skiddles, the lost Skiddles, was in the philanthropist's arms. Mrs. Bailey shut the door with a troubled face.

"I see it's your dog, sir," she said, "but I hope you won't be thinking that Jimmy or I—"

"Madam," interrupted Mr. Carter, "I could not be so foolish. On the contrary, I owe you a thousand thanks."

Mrs. Bailey looked more cheerful. "Poor little Billy!" she said. "It'll come hard on him, losing Pete just at Christmas time. But the boys are so good to him, I dare say he'll forget it."

"Who are these boys?" inquired the philanthropist. "Isn't their action—somewhat unusual?"

"It's Miss Gray's club at the settlement, sir," explained Mrs. Bailey. "Every Christmas they do this for somebody. It's not charity; Billy and I don't need charity, or take it. It's just friendliness. They're good boys."

"I see," said the philanthropist. He was still wondering about it, though, when the door opened again, and Jimmy thrust out a face shining with anticipation.

"All ready, mister!" he said. "Bill's waitin' for you!"

"Jimmy," began Mrs. Bailey, about to explain, "the gentleman—"

But the philanthropist held up his hand, interrupting her. "You'll let me see your son, Mrs. Bailey?" he asked, gently.

"Why, certainly, sir."

Mr. Carter put Skiddles down and walked slowly into the inner room. The bed stood with its side toward him. On it lay a small boy of seven, rigid of body, but with his arms free and his face lighted with joy. "Hello, Santa Claus!" he piped, in a voice shrill with excitement.

"Hello, Bill!" answered the philanthropist, sedately.

The boy turned his eyes on Jimmy.

"He knows my name," he said, with glee.

"He knows everybody's name," said Jimmy. "Now you tell him what you want, Bill, and he'll bring it tomorrow."

"How would you like," said the philanthropist, reflectively, "an—an—" he hesitated, it seemed so incongruous with that stiff figure on the bed—"an air-gun?"

"I guess yes," said Bill, happily.

"And a train of cars," broke in the impatient Jimmy, "that goes like sixty when you wind her?"

"Hi!" said Bill.

The philanthropist solemnly made notes of this.

"How about," he remarked, inquiringly, "a tree?"

"Honest?" said Bill.

"I think it can be managed," said Santa Claus. He advanced to the bedside. "I'm glad to have seen you, Bill. You know how busy I am, but I hope—I hope to see you again."

"Not till next year, of course," warned Jimmy.

"Not till then, of course," assented Santa Claus. "And now, good-bye."

"You forgot to ask him if he'd been a good boy," suggested Jimmy.

"I have," said Bill. "I've been fine. You ask mother."

"She gives you—she gives you both a high character," said Santa Claus. "Good-bye again," and so saying he withdrew. Skiddles followed him out. The philanthropist closed the door of the bedroom, and then turned to Mrs. Bailey.

She was regarding him with awestruck eyes.

"Oh, sir," she said, "I know now who you are—the Mr. Carter that gives so much away to people!"

The philanthropist nodded, deprecatingly.

"Just so, Mrs. Bailey," he said. "And there is one gift—or loan rather—which I should like to make to you. I should like to leave the little dog with you till after the holidays. I'm afraid I'll have to claim him then; but if you'll keep him till after Christmas—and let me find, perhaps, another dog for Billy—I shall be much obliged."

Again the door of the bedroom opened, and Jimmy emerged quietly.

"Bill wants the pup," he explained.

"Pete! Pete!" came the piping but happy voice from the inner room.

Skiddles hesitated. Mr. Carter made no sign.

"Pete! Pete!" shrilled the voice again.

Slowly, very slowly, Skiddles turned and went back into the bedroom.

"You see," said Mr. Carter, smiling, "he won't be too unhappy away from me, Mrs. Bailey."

On his way home the philanthropist saw even more evidences of Christmas gaiety along the streets than before. He stepped out briskly, in spite of his sixty-eight years; he even hummed a little tune.

When he reached the house on the avenue he found his secretary still at work.

"Oh, by the way, Mr. Mathews," he said, "did you send that letter to the woman, saying I never paid attention to personal appeals? No? Then write her, please, enclosing my check for two hundred dollars, and wish her a very Merry Christmas in my name, will you? And hereafter will you always let me see such letters as that one—of course after careful investigation? I fancy perhaps I may have been too rigid in the past."

"Certainly, sir," answered the bewildered secretary. He began fumbling excitedly for his note-book.

"I found the little dog," continued the philanthropist. "You will be glad to know that."

"You have found him?" cried the secretary. "Have you got him back, Mr. Carter? Where was he?"

"He was—detained—on Oak Street, I believe," said the philanthropist. "No, I have not got him back yet. I have left him with a young boy till after the holidays."

He settled himself to his papers, for philanthropists must toil even on the twenty-fourth of December, but the secretary shook his head in a daze. "I wonder what's happened?" he said to himself.

Christmas Day at Sea

Joseph Conrad

Theologically Christmas Day is the greatest occasion for rejoicing offered to sinful mankind; but this aspect of it is so august and so great that the human mind refuses to contemplate it steadily, perhaps because of its own littleness, for which, of course, it is in no way to blame. It prefers to concentrate its attention on ceremonial observances, expressive generally of goodwill and festivity, such, for instance, as giving presents and eating plum-puddings. It may be said at once here that from that conventional point of view the spirit of Christmas Day at sea appears distinctly weak. The opportunities, the materials too, are lacking. Of course, the ship's company get a plum-pudding of some sort, and when the captain appears on deck for the first time the officer of the morning watch greets him with a "Merry Christmas, sir," in a tone only moderately effusive. Anything more would be, owing to the difference in station, not correct. Normally he may expect a return for this in the shape of a "the same to you" of a nicely graduated heartiness. He does not get it always, however.

On Christmas morning, many years ago (I was young then and anxious to do the correct thing), my conventional greeting was met by a grimly scathing "Looks like it, doesn't it?" from my captain. Nothing more. A three days' more or less thick weather had turned frankly into a dense fog, and I had him called according to orders. We were in the chops of the Channel, with the Scilly Islands on a vague bearing within thirty miles of us, and not a breath of wind anywhere. There the ship remained wrapped up in a damp blanket and as motionless as a post stuck right in the way of the wretched steamboats groping blindly in and out of the Channel. I felt I had behaved tactlessly; yet how rude it would have been to have withheld the season's greetings from my captain!

It is very difficult to know what is the right thing to do when one is young. I suffered exceedingly from my gaucherie; but imagine my disgust when in less than half an hour we had the narrowest possible escape from a collision with a steamer which, without the slightest warning sound, appeared like a vague dark blot in the fog on our bow. She only took on the shape of a ship as she passed within twenty yards of the end of our jib-boom, terrifying us with the furious screeching of her whistle. Her form melted into nothing, long before the end of the beastly noise, but I hope that her people heard the simultaneous yell of execration from thirty-six throats which we sent after her by way of a Christmas greeting. Nothing more at variance with the spirit of peace and goodwill could be imagined; and I must add that I never saw a whole ship's company get so much affected by one of the "close calls" of the sea. We remained jumpy all the morning and consumed our Christmas puddings at noon with restless eyes and straining ears as if under the shadow of some impending marine calamity or other.

On shore, of course, a calamity at Christmastime would hardly take any other shape than that of an avalanche—avalanche of unpaid bills. I think that it is the absence of that kind of danger which makes Christmas at sea rather agreeable on the whole. An additional charm consists in there being no worry about presents. Presents ought to be unexpected things. The giving and receiving of presents at appointed times seems to me a hypocritical ceremony, like exchanging gifts of Dead Sea fruit in proof of sham of good-fellowship. But the sea of which I write here is a live sea; the fruits one chances to gather on it may be salt as tears or bitter as death, but they never taste like ashes in the mouth.

In all my twenty years of wandering over the restless waters of the globe I can only remember one Christmas Day celebrated by a present given or received. It was, in my view, a proper live sea transaction, no offering of Dead Sea fruit; and in its unexpectedness perhaps worth recording. Let me tell you first that it happened in the year 1879, long before there was any thought of wireless messages, and when an inspired person trying to prophesy broadcasting would have been regarded as a particularly offensive nuisance and probably sent to a rest-cure home. We used to call them madhouses then, in our rude, cave-man way.

The daybreak of Christmas Day in the year 1879 was fine. The sun began to shine some time about four o'clock over the somber expanse of the Southern Ocean in latitude 51; and shortly afterwards a sail was sighted ahead. The wind was light, but a heavy swell was running. Presently I wished a "Merry Christmas" to my captain. He looked still sleepy, but amiable. I reported the distant sail to him and ventured the opinion that there was something wrong with her. He said, "Wrong?" in an incredulous tone. I pointed out that she had all her upper sails furled and that she was brought to the wind, which, in that region of the world, could not be accounted for on any other theory. He took the glasses from me, directed them towards her stripped masts resembling three Swedish safety matches, flying up and down and waggling to and fro ridiculously in that heaving and austere wilderness of countless water-hills, and returned them to me without a word. He only yawned. This marked display of callousness gave me a shock. In those days I was generally inexperienced and still a comparative stranger in that particular region of the world of waters.

The captain, as is a captain's way, disappeared from the deck; and after a time our carpenter came up the poop-ladder carrying an empty small wooden keg, of the sort in which certain ship's provisions are packed. I said, surprised, "What do you mean by lugging this thing up here, Chips?"—"Captain's orders, sir," he explained shortly.

I did not like to question him further, and so we only exchanged Christmas greetings and he went away. The next person to speak to me was the steward. He came running up the companion-stairs: "Have you any old newspapers in your room, sir?"

We had left Sydney, N. S. W., eighteen days before. There were several old Sydney Heralds, Telegraphs and Bulletin in my cabin, besides a few home papers received by the last mail. "Why do you ask, steward?" I inquired naturally. "The captain would like to have them," he said.

And even then I did not understand the inwardness of these eccentricities. I was only lost in astonishment at them. It was eight o'clock before we had closed with that ship, which, under her short canvas and heading nowhere in particular, seemed to be loafing aimlessly on the very threshold of the gloomy home of storms. But long before that hour I had learned from the number of the boats she carried that this nonchalant ship was a whaler. She was the first whaler I had ever seen. She had hoisted the Stars and Stripes at her peak, and her signal flags had told us already that her name was: "Alaska—two years out from New York— east from Honolulu—two hundred and fifteen days on the cruising-ground."

We passed, sailing slowly, within a hundred yards of her; and just as our steward started ringing the breakfast-bell, the captain and I held aloft, in good view of the figures watching us over her stern, the keg, properly headed up and containing, besides an enormous bundle of old newspapers, two boxes of figs in honour of the day. We flung it far out over the rail. Instantly our ship, sliding down the slope of a high swell, left it far behind in our wake. On board the Alaska a man in a fur cap flourished an arm; another, a much be-whiskered person, ran forward suddenly. I never saw anything so ready and so smart as the way that whaler, rolling desperately all the time, lowered one of her boats. The Southern Ocean went on tossing the two ships like a juggler his gilt balls, and the microscopic white spec of the boat seemed to come into the game instantly, as if shot out from a catapult on the enormous and lonely stage. That Yankee whaler lost not a moment in picking up her Christmas present from the English wool-clipper.

Before we had increased the distance very much she dipped her ensign in thanks, and asked to be reported "All well, with a catch of three fish." I suppose it paid them for two hundred and fifteen days of risk and toil, away from the sounds and sights of the inhabited world, like outcasts devoted, beyond the confines of mankind's life, to some enchanted and lonely penance.

Christmas Days at sea are a varied character, fair to middling and down to plainly atrocious. In this statement I do not include Christmas Days on board passenger ships. A passenger is, of course, a brother (or sister), and quite a nice person in a way, but his Christmas Days are, I suppose, what he wants them to be: the conventional festivities of an expensive hotel included in the price of his ticket.

To Springvale for Christmas

ZONA GALE

✳

When President Arthur Tilton of Briarcliff College, who usually used a two-cent stamp, said, "Get me Chicago, please," his secretary was impressed, looked for vast educational problems to be in the making, and heard instead:

"Ed? Well, Ed, you and Rick and Grace and I are going out to Springvale for Christmas . . . Yes, well, I've got a family too, you recall. But Mother was seventy last fall and—Do you realize that it's eleven years since we all spent Christmas with her? Grace has been every year. She's going this year. And so are we! And we take her the best Christmas she ever had, too. Ed, Mother was seventy last fall . . ."

At dinner, he asked his wife what would be a suitable gift, a very special gift, for a woman of seventy. And she said: "Oh, your mother. Well, dear, I should think the material for a good wool dress would be right. I'll select it for you, if you like . . ." He said that he would see, and he did not reopen the subject.

In town on December twenty-fourth he timed his arrival to allow him an hour in a shop. There he bought a silver-gray silk of a fineness and a lightness which pleased him and at a price which made him comfortably guilty. And at the shop, Ed, who was Edward McKillop Tilton, head of a law firm, picked him up.

"Where's your present?" Arthur demanded.

Edward drew a case from his pocket and showed him a tiny gold wristwatch of decent manufacture and explained: "I expect you'll think I'm a fool, but you know that Mother has told time for fifty years by the kitchen clock, or else the shield of the black marble parlor angel who never goes—you get the idea?—and so I bought her this."

At the station was Grace, and the boy who bore her bag bore also a parcel of great dimensions.

"Mother already has a feather bed," Arthur reminded her.

"They won't let you take an automobile into the coach," Edward warned her.

"It's a rug for the parlor," Grace told them. "You know it is a parlor—one of the few left in the Mississippi Valley. And Mother has had that ingrain down since before we left home . . ."

Grace's eyes were misted. Why would women always do that? This was no occasion for sentiment. This was a merry Christmas.

"Very nice. And Ricky'd better look sharp," said Edward dryly.

Ricky never did look sharp. About trains he was conspicuously ignorant. He had no occupation. Some said that he "wrote," but no one had ever seen anything that he had written. He lived in town—no one knew how—never accepted a cent from his brothers and was beloved of everyone, most of all of his mother.

"Ricky won't bring anything, of course," they said.

But when the train pulled out without him, observably, a porter came staggering through the cars carrying two great suitcases among brothers and sister and rug. "I had only a minute to spare," he said regretfully. "If I'd had two, I could have snatched some flowers. I flung 'em my card and told 'em to send 'em."

"Why are you taking so many lugs?" they wanted to know.

Ricky focused on the suitcases. "Just necessities," he said. "Just the presents. I didn't have room for anything else."

"Presents! What?"

"Well," said Ricky, "I'm taking books. I know Mother doesn't care much for books, but the bookstore's the only place I can get trusted."

They turned over his books: fiction, travels, biography, a new illustrated edition of the Bible—they were willing to admire his selection. And Grace said confusedly but appreciatively: "You know, the parlor bookcase has never had a thing in it excepting a green curtain over it!"

And they were all borne forward, well pleased.

Springvale has eight hundred inhabitants. As they drove through the principal street at six o'clock on that evening of December twenty-fourth, all that they expected to see abroad was the popcorn wagon and a cat or two. Instead they counted seven automobiles and estimated thirty souls, and no one paid the slightest attention to them as strangers. Springvale was becoming metropolitan. There was a new church on one corner and a store building bore the sign PUBLIC LIBRARY. Even the little hotel had a rubber plant in the window and a strip of cretonne overhead.

The three men believed themselves to be a surprise. But, mindful of the panic to be occasioned by four appetites precipitated into a Springvale ménage, Grace had told. Therefore the parlor was lighted and heated, there was in the air of the passage an odor of brown gravy which, no butler's pantry ever having inhibited, seemed a permanent savory. By the happiest chance, Mrs. Tilton had not heard their arrival nor—the parlor angel being in her customary eclipse and the kitchen grandfather's clock wrong—had she begun to look for them. They slipped in, they followed Grace down the hall, they entered upon her in her gray gingham apron worn over her best blue serge, and they saw her first in profile, frosting a lemon pie. With some assistance from her, they all took her in their arms at once.

"Aren't you surprised?" cried Edward in amazement.

"I haven't got over being surprised," she said placidly, "since I first heard you were coming!"

She gazed at them tenderly, with flour on her chin, and then said: "There's something you won't like. We're going to have the family dinner tonight."

Their clamor that they would entirely like that did not change her look.

"Our church couldn't pay the minister this winter," she said, "on account of the new church building. So the minister and his wife are boarding around with the congregation. Tomorrow's their day to come here for a week. It's a hard life, and I didn't have the heart to change 'em."

Her family covered their regret as best they could and entered upon her little feast. At the head of the table, with her four "children" about her, and Father's armchair left vacant, they perceived that she was not quite the figure they had been thinking her. In this interval they had grown to think of her as a pathetic figure. Not because their father had died, not because she insisted on Springvale as a residence, not because of her eyes. Just pathetic. Mothers of grown children, they might have given themselves the suggestion, were always pathetic. But here was Mother, a definite person, with poise and with ideas, who might be proud of her offspring, but who, in her heart, never forgot that they were her offspring and that she was the parent stock.

"I wouldn't eat two pieces of that pie," she said to President Tilton; "it's pretty rich." And he answered humbly: "Very well, Mother." And she took with composure Ricky's light chant:

"Now, you must remember, wherever you are,
That you are the jam, but your mother's the jar."

"Certainly, my children," she said. "And I'm about to tell you when you may have your Christmas presents. Not tonight. Christmas Eve is no proper time for presents. It's stealing a day outright! And you miss the fun of looking forward all night long. The only proper time for the presents is after breakfast on Christmas morning, after the dishes are washed. The minister and his wife may get here any time from nine on. That means we've got to get to bed early!"

President Arthur Tilton lay in his bed looking at the muslin curtain on which the streetlamp threw the shadow of a bare elm which he remembered. He thought: *She's a pioneer spirit. She's the kind who used to go ahead anyway, even if they had missed the emigrant party, and who used to cross the plains alone. She's the backbone of the world. I wish I could megaphone that to the students at Briar-cliff who think their mothers "try to boss" them!*

"Don't leave your windows open too far," he heard from the hall. "The wind's changed."

In the light of a snowy morning the home parlor showed the cluttered com-monplace of a room whose furniture and ornaments were not believed to be beautiful and most of them known not to be useful. Yet when—after the dishes were washed—these five came to the leather chair which bore the gifts, the mo-ment was intensely satisfactory. This in spite of the sense of haste with which the parcels were attacked—lest the minister and his wife arrive in their midst.

"That's one reason," Mrs. Tilton said, "why I want to leave part of my Christmas for you until I take you to the train tonight. Do you care?"

"I'll leave a present I know about until then too," said Ricky. "May I?"

"Come on now, though," said President Arthur Tilton. "I want to see Mother get her dolls."

It was well that they were not of an age to look for exclamations of delight from Mother. To every gift her reaction was one of startled rebuke.

"Grace! How could you? All that money! Oh, it's beautiful! But the old one would have done me all my life . . . Why, Edward! You extravagant boy! I never had a watch in my life. You ought not to have gone to all that expense. Arthur Tilton! A silk dress! What a firm piece of goods! I don't know what to say to you—you're all too good to me!"

At Ricky's books she stared and said: "My dear boy, you've been very reck-less. Here are more books than I can ever read—now. Why, that's almost more than they've got to start the new library with. And you spent all that money on me!"

It dampened their complacence, but they understood her concealed delight and forgave her an honest regret of their modest prodigality. For, when they opened her gifts for them, they felt the same reluctance to take the hours and hours of patient knitting for which these stood.

"Hush, and hurry," was her comment, "or the minister'll get us!"

The minister and his wife, however, were late. The second side of the turkey was ready and the mince pie hot when, toward noon, they came to the door—a faint little woman and a thin man with beautiful, exhausted eyes. They were both in some light glow of excitement and disregarded Mrs. Tilton's efforts to take their coats.

"No," said the minister's wife. "No. We do beg your pardon. But we find we have to go into the country this morning."

"It is absolutely necessary that we go into the country," said the minister earnestly. "This morning," he added impressively.

"Into the country! You're going to be here for dinner."

They were firm. They had to go into the country. They shook hands almost tenderly with these four guests. "We just heard about you in the post office," they said. "Merry Christmas—oh, merry Christmas! We'll be back about dark."

They left their two shabby suitcases on the hall floor and went away.

"All the clothes they've got between them would hardly fill these up," said Mrs. Tilton mournfully. "Why on earth do you suppose they'd turn their back on a dinner that smells so good and go off into the country at noon on Christmas Day? They wouldn't do that for another invitation. Likely somebody's sick," she ended, her puzzled look denying her tone of finality.

"Well, thank the Lord for the call to the country," said Ricky shamelessly. "It saved our day."

They had their Christmas dinner; they had their afternoon—safe and happy and uninterrupted. Five commonplace-looking folk in a commonplace-looking house, but the eye of love knew that this was not all. In the wide sea of their routine they had found and taken for their own this island day, unforgettable.

"I thought it was going to be a gay day," said Ricky at its close, "but it hasn't. It's been heavenly! Mother, shall we give them the rest of their presents now, you and I?"

"Not yet," she told them. "Ricky, I want to whisper to you."

She looked so guilty that they all laughed at her. Ricky was laughing when he came back from that brief privacy. He was still laughing mysteriously when his mother turned from a telephone call.

"What do you think?" she cried. "That was the woman that brought me my turkey. She knew the minister and his wife were to be with me today. She wants to know why they've been eating a lunch in a cutter out that way. Do you suppose . . ."

They all looked at one another doubtfully, then in abrupt conviction. "They went because they wanted us to have the day to ourselves!"

"Arthur," said Mrs. Tilton with immense determination, "let me whisper to you, too." And from that moment's privacy he also returned smiling, but a bit ruefully.

"Mother ought to be the president of a university," he said.

"Mother ought to be the head of a law firm," said Edward.

"Mother ought to write a book about herself," said Ricky.

Mother's Mother," said Grace, "and that's enough. But you're all so mysterious, except me."

"Grace," said Mrs. Tilton, "you remind me that I want to whisper to you."

Their train left in the late afternoon. Through the white sheets they walked to the station, the somber little woman, the buoyant, capable daughter, the three big sons. She drew them to seclusion down by the baggage room and gave them four envelopes.

"Here's the rest of my Christmas for you," she said. "I'd rather you'd open it on the train. Now, Ricky, what's yours?"

She was firm to their protests. The train was whistling when Ricky owned up that the rest of his Christmas present for his mother was a brand-new daughter, to be acquired as soon as his new book was off the press. "We're going to marry on the advance royalty," he said importantly, "and live on . . ." The rest was lost in the roar of the express.

"Edward!" shouted Mrs. Tilton. "Come here. I want to whisper . . ."

She was obliged to shout it, whatever it was. But Edward heard, and nodded, and kissed her. There was time for her to slip something in Ricky's pocket and for the other good-bys, and then the train drew out. From the other platform they saw her brave, calm face against the background of the little town. A mother of "grown children" pathetic? She seemed to them at that moment the one supremely triumphant figure in life.

They opened their envelopes soberly and sat soberly over the contents. The note, scribbled to Grace, explained: Mother wanted to divide up now what she had had for them in her will. She would keep one house and live on the rent from the other one, and "here's the rest." They laughed at her postscript:

"Don't argue. I ought to give the most—I'm the mother."

"And look at her," said Edward solemnly. "As soon as she heard about Ricky, there at the station, she whispered to me that she wanted to send Ricky's sweetheart the watch I'd just given her. Took it off her wrist then and there."

"That must be what she slipped in my pocket," said Ricky.

It was.

"She asked me," he said, "if I minded if she gave those books to the new Springvale Public Library."

"She asked me," said Grace, "if I cared if she gave the new rug to the new church that can't pay its minister."

President Arthur Tilton shouted with laughter. "When we heard where the minister and his wife ate their Christmas dinner," he said, "she whispered to ask me whether she might give the silk dress to her when they get back tonight."

All this they knew by the time the train reached the crossing where they could look back on Springvale. On the slope of the hill lay the little cemetery, and Ricky said, "And she told me that if my flowers got there before dark, she'd take them up to the cemetery for Christmas for Father. By night she won't have even a flower left to tell her we've been there."

"Not even the second side of the turkey," said Grace, "and yet I think . . ."

"So do I," her brothers said.

Three Stockings

JAN STRUTHER

However much one groaned about it beforehand, however much one hated making arrangements and doing up parcels and ordering several days' meals in advance—when it actually happened Christmas Day was always fun.

It began in the same way every year: the handle of her bedroom door being turned just loudly enough to wake her up, but softly enough not to count as waking her up on purpose; Toby glimmering like a moth in the dark doorway, clutching a nobbly Christmas stocking in one hand and holding up his pyjama trousers with the other. (He insisted upon pyjamas, but he had not yet outgrown his sleeping-suit figure.)

"Toby! It's only just after six. I did say not till seven."

"But, Mummy, I can't tell the time. " He was barefoot and shivering, and his eyes were like stars.

"Come here and get warm, you little goat." He was into her bed in a flash, stocking and all. The tail of a clockwork dog scratched her shoulder. A few moments later another head appeared round the door, a little higher up.

"Judy, darling, it's too early, honestly."

"I know, but I heard Toby come in, so I knew you must be awake."

"All right, you can come into bed, but you've got to keep quiet for a bit. Daddy's still asleep."

And then a third head, higher up still, and Vin's voice, even deeper than it had been at Long Leave.

"I say, are the others in here? I thought I heard them."

He curled himself up on the foot of his father's bed. And by that time, of course, Clem was awake too. The old transparent stratagem had worked to perfection once more: there was nothing for it but to switch on the lights, shut the windows, and admit that Christmas Day had insidiously but definitely begun.

The three right hands—Vin's strong and broad, Judy's thin and flexible, Toby's still a star-fish—plunged in and out of the three distorted stockings, until there was nothing left but the time-hallowed tangerine in the toe. (It was curious how that tradition lingered, even nowadays when children had a good supply of fruit all the year round.) Their methods were as different as their hands.

Vin, with little grunts of approval, examined each object carefully as he drew it out, exploring all its possibilities before he went on to the next. Judy, talking the whole time, pulled all her treasures out in a heap, took a quick glance at them and went straight for the one she liked best—a minikin baby in a wicker cradle. Toby pulled all his out, too, but he arranged them in a neat pattern on the eider-down and looked at them for a long time in complete silence. Then he picked up one of them—a big glass marble with coloured squirls inside—and put it by itself a little way off. After that he played with the other toys, appreciatively enough; but from time to time his eyes would stray towards the glass marble, as though to make sure it was still waiting for him.

Mrs. Miniver watched him with a mixture of delight and misgiving. It was her own favourite approach to life: but the trouble was that sometimes the marble rolled away. Judy's was safer; Vin's, on the whole, the wisest of the three.

To the banquet of real presents which was waiting downstairs, covered with a red and white dust-sheet, the stocking-toys, of course, were only an aperitif; but they had a special and exciting quality of their own. Perhaps it was the atmosphere in which they were opened—the chill, the black window-panes, the unfamiliar hour; perhaps it was the powerful charm of the miniature, of toy toys, of smallness squared; perhaps it was the sense of limitation within a strict form, which gives to both the filler and the emptier of a Christmas stocking something of the same enjoyment which is experienced by the writer and the reader of a sonnet; or perhaps it was merely that the spell of the old legend still persisted, even though for everybody in the room except Toby the legend itself was outworn.

There were cross-currents of pleasure, too: smiling glances exchanged by her and Vin about the two younger children (she remembered suddenly, having been an eldest child, the unsurpassable sense of grandeur that such glances gave one); and by her and Clem, because they were both grown-ups; and by her and Judy, because they were both women; and by her and Toby, because they were both the kind that leaves the glass marble till the end. The room was laced with an invis-ible network of affectionate understanding.

This was one of the moments, thought Mrs. Miniver, which paid off at a single stroke all the accumulations on the debit side of parenthood: the morning sickness and the quite astonishing pain; the pram in the passage, the cold mulish glint in the cook's eye; the holiday nurse who had been in the best families; the pungent white mice, the shrivelled caterpillars; the plasticine on the door-han-dles, the face-flannels in the bathroom, the nameless horrors down the crevices of armchairs; the alarms and emergencies, the swallowed button, the inexplicable earache, the ominous rash appearing on the eve of a journey; the school bills and the dentists' bills; the shortened step, the tempered pace, the emotional compromises, the divided loyalties, the adventures continually forsworn.

And now Vin was eating his tangerine, pig by pig; Judy had undressed the black baby and was putting on its frock again back to front; Toby was turning the glass marble round and round against the light, trying to count the squirls. There were sounds of movement in the house; they were within measurable distance of the blessed chink of early morning tea. Mrs. Miniver looked towards the window. The dark sky had already paled a little in its frame of cherry-pink chintz. Eternity framed in domesticity. Never mind. One had to frame it in something, to see it at all.

❄

David's Star of Bethlehem

CHRISTINE WHITING PARMENTER

Scott Carson reached home in a bad humor. Nancy, slipping a telltale bit of red ribbon into her workbasket, realized this as soon as he came in.

It was the twenty-first of December, and a white Christmas was promised. Snow had been falling for hours, and in most of the houses wreaths were already in the windows. It was what one calls "a Christmasy-feeling day," yet, save for that red ribbon in Nancy's basket, there was no sign in the Carson home of the approaching festival.

Scott said, kissing her absentmindedly and slumping into a big chair, "This snow is the very limit. If the wind starts blowing there'll be a fierce time with the traffic. My train was twenty minutes late as it is, and—There's the bell. Who can it be at this hour? I want my dinner."

"I'll go to the door," said Nancy hurriedly, as he started up. "Selma's putting dinner on the table now." Relaxing into his chair Scott heard her open the front door, say something about the storm and, after a moment, wish someone a Merry Christmas.

A Merry Christmas! He wondered that she could say it so calmly. Three years ago on Christmas morning, they had lost their boy—swiftly—terribly without warning. Meningitis, the doctor said. Only a few hours before the child had seemed a healthy, happy youngster, helping them trim the tree; hoping, with a twinkle in the brown eyes so like his mother's, that Santa Claus would remember the fact that he wanted skis! He had gone happily to be after Nancy had read them "The Night Before Christmas," a custom of early childhood's days that the eleven-year-old lad still clung to. Later his mother remembered, with a pang, that when she kissed him good night he had said his head felt "kind of funny." But she had left him lightheartedly enough and gone down to help Scott fill the stockings. Santa had not forgotten the skis; but Jimmy never saw them.

Three years—and the memory still hurt so much that the very thought of Christmas was agony to Scott Carson. Jimmy had slipped away just as the carolers stopped innocently beneath his window, their voices rising clear and penetrating on the dawn-sweet air:

"Silent night—holy night . . ."

Scott arose suddenly. He must not live over that time again. "Who was it?"

he asked gruffly as Nancy joined him, and understanding the gruffness she answered tactfully, "Only the expressman."

"What'd he bring?"

"Just a—a package."

"One naturally supposes that," replied her husband, with a touch of sarcasm. Then, suspicion gripping him, he burst out, "Look here! If you've been getting a Christmas gift for me, I—I won't have it. I told you I wanted to forget Christmas. I—"

"I know, dear," she broke in hastily. "The package was only from Aunt Mary."

"Didn't you tell her we weren't keeping Christmas?" he demanded irritably.

"Yes, Scott; but—but you know Aunt Mary! Come now, dinner's on and I think it's a good one. You'll feel better after you eat."

But Scott found it unaccountably hard to eat; and later, when Nancy was reading aloud in an effort to soothe him, he could not follow. She had chosen something humorous and diverting; but in the midst of a paragraph he spoke, and she knew that he had not been listening.

"Nancy," he said, "is there any place—any place on God's earth where we can get away from Christmas?"

She looked up, answering with sweet gentleness, "It would be a hard place to find, Scott."

He faced her suddenly. "I feel as if I couldn't stand it—the trees—the carols—the merrymaking, you know. Oh, if I could only sleep this week away! But . . . I've been thinking . . . Would—would you consider for one moment going up to camp with me for a day or two? I'd go alone, but—"

"Alone!" she echoed. "Up there in the wilderness at Christmas time? Do you think I'd let you?"

"But it would be hard for you, dear, cold and uncomfortable. I'm a brute to ask it, and yet—"

Nancy was thinking rapidly. They could not escape Christmas, of course. No change of locality could make them forget the anniversary of the day that Jimmy went away. But she was worried about Scott, and the change of scene might help him over the difficult hours ahead. The camp, situated on the mountain a mile from any neighbors, would at least be isolated. There was plenty of bedding, and a big fireplace. It was worth trying.

She said, cheerfully, "I'll go with you, dear. Perhaps the change will make things easier for both of us."

This was Tuesday, and on Thursday afternoon they stepped off the northbound train and stood on the platform watching it vanish into the mountains. The day was crisp and cold. "Two above," the station master told them as they went into the box of a station and moved instinctively toward the red-hot "air-tight" which gave forth grateful warmth.

"I sent a telegram yesterday to Clem Hawkins, over on the mountain road," said Scott. "I know you don't deliver a message so far off; but I took a chance. Do you know if he got it?"

"Yep. Clem don't have a 'phone, but the boy come down for some groceries and I sent it up. If I was you, though, I'd stay to the Central House. Seems as if it would be more cheerful—Christmas time."

"I guess we'll be comfortable enough if Hawkins airs out, and lights a fire," replied Scott, his face hardening at this innocent mention of the holiday. "Is there anyone around here who'll take us up? I'll pay well for it, of course."

"Iry Morse'll go; but you'll have to walk from Hawkinses. The road ain't dug out beyond . . . There's Iry now. You wait, an' I'll holler to him. Hey, Iry!" he called, going to the door, "Will you carry these folks up to the Hawkinses? They'll pay for it."

"Iry," a ruddy-faced young farmer, obligingly appeared, his gray work horse hitched to a one-seated sleigh of ancient and uncomfortable design.

"Have to sit three on a seat," he explained cheerfully; "but we'll be all the warmer for it. Tuck the buffalo robe 'round the lady's feet, mister, and you and me'll use the horse blanket. Want to stop to the store for provisions?"

"Yes. I brought some canned stuff, but we'll need other things," said Nancy. "I've made a list."

"Well, you got good courage," grinned the station master. "I hope you don't get froze to death up in the woods. Merry Christmas to yer, anyhow!"

"The same to you!" responded Nancy, smiling; and noted with a stab of pain that her husband's sensitive lips were trembling.

Under Ira's cheerful conversation, however, Scott relaxed. They talked of crops, the neighbors, and local politics—safe subjects all; but as they passed the district school, where a half-dozen sleighs or flivers were parked, the man explained: "Folks decoratin' the school for the doin's tomorrow afternoon. Christmas tree for the kids, and pieces spoke, and singin'. We got a real live schoolma'am this year, believe me!"

They had reached the road that wound up the mountain toward the Hawkins farm, and as they plodded on, a sudden wind arose that cut their faces. Snow creaked under the runners, and as the sun sank behind the mountain Nancy shivered, not so much with cold as with a sense of loneliness and isolation. It was Scott's voice that roused her:

"Should we have brought snowshoes? I didn't realize that we couldn't be carried all the way."

"Guess you'll get there all right," said Ira. "Snow's packed hard as a drum-head, and it ain't likely to thaw yet a while. Here you are," as he drew up before the weather-beaten, unpainted farmhouse. "You better step inside a minute and warm up."

A shrewish-looking woman was already at the door, opening it but a crack, in order to keep out fresh air and cold.

"I think," said Nancy, with a glance at the deepening shadows, "that we'd better keep right on. I wonder if there's anybody here who'd help carry our bags and provisions."

"There ain't," answered the woman, stepping outside and pulling a faded gray sweater around her shoulders. "Clem's gone to East Conroy with the eggs, and Dave's up to the camp keepin' yer fire goin'. You can take the sled and carry yer stuff on that. There 'tis, by the gate. Dave'll bring it back when he comes. An' tell him to hurry. Like as not, Clem won't get back in time fer milkin'."

"I thought Dave was goin' to help Teacher decorate the school this after-noon," ventured Ira. He was unloading their things as he spoke and roping them to the sled.

"So'd he," responded the woman; "but there wa'n't no one else to light that fire, was they? Guess it won't hurt him none to work for his livin' like other folks. That new schoolma'am, she thinks o' nothing but—"

"Oh, look here!" said the young man, straightening up, a belligerent light in his blue eyes, "it's Christmas! Can Dave go back with me if I stop and milk for him? They'll be workin' all evenin'—lots o' fun for a kid like him, and—"

"No, he can't!" snapped the woman. "His head's enough turned now with speakin' pieces and singin' silly songs. You better be gettin' on, folks. I can't stand here talkin' till mornin'."

She slammed the door, while Ira glared after her retreating figure, kicked the gatepost to relieve his feelings, and then grinned sheepishly.

"Some grouch! Why, she didn't even ask you in to get warm! Well, I wouldn't loiter if I was you. And send that kid right back, or he'll get worse'n a tongue-lashin'. Well, good-bye to you, folks. Hope you have a merry Christmas."

The tramp up the mountain passed almost entirely in silence, for it took their united energy to drag the sled up that steep grade against the wind. Scott drew a breath of relief when they beheld the camp, a spiral of smoke rising from its big stone chimney like a welcome promise of warmth.

"Looks good, doesn't it? But it'll be dark before that boy gets home. I wonder how old—"

They stopped simultaneously as a clear, sweet voice sounded from within the cabin:

"Silent night . . . holy night . . ."

"My God!"

Scott's face went suddenly dead white. He threw out a hand as if to brush something away, but Nancy caught it in hers, pulling it close against her wildly beating heart.

"All is calm . . . all is bright."

The childish treble came weirdly from within, while Nancy cried, "Scott—dearest, don't let go! It's only the little boy singing the carols he's learned in school. Don't you see? Come! Pull yourself together. We must go in."

Even as she spoke the door swung open, and through blurred vision they beheld the figure of a boy standing on the threshold. He was a slim little boy with an old, oddly wistful face, and big brown eyes under a thatch of yellow hair.

"You the city folks that was comin' up? Here, I'll help carry in yer things."

Before either could protest he was down on his knees in the snow, untying Ira's knots with skillful fingers. He would have lifted the heavy suitcase himself, had not Scott, jerked back to the present by the boy's action, interfered.

"I'll carry that in." His voice sounded queer and shaky. "You take the basket. We're late, I'm afraid. You'd better hurry home before it gets too dark. Your mother said—"

"I don't mind the dark," said the boy quietly, as they went within. "I'll coast most o' the way down, anyhow. Guess you heard me singin' when you come along." He smiled, a shy, embarrassed smile as he explained: "It was a good chance to practice the Christmas carols. They won't let me, 'round home. We're goin' to have a show at the school tomorrow. I'm one o' the three kings—you know—'We three kings of Orient are.' I sing the first verse all by myself," he added with childish pride.

There followed a moment's silence. Nancy was fighting a desire to put her arms about the slim boyish figure, while Scott had turned away, unbuckling the straps of his suitcase with fumbling hands. Then Nancy said, "I'm afraid we've kept you from helping at the school this afternoon. I'm so sorry."

The boy drew a resigned breath that struck her as strangely unchildlike.

"You needn't to mind, ma'am. Maybe they wouldn't have let me go anyway; and I've got tomorrow to think about. I—I been reading one o' your books. I like to read."

"What book was it? Would you like to take it home with you for a—" She glanced at Scott, still on his knees by the suit case, and finished hurriedly—"a Christmas gift?"

"Gee! Wouldn't I!" His wistful eyes brightened, then clouded. "Is there a place maybe where I could hide it 'round here? They don't like me to read much to home. They," (a hard look crept into his young eyes), "they burned up the book Teacher gave me a while back. It was 'David Copperfield,' and I hadn't got it finished."

There came a crash as Scott, rising suddenly, upset a chair. The child jumped, and then laughed at himself for being startled.

"Look here, sonny," said Scott huskily, "you must be getting home. Can you bring us some milk tomorrow? I'll find a place to hide your book and tell you about it then. Haven't you got a warmer coat than this?"

He lifted a shabby jacket from the settle and held it out while the boy slipped into it.

"Thanks, mister," he said. "It's hard gettin' it on because it's tore inside. They's only one button," he added, as Scott groped for them. "She don't get much time to sew 'em on. I'll bring up the milk tomorrow mornin'. I got to hurry now or I'll get fits! Thanks for the book ma'am. I'd like it better'n the dancing flames."

Standing at the window Nancy watched him start out in the fast descending dusk. It hurt her to think of that lonely walk; but she thrust the thought aside and turned to Scott, who had lighted a fire on the hearth and seemed absorbed in the dancing flames.

"That's good!" she said cheerfully. "I'll get things started for supper, and then make the bed. I'm weary enough to turn in early. You might bring me the canned stuff in your suitcase, Scott. A hot soup ought to taste good tonight."

She took an apron from her bag and moved toward the tiny kitchen. Dave evidently knew how to build a fire. The stove lids were almost red, and the kettle was singing. Nancy went about her preparations deftly, tired though she was from the unaccustomed tramp, while Scott opened a can of soup, toasted some bread, and carried their meal on a tray to the settles before the hearthfire. It was all very cozy and "Christmasy," thought Nancy, with the wind blustering outside and the flames leaping up the chimney. But she was strangely quiet. The thought of that lonely little figure trudging off in the gray dusk persisted, despite her efforts to forget. It was Scott who spoke, saying out of a silence, "I wonder how old he is."

"The—the little boy?"

He nodded, and she answered gently, "He seemed no older than—I mean, he seemed very young to be milking cows and doing chores."

Again Scott nodded, and a moment passed before he said, "The work wouldn't hurt him though, if he were strong enough; but—did you notice, Nancy, he didn't look half fed? He is an intelligent little chap, though, and his voice—Good lord!" he broke off suddenly, "how can a shrew like that bring such a child into the world? To burn his book! Nancy, I can't understand how things are ordered. Here's that poor boy struggling for development in an unhappy atmosphere—and our Jimmy, who had love, and understanding, and—Tell me, why is it?"

She stretched out a tender hand; but the question remained unanswered, and the meal was finished in silence.

Dave did not come with the milk next morning. They waited till nearly noon, and then tramped off in the snow-clad, pine-scented woods. It was a glorious day, with diamonds sparkling on every fir tree, and they came back refreshed, and ravenous for the delayed meal. Scott wiped the dishes, whistling as he worked. It struck his wife that he hadn't whistled like that for months. Later, the last kitchen rites accomplished, she went to the window, where he stood gazing down the trail.

"He won't come now, Scott."

"The kid? It's not three yet, Nancy."

"But the party begins at four. I suppose everyone for miles around will be there. I wish—" she was about to add that she wished they could have gone too, but something in Scott's face stopped the words. She said instead, "Do you think we'd better go for the milk ourselves?"

"What's the use? They'll all be at the shindig, even that sour-faced woman, I suppose, but somehow—I feel worried about the boy. If he isn't here bright and early in the morning I'll go down and see what's happened. Looks as if it were clouding up again, doesn't it? Perhaps we'll get snowed in!"

Big, lazy-looking snowflakes were already beginning to drift down. Scott piled more wood on the fire, and stretched out on the settle for a nap. But Nancy was restless. She found herself standing repeatedly at the window looking at the snow. She was there when at last Scott stirred and wakened. He sat up blinking, and asked, noting the twilight, "How long have I been asleep?"

Nancy laughed, relieved to hear his voice after the long stillness.

"It's after five."

"Good thunder!" he arose, putting an arm across her shoulders. "Poor girl! I haven't been much company on this trip! But I didn't sleep well last night, couldn't get that boy out of my mind. Why, look!" Scott was staring out of the window into the growing dusk. "Here he is now! I thought you said—"

He was already at the door, flinging it wide in welcome as he went out to lift the box of milk jars from the sled. It seemed to Nancy, as the child stepped inside, that he looked subtly different—discouraged, she would have said of an older person; and when he raised his eyes she saw the unmistakable signs of recent tears.

"Oh, David!" she exclaimed, "why aren't you at the party?"

"I didn't go."

The boy seemed curiously to have withdrawn into himself. His answer was like a gentle "none of your business"; but Nancy was not without a knowledge of boy nature. She thought, "He's hurt—dreadfully. He's afraid to talk for fear he'll cry; but he'll feel better to get it off his mind." She said, drawing him toward the cheerful hearthfire, "But why not, Dave?"

He swallowed, pulling himself together with an heroic effort.

"I had ter milk. The folks have gone to Conroy to Gramma Hawkins's! I like Gramma Hawkins. She told 'em to be sure an' bring me; but there wasn't no one else ter milk, so . . . so . . . ."

It was Scott who came to the rescue as David's voice failed suddenly.

"Are you telling us that your people have gone away, for Christmas, leaving you home alone?"

The boy nodded, winking back tears as he managed a pathetic smile.

"Oh, I wouldn't ha' minded so much if—if it hadn't been for the doin's at the school. Miss Mary was countin' on me ter sing, and speak a piece. I don't know who they could ha' got to be that wise man." His face hardened in a way not good to see in a little boy, and he burst out angrily, "Oh, I'd have gone—after they got off! Darn 'em! But they hung 'round till almost four, and —and then I went for my good suit they—they'd hid it—or carried it away! . . . And there was a Christmas tree . . . ."

His voice faltered again, while Nancy found herself speechless before what she recognized as a devastating disappointment. She glanced at Scott, and was frightened at the consuming anger in his face; but he came forward calmly, laying a steady hand on the boy's shoulder. He said, and, knowing what the words cost him, Nancy's heart went out to her husband in adoring gratitude, "Buck up, old scout! We'll have a Christmas tree! And we'll have a party too, you and Mother and I—darned if we don't! You can speak your piece and sing your carols for us. And mother will read us 'The'"—for an appreciable moment Scott's voice faltered, but he went on gamely—"'The Night Before Christmas.' Did you ever hear it? And I know some stunts that'll make your eyes shine. We'll have our party tomorrow, Christmas Day, sonny; but now" (he was stooping for his overshoes as he spoke), "now we'll go after that tree before it gets too dark! Come on, Mother. We want you, too!"

Mother! Scott hadn't called her that since Jimmy left them! Through tear-blinded eyes Nancy groped for her coat in the diminutive closet. Darkness was coming swiftly as they went into the snowy forest, but they found their tree, and stopped to cut fragrant green branches for decoration. Not till the tree stood proudly in its corner did they remember the lack of tinsel trimmings; but Scott brushed this aside as a mere nothing.

"We've got pop corn, and nothing's prettier. Give us a bite of supper, Nancy, and then I'm going to the village."

"The village! At this hour?"

"You take my sled, mister," cried David, and they saw that his eyes were happy once more, and child-like. "You can coast 'most all the way, like lightning! I'll pop the corn. I'd love to! Gee! It's lucky I milked before I come away!"

The hours that followed passed like magic to Nancy Carson. Veritable wonders were wrought in that small cabin; and oh, it was good to be planning and playing again with a little boy! Not till the child, who had been up since dawn, had dropped asleep on the settle from sheer weariness, did she add the finishing touches to the scene.

"It's like a picture of Christmas," she murmured happily. "The tree, so green and slender with its snowy trimmings—the cone-laden pine at the windows—the bulging stocking at the fireplace, and—and the sleeping boy. I wonder—"

She turned, startled by a step on the creaking snow outside, but it was Scott, of course. He came in quietly, not laden with bundles as she'd expected, but empty-handed. There was, she thought, a strange excitement in his manner as he glanced 'round the fire-lit room, his eyes resting for a moment on David's peaceful face. Then he saw the well-filled stocking at the mantel, and his eyes came back unswerving to hers.

"Nancy! Is—is it—?"

She drew nearer, and put her arms about him.

"Yes, dear, it's—Jimmy's—just as we filled it on Christmas Eve three years ago. You see, I couldn't quite bear to leave it behind us when we came away, lying there in his drawer so lonely—at Christmas time. Tell me you don't mind, Scott—won't you? We have our memories, but David—he has so little. That dreadful mother, and—"

Scott cleared his throat; swallowed, and said gently, "He has, I think, the loveliest mother in the world!"

"What do you mean?"

He drew her down onto the settle that faced the sleeping boy, and answered, "Listen, Nancy. I went to the schoolhouse. I thought perhaps they'd give me something to trim the tree. The party was over, but the teacher was there with Ira Morse, clearing things away. I told them about David—why he hadn't shown up; and asked some questions. Nancy—what do you think? That Hawkins woman isn't the child's mother! I knew it!"

"Nobody around here ever saw her. She died when David was a baby, and his father, half crazed, the natives thought, with grief, brought the child here, and lived like a hermit on the mountain. He died when Dave was about six, and as no one claimed the youngster, and there was no orphan asylum within miles, he was sent to the poor farm, and stayed there until last year, when Clem Hawkins wanted a boy to help do chores, and Dave was the cheapest thing in sight. Guess you wonder where I've been all this time? Well, I've been interviewing the overseer of the poor—destroying red tape by the yard—resorting to bribery and corruption! But—Hello, old man, did I wake you up?"

David, roused suddenly, rubbed his eyes. Then, spying the stocking, he wakened thoroughly and asked, "Say! Is—is it Christmas?"

Scott laughed, and glanced at his watch.

"It will be, in twelve minutes. Come here, sonny."

He drew the boy onto his knee, and went on quietly: "The stores were closed, David, when I reached the village. I couldn't buy you a Christmas gift, you see. But I thought if we gave you a real mother, and—and a father—"

"Oh, Scott!"

It was a cry of rapture from Nancy. She had, of course, suspected the ending to his story, but not until that moment had she let herself really believe it. Then, seeing the child's bewilderment, she explained, "He means, dear, that you're our boy now—for always."

David looked up, his brown eyes big with wonder.

"And I needn't go back to Hawkins's? Not ever?"

"Not ever," Scott promised, while his throat tightened at the relief in the boy's voice.

"And I'll have folks, same as the other kids?"

"You've guessed right." The new father spoke lightly in an effort to conceal his feeling. 'That is, if you think we'll do!" he added, smiling.

"Oh, you'll—"

Suddenly inarticulate, David turned, throwing his thin arms around Scott's neck in a strangling, boylike hug. Then, a bit ashamed because such things were new to him, he slipped away, standing with his back to them at the window, trying, they saw with understanding hearts, to visualize this unbelievable thing that had come, a miracle, into his starved life. When after a silence they joined him, the candle on the table flared up for a protesting moment, and then went out. Only starlight and firelight lit the cabin now; and Nancy, peering into the night, said gently, "How beautifully it has cleared! I think I never saw the stars so bright."

"Christmas stars," Scott reminded her and, knowing the memory that brought the roughness to his voice, she caught and clasped his hand.

It was David who spoke next. He was leaning close to the window, his elbows resting on the sill, his face cupped in his two hands. He seemed to have forgotten them as he said, dreamily, "It's Christmas . . . Silent night . . . holy night . . . like the son. I wonder—"

He looked up trustfully into the faces above him—"I wonder if—if maybe one of them stars isn't the Star of Bethlehem!"

The Christmas Rose

LIZZIE DEAS

Legend has it that the Magi laid their rich offerings of myrrh, frankincense, and gold by the bed of the sleeping Christ Child, while a shepherd maiden stood outside the door, quietly weeping.

She, too, had sought the Christ Child. She, too, desired to bring him gifts. But she had nothing to offer, for she was very poor indeed. In vain she had searched the countryside over for one little flower to bring Him, but she could find neither bloom nor leaf, for the winter had been cold.

And as she stood there weeping, an angel passing saw her sorrow, and stooping he brushed aside the snow at her feet. And there sprang up on the spot a cluster of beautiful winter roses,—waxen white with pink tipped petals.

"Nor myrrh, nor frankincense, nor gold," said the angel, "is offering more meet for the Christ Child than these pure Christmas Roses."

Joyfully the shepherd maiden gathered the flowers and made her offering to the Holy Child.

Rather Late for Christmas

Mary Ellen Chase

D uring those confusing days before Christmas, while I wrap gifts for
sisters and brothers, brothers-in-law and sisters-in-law, nephews and
nieces, aunts and great-aunts, neighbors and friends, the milkman,
the postman, the paper boy, the cook and the cook's children. The cleaning
woman and the cleaning woman's children, I remember my grandmother, who
in the twenty years I knew her wrapped Christmas gifts for no one at all. My
grandmother never stood half submerged in a jungle of silver cord, gold cord,
red ribbon, tinsel ribbon, white tissue paper, red tissue paper, paper marked
with Aberdeens or angels. She viewed with fine scorn all such pre-Christmas
frenzy. I remember her again when my January bills weigh down my desk and
my disposition. My grandmother in all those years never bought a Christmas gift
for anyone, although she gave many. Nor did she make her Christmas gifts by the
labor of her hands, which were almost never idle.

To be sure, she spent most of her waking hours during twelve months of
the year in making gifts, but they were not for Christmas. She made yards upon
yards of tatting, fashioned hundreds of tea cozies, tidies, and table mats, hem-
stitched innumerable handkerchiefs, crocheted fine filet for pillowcases and
sheets, knit countless scalloped bands of white lace for the legs of white cotton
drawers, and countless stockings, gloves, mittens, scarfs, sacques, and shawls.
These creations were all gifts, yet they were never given at Christmas. Instead,
they were presented at odd moments to all sorts of odd and sundry persons—to
the gardener, the minister's wife, a surprised boy coasting down the hill, the
village schoolmistresses, the stage driver, a chance Syrian peddler, the fishman,
the paperhangers, and unknown woman distributing religious literature at the
back door, the sexton. Moreover, none of my grandmother's many acquaintances
ever called upon her without departing from her door richer, or at least more
encumbered, than when she entered it; nor did my grandmother ever set out
empty-handed to return those calls.

My grandmother's nature was essentially dramatic. She loved all sudden,
surprising, unexpected things; but she loved them only if either she or God
instigated them. Quite illogically she denied this privilege to others. She was

distinctly irritated if anyone took her unawares either by a sudden gift or by an unexpected piece of news. She was so filled with life herself that she forever wanted to dispense rather than to receive, to initiate rather than to be initiated.

She loved sudden changes of weather, blizzards, line gales, the excitement of continuous winter cold, northern lights, falling stars; and during many years of her long and abundant life she had had her fill of such abrupt and whimsical behavior on the part of God. For she had spent much of her life at sea, where holidays were mere points in time, unprepared for, often even unnoticed, slipping upon one like all other days, recalled if wind and weather were kind, forgotten if God had other and more immediate means of attracting one's attention to His power and His might. She had spent Christmas in all kinds of strange places: off Cape Horn in a gale; running before the trades somewhere a thousand miles off Africa; in a typhoon off the Chinese coast; in the doldrums, where the twenty-fifth of December was but twenty-four hours in a succession of motionless days; in the bitter cold of a winter storm too near the treacherous cliffs of southern Ireland for comfort or security. Small wonder that she would find it difficult, after her half-reluctant return to village life, to tie up Christmas in a neat parcel and to label it with a date.

As children we were forever asking our grandmother about these Christmases at sea.

"Didn't you give any presents at all, Grandmother? Not to the sailors or even to Grandfather."

"The sailors," said my grandmother, "had a tot of run all around in the dog-watch if the weather was fair. That was the sailors' present."

We always smiled over "tot." This facetious, trifling word attached to one of such enormity as "run" in those days of temperance agitation seemed impious to say the least. "What is a tot of rum, Grandmother?"

"A tot," answered my grandmother with great dignity, "is an indeterminate quantity."

"Did the sailors sing Christmas carols when they had the tot?"

"They did not. They sang songs which no child should ever know."

"Then did you and Grandfather have no presents at all, Grandmother?"

"Whenever we got to port we had our presents; that is, if we did not forget that we had had not Christmas. We had Christmas in January or even March. Christmas, children, is not a date. It is a state of mind."

Christmas to my grandmother was always a state of mind. Once she had left the sea, once she was securely on land, where the behavior of God was less exciting, she began to supplement Providence and Fate by engendering excitement in those about her. Her objection to Christmas lay in the fact that it was a day of expectation, when no one could possibly be taken by surprise. She endured it with forbearance, but she disliked it heartily.

Unlike most women of her generation, she cared not a whit for tradition or convention; but she remained to the end of her days the unwilling prey of both. Unlike most women of any generation, she scorned possessions, and she saw to it that she suffered them briefly. We knew from the beginning the fate of the gifts we annually bestowed upon her; yet we followed the admonition and example of our parents in bestowing them. From our scanty Christmas allowance of two dollars each with which to purchase presents for a family of ten, we set aside a generous portion for Grandmother's gift. She was always with us at Christmas and received our offerings without evident annoyance, knowing that what she must endure for a brief season she could triumph over in the days to come.

As we grew older and were allowed at length to select our gifts free from parental supervision, we began to face the situation precisely as it was. Instead of black silk gloves for Grandmother, we chose for her our own favorite perfumery; we substituted plain white handkerchiefs for the black-edged ones which she normally carried; a box of chocolates took the place of one of peppermints; a book called Daily Thoughts for Daily Needs was discarded in favor of a story by Anna Katharine Green.

My grandmother waited for a fortnight or longer after Christmas before she proffered her gifts to family, neighbors, and friends. By early January, she concluded, expectation would have vanished and satiety be forgotten; in other words, the first fine careless rapture of sudden surprise and pleasure might again be abroad in the world. She invariably chose a dull or dark day upon which to deliver her presents. Around three o'clock on some dreary afternoon was her time for setting forth. Over her coat she tied one of her stout aprons of black sateen, and in its capacious lap she cast all her own unwanted gifts—a black silk umbrella, odd bits of silver and jewelry, gloves, handkerchiefs, stockings, books, candies, Florida water, underwear, bedroom slippers, perfumeries, knickknacks of every sort; even the family photographs were not excluded! Thus she started upon her rounds, returning at suppertime empty-handed and radiant.

I remember how once as children we met her thus burdened on our way home from school.

"You're rather late for Christmas, Grandmother," we ventured together.

"So, my dears, were the Three Wise Men!" she said.

The many days foretold by the Preacher for the return of bread thus cast upon the waters have in the case of my grandmother not yet elapsed. For, although she has long since gone where possessions are of no account, and where, for all we know, life is a succession of quick surprises, I receive from time to time the actual return of her Christmas gifts so freely and curiously dispensed. Only last Christmas a package revealed a silver pie knife marked with her initials, and presented to her, I remembered with a start, through the combined sacrificial resources of our entire family fully thirty years before. An accompanying note bore words:

> Your grandmother brought this knife to my mother twenty-eight years ago as a Christmas gift. I remember how she came one rainy afternoon in January with the present in her apron. I found it recently among certain of my mother's things, and knowing your grandmother's strange ways as to Christmas gifts, I feel that honesty demands its return to you. You may be interested in this card which accompanied it.

Tied to the silver pie knife by a bit of red ribbon obviously salvaged long ago from Christmas plenty was a card inscribed on both sides. On one side was written: To Grandmother with Christmas love from her children and grandchildren, and on the other: To my dear friend, Lizzie Osgood, with daily love from Eliza Ann Chase.

The Star

FLORENCE M. KINGSLEY

nce upon a time in a country far away, there lived a little girl named Ruth. Ruth's home was not at all like our houses, for she lived in a little tower on top of the great stone wall that surrounded the town of Bethlehem.

Ruth's father was the hotelkeeper—the Bible says the "innkeeper." This inn was not at all like our hotels of today. There was a great open yard, which was called the courtyard. All about this yard were little rooms, and each traveler who came to the hotel rented one.

This inn stood near the great stone wall of the city, so that as Ruth stood one night, looking out of the tower window, she looked directly into the courtyard. It was truly a strange sight that met her eyes. So many people were coming to the inn, for the king had made a law that every man should return to the city where his father used to live to be counted and to pay taxes.

Some of the people came on the backs of camels, with great rolls of bedding and their dishes for cooking upon the back of the beast. Some came on little donkeys, and on their backs, too, were the bedding and the dishes. Some people came walking—slowly, for they were very tired.

As Ruth looked down into the courtyard, she saw camels being led to their places by their masters; she heard the snap of the whips; she saw the sparks shoot up from the fires that were kindled in the courtyard where each person was preparing for his own supper; she heard the cries of the tired, hungry, little children.

Presently her mother, who was cooking supper, came over to the window and said, "Ruthie, thou shalt hide in the house until all those people are gone. Dost thou understand?"

"Yes, my mother," said the child, and she left the window to follow her mother back to the stove, limping painfully, for little Ruth was a cripple. Her mother stooped suddenly and caught the child in her arms.

"My poor little lamb. It was a mule's kick, just six years ago, that hurt your poor back and made you lame."

"Never mind, my mother. My back does not ache today, and lately, when the light of the strange new star has shone down upon my bed, my back has felt so much stronger, and I have felt so happy, as though I could climb above the stars!"

Her mother shook her head sadly. "Thou art not likely to climb much, now or ever, but come, the supper is ready; let us go and find your father. I wonder what keeps him?"

They found the father standing at the gate of the courtyard, talking to a man and woman who had just arrived. The man was tall, with a long beard, and he led by a rope a snow-white mule, on which sat the drooping figure of the woman. As Ruth and her mother came near, they heard the father say, "But I tell thee that there is no more room in the inn. Hast thou no friends where thou canst go to spend the night?" The man shook his head. "No, none," he answered. "I care not for myself, but my poor wife." Little Ruth pulled at her mother's dress. "Mother, the oxen sleep out under the stars warm nights, and the straw is clean and warm; I have made a bed there for my little lamb."

Ruth's mother bowed before the tall man. "Thou didst hear the child. It is as she says—the straw is clean and warm." The tall man bowed his head. "We shall be very glad to stay," and he helped the sweet-faced woman down from the donkey's back and led her away to the cave-stable, while little Ruth and her mother hurried up the stairs that they might send a bowl of porridge to the sweet-faced woman and a cup of milk, as well.

That night when little Ruth lay down on her bed, the rays of the beautiful new star shone through the window more brightly than before. They seemed to soothe the tired, aching shoulders. She fell asleep and dreamed that the beautiful, bright star burst, and out of it came countless angels, who sang in the night: "Glory to God in the highest, peace on earth, good-will toward men."

And then it was morning and her mother was bending over her, saying, "Awake, awake, little Ruth. Mother has something to tell thee." Then as her eyes opened slowly her mother said, "Angels came in the night, little one, and left a Baby to lay beside your little white lamb in the manger."

That afternoon Ruth went with her mother to the fountain. The mother turned to talk to the other women of the town about the strange things heard and seen the night before, but Ruth went on and sat down by the edge of the fountain. The child was not frightened, for strangers came often to the well; but never before had she seen men who looked like the three who now came toward her. The first one, a tall man with a long, white beard, came close to Ruth and said, "Canst thou tell us, child, where is born He that is called King of the Jews?"

"I know of no king," answered Ruth, "but last night while the star was shining, the angels brought a baby to lie beside my little white lamb in the manger." The stranger bowed his head. "That must be He. Wilt thou show me the way to Him, my child?" So Ruth ran and her mother led the three men to the cave, "and when they saw the Child, they rejoiced with exceeding great joy, and opening their gifts, they presented unto Him gold and frankincense and myrrh," with wonderful jewels, so that Ruth's mother's eyes opened with wonder, but little Ruth saw only the Baby, who lay asleep on His mother's breast.

If I might only hold Him in my arms, thought she, but she was afraid to ask.

After a few days, the strangers left Bethlehem, all but the three—the man, whose name was Joseph, and Mary his wife, and the Baby. Then, as of old, little Ruth played about the courtyard, and the white lamb frolicked at her side. Often she dropped to her knees to press the little woolly white head against her breast, while she murmured: "My little lamb, my very, very own. I love you, lambie," and then together they would steal over to the entrance of the cave to peep in at the Baby, and always Ruth thought, *If I might only touch His hand.* But she was afraid to ask.

One night as she lay in her bed she thought to herself: *Oh, I wish I had a beautiful gift for Him, such as the wise men brought; but I have nothing at all to offer, and I love Him so much.* Just then the light of the star, which was nightly fading, fell across the foot of the bed and shone full upon the white lamb which lay asleep at her feet—and then she thought of something.

The next morning she arose with her face shining with joy. She dressed carefully and with the white lamb held close to her breast, went slowly and painfully down the stairway and over to the door of the cave. "I have come," she said, "to worship Him, and I have brought Him—my little, white lamb." The mother smiled at the lame child, then she lifted the Baby from her breast and placed Him in the arms of the little maid who knelt at her feet.

A few days later an angel came to the father, Joseph, and told him to take the Baby and hurry into the land of Egypt, for the wicked king wanted to do Him harm; and so these three—the father, the mother, and the Baby—went by night to that far country of Egypt. And the star grew dimmer and dimmer and passed away forever from the skies of Bethlehem; but little Ruth grew straight and strong and beautiful as the almond trees in the orchard, and all the people who saw her were amazed, for Ruth was once a cripple.

"It was the light of the strange star," her mother said; but little Ruth knew it was the touch of the blessed Christ Child, who was once folded against her heart.

Carols in the Cotswolds

LAURIE LEE

Towards Christmas, there was heavy snow, which raised the roads to the tops of the hedges. There were tons of the lovely stuff, plastic, pure, all-purpose, which nobody owned, which one could carve or tunnel, eat, or just throw about. It covered the hills and cut off the villages, but nobody thought of rescues; for there was hay in the barns and flour in the kitchens, the women baked bread, the cattle were fed and sheltered—we'd been cut off before, after all.

The week before Christmas, when snow seemed to lie thickest, was the moment for carol singing; and when I think back to those nights it is to the crunch of snow and to the lights of the lanterns on it. Carol singing in my village was a special tithe for the boys; the girls had little to do with it. Like haymaking, blackberrying, stone clearing, and wishing people a happy Easter, it was one of our season perks.

By instinct we knew just when to begin it; a day too soon and we should have been welcome, a day too late and we should have received lean looks from people whose bounty was already exhausted. When the true moment came, exactly balanced, we recognized it and were ready.

So as soon as the wood had been stacked in the oven to dry for the morning fire, we put on our scarves and went out through the streets, calling loudly between our hands, till the various boys who knew the signal ran out from their houses to join us. One by one they came stumbling over the snow, swinging their lanterns round their heads, shouting and coughing horribly.

"Coming carol barking then?"

We were the Church Choir, so no answer was necessary. For a year we had praised the Lord out of key, and as a reward for this service we now had the right to visit all the big houses, to sing our carols and collect our tribute.

To work them all in meant a five-mile foot journey over wild and generally snowed-up country. So the first thing we did was to plan our route; a formality; as the route never changed. All the same, we blew on our fingers and argued; and then we chose our leader. This was not binding, for we all fancied ourselves as leaders, and he who started the night in that position usually trailed home with a bloody nose.

Eight of us set out that night. There was Sixpence the Simple, who had never sung in his life (he just worked his mouth in church); the brothers Horace and Boney, who were always fighting everybody and always getting the worst of it; Clergy Green, the preaching maniac; Walt the Bully, and my two brothers. As we went down the lane other boys, from other villages, were already about the hills, bawling "Kingwenslush," and shouting through keyholes "Knock on the knocker! Ring at the bell! Give us a penny for singing so well!" They weren't an approved charity as we were, the choir; but competition was in the air.

Our first call as usual was the house of the Squire, and we trooped nervously down his drive. For light we had candles in marmalade jars suspended on loops of string, and they threw pale gleams on the towering snowdrifts that stood on each side of the drive. A blizzard was blowing but we were well wrapped up, with army puttees on our legs, woolen hats on our heads, and several scarves round our ears. As we approached the Big House across its white silent lawns, we too grew respectfully silent. The lake nearby was stiff and black, the waterfall frozen and still. We arranged ourselves shuffling round the big front door, then knocked and announced the choir.

A maid bore the tiding of our arrival away into the echoing distances of the house, and while we waited we cleared our throats noisily. Then she came back, and the door was left ajar for us, and we were bidden to begin. We brought no music; the carols were in our heads. "Let's give 'em 'Wild Shepherds,'" said Jack. We began in confusion, plunging into a wreckage of keys, of different words and tempos; but we gathered our strength; he who sang loudest took the rest of us with him, and the carol took shape, if not sweetness.

This huge stone house, with its ivied walls, was always a mystery to us. What were those gables, those rooms and attics, those narrow windows veiled by the cedar trees? As we sang "Wild Shepherds" we craned our necks, gaping into the lamplit hall which we had never entered; staring at the muskets and untenanted chairs, the great tapestries furred by dust—until suddenly, on the stairs, we saw the old Squire himself standing and listening with his head on one side.

He didn't move until we'd finished; then slowly he tottered towards us, dropped two coins in our box with a trembling hand, scratched his name in the book we carried, gave us each a long look with his moist blind eyes, then turned away in silence. As though released from a spell we took a few sedate steps, then broke into a run for the gate. We didn't stop till we were out of the grounds.

Impatient, at last, to discover the extent of his bounty, we squatted by the cow sheds, held our lanterns over the book, and saw that he had written "Two Shillings." This was quite a good start. No one of any worth in the district would dare to give us less than the Squire.

So with money in the box, we pushed on up the valley, pouring scorn on each other's performance. Confident now, we began to consider our quality and whether one carol was not better suited to us than another. Horace, Walt said, shouldn't sing at all; his voice was beginning to break. Horace disputed this and there was a brief token battle—they fought as they walked, kicking up divots of snow, then they forgot it, and Horace still sang.

Steadily we worked through the length of the valley, going from house to house, visiting the lesser and the greater gentry—the farmers, the doctors, the merchants, the majors, and other exalted persons. It was freezing hard and blowing too; yet not for a moment did we feel the cold. The snow blew into our faces, into our eyes and mouths, soaked through our puttees, got into our boots, and dripped from our woolen caps. But we did not care. The collecting box grew heavier, and the list of names in the book longer and more extravagant, each trying to outdo the other.

Mile after mile we went, fighting against the wind, falling into snowdrifts, and navigating by the lights of the houses. And yet we never saw our audience. We called at house after house; we sang in courtyards and porches, outside windows, or in the damp gloom of hallways; we heard voices from hidden rooms; we smelled rich clothes and strange hot food; we saw maids bearing in dishes or carrying away coffee cups; we received nuts, cakes, figs, preserved ginger, dates, cough drops, and money; but we never once saw our patrons. We sang, as it were, at the castle walls and, apart from the Squire, who had shown himself to prove that he was still alive, we never expected it otherwise.

As the night drew on there was trouble with Boney. "Noel," for instance, had a rousing harmony which Boney persisted in singing, and singing flat. The others forbade him to sing it at all, and Boney said he would fight us. Picking himself up he agreed we were right, then he disappeared altogether. He just turned away and walked into the snow and wouldn't answer when we called him back. Much later, as we reached a far point up the valley, somebody said "Hark!" and we stopped to listen. Far away across the fields from the distant village came the sound of a frail voice singing, singing "Noel," and singing it flat—it was Boney, branching out on his own.

We approached our last house high up on the hill, the place of Joseph the farmer. For him we had chosen a special carol, which was about the other Joseph, so that we always felt that singing it added a spicy cheek to the night. The last stretch of country to reach his farm was perhaps the most difficult of all. In these rough bare lanes, open to all winds, sheep were buried and wagons lost. Huddled together, we tramped in one another's footsteps, powdered snow blew into our screwed-up eyes, the candles burned low, some blew out altogether, and we talked loudly above the gale.

Crossing, at last, the frozen millstream—whose wheel in summer still turned a barren mechanism—we climbed up to Joseph's farm. Sheltered by trees, warm on its bed of snow, it seemed always to be like this. As always it was late; as always this was our final call. The snow had a fine crust upon it, and the old trees sparkled like tinsel. We grouped ourselves round the farmhouse porch. The sky cleared, and broad streams of stars ran down over the valley and away to Wales. On Slad's white slopes, seen through the black sticks of its woods, some red lamps still burned in the windows.

Everything was quiet; everywhere there was the faint crackling silence of the winter night. We started singing, and we were all moved by the words and the sudden trueness of our voices. Pure, very clear, and breathless we sang:

> "As Joseph was a-walking
> He heard an angel sing,
> 'This night shall be the birth-time
> Of Christ the Heavenly King.
> He neither shall be borned
> In Housen nor in ball,
> But in an ox's stall . . .'"

And two thousand Christmases became real to us then; the houses, the halls, the places of paradise had all been visited; the stars were bright to guide the Kings through the snow; and across the farmyard we could hear the beasts in their stalls. We were given roast apples and hot mince pies, in our nostrils were spices like myrrh, and in our wooden box, as we headed back for the village, there were golden gifts for all.

The Promise

Maud Lindsay

There was once a harper who played such beautiful music and sang such beautiful songs that his fame spread throughout the whole land, and at last the king heard of him and sent messengers to bring him to the palace.

"I will neither eat nor sleep till I have seen your face and heard the sound of your harp." This was the message the king sent to the harper.

The messengers said it over and over until they knew it by heart. When they reached the harper's house, they called:

"Hail, harper! Come and listen, for we have something to tell you that will make you glad."

But when the harper heard the king's message, he was sad, for he had a wife and a child and a little brown dog. He was sorry to leave them, and they were sorry to have him go.

"Stay with us," they begged; but the harper said:

"I must go, for it would be discourtesy to disappoint the king. But as sure as holly berries are red and pine is green, I will come back by Christmas Day to eat my share of the Christmas pudding and sing the Christmas songs by my own fireside."

And when he had promised this, he hung his harp upon his back and went away with the messengers to the king's palace.

When he got there, the king welcomed him with joy, and many things were done in his honor. He slept on a bed of softest down and ate from a plate of gold at the king's own table; and when he sang everybody and everything, from the king himself to the mouse in the palace pantry, stood still to listen.

No matter what he was doing, however, feasting or resting, singing or listening to praises, he never forgot the promise that he had made to his wife and his child and his little brown dog, and when the day before Christmas came, he took his harp in his hand and went to bid the king good-bye.

Now the king was loath to have the harper leave him. That means the king did not want the harper to leave him, and he said to him, "I will give you a horse as white as milk, as glossy as satin, and as fleet as a deer, if you will stay to play and sing before my throne on Christmas Day."

But the harper answered, "I cannot stay, for I have a wife and a child and a little brown dog. And I have promised them to be at home by Christmas Day to eat my share of the Christmas pudding and sing the Christmas songs by my own fireside."

Then the king said, "If you will stay to play and sing before my throne on Christmas Day, I will give to you a wonderful tree that summer or winter is never bare; and silver and gold will fall for you whenever you shake this little tree."

But the harper said, "I must not stay, for my wife and my child and my little brown dog are waiting for me, and I have promised them to be at home by Christmas Day to eat my share of the Christmas pudding and sing the Christmas songs by my own fireside."

Then the king said, "If you will stay on Christmas Day one tune to play and one song to sing, I will give you a velvet robe to wear, and you may sit beside me here with a ring on your finger and a crown on your head."

But the harper answered, "I will not stay, for my wife and my child and my little brown dog are watching for me; and I have promised them to be at home on Christmas Day to eat my share of the Christmas pudding and sing the Christmas songs by my own fireside."

And he wrapped his old cloak about him and he hung his harp upon his back and went out from the king's palace without another word. Even the king could not make the harper stay at the palace.

He had not gone far when the little white snowflakes came fluttering down from the skies.

"Harper, stay!" they seemed to say.

"Do not venture out today!"

But the harper said, "The snow may fall, but I must go, for I have a wife and a child and a little brown dog, and I have promised them to be at home by Christmas Day to eat my share of the Christmas pudding and sing the Christmas songs by my own fireside."

Then the snow fell thick and the snow fell fast. The hills and the valleys, the hedges and hollows, were white. The paths were all hidden and there were drifts like mountains on the king's highway. The harper stumbled and the harper fell, but he would not turn back; and as he traveled, he met the wind.

"Brother Harper, turn, I pray;

Do not journey on today!" sang the wind, but the harper would not listen.

"Snows may fall and winds may blow, but I must go on," he said, "for I have a wife and a child and a little brown dog; and I have promised them to be at home by Christmas Day to eat my share of the Christmas pudding and sing the Christmas songs by my own fireside."

Then the wind blew an icy blast. The snow froze on the ground and the water froze in the rivers. The harper's breath froze in the air and icicles as long as the king's sword hung from the rocks on the king's highway. The harper shivered and the harper shook, but he would not turn back; and by and by he came to the forest that lay between them and his home.

The trees of the forest were creaking and bending in the wind, and every one of them seemed to say:

"Darkness gathers, night is near;
Harper, stop! Don't venture here!"

But the harper would not stop. "Snows may fall, winds may blow, and night may come, but I have promised to be at home by Christmas Day, because I have a wife and a child and a little brown dog. And I want to eat my share of the Christmas pudding and sing the Christmas songs by my own fireside. I must go on."

And on he went till the last glimmer of daylight faded and there was darkness everywhere. But the harper was not afraid of the dark.

"If I cannot see, I can sing," he said. And he sang in the forest joyously:

> "Sing glory, glory, glory
> And bless God's holy name,
> For it was on Christmas morning
> The little Jesus came.
> He wore no robes. No crown of gold
> Was on His head that morn;
> But herald angels sang for joy
> To tell a king was born."

The snow ceased its falling; the wind ceased its blowing. The trees of the forest bowed down to listen, and lo! dear children, as he sang the darkness turned to wondrous light, and close at hand the harper saw the open doorway of his home.

The wife, the child, and the little brown dog were watching and waiting. They welcomed the harper with great joy. The holly berries were red in the Christmas wreaths; their tree was a young green pine; the Christmas pudding was full of plums; and the harper was happier than a king as he sat by his own fireside to sing:

"O glory, glory, glory!
We praise God's holy name;
For 'twas to bring His wondrous love
That little Jesus came.
And in His praise our songs we sing,
And in His name we pray;
God bless us all for Jesus' sake,
This happy Christmas Day."

When the Wise Man Appeared

William Ashley Anderson

he battery in the car had gone dead; and it turned out to be a bitterly cold night, vast and empty, a ringing void domed with icy stars. Over Hallet's Hill the evening star danced like tinsel on the tip of a Christmas tree. The still air was resonant as the inside of an iron bell; but within our snug farmhouse it was mellow with the warmth of three cherry-red stoves. The dinner things had been pushed back, and I was feeling relaxed and content, lazily smoking a cigarette, when Bruce came into the room.

He had gone upstairs in heavy boots and flannel cruiser's shirt. He reappeared in a long white nightgown with a purple cloak of Tintexed cotton over his shoulders. In one hand he held a tall crown of yellow pasteboard and tinsel. From the other swung an ornate censer. His boots had been replaced by thin flapping sandals.

"What in the world are you supposed to be?" I asked.

My wife looked at him critically. There was both concern and tenderness in the look. Women always look tenderly at Bruce; and then, of course, she had more than a hand in his costuming. She said indignantly:

"He's one of the Wise Men of the East!"

Virginia, my daughter, put both hands to her face, ready to stifle an hysterical shriek because Bruce, who is small for fourteen, likes to be grouped with men, swinging a double-edged axe with the best of them and handling a twelve-gauge as if it were a BB gun. With a tight voice she managed to say:

"Have you got matches for that thing?"

With considerable difficulty Bruce raised his skirts and produced a box from his pants pocket.

"He'll be ready," said my wife, "whatever happens!" She looked at me, and I thought again how lovely she is. That did me no good. Her look was an urgent reminder. I felt all the chill of the night air run up my spine, suddenly remembering that I had promised to get the boy to the school-house in town in good time for the Christmas pageant. I shuddered and groaned and went out into the night pulling on a heavy coat.

By one of those freaks of mechanical whimsy that baffle man, its maker, the engine caught at the first turn of the crank, and off we went with a bang, bouncing and roaring across the rough frozen field. That was a trick of the devil.

At the turn by the barn the generator couldn't pick up enough current; and there the engine died. My heart sank with its last long sigh. I looked out the side of my eyes at Bruce, sitting there saying nothing, making me think what a kid he still is, with the crown and censer clasped in his arms, staring down that long endless lane that disappeared in the lonely hills.

It was a moment of deep breathless silence. The hills walled us in from all hope of neighborly assistance. Hallet's place was more than a mile and a half away, and the nearest turn of Route 90, even with the thin chance of a lift, was more than two miles away. Still, what could I do about it? I felt as helpless as a kid myself—and I had promised to get him there on time.

Well, I thought, it's not tragically important. Bruce said nothing, but his eyes were wide, staring now at the big star twinkling just over the ragged edge of the mountain. Then a strange and uneasy feeling stirred in me, because I knew the boy was praying. He had made his promises too!

Before I could move, he dropped his crown and censer and scrambled out of the car, stumbling over his skirts. But all his straining and heaving at the crank was useless. I strained and heaved in turn and was equally impotent. When we weren't sweating we were shivering. The still air cut like knives. The cold metal clung to our hands. Every deep breath rasped my lungs until I sputtered.

Ordinarily we might have pushed the car to the edge of the rise and rolled it down the hill in gear; but the grease stuck like cement, and we couldn't budge it. After a while I straightened my cramped back and guessed I'd smoke a cigarette while I thought it over. When I struck a light with fumbling hands and looked up through the smoke Bruce was scuttling down the lane, one hand holding his skirts, one hand swinging the censer, the high golden crown perched cock-eyed on his head. I hesitated between laughing at him and yelling for him to stop. At the moment it seemed that this was about the only thing he could do. As for me, there wasn't anything I could do. Then I thought of the expression on his face as he prayed, and I felt mean, realizing that a man's view and a boy's view are not necessarily the same.

I threw the cigarette away and began once more to crank.

I don't know how long the struggle lasted, but all at once the engine sneezed. With hands clenched and eyes closed I straightened slowly and held my breath. The engine began to cough throatily. I scrambled frenziedly into the car.

Just about where Fifth Street enters Stroudsburg I overtook Bruce. There was a twist at my innards at the sight of that small figure trudging along with cock-eyed crown on his head and the censer hugged to his stomach. A long sigh went out of me as he turned his face into the lights with a white-lipped grin. His gown was torn and he shivered violently.

"You shouldn't have gone off that way," I growled. "It's too cold. It's terribly cold!"

"I put twigs in the censer," he said, "and made a fire. I kept warm enough."

"But look at your feet! You might have frozen them!"

"It wasn't so bad. I took a bearing on the star and made a short cut across Lasoine's farm. It came out right back there by the new cottage."

After that I was too busy putting on speed to say much. We arrived at the school on time. I stood in back and watched.

A good many years have passed since I last saw the story of Bethlehem and the homage of the Three Wise Men presented by children at Christmastime. It had become so old a story to me that it seemed strange to realize that to them it was new.

When I saw Bruce walking stiff-legged on cut and chilblained feet with his two companions on the stage, kneeling by the crèche, declaiming his studied lines, first I regretted my laughter at the dinner table, then an uneasy awe rose up within me.

Going home we stopped at a garage for antifreeze and at a soda counter for hot chocolate, and I said nothing but commonplace things. As we rolled comfortably out Fifth Street Bruce showed me where the shortcut came out.

"That's where the Thompsons lived," I said, "before the place burned down."

"I know," said Bruce; "where the boy was burned to death."

A new house had been built on the old foundations and people were again living there.

"They've got lights burning."

As we passed the Lasoine farm there were lights burning there, too. I thought this was strange, because since George Lasoine had gone off to war the old grandmother, who had lost her youngest son in the first war, had sort of shriveled up, and a gloom lay over the house; but as I slowed down I could see Lou Lasoine through the kitchen window, smoking his pipe and smiling at the two women talking, so I sensed everything was all right.

So far as I knew that was about all there was to the evening; but on Christmas Day the Good Farmer's Wife came by with gifts of mincemeat made from venison and a jug of sassafras cider. She had shaken off her customary pessimism and was full of bounce and high-pitched talk. I heard the laughter and ejaculations in the kitchen where my wife was supervising the Christmas feast; and since I have a weakness for the racy gossip of the countryside, I drifted toward the kitchen too.

"You must hear this!" said my wife, drawing me in.

The Farmer's Wife looked at me with a glittering but wary eye.

"You hain't agoin' to believe it either," she said. "Just the same I'm tellin' you, folks up here in the hills see things and they do believe."

"What have you been seeing?"

"It was old Mrs. Lasoine. Last Tuesday night when she was a-feelin' awful low she thought she heard something back of the barn and she looked out. Now I'll say this for the old lady—she's got good vision. That she has! Plenty good! There warn't no moonlight, but if you recollect it was a bright starry night. And there she saw, plain as her own husband, one of the Wise Men of the Bible come a-walkin' along the hill with a gold crown on his head, a-swingin; one of them pots with smoke in them—"

My mouth opened and I looked at Rosamunde, and Rosamunde looked at me; but before I could say anything, the Farmer's Wife hurried on:

"Now don't you start a-laughin'—not yet!—'cause that hain't the long and short of it! There's other testimony! The Thompsons. You know the ones whose oldest boy was burned in the fire? Well, there it was the children. First, they heard him, they heard him a-singin' 'Come All Ye Faithful' plain as day. They went runnin' to the window and they seen the Wise Man a-walkin' in the starlight across the lane, gold crown and robes and firepot and all! Well, my goodness, they put up such a shoutin' and a yellin' that their parents come a-runnin'. But by then it was too late. He was gone. Just disappeared. Afterward they went out and looked but couldn't find hide nor hair—"

"Did they see any other signs?" I asked faintly.

The Farmer's Wife scoffed.

"Old folks and children see things which maybe we can't. All I can say is this. Lasoines and Thompsons don't even know each other. But old lady Lasoine was heartsick and lonely and a-prayin' about her lost boy, and the Thompsons was heartsick and lonely because this was the first Christmas in the new house without Harry, and you dassen't say they wasn't a-prayin' too! Maybe you don't believe that amounts to anythin'—but I'm tellin' you it was a comfort to them to see and believe!"

I swallowed hard, recalling the look on Bruce's face as he stared at the star, when I knew he was praying that he might not fail his friends. Well, not daring to look at my wife, I said with all the sincerity one can feel:

"Yes, I believe God was close that night."

For the first time in her garrulous life the Farmer's Wife was stricken dumb. She looked at me as if an even greater miracle had been performed before her very eyes.

'Twas the Night before Christmas

CLEMENT C. MOORE

'Twas the night before Christmas, when all through the house
Not a creature was stirring, not even a mouse;
The stockings were hung by the chimney with care
In hopes that St. Nicholas soon would be there;

The children were nestled all snug in their beds,
While visions of sugar-plums danced in their heads;
And mamma in her kerchief, and I in my cap,
Had just settled our brains for a long winter's nap,

When out on the lawn there arose such a clatter,
I sprang from the bed to see what was the matter.
Away to the window I flew like a flash,
Tore open the shutters and threw up the sash.

The moon on the breast of the new-fallen snow
Gave the lustre of mid-day to objects below,
When, what to my wondering eyes should appear,
But a miniature sleigh, and eight tiny reindeer,

With a little old driver, so lively and quick,
I knew in a moment it must be St. Nick.
More rapid than eagles his coursers they came,
And he whistled, and shouted, and called them by name:

"Now, Dasher! now, Dancer! now, Prancer and Vixen!
On, Comet! on, Cupid! on, Donder and Blitzen!
To the top of the porch! to the top of the wall!
Now dash away! dash away! dash away all!"

As dry leaves that before the wild hurricane fly,
When they meet with an obstacle, mount to the sky;

So up to the house-top the coursers they flew,
With the sleigh full of toys, and St. Nicholas too.

And then, in a twinkling, I heard on the roof
The prancing and pawing of each little hoof.
As I drew in my head, and was turning around,
Down the chimney St. Nicholas came with a bound.

He was dressed all in fur, from his head to his foot,
And his clothes were all tarnished with ashes and soot;
A bundle of toys he had flung on his back,
And he looked like a peddler just opening his pack.

His eyes—how they twinkled! his dimples how merry!
His cheeks were like roses, his nose like a cherry!
His droll little mouth was drawn up like a bow,
And the beard of his chin was as white as the snow;

The stump of a pipe he held tight in his teeth,
And the smoke it encircled his head like a wreath;
He had a broad face and a little round belly,
That shook when he laughed, like a bowlful of jelly.

He was chubby and plump, a right jolly old elf,
And I laughed when I saw him, in spite of myself;
A wink of his eye and a twist of his head,
Soon gave me to know I had nothing to dread;

He spoke not a word, but went straight to his work,
And filled all the stockings; then turned with a jerk,
And laying his finger aside of his nose,
And giving a nod, up the chimney he rose;

He sprang to his sleigh, to his team gave a whistle,
And away they all flew like the down of a thistle.
'But I heard him exclaim, ere he drove out of sight,
"Happy Christmas to all, and to all a good-night."

Susie's Letter from Santa

MARK TWAIN

Palace of Nicholas
In the Moon
Christmas Morning

My Dear Susie Clemens:

I have received and read all the letters which you and your little sister have written me by the hands of your mother and your nurses; I have also read those which you little people have written me with your own hands—for although you did not use any characters that are in grown people's alphabet, you used the characters that all children in all lands on earth and in the twinkling stars use; and as all my subjects in the moon are children and use no characters but that, you will easily understand that I can read your and your baby sister's jagged and fantastic marks without any trouble at all. But I had trouble with those letters which you dictated through your mother and your nurses, for I am a foreigner and cannot read English writing well. You will find that I made no mistakes about the things which you and the baby ordered in your own letters—I went down your chimney at midnight when you were asleep and delivered them all myself—and kissed both of you, too, because you are good children, well trained, nice mannered, and about the most obedient little people I ever saw. But in the letter which you dictated there were some words which I could not make out for certain, and one or two small orders which I could not fill because we ran out of stock. Our last lot of kitchen furniture for dolls has just gone to a very poor little child in the North Star away up in the old country above the Big Dipper. Your mama can show you that star and you will say: "Little Snow Flake" (for that is the child's name), "I'm glad you got that furniture, for you need it more than I." That is, you must write that, with your own hand, and Snow Flake will write you an answer. If you only spoke it she wouldn't hear you. Make your letter light and thin, for the distance is great and postage very heavy.

There was a word or two in your mama's letter which I couldn't be certain of. I took it to be "a trunk full of doll's clothes." Is that it? I will call at your kitchen door about nine o'clock this morning to inquire. But I must not see anybody and I must not speak to anybody but you. When the kitchen doorbell rings, George must be blindfolded and sent to open the door. Then he must go back to the dining room or the china closet and take the cook with him. You must tell

George he must walk on tiptoe and not speak—otherwise he will die someday. Then you must go up to the nursery and stand on a chair or the nurse's bed and put your ear to the speaking tube that leads down to the kitchen and when I whistle through it you must speak in the tube and say, "Welcome, Santa Claus!" then I will ask whether it was a trunk you ordered or not. If you say it was, I shall ask you what color you want the trunk to be. Your mama will help you to name a nice color, and then you must tell me every single thing in detail which you want the trunk to contain. Then when I say "Good-bye and a merry Christmas to my little Susie Clemens," you must say "Good-bye, good old Santa Claus, I thank you very much and please tell that little Snow Flake I will look at her star tonight and she must look down here—I will be right in the west bay window; and every fine night I will look at her star and say, 'I know somebody up there and like her, too.'" Then you must go down into the library and make George close the doors that open into the main hall and everybody must keep still for a little while. Then while you are waiting I will go to the moon and get those things and in a few minutes I will come down the chimney that belongs to the fireplace that is in the hall—if it is a trunk you want—because I couldn't get such a large thing as a trunk down the nursery chimney, you know.

People may talk if they want, till they hear my footsteps in the hall. Then you tell them to keep quiet a little while until I go up the chimney. Maybe you will not hear my footsteps at all—so you may go now and then and peep through the dining-room doors, and by and by you will see that which you want, right under the piano in the drawing room—for I shall put it there. If I should leave any snow in the hall, you must tell George to sweep it into the fireplace, for I haven't time to do such things. George must not use a broom, but a rag—or he will die someday. You watch George and don't let him run into danger. If my boot should leave a stain on the marble, George must not holystone it away. Leave it there always in memory of my visit; and whenever you look at it or show it to anybody you must let it remind you to be a good little girl. Whenever you are naughty and somebody points to that mark which your good old Santa Claus's boot made on the marble, what will you say, little sweetheart?

Good-bye for a few minutes, till I come down and ring the kitchen doorbell.

Your loving Santa Claus
Whom people sometimes call
"The Man in the Moon"

My First Christmas Tree

Hamlin Garland

I will begin by saying that we never had a Christmas tree in our house in the Wisconsin coulee; indeed, my father never saw one in a family circle till he saw that which I set up for my own children last year. But we celebrated Christmas in those days, always, and I cannot remember a time when we did not all hang up our stockings for "Sandy Claws" to fill. As I look back upon those days it seems as if the snows were always deep, the night skies crystal clear, and the stars especially lustrous with frosty sparkles of blue and yellow fire, and probably this was so, for we lived in a northern land where winter was usually stern and always long.

I recall one Christmas when "Sandy" brought me a sled and a horse that stood on rollers—a wonderful tin horse, which I very shortly split in two in order to see what his insides were. Father traded a cord of wood for the sled, and the horse cost twenty cents, but they made the day wonderful.

Another notable Christmas Day, as I stood in our front yard, mid-leg-deep in snow, a neighbor drove by closely muffled in furs, while behind his seat his son, a lad of twelve or fifteen, stood beside a barrel of apples, and as he passed he hurled a glorious big one at me. It missed me, but bored a deep, round hole in the soft snow. I thrill yet with the remembered joy of burrowing for that delicious bomb. Nothing will ever smell quite as good as that Winesap or Northern Spy or whatever it was. It was wayward impulse on the part of the boy in the sleigh, but it warms my heart after more than forty years.

We had no chimney in our home, but the stocking hanging was a ceremony nevertheless. My parents, and especially my mother, entered into it with the best of humor. They always put up their own stockings or permitted us to do it for them, and they always laughed the next morning when they found potatoes or ears of corn in them. I can see now that my mother's laugh had a tear in it, for she loved pretty things and seldom got any during the years that we lived in the coulee.

When I was ten years old, we moved to Mitchell County, an Iowa prairie land, and there we prospered in such ways that our stocking always held toys of some sort, and even my mother's stocking occasionally sagged with a simple piece of jewelry or a new comb or brush. But the thought of a family tree remained the luxury of millionaire city dwellers; indeed it was not till my fifteenth or sixteenth year that our Sunday school rose to the extravagance of a tree, and it is of this wondrous festival that I write.

The land about us was only partly cultivated at this time, and our district schoolhouse, a bare little box, was set bleakly on the prairie; but the Burr Oak schoolhouse was not only larger, but it stood beneath great oaks as well and possessed the charm of a forest background through which a stream ran silently. It was our chief social center. There on a Sunday a regular preacher held "divine service" with Sunday school as a sequence. At night—usually on Friday nights— the young people met in "lyceums," as we called them, to debate great questions or to "speak pieces" and read essays, and here it was that I saw my first Christmas tree.

I walked to that tree across four miles of moonlit snow. Snow? No, it was a floor of diamonds, a magical world, so beautiful that my heart still aches with the wonder of it and with the regret that it has all gone—gone with the keen eyes and the bounding pulses of the boy.

Our home at the time was a small frame house on the prairie almost directly west of the Burr Oak grove, and as it was too cold to take the horses out, my brother and I, with our tall boots, our visored caps and our long woolen mufflers, started forth afoot defiant of the cold. We left the gate on the trot, bound for a sight of the glittering unknown. The snow was deep and we moved side by side in the grooves made by the hoofs of the horses, setting our feet in the shine left by the broad shoes of the wood sleighs whose going had smoothed the way for us. Our breaths rose like smoke in the still air. It must have been ten below zero, but that did not trouble us in those days, and at last we came in sight of the lights, in sound of the singing, the laughter, the bells of the feast.

It was a poor little building without tower or bell and its low walls had but three windows on a side, and yet it seemed very imposing to me that night as I crossed the threshold and faced the strange people who packed it to the door. I say "strange people," for though I had seen most of them many times, they all seemed somehow alien to me that night; therefore I stood against the wall and gazed with open-eyed marveling at the shining pine which stood where the pulpit was wont to be. I was made to feel the more embarrassed by reason of the remark of a boy who accused me of having forgotten to comb my hair.

This was not true, but the cap I wore always matted my hair down over my brow, and then, when I lifted it off, invariably disarranged it completely. Nevertheless, I felt guilty—and hot. I don't suppose my hair was artistically barbered that night—I rather guess Mother had used the shears—and I can believe that I looked the half-wild colt that I was; but there was no call for that youth to direct attention to my unavoidable shagginess.

I don't think the tree had many candles, and I don't remember that it glittered with golden apples. But it was loaded with presents, and the girls coming and going clothed in bright garments made me forget my own looks—I think they made me forget to remove my overcoat, which was a sodden thing of poor cut and worse quality. I think I must have stood agape for nearly two hours listening to the songs, noting every motion of Adoniram Burtsch and Asa Walker as they directed the ceremonies and prepared the way for the great event—that is to say, for the coming of Santa Clause himself.

A furious jingling of bells, a loud voice outside, the lifting of a window, the nearer clash of bells, and the dear old saint appeared (in the person of Stephen Bartle) clothed in a red robe, a belt of sleigh bells, and a long white beard. The children cried out, "Oh!" The girls tittered and shrieked with excitement, and the boys laughed and clapped their hands. Then "Sandy" made a little speech about being glad to see us all, but as he had many other places to visit, and as there were a great many presents to distribute, he guessed he'd have to ask some of the many pretty girls to help him. So he called upon Betty Burtch and Hattie Knapp—and I for one admired his tastes, for they were the most popular maids of the school.

They came up blushing, and a little bewildered by the blasé of publicity thus blown upon them. But their native dignity asserted itself, and the distribution of the presents began. I have a notion now that the fruit upon the tree was mostly bags of popcorn and "corny copias" of candy, but as my brother and I stood there that night and saw everybody, even the rowdiest boy, getting something we felt aggrieved and rebellious. We forgot that we had come from afar—we only knew that we were being left out.

But suddenly, in the midst of our gloom, my brother's name was called, and a lovely girl with a gentle smile handed him a bag of popcorn. My heart glowed with gratitude. Somebody had thought of us, and when she came to me, saying sweetly, "Here's something for you," I had not words to thank her. This happened nearly forty years ago, but her smile, her outstretched hand, her sympathetic eyes are vividly before me as I write. She was sorry for the shock-headed boy who stood against the wall, and her pity made the little box of candy a casket of pearls. The fact that I swallowed the jewels on the road home does not take from the reality of my adoration.

At last I had to take my final glimpse of that wondrous tree, and I well remember that walk home. My brother and I traveled in wordless companion-ship. The moon was sinking toward the west, and the snow crust gleamed with a million fairy lamps. The sentinel watchdogs barked from lonely farmhouses, and the wolves answered from the ridges. Now and then sleighs passed us with lovers sitting two and two, and the bells on their horses had the remote music of romance to us whose boots drummed like clogs of wood upon the icy road.

Our house was dark as we approached and entered it, but how deliciously warm it seemed after the pitiless wind. I confess we made straight for the cupboard for a mince pie, a doughnut, and a bowl of milk.

As I write this there stands in my library a thick-branched, beautifully taper-ing fir tree covered with the gold and purple apples of Hesperides, together with crystal ice points, green and red and yellow candles, clusters of gilded grapes, wreaths of metallic frost, and glittering angels swinging in ecstasy; but I doubt if my children will ever know the keen pleasure (that is almost pain) which came to my brother and to me in those Christmas days when an orange was not a breakfast fruit, but a casket of incense and of spice, a message from the sunlands of the South.

That was our compensation—we brought to our Christmas time a keen ap-petite and empty hands. And the lesson of it all is, if we are seeking a lesson, that it is better to give to those who want than to those for whom "we ought to do something because they did something for us last year."

The Fir Tree

HANS CHRISTIAN ANDERSEN

✳

Out in the woods stood a nice little Fir tree. The place he had was a very good one; the sun shone on him; as to fresh air, there was enough of that, and round him grew many large-sized comrades, pine as well as firs. But the little Fir wanted so very much to be a grown-up tree.

He did not think of the warm sun and of the fresh air; and he did not care for the little cottage children that ran about and prattled when they were in the woods looking for wild strawberries. The children often came with a whole pitcherful of berries, or a long row of them threaded on a straw, and sat down near the young Tree and said, "Oh, how pretty he is! What a nice little Fir!" But this was what the Tree could not bear to hear.

At the end of the year he had shot up a good deal, and after another year he was another long bit taller; for with fir trees one can always tell by the shoots how may years old they are.

"Oh, were I but such a high tree as the others are!" sighed he. "Then I should be able to spread out my branches and with the tops look into the wide world! Then would the birds build nests among branches; and when there was a breeze I could bend with as much stateliness as the others!"

Neither the sunbeams, nor the birds, nor the red clouds which morning and evening sailed above him gave the little Tree any pleasure.

In winter, when the snow lay glittering on the ground, a hare would often come leaping along and jump right over the little Tree. Oh, that made him so angry! But two winters were past, and in the third the Tree was so large that the hare was obliged to go around it. "To grow and grow, to get older and be tall," thought the Tree—"that, after all, is the most delightful thing in the world!"

In autumn the woodcutters always came and felled some of the largest trees. This happened every year; and the young Fir tree, that had now grown to a very comely size, trembled at the sight; for the magnificent great trees fell to the earth with noise and cracking, the branches were lopped off, and the trees looked long and bare; they were hardly to be recognized; and then they were laid in carts, and the horses dragged them out of the woods.

Where did they go to? What became of them?

In spring, when the Swallows and the Storks came, the Tree asked them, "Don't you know where they have been taken? Have you not met them anywhere?"

The Swallows did not know anything about it; but the Stork looked musing, nodded his head, and said, "Yes, I think I know. I met many ships as I was flying hither from Egypt; on the ships were magnificent masts, and I venture to assert that it was they that smelt so of fir. I may congratulate you, for they lifted themselves on high most majestically!"

"Oh, were I but old enough to fly across the sea! But how does the sea look in reality? What is it like?"

"That would take a long time to explain," said the Stork; and with these words off he went.

"Rejoice in thy growth!" said the Sunbeams; "rejoice in the vigorous growth and in the fresh life that moveth within thee!"

And the Wind kissed the Tree, and the Dew wept tears over him, but the Fir understood it not.

When Christmas came, quite young trees were cut down, trees which often were not even as large or of the same age as this Fir tree who could never rest but always wanted to be off. These young trees, and they were always the finest-looking, retained their branches; they were laid on carts, and the horses drew them out of the woods.

"Where are they going to?" asked the Fir. "We have peeped in at the windows in the town below! We know whither they are taken! The greatest splendor and the greatest magnificence one can imagine await them. We peeped through the windows and saw them planted in the middle of the warm room, and ornamented with the most splendid things—with gilded apples, with gingerbread, with toys, and many hundred lights!"

"And then?" asked the Fir tree, trembling in every bough. "And then? What happens then?"

"We did not see anything more; it was incomparably beautiful."

"I would fain know if I am destined for so glorious a career," cried the Tree, rejoicing. That is still better than to cross the sea! What a longing do I suffer! Were Christmas but come! I am now tall, and my branches spread like the others that were carried off last year! Oh, were I but already on the cart! Were I in the warm room with all the splendor and magnificence! Yes; then something better, something still grander, will surely follow, or wherefore should they thus ornament me? Something better, something still grander, must follow—but what? Oh, how I long, how I suffer! I do not know myself what is the matter with me!"

"Rejoice in our presence!" said the Air and the Sunlight; "rejoice in thy own fresh youth!"

But the Tree did not rejoice at all; he grew and grew, and was green both winter and summer. People that saw him said, "What a fine tree!" and toward Christmas he was one of the first that was cut down. The ax struck deep into the very pith; the tree fell to the earth with a sigh; he felt a pang—it was like a swoon; he could not think of happiness, for he was sorrowful at being separated from his home, from the place where he had sprung up. He well knew that he should never see his dear old comrades, the little bushes and flowers around him, anymore, perhaps not even the birds! The departure was not at all agreeable.

The Tree only came to himself when he was unloaded in a courtyard with the other trees, and heard a man say, "That one is splendid; we don't want the others." Then two servants came in rich livery and carried the Fir tree into a large and splendid drawing room. Portraits were hanging on the walls, and near the white porcelain stove stood two large Chinese vases with lions on the covers. There, too, were large easy chairs, silken sofas, large tables full of picture books and full of toys worth hundreds and hundreds of crowns—at least the children said so. And the Fir tree was stuck upright in a cask that was filled with sand; but no one could see that it was a cask, for green cloth was hung all around it, and it stood on a large, gaily colored carpet. Oh, how the tree quivered! What was to happen? The servants as well as the young ladies decorated it. On one branch there hung little nets cut out of colored paper, and each net was filled with sugarplums; and among the other boughs gilded apples and walnuts were suspended, looking as though they had grown there, and little blue and white tapers were placed among the leaves. Dolls that looked for all the world like men—the Tree had never beheld such before—were seen among the foliage, and at the very top a large star of gold tinsel was fixed. It was really splendid—beyond description splendid.

"This evening!" said they all; "how it will shine this evening!"

"Oh," thought the Tree, "if the evening were but come! If the tapers were but lighted! And then I wonder what will happen! Perhaps the other trees from the forest will come to look at me! Perhaps the sparrows will beat against the windowpanes! I wonder if I shall take root here and winter and summer stand covered with ornaments."

He knew very much about the matter! But he was so impatient that for sheer longing he got a pain in his back, and this with trees is the same thing as a headache with us.

The candles were now lighted. What brightness! What splendor! The Tree trembled so in every bough that one of the tapers set fire to the foliage. It blazed up splendidly.

"Help! Help!" cried the young ladies, and they quickly put out the fire.

Now the Tree did not even dare tremble. What a state he was in! He was so uneasy lest he should lose something of his splendor that he was quite bewildered amid the glare and the brightness, when suddenly both doors opened and a troop of children rushed in as if they would upset the Tree. The older persons followed quietly; the little ones stood quite still. But it was only for a moment; then they shouted so that the whole place re-echoed with their rejoicing; they danced round the Tree, and one present after the other was pulled off.

"What are they about?" thought the Tree. "What is to happen now?" And the lights burned down to the very branches, and as they burned down they were put out one after the other, and then the children had permission to plunder the Tree. So they fell upon it with such violence that all its branches cracked; if it had not been fixed firmly in the cask it would certainly have tumbled down.

The children danced about with their beautiful playthings; no one looked at the Tree except the old nurse, who peeped between the branches; but it was only to see if there was a fig or an apple left that had been forgotten.

"A story! A story!" cried the children, drawing a little fat man toward the Tree. He seated himself under it and said, "Now we are in the shade, and the Tree can listen too. But I shall tell only one story. Now which will you have: that about Ivedy-Avedy, or about Klumpy-Dumpy who tumbled downstairs, and yet after all came to the throne and married the princess?"

"Ivedy-Avedy," cried some; "Klumpy-Dumpy," cried the others. There was such a bawling and screaming. The Fir tree alone was silent, and he thought to himself, "Am I not to bawl with the rest—am I to do nothing whatever?" for he was one of the company and had done what he had to do.

And the man told about Klumpy-Dumpy that tumbled down, who notwithstanding came to the throne and at last married the princess. And the children clapped their hands and cried out, "Oh, go on! Do go on!" They wanted to hear about Ivedy-Avedy, too, but the little man only told them about Klumpy-Dumpy. The Fir tree stood quite still and absorbed in thought; the birds in the woods had never related the like of this.

"Klumpy-Dumpy fell downstairs, and yet he married the princess! Yes, yes! That's the way of the world!" thought the Fir tree, and believed it all, because the man who told the story was so good-looking. "Well, well! Who knows, perhaps I may fall downstairs, too, and get a princess as a wife!" And he looked forward with joy to the morrow, when he hoped to be decked out again with lights, playthings, fruits, and tinsel.

"I won't tremble tomorrow!" thought the Fir tree. "I will enjoy to the full all my splendor! Tomorrow I shall hear again the story of Klumpy-Dumpy, and perhaps that of Ivedy-Avedy, too." And the whole night the Tree stood still and in deep thought.

In the morning the servant and the housemaid came in.

"Now, then, the splendor will begin again," thought the Fir, but they dragged him out of the room, and up the stairs into the loft; and here in a dark corner, where no daylight could enter, they left him. "What's the meaning of this?" thought the Tree. "What am I to do here? What shall I hear now, I wonder?" and he leaned against the wall, lost in reverie. Time enough had he, too, for his reflections, for days and nights passed on, and nobody came up; and when at last somebody did come it was only to put some great trunks in a corner out of the way. There stood the Tree, quite hidden; it seemed as if he had been entirely forgotten.

"'Tis now winter out-of-doors!" thought the Tree. "The earth is hard and covered with snow; men cannot plant me now, and therefore I have been put up here under shelter till the springtime comes! How thoughtful that is! How kind man is, after all! If it only were not too dark here and so terribly lonely! Not even a hare. And out in the woods it was so pleasant when the snow was on the ground, and the hare leaped by; yes, even when he jumped over me; but I did not like it then. It is really terribly lonely here!"

"Squeak! Squeak!" said a little Mouse, at the same moment peeping out of his hole. And then another little one came. They snuffed about the Fir tree and rustled among the branches.

"It is dreadfully cold," said the mouse. "But for that, it would be delightful here, old Fir, wouldn't it?"

"I am by no means old," said the Fir tree. "There's many a one considerably older than I am."

"Where do you come from," asked the Mice, "and what can you do?" They were so extremely curious. "Tell us about the most beautiful spot on the earth. Have you never been there? Were you never in the larder where cheeses lie on the shelves and hams hang from above, where one dances about on tallow candles; that place where one enters lean and comes out again fat and portly?"

"I know no such a place," said the Tree. "But I know the woods, where the sun shines, and where the little birds sing." And then he told all about his youth; and the little Mice had never heard the life before; and they listened and said, "Well, to be sure! How much you have seen! How happy you must have been!"

"I!" said the Fir tree, thinking over what he had himself related. "Yes, in reality those were happy times." And then he told about Christmas Eve, when he was decked out with cakes and candles.

"Oh," said the little Mice, "how fortunate you have been, old Fir tree!"

"I am by no means old," said he. "I came from the woods this winter; I am in my prime, and am only rather short for my age."

"What delightful stories you know!" said the Mice; and the next night they came with four other little Mice, who were to hear what the Tree recounted; and the more he related the more plainly he remembered all himself; and it appeared as if those times had really been happy times. "But they may still come—they may still come. Klumpy-Dumpy fell downstairs, and yet he got a princess!" and he thought at the moment of a nice little Birch tree growing out in the woods; to the Fir that would be a real charming princess.

"Who is Klumpy-Dumpy?" asked the Mice. So then the Fir tree told the whole fairy tale, for he could remember every single word of it; and the little Mice jumped for joy up to the very top of the Tree. The next night two more Mice came, and on Sunday two Rats, even; but, they said the stories were not interesting, which vexed the little Mice; and they, too, now began to think them not so very amusing, either.

"Do you know only one story?" asked the Rats.

"Only that one," answered the Tree. "I heard it on my happiest evening; but I did not then know how happy I was."

"It is a very stupid story! Don't you know one about bacon and tallow candles? Can't you tell any larder stories?"

"No," said the Tree.

"Then good-by," said the Rats; and they went home.

At last the little Mice stayed away also; and the Tree sighed. "After all, it was very pleasant when the sleek little Mice sat around me and listened to what I told them. Now that, too, is over. But I will take good care to enjoy myself when I am brought out again."

But when was that to be? Why, one morning there came a quantity of people and set to work in the loft. The trunks were moved, the Tree was pulled out and thrown—rather hard, it is true—down on the floor, but a man drew him toward the stairs, where the daylight shone.

"Now a merry life will begin again," thought the Tree. He felt the fresh air, the first sunbeam—and now he was out in the courtyard. All passed so quickly, there was so much going on around him, that the Tree quite forgot to look to himself. The court adjoined a garden, and all was in flower; the roses hung so fresh and odorous over the balustrade, the lindens were in blossom, the Swallows flew by and said, "Quirre-vit! My husband is come!" but it was not the Fir tree that they meant.

"Now, then, I shall really enjoy life," said he, exultingly, and—spread out his branches; but alas! they were all withered and yellow. It was in a corner that he lay, among weeds and nettles. The golden star of tinsel was still on the top of the Tree, and glittered in the sunshine.

In the courtyard some of the merry children were playing who had danced at Christmas round the Fir tree and were so glad at the sight of him. One of the youngest ran and tore off the golden star.

"Only look what is still on the ugly old Christmas tree!" said he, trampling on the branches so that they all cracked beneath his feet.

And the tree beheld all the beauty of the flowers and the freshness in the garden; he beheld himself and wished he had remained in his dark corner in the loft; he thought of his first youth in the wood, of the merry Christmas Eve, and of the little Mice who had listened with so much pleasure to the story of Klumpy-Dumpy.

"'Tis over! 'Tis past!" said the poor Tree. "Had I but rejoiced when I had reason to do so! But now 'tis past, 'tis past!"

And the gardener's boy chopped the Tree into small pieces; there was a heap lying there. The wood flamed up splendidly under the large brewing cauldron, and it sighed so deeply! Each sigh was like a shot.

The boys played about in the court, and the youngest wore the gold star on his breast which the Tree had had on the happiest evening of his life. However, that was over now—the Tree gone, the story at an end. All, all was over; every tale must end at last.

Christmas at Orchard House

Louisa May Alcott

"Christmas won't be Christmas without any presents," grumbled Jo, lying on the rug.

"It's so dreadful to be poor!" sighed Meg, looking down at her old dress.

"I don't think it's fair for some girls to have plenty of pretty things, and other girls nothing at all," added little Amy, with an injured sniff.

"We've got Father and Mother and each other," said Beth contentedly, from her corner.

The four young faces on which the firelight shone brightened at the cheerful words but darkened again as Jo said sadly—"We haven't got Father, and shall not have him for a long time." She didn't say "perhaps never," but each silently added it, thinking of Father far away, where the fighting was.

Nobody spoke for a minute; then Meg said in an altered tone, "You know the reason Mother proposed not having any presents this Christmas was because it is going to be a hard winter for everyone; and she thinks we ought not to spend money for pleasure, when our men are suffering so in the army. We can't do much, but we can make our little sacrifices and ought to do it gladly. But I am afraid I don't." And Meg shook her head as she thought regretfully of all the pretty things she wanted.

"But I don't think the little we should spend would do any good. We've each got a dollar, and the army wouldn't be much helped by our giving that. I agree not to expect anything from Mother or you, but I do want to buy Undine and Sintram for myself; I've wanted to so long," said Jo, who was a bookworm.

"I planned to spend mine on new music," said Beth, with a little sigh, which no one heard but the hearth brush and kettle holder.

"I shall get a nice box of Faber's drawing pencils; I really need them," said Amy decidedly.

"Mother didn't say anything about our money, and she won't wish us to give up everything. Let's each buy what we want and have a little fun; I'm sure we work hard enough to earn it," cried Jo, examining the heels of her shoes in a gentlemanly manner.

"I know I do—teaching those tiresome children nearly all day, when I'm longing to enjoy myself at home," began Meg, in the complaining tone again.

"You don't have half such a hard time as I do," said Jo. "How would you like to be shut up for hours with a nervous, fussy, old lady, who keeps you trotting, is never satisfied, and worries you till you're ready to fly out of the window or cry?"

"It's naughty to fret; but I do think washing dishes and keeping things tidy is the worst work in the world. It makes me cross, and my hands get stiff, I can't practise well at all," and Beth looked at her rough hands with a sigh that anyone could hear that time.

"I don't believe any of you suffer as I do," cried Amy, "for you don't have to go to school with impertinent girls who plague you if you don't know your lessons, and laugh at your dresses, and label your father if he isn't rich, and insult you when your nose isn't nice."

"If you mean libel, I'd say so, and not talk about labels, as if Papa was a pickle bottle," advised Jo, laughing.

"I know what I mean, and you needn't be statirical [sic] about it. It's proper to use good words, and improve your vocabilary [sic]," returned Amy, with dignity.

"Don't peck at one another, children. Don't you wish we had the money Papa lost when we were little, Jo? Dear me! How happy and good we'd be, if we had no worries!" said Meg, who could remember better times.

"You said, the other day, you thought we were a deal happier than the King children, for they were fighting and fretting all the time, in spite of their money."

"So I did, Beth. Well, I think we are; for, though we do have to work, we make fun for ourselves, and are a pretty jolly set, as Jo would say!"

"Jo does use such slang words!" observed Amy, with a reproving look at the long figure stretched on the rug. Jo immediately sat up, put her hands in her pockets, and began to whistle.

"Don't Jo; it's so boyish!"

"That's why I do it."

"I detest rude, unladylike girls!"

"I hate affected, niminy-piminy chits!"

"'Birds in their little nests agree,'" sang Beth, the peacemaker, with such a funny face that both sharp voices softened to a laugh, and the "pecking" ended for that time.

"Really, girls, you are both to be blamed," said Meg, beginning to lecture in her elder-sisterly fashion. "You are old enough to leave off boyish tricks, and to behave better, Josephine. It didn't matter so much when you were a little girl, but now you are so tall and turn up your hair; you should remember that you are a young lady."

"I'm not! And if turning up my hair makes me one, I'll wear it in two tails till I'm twenty," cried Jo, pulling off her net, and shaking down a chestnut mane. "I hate to think I've got to grow up, and be Miss March, and wear long gowns, and look as prim as a China-aster! It's bad enough to be a girl, anyway, when I like boys' games and work and manners! I can't get over my disappointment in not being a boy; and it's worse than ever now, for I'm dying to go and fight with Papa, and I can only stay at home and knit, like a poky old woman!" And Jo shook the blue army sock till the needles rattled like castanets, and her ball bounded across the room.

"Poor Jo! It's too bad, but it can't be helped; so you must try to be contented with making your name boyish, and playing brother to us girls," said Beth, stroking the rough head at her knee with a hand that all the dishwashing and dusting in the world could not make ungentle in its touch.

"As for you, Amy," continued Meg, "you are altogether too particular and prim. Your airs are funny now; but you'll grow up an affected little goose, if you don't care. I like your nice manners and refined ways of speaking, when you don't try to be elegant; but your absurd words are as bad as Jo's slang."

"If Jo is a tomboy and Amy a goose, what am I, please?" asked Beth, ready to share the lecture.

"You're a dear, and nothing else," answered Meg warmly; and no one contradicted her, for the "Mouse" was the pet of the family.

As young readers like to know "how people look," we will take this moment to give them a little sketch of the four sisters, who sat knitting away in the twilight, while the December snow fell quietly without, and the fire crackled cheerfully within. It was a comfortable old room, though the carpet was faded and the furniture very plain; for a good picture or two hung on the walls, book filled recesses, chrysanthemums and Christmas roses bloomed in the windows, and a pleasant atmosphere of home—peace pervaded it.

Margaret, the eldest of the four, was sixteen, and very pretty, being plump and fair, with large eyes, plenty of soft, brown hair, a sweet mouth, and white hands, of which she was rather vain. Fifteen-year-old Jo was very tall, thin, and brown, and reminded one of a colt; for she never seemed to know what to do with her long limbs, which were very much in her way. She had a decided mouth, a comical nose, and sharp, gray eyes, which appeared to see everything and were by turns fierce, funny, or thoughtful. Her long, thick hair was her one beauty; but it was usually bundled into a net, to be out of her way. Round shoulders had Jo, big hands and feet, a flyaway look to her clothes, and the uncomfortable appearance of a girl who was rapidly shooting up into a woman, and didn't like it. Elizabeth—or Beth, as everyone called her "Little Tranquility," and the name suited her excellently; for she seemed to live in a happy world of her own, only venturing out to meet the few whom she trusted and loved. Amy, though the youngest, was a most important person—in her own opinion at least. A regular snow-maiden, with blue eyes, and yellow hair, curling on her shoulders, pale and slender, and always carrying herself like a young lady mindful of her manners. What the characters of the four sisters were, we will leave to be found out.

The clock struck six; and, having swept up the hearth, Beth put a pair of slippers down to warm. Somehow the sight of the old shoes had a good effect upon the girls; for Mother was coming, and everyone brightened to welcome her. Meg stopped lecturing, and lighted the lamp. Amy got out of the easy chair without being asked, and Jo forgot how tired she was as she sat up to hold the slippers nearer the blaze.

"They are quite worn out; Marmee must have a new pair."

"I thought I'd get her some with my dollar," said Beth.

"No, I shall!" cried Amy.

"I'm the oldest," began Meg, but Jo cut in with a decided—"I'm the man of the family now Papa is away, and I shall provide the slippers, for he told me to take special care of mother while he was gone."

"I'll tell you what we'll do," said Beth; "let's each get her something for Christmas and not get anything for ourselves."

"That's like you, dear! What will we get?" exclaimed Jo.

Everyone thought soberly for a minute; then Meg announced, as if the idea was suggested by the sight of her own pretty hands, "I shall give her a nice pair of gloves."

"Army shoes, best to be had," cried Jo.

"Some handkerchiefs, all hemmed," said Beth.

"I'll get a little bottle of cologne; she likes it, and it won't cost much, so I'll have some left to buy my pencils," added Amy.

"How will we give the things?" asked Meg.

"Put them on the table, and bring her in and see her open the bundles. Don't you remember how we used to do on our birthdays?" answered Jo.

"I used to be so frightened when it was my turn to sit in the big chair with the crown on, and see you all come marching round to give presents, with a kiss. I like the things and the kisses, but it was dreadful to have you sit looking at me while I opened the bundles," said Beth, who was toasting her face and the bread for tea, at the same time.

"Let Marmee think we are getting things for ourselves, and then surprise her. We must go shopping tomorrow afternoon, Meg; there is so much to do about the play for Christmas night," said Jo, marching up and down, with her hands behind her back and her nose in the air.

"I don't mean to act any more after this time; I'm getting too old for such things," observed Meg, who was as much a child as ever about "dressing-up" frolics.

"You won't stop, I know, as long as you can trail round in a white gown with your hair down, and wear gold-paper jewelry. You are the best actress we've got, and there'll be an end of everything if you quit the boards," said Jo. "We ought to rehearse tonight. Come here, Amy, and do the fainting scene, for you are as stiff as a poker in that."

"I can't help it; I never saw anyone faint, and I don't choose to make myself all black and blue, tumbling flat as you do. If I can go down easily, I'll drop; if I can't, I shall fall into a chair and be graceful; I don't care if Hugo does come at me with a pistol," returned Amy, who was not gifted with dramatic power, but was chosen because she was small enough to be borne out shrieking by the villain of the piece.

"Do it this way; clasp your hands so, and stagger across the room, crying frantically, 'Roderigo! Save me! Save me!'" and away went Jo, with a melodramatic scream which was truly thrilling.

Amy followed, but she poked her hands out stiffly before her and jerked herself along as if she went by machinery; and her "Ow!" was more suggestive of pins being run into her than of fear and anguish. Jo gave a despairing groan, and Meg laughed outright, while Beth let her bread burn as she watched the fun, with interest.

"It's no use! Do the best you can when the time comes, and if the audience laughs, don't blame me. Come on, Meg."

Then things went smoothly, for Don Pedro defied the world in a speech of two pages without a single break; Hagar, the witch, chanted an awful incantation over her kettleful of simmering toads, with weird effect; Roderigo rent his chains asunder manfully, and Hugo died in agonies of remorse and arsenic, with a wild, "Ha! Ha!"

"It's the best we've had yet," said Meg, as the dead villain sat up and rubbed his elbows.

"I don't see how you can write and act such splendid things, Jo. You're a regular Shakespeare!" exclaimed Beth, who firmly believed that her sisters were gifted with wonderful genius in all things.

Not quite," replied Jo modestly. "I do think, 'The Witch's Curse, and Operatic Tragedy' is rather a nice thing; but I'd like to try 'Macbeth,' if we only had a trap door for Banquo. I always wanted to do the killing part. 'Is that a dagger that I see before me?'" muttered Jo, rolling her eyes and clutching at the air, as she had seen a famous tragedian do.

"No, it's the toasting fork, with mother's shoe on it instead of the bread. Beth's stage-struck!" cried Meg, and the rehearsal ended in a general burst of laughter.

II
A MERRY CHRISTMAS

Jo was the first to wake in the gray dawn of Christmas morning. No stockings hung at the fireplace, and for a moment she felt as much disappointed as she did long ago, when her little sock fell down because it was crammed so full of goodies. Then she remembered her mother's promise and, slipping her hand under her pillow, drew out a little crimson-covered book. She knew it very well, for it was that beautiful old story of the best life ever lived, and Jo felt that it was a true guidebook for any pilgrim going on a long journey. She woke Meg with a "Merry Christmas," and bade her see what was under her pillow. A greencovered book appeared, with the same picture inside, and a few words written by their mother, which made their one present very precious in their eyes. Presently Beth and Amy woke to rummage and find their little books also, one dove-colored, the other blue, and all sat looking at and talking about them, while the east grew rosy with the coming day.

In spite of her small vanities, Margaret had a sweet and pious nature, which unconsciously influenced her sisters, especially Jo, who loved her very tenderly, and obeyed her because her advice was so gently given.

"Girls," said Meg seriously, looking from the tumbled head beside her to the two little night-capped ones in the room beyond, "Mother wants us to read and love and mind these books, and we must begin at once. We used to be faithful about it, but since Father went away and all this war trouble unsettled us, we have neglected many things. You can do as you please, but I shall keep my book on the table here and read a little every morning as soon as I wake, for I know it will do me good and help me through the day."

Then she opened her new book and began to read. Jo put her arm round her and, leaning cheek to cheek, read also, with the quiet expression so seldom seen on her restless face.

"How good Meg is! Come, Amy, let's do as they do. I'll help you with the hard words, and they'll explain things if we don't understand," whispered Beth, very much impressed by the pretty books and her sisters' example.

"I'm glad mine is blue," said Amy. and then the rooms were very still while the pages were softly turned, and the winter sunshine crept in to touch the bright heads and serious faces with a Christmas greeting.

"Where is Mother?" asked Meg, as she and Jo ran down to thank her for their gifts, half an hour later.

"Goodness only knows. Some poor creeter came a-beggin', and your ma went straight off to see what was needed. There never was such a woman for givin' away vittles and drink, clothes and firin'," replied Hannah, who had lived with the family since Meg was born, and was considered by them all more as a friend than a servant.

"She will be back soon, I think, so fry your cakes, and have everything ready," said Meg, looking over the presents which were collected in a basket and kept under the sofa, ready to be produced at the proper time. "Why, where is Amy's bottle of cologne?" she added, as the little flask did not appear.

"She took it out a minute ago, and went off with it to put a ribbon on it, or some such notion," replied Jo, dancing about the room to take the first stiffness off the new army slippers.

"How nice my handkerchiefs look, don't they? Hannah washed and ironed them for me, and I marked them all myself," said Beth, looking proudly at the somewhat uneven letters which had cost her such labor.

"Bless the child! She's gone and put 'Mother' on them instead of 'M. March'. How funny!" cried Jo, taking one up.

"Isn't that right? I thought it was better to do it so, because Meg's initials are M. M., and I don't want anyone to use these but Marmee," said Beth, looking troubled.

"It's all right, dear, and a very pretty idea, quite sensible too, for no one can ever mistake them now. It will please her very much, I know," said Meg, with a frown for Jo and a smile for Beth.

"There's Mother. Hide the basket, quick!" cried Jo, as a door slammed and steps sounded in the hall.

Amy came in hastily, and looked rather abashed when she saw her sisters all waiting for her.

"Where have you been, and what are you hiding behind you?" asked Meg, surprised to see, by her hood and cloak, that lazy Amy had been out so early.

"Don't laugh at me, Jo! I didn't mean anyone should know till the time came. I only meant to change the little bottle for a big one, and I gave all my money to get it, and I'm truly trying not to be selfish any more."

As she spoke, Amy showed the handsome flask which replaced the cheap one, and looked so earnest and humble in her little effort to forget herself that Meg hugged her on the spot, and Jo pronounced her 'a trump', while Beth ran to the window, and picked her finest rose to ornament the stately bottle.

"You see I felt ashamed of my present, after reading and talking about being good this morning, so I ran round the corner and changed it the minute I was up, and I'm so glad, for mine is the handsomest now."

Another bang of the street door sent the basket under the sofa, and the girls to the table, eager for breakfast.

"Merry Christmas, Marmee! Many of them! Thank you for our books. We read some, and mean to every day," they all cried in chorus.

"Merry Christmas, little daughters! I'm glad you began at once, and hope you will keep on. But I want to say one word before we sit down. Not far away from here lies a poor woman with a little newborn baby. Six children are huddled into one bed to keep from freezing, for they have no fire. There is nothing to eat over there, and the oldest boy came to tell me they were suffering hunger and cold. My girls, will you give them your breakfast as a Christmas present?"

They were all unusually hungry, having waited nearly an hour, and for a minute no one spoke, only a minute, for Jo exclaimed impetuously, "I'm so glad you came before we began!"

"May I go and help carry the things to the poor little children?" asked Beth eagerly.

"I shall take the cream and the muffins," added Amy, heroically giving up the article she most liked.

Meg was already covering the buckwheats, and piling the bread into one big plate.

"I thought you'd do it," said Mrs. March, smiling as if satisfied. "You shall all go and help me, and when we come back we will have bread and milk for breakfast, and make it up at dinnertime."

They were soon ready, and the procession set out. Fortunately it was early, and they went through back streets, so few people saw them, and no one laughed at the queer party.

A poor, bare, miserable room it was, with broken windows, no fire, ragged bedclothes, a sick mother, wailing baby, and a group of pale, hungry children cuddled under one old quilt, trying to keep warm.

How the big eyes stared and the blue lips smiled as the girls went in.

"Ach, mein Gott! It is good angels come to us!" said the poor woman, crying for joy.

"Funny angels in hoods and mittens," said Jo, and set them to laughing.

In a few minutes it really did seem as if kind spirits had been at work there. Hannah, who had carried wood, made a fire, and stopped up the broken panes with old hats and her own cloak. Mrs. March gave the mother tea and gruel, and comforted her with promises of help, while she dressed the little baby as tenderly as if it had been her own. The girls meantime spread the table, set the children round the fire, and fed them like so many hungry birds, laughing, talking, and trying to understand the funny broken English.

"Das ist gut!" "Die Engel-kinder!" cried the poor things as they ate and warmed their purple hands at the comfortable blaze.

The girls had never been called angel children before, and thought it very agreeable, especially Jo, who had been considered a 'Sancho' ever since she was born. That was a very happy breakfast, though they didn't get any of it. And when they went away, leaving comfort behind, I think there were not in all the city four merrier people than the hungry little girls who gave away their breakfasts and contented themselves with bread and milk on Christmas morning.

"That's loving our neighbor better than ourselves, and I like it," said Meg, as they set out their presents while their mother was upstairs collecting clothes for the poor Hummels.

Not a very splendid show, but there was a great deal of love done up in the few little bundles, and the tall vase of red roses, white chrysanthemums, and trailing vines, which stood in the middle, gave quite an elegant air to the table.

"She's coming! Strike up, Beth! Open the door, Amy! Three cheers for Marmee!" cried Jo, prancing about while Meg went to conduct Mother to the seat of honor.

Beth played her gayest march, Amy threw open the door, and Meg enacted escort with great dignity. Mrs. March was both surprised and touched, and smiled with her eyes full as she examined her presents and read the little notes which accompanied them. The slippers went on at once, a new handkerchief was slipped into her pocket, well scented with Amy's cologne, the rose was fastened in her bosom, and the nice gloves were pronounced a perfect fit.

There was a good deal of laughing and kissing and explaining, in the simple, loving fashion which makes these home festivals so pleasant at the time, so sweet to remember long afterward, and then all fell to work.

The morning charities and ceremonies took so much time that the rest of the day was devoted to preparations for the evening festivities. Being still too young to go often to the theater, and not rich enough to afford any great outlay for private performances, the girls put their wits to work, and necessity being the mother of invention, made whatever they needed. Very clever were some of their productions, pasteboard guitars, antique lamps made of old-fashioned butter boats covered with silver paper, gorgeous robes of old cotton, glittering with tin spangles from a pickle factory, and armor covered with the same useful diamond shaped bits left in sheets when the lids of preserve pots were cut out. The big chamber was the scene of many innocent revels.

No gentlemen were admitted, so Jo played male parts to her heart's content and took immense satisfaction in a pair of russet leather boots given her by a friend, who knew a lady who knew an actor. These boots, an old foil, and a slashed doublet once used by an artist for some picture, were Jo's chief treasures and appeared on all occasions. The smallness of the company made it necessary for the two principal actors to take several parts apiece, and they certainly deserved some credit for the hard work they did in learning three or four different parts, whisking in and out of various costumes, and managing the stage besides. It was excellent drill for their memories, a harmless amusement, and employed many hours which otherwise would have been idle, lonely, or spent in less profitable society.

On Christmas night, a dozen girls piled onto the bed which was the dress circle, and sat before the blue and yellow chintz curtains in a most flattering state of expectancy. There was a good deal of rustling and whispering behind the curtain, a trifle of lamp smoke, and an occasional giggle from Amy, who was apt to get hysterical in the excitement of the moment. Presently a bell sounded, the curtains flew apart, and the Operatic Tragedy began.

"A gloomy wood," according to the one playbill, was represented by a few shrubs in pots, green baize on the floor, and a cave in the distance. This cave was made with a clothes horse for a roof, bureaus for walls, and in it was a small furnace in full blast, with a black pot on it and an old witch bending over it. The stage was dark and the glow of the furnace had a fine effect, especially as real steam issued from the kettle when the witch took off the cover. A moment was allowed for the first thrill to subside, then Hugo, the villain, stalked in with a clanking sword at his side, a slouching hat, black beard, mysterious cloak, and the boots. After pacing to and fro in much agitation, he struck his forehead, and burst out in a wild strain, singing of his hatred for Roderigo, his love for Zara, and his pleasing resolution to kill the one and win the other. The gruff tones of Hugo's voice, with an occasional shout when his feelings overcame him, were very impressive, and the audience applauded the moment he paused for breath. Bowing with the air of one accustomed to public praise, he stole to the cavern and ordered Hagar to come forth with a commanding, "What ho, minion! I need thee!"

Out came Meg, with gray horsehair hanging about her face, a red and black robe, a staff, and cabalistic signs upon her cloak. Hugo demanded a potion to make Zara adore him, and one to destroy Roderigo. Hagar, in a fine dramatic melody, promised both, and proceeded to call up the spirit who would bring the love philter.

> "Hither, hither, from thy home,
> Airy sprite, I bid thee come!
> Born of roses, fed on dew,
> Charms and potions canst thou brew?
> Bring me here, with elfin speed,
> The fragrant philter which I need.
> Make it sweet and swift and strong,
> Spirit, answer now my song!"

A soft strain of music sounded, and then at the back of the cave appeared a little figure in cloudy white, with glittering wings, golden hair, and a garland of roses on its head. Waving a wand, it sang:

> "Hither I come,
> From my airy home,
> Afar in the silver moon.
> Take the magic spell,
> And use it well,
> Or its power will vanish soon!"

And dropping a small, gilded bottle at the witch's feet, the spirit vanished. Another chant from Hagar produced another apparition, not a lovely one, for with a bang an ugly black imp appeared and, having croaked a reply, tossed a dark bottle at Hugo and disappeared with a mocking laugh. Having warbled his thanks and put the potions in his boots, Hugo departed, and Hagar informed the audience that as he had killed a few of her friends in times past, she had cursed him, and intends to thwart his plans, and be revenged on him. Then the curtain fell, and the audience reposed and ate candy while discussing the merits of the play.

A good deal of hammering went on before the curtain rose again, but when it became evident what a masterpiece of stage carpentry had been got up, no one murmured at the delay. It was truly superb. A tower rose to the ceiling, halfway up appeared a window with a lamp burning in it, and behind the white curtain appeared Zara in a lovely blue and silver dress, waiting for Roderigo. He came in gorgeous array, with plumed cap, red cloak, chestnut lovelocks, a guitar, and the boots, of course. Kneeling at the foot of the tower, he sang a serenade in melting tones. Zara replied and, after a musical dialogue, consented to fly. Then came the grand effect of the play. Roderigo produced a rope ladder, with five steps to it, threw up one end, and invited Zara to descend. Timidly she crept from her lattice, put her hand on Roderigo's shoulder, and was about to leap gracefully down when "Alas! Alas for Zara!" she forgot her train. It caught in the window, the tower tottered, leaned forward, fell with a crash, and buried the unhappy lovers in the ruins.

A universal shriek arose as the russet boots waved wildly from the wreck and a golden head emerged, exclaiming, "I told you so! I told you so!" With wonderful presence of mind, Don Pedro, the cruel sire, rushed in, dragged out his daughter, with a hasty aside—

"Don't laugh! Act as if it was all right!" and, ordering Roderigo up, banished him from the kingdom with wrath and scorn. Though decidedly shaken by the fall from the tower upon him, Roderigo defied the old gentleman and refused to stir. This dauntless example fired Zara. She also defied her sire, and he ordered them both to the deepest dungeons of the castle. A stout little retainer came in with chains and led them away, looking very much frightened and evidently forgetting the speech he ought to have made.

Act third was the castle hall, and here Hagar appeared, having come to free the lovers and finish Hugo. She hears him coming and hides, sees him put the potions into two cups of wine and bid the timid little servant, "Bear them to the captives in their cells, and tell them I shall come anon." The servant takes Hugo aside to tell him something, and Hagar changes the cups for two others which are harmless. Ferdinando, the 'minion', carries them away, and Hagar puts back the cup which holds the poison meant for Roderigo. Hugo, getting thirsty after a long warble, drinks it, loses his wits, and after a good deal of clutching and stamping, falls flat and dies, while Hagar informs him what she has done in a song of exquisite power and melody.

This was a truly thrilling scene, though some persons might have thought that the sudden tumbling down of a quantity of long red hair rather marred the effect of the villain's death. He was called before the curtain, and with great propriety appeared, leading Hagar, whose singing was considered more wonderful than all the rest of the performance put together.

Act fourth displayed the despairing Roderigo on the point of stabbing himself because he has been told that Zara has deserted him. Just as the dagger is at his heart, a lovely song is sung under his window, informing him that Zara is true but in danger, and he can save her if he will. A key is thrown in, which unlocks the door, and in a spasm of rapture he tears off his chains and rushes away to find and rescue his lady love.

Act fifth opened with a stormy scene between Zara and Don Pedro. He wishes her to go into a convent, but she won't hear of it, and after a touching appeal, is about to faint when Roderigo dashes in and demands her hand. Don Pedro refuses, because he is not rich. They shout and gesticulate tremendously but cannot agree, and Rodrigo is about to bear away the exhausted Zara, when the timid servant enters with a letter and a bag from Hagar, who has mysteriously disappeared. The latter informs the party that she bequeaths untold wealth to the young pair and an awful doom to Don Pedro, if he doesn't make them happy. The bag is opened, and several quarts of tin money shower down upon the stage till it is quite glorified with the glitter. This entirely softens the stern sire. He consents without a murmur, all join in a joyful chorus, and the curtain falls upon the lovers kneeling to receive Don Pedro's blessing in attitudes of the most romantic grace.

Tumultuous applause followed but received an unexpected check, for the cot bed, on which the dress circle was built, suddenly shut up and extinguished the enthusiastic audience. Roderigo and Don Pedro flew to the rescue, and all were taken out unhurt, though many were speechless with laughter. The excitement had hardly subsided when Hannah appeared, with "Mrs. March's compliments, and would the ladies walk down to supper."

This was a surprise even to the actors, and when they saw the table, they looked at one another in rapturous amazement. It was like Marmee to get up a little treat for them, but anything so fine as this was unheard of since the departed days of plenty. There was ice cream, actually two dishes of it, pink and white, and cake and fruit and distracting French bonbons and, in the middle of the table, four great bouquets of hot house flowers.

It quite took their breath away, and they stared first at the table and then at their mother, who looked as if she enjoyed it immensely.

"Is it fairies?" asked Amy.

"Santa Claus," said Beth.

"Mother did it." And Meg smiled her sweetest, in spite of her gray beard and white eyebrows.

"Aunt March had a good fit and sent the supper," cried Jo, with a sudden inspiration.

"All wrong. Old Mr. Laurence sent it," replied Mrs. March.

"The Laurence boy's grandfather! What in the world put such a thing into his head? We don't know him!" exclaimed Meg.

"Hannah told one of his servants about your breakfast party. He is an odd old gentleman, but that pleased him. He knew my father years ago, and he sent me a polite note this afternoon, saying he hoped I would allow him to express his friendly feeling toward my children by sending them a few trifles in honor of the day. I could not refuse, and so you have a little feast at night to make up for the bread-and-milk breakfast."

"That boy put it into his head, I know he did! He's a capital fellow, and I wish we could get acquainted. He looks as if he'd like to know us but he's bashful, and Meg is so prim she won't let me speak to him when we pass," said Jo, as the plates went round, and the ice began to melt out of sight, with ohs! and ahs! of satisfaction.

"You mean the people who live in the big house next door, don't you?" asked one of the girls. "My mother knows old Mr. Laurence, but says he's very proud and doesn't like to mix with his neighbors. He keeps his grandson shut up, when he isn't riding or walking with his tutor, and makes him study very hard. We invited him to our party, but he didn't come. Mother says he's very nice, though he never speaks to us girls."

"Our cat ran away once, and he brought her back, and we talked over the fence, and were getting on capitally, all about cricket, and so on, when he saw Meg coming, and walked off. I mean to know him some day, for he needs fun, I'm sure he does," said Jo decidedly.

"I like his manners, and he looks like a little gentleman, so I've no objection to your knowing him, if a proper opportunity comes. He brought the flowers himself, and I should have asked him in, if I had been sure what was going on upstairs. He looked so wistful as he went away, hearing the frolic and evidently having none of his own."

"It's a mercy you didn't, Mother!" laughed Jo, looking at her boots. "But we'll have another play sometime that he can see. Perhaps he'll help act. Wouldn't that be jolly?"

"I never had such a fine bouquet before! How pretty it is!" And Meg examined her flowers with great interest.

"They are lovely. But Beth's roses are sweeter to me," said Mrs. March, smelling the half-dead posy in her belt.

Beth nestled up to her, and whispered softly, "I wish I could send my bunch to Father. I'm afraid he isn't having such a merry Christmas as we are."

❄

The Noel Candle

CLEMENT C. MOORE

I t was Christmas Eve in Rheims, nearly five hundred years ago. The great cathedral towered high above the city, its spires seemed to reach to the very skies, and the square in front of the church was thronged with people, celebrating the joyous Noel, the Christmas time. Children darted here and there through the crowd, shrieking with laughter. On one corner a group of well-dressed youths and maidens were dancing to the music of a lute and tambourine; in another a number of boys sang old carols. Others strolled about in groups of two or three, chatting and laughing, while the older and more serious went their way, candle in hand, toward the cathedral, where masses were being chanted in Latin. Though these churchgoers were more quiet, it was evident that they were happy, for their faces shone with contentment. It did not seem that there could be, in all the city of Rheims, one sad or lonely heart.

Yet there were four. Three of them dwelt in a squalid hovel by the riverside, a tiny shed or lean-to which stood beside a stable. Though its outward appearance was so dismal, once within the door, one might have been surprised to see how neat and trim it was kept. There was but one room which served at once as living room, dining room, bedroom and kitchen for three people. The rough stone floor was carefully swept and polished. In one corner lay a straw-filled mattress, but the covers drawn over it, though patched and darned in a dozen places, were spotlessly clean. A rude table, a broken chair, a stool and a clumsy bench completed the furniture of the room. In a far corner stood a small charcoal brazier, whose feeble fire served not only to cook meals, but to warm the dwellers in the hut. Some cracked earthen kettles hung beside it.

The one touch of brightness and beauty in the little room was supplied by a tiny shrine, built on a shelf at the rear wall. A few field flowers in a bowl stood before it, and from the edge of the shelf hung a silken sash which once held a knight's shield. It was of scarlet, heavily embroidered in gold, and bore a devise of a lion, surmounted by the lily of France.

Three people were in the room. A young woman was bending over a small spinning wheel, a boy of seven was setting the table with their few cracked dishes, and a girl a year or so older was leaning over a kettle on the brazier, stirring its contents from time to time. The lady, whose beauty seemed to shine in the poor room, despite her shabby clothing, was Madame la Comtesse Marie de

Malincourt, and the boy and girl, her son and daughter, Louis and Jeanne.

As she worked the lady was thinking sadly of that Christmas Eve only a year before, when all had been so different. Then she had lived in a great castle, and on the eve of Noel, as she had done for a half dozen years before, she and her husband and the children had gone down to the castle gate to greet the crowd that had assembled. The old, the ailing, and the poor had gathered there, and that meant nearly all the village. Out among the crowd they had gone, followed by a dozen servants, laden down like beasts of burden and to each villager the lady had made gifts of warm clothing, of healing herbs, and of wholesome food. Even Louis and Jeanne, young as they were, had given from their store of toys and baubles to the children of the village.

Then the tide of war had swept over their happy valley; the castle had been attacked, defended, and lost, then sacked and pillaged by the victors. Lady Marie had even seen them lead her husband away a prisoner. She had fled with her children, down a secret passage out into the night and away to the village. She found it deserted, the villagers driven out before the sword.

During the months that had ensued the three had been wandering along the highway. Bit by bit Lady Marie had given her jewels and trinkets, then those of the children, in exchange for food and lodging. Even her velvet robe, with its soft fur mantle, had gone to the wife of a rich burgher, and the pretty clothing of Louis and Jeanne had long since been replaced with coarse peasant garb. One thing alone remained of all their riches—the cover of her husband's shield, which little Louis had brought from the castle that dreadful night. "Father gave it to me to keep until he came back," he said, and through all the terrors of flight he had clung to it. It was very dear to them all. It seemed a bit of their old life, and a constant reminder of the dear lost father.

"Mother," said Jeanne suddenly, interrupting the current of her mother's sad thoughts, "it is Noel tonight."

"Yes, my child," Lady Marie answered with a sigh, "but there will be no toys, or sweets, or pretty things for thee or little Louis this Noel."

"We want them not," the children answered, almost in unison. "We have thee, dear mother, and we can keep the Noel in our hearts," added Jeanne.

Her mother looked up from the wheel and smiled at her. "Yes, though life is hard," she said, "still, we have each other, and though we are sad, perhaps there are other hearts in Rheims that grieve tonight. I wish I might give, as once I did, to the poor, but I have nothing to give. We have ourselves become the poor." She resumed her work, but there was silence in the room save for the whir of the wheel.

"Mother," Jeanne spoke again excitedly, "I know something we can give." As she talked she caught up the small tallow dip candle from the table and hurried with it to the one window of the hut.

"See," she went on, "I will put it here—on the sill—so—and perhaps someone who passes, someone like ourselves lonely and forlorn will be the happier for my little gift of light. There—see how it shines out on the snow, and she stood back to survey her work.

"You are a good child, Jeanne," said Lady Marie, then, sighing, she resumed her work, her silence, her sad thoughts.

Down in the great square, among all the lights and gayety, was another sad heart. It beat in the breast of a little lad of nine, a boy whose clothes were shabby and ragged, whose bare feet were thrust into clumsy wooden sabots, and with no covering on his head but his own fair hair. He was utterly alone, without money, without friends, cold, hungry, miserable. When it seemed he could bear this no longer he tried to tell his story to some of the smiling people he saw about him. Surely among so many he would find friends. But no one took any interest in him, other than to frown at him, or elbow him roughly out of the way, and one man shook him by the shoulder, and called him a beggar.

He left the square at last in utter discouragement, and began to tramp the streets, stopping now and then at splendid dwellings through whose windows streamed bright lights like a welcoming smile. But there was no welcome for the lonely child. Fat, well-dressed servants turned him away with angry words, and threatened him with their dogs.

It was dark in the streets of Rheims now, and the air was growing colder, but the child tramped on, trying desperately to find shelter before the night closed in. At last, far off down by the river, he saw a tiny gleam of light appear suddenly at a window, and he hurried toward it. As he neared it, the boy saw that it was only a small tallow dip at the window of a hovel, the poorest and meanest hut in all Rheims, but the steady light of the tiny flame brought a sudden glow to his heart, and he ran forward and knocked at the door.

It was opened in an instant by a little girl, and at once the other two in the room had risen to greet him. In another moment he found himself seated on a stool beside the charcoal brazier. The little girl was rubbing one of his cold hands in her two warm palms, while her brother was holding the other, and a beautiful woman, kneeling at his feet, drew off the wooden shoes, and chafed his icy feet. When he was thoroughly warmed, the little girl dashed up into three bowls and a cracked cup the stew which had been simmering on the fire. There was only a little of it, a scant meal for themselves, but she passed the fullest bowl to the stranger and made room for him beside her on the bench.

After a word of blessing, they ate their stew, and never had the thin soup tasted so rich or so satisfying to the countess and her children. As they finished, a sudden glowing light filled the room, greater than the brightness of a thousand candles. There was a sound of angel voices, and the stranger child had grown so radiant they could scarcely bear to look at him.

"Thou, with thy little candle, has lighted the Christ-child on his way to heaven," said their unknown guest, his hand on the door latch. "This night shall thy dearest wish be granted thee," and in another instant he was gone.

The countess and her children fell on their knees and prayed, and there they still were, almost a quarter of an hour later, when a knight in armor gently pushed open the door and entered the hut.

"Marie! Jeanne! Louis!" he cried in a voice of love and longing. "Do you not know me after all these weary months of prison and battle, and then of search for thee?"

Immediately his family were clustered about him, and their kisses and embraces were his answer.

"But, father, how did you find us here," cried little Louis at last, when the first raptures of welcome were over.

"A ragged lad I met on the highway told me ye dwelt here," answered the knight.

"The Christ-child," said Lady Marie reverently, and told him the story.

And so, forever after, they and all their descendants, have burned a candle in the window on the eve of Noel, to light the lonely Christ-child on his way.

A Christmas Carol

CHARLES DICKENS

✳

MARLEY'S GHOST

Marley was dead, to begin with. There is no doubt whatever about that. The register of his burial was signed by the clergyman, the clerk, the undertaker, and the chief mourner. Scrooge signed it. And Scrooge's name was good upon 'Change for anything he chose to put his hand to. Old Marley was as dead as a doornail!

Mind! I don't mean to say that I know what is particularly dead about a doornail. I'd be inclined, myself, to regard a coffin nail as the deadest piece of ironmongery in the trade. But the wisdom of our ancestors is in the simile. You will therefore permit me to repeat, emphatically, that Marley was as dead as a doornail. This must be distinctly understood, or nothing wonderful can come of the story I am going to relate.

Scrooge knew he was dead? Of course he did. Scrooge and he were partners for I don't know how many years. Scrooge was his sole executor, his sole legatee, his sole friend and sole mourner. And even Scrooge was not so dreadfully cut up by the sad event but that he was an excellent man of business on the very day of the funeral, and solemnized it with an undoubted bargain.

Scrooge never painted out old Marley's name. There it stood, years afterwards, above the warehouse door: Scrooge and Marley. Sometimes people new to the business called Scrooge Scrooge, and sometimes Marley, but he answered to both names. It was all the same to him.

Oh! But he was a tightfisted hand at the grindstone, Scrooge! a squeezing, wrenching, grasping, scraping, covetous old sinner! Hard and sharp as flint, from which no steel had ever struck out generous fire; secret, and self-contained, and solitary as an oyster. The cold within him froze his old features, nipped his pointed nose, shriveled his cheek, stiffened his gait; made his eyes red, his thin lips blue; and spoke out in his grating voice. A frosty rime was on his head, and on his eyebrows, and his wiry chin. He carried his own low temperature with him; he iced his office in the dog days, and didn't thaw it one degree at Christmas.

Nobody every stopped him in the street to say, with gladsome looks, "My dear Scrooge, how are you?" No beggars implored him to bestow a trifle, no children asked him what it was o'clock, no man or woman ever inquired the way to such and such a place, of Scrooge. Even the blind men's dogs appeared to know him; and, when they saw him coming, would tug their owners into doorways, and then wag their tails as though they said, "No eye at all is better than an evil eye, dark master!"

But what did Scrooge care? He liked to edge his way along the crowded paths of life, warning all human sympathy to keep its distance.

Once upon a time—of all the good days in the year, on Christmas Eve— old Scrooge sat busy in his countinghouse. It was bleak, biting, foggy weather. He could hear the people in the court outside go wheezing up and down, beating their hands upon their breasts, and stamping their feet to warm them. The City clocks had only just gone three, but it was dark already. The fog came pouring in at every clink and keyhole, and was so dense without, that, although the court was of the narrowest, the houses opposite were mere phantoms.

Scrooge's door was open, that he might keep his eye upon his clerk, who in a dismal little cell, a sort of tank, was copying letters. Scrooge had a very small fire, but the clerk's fire was so much smaller that it looked like one coal. He couldn't replenish it, for Scrooge kept the coalbox in his own room; so he wore his white comforter, and tried to warm himself at the candle; in which effort, not being a man of strong imagination, he failed.

"A merry Christmas, uncle! God save you!" cried a cheerful voice. It was the voice of Scrooge's nephew, who came upon him so quickly that this was the first intimation he had of his approach.

"Bah!" said Scrooge. "Humbug!"

He had so heated himself with rapid walking in the fog and frost, this nephew of Scrooge's, that he was all in a glow; his face was ruddy and handsome; his eyes sparkled.

"Christmas a humbug, uncle!" said Scrooge's nephew. "You don't mean that, I am sure?"

"I do," said Scrooge. "Merry Christmas! What right have you to be merry? You're poor enough."

"Come, then," returned the nephew gaily. "What right have you to be dismal? You're rich enough."

Scrooge, having no better answer ready, said, "Bah!" again; and followed it up with "Humbug!"

"Don't be cross, uncle," said the nephew.

"What else can I be when I live in such a world of fools as this? Merry Christmas! Out upon merry Christmas! What's Christmastime to you but a time for paying bills without money; a time for finding yourself a year older, and not an hour richer? If I could work my will," said Scrooge indignantly, "every idiot who goes about with 'Merry Christmas' on his lips should be boiled with his own pudding, and buried with a stake of holly through his heart. He should!"

"Uncle!" pleaded the nephew.

"Nephew!" returned the uncle sternly, "keep Christmas in your own way, and let me keep it in mine."

"Keep it!" repeated Scrooge's nephew. "But you don't keep it."

"Let me leave it alone, then," said Scrooge. "Much good it has ever done you!"

"There are many good things from which I have not profited, I daresay," returned the nephew; "Christmas among them. But I am sure I have always thought of Christmas as a good time; a kind, forgiving, charitable, pleasant time; the only time I know of, in the long calendar of the year, when men seem by one consent to open their shut-up hearts freely. And therefore, though it has never put a scrap of gold in my pocket, I believe that it has done me good; and I say, God bless it!"

The clerk in the tank involuntarily applauded. Becoming immediately sensible of the impropriety, he poked the fire, and extinguished the last frail spark forever.

"Let me hear another sound from you," said Scrooge, "and you'll keep your Christmas by losing your situation! You're quite a powerful speaker, sir," he added, turning to his nephew. "I wonder you don't go into Parliament."

"Don't be angry, uncle," the nephew repeated. "Come! Dine with us tomorrow."

Scrooge said that he would see him—Yes, indeed he did. He said that he would see him in that extremity first.

"But why?" cried Scrooge's nephew. "Why?"

"Why did you get married?" said Scrooge.

"Because I fell in love."

"Because you fell in love!" growled Scrooge, as if that were the only one thing in the world more ridiculous than a merry Christmas. "Good afternoon!"

"I am sorry to find you so resolute. But I'll keep my Christmas humor to the last. A merry Christmas, uncle!"

"Good afternoon!" said Scrooge.

"And a happy New Year!"

"Good afternoon!" said Scrooge.

His nephew left the room without an angry word, notwithstanding. He stopped at the outer door to bestow the greetings of the season on the clerk, who, cold as he was, was warmer than Scrooge; for he returned them cordially.

"There's another," muttered Scrooge: "my clerk, with fifteen shillings a week, and a wife and family, talking about a merry Christmas. I'll retire to Bedlam."

The clerk, in letting Scrooge's nephew out, had let two other people in. They were portly gentlemen, pleasant to behold, and now stood, with their hats off, in Scrooge's office.

"Scrooge and Marley's, I believe," said one of the gentlemen. "Have I the pleasure of addressing Mr. Scrooge, or Mr. Marley?"

"Mr. Marley has been dead these seven years," Scrooge replied. "He died seven years ago, this very night."

"We have no doubt his liberality is well represented by his surviving partner," said the gentleman, presenting his credentials.

It certainly was; for they had been two kindred spirits. At the ominous word "liberality," Scrooge frowned.

"At this festive season of the year, Mr. Scrooge," the gentleman continued, taking up a pen, "it is more than usually desirable that we should make some slight provision for the poor and destitute, who suffer greatly at the present time. Many thousands are in want of common comforts, sir."

"Are there no prisons?" asked Scrooge.

"Plenty of prisons," said the gentleman, laying down the pen.

"And the workhouses?" demanded Scrooge. "Are they still in operation?"

"They are. I wish I could say they were not."

"The Treadmill and the Poor Law are in full vigor, then?" said Scrooge.

"Both very busy, sir."

"I am very glad to hear it," said Scrooge.

"Since they scarcely furnish Christian cheer to the multitude," returned the gentleman, "a few of us are endeavoring to raise a fund to buy the Poor some meat and drink, and means of warmth. This is the time, of all others, when Want is keenly felt, and Abundance rejoices. What shall I put you down for?"

"Nothing!" said Scrooge. "I don't make merry myself at Christmas, and I can't afford to make idle people merry. I help to support the establishments

I have mentioned—they cost enough: and those who are badly off must go there."

"Many can't go there; and many would rather die!"

"If they would rather die," said Scrooge, "they had better do it, and decrease the surplus population. Good afternoon, gentlemen!"

Seeing clearly that it would be useless to pursue their point, the gentlemen withdrew and Scrooge resumed his labors with an improved opinion of himself.

Meanwhile the fog and darkness thickened so that people ran about with flaring links, proffering their services to go before horses and carriages. The ancient tower of a church, whose gruff old bell was always peeping slyly down at Scrooge out of a Gothic window in the wall, became invisible, and struck the hours and quarters in the clouds with tremulous vibrations. The cold became intense. At the corner of the court, some laborers, repairing the gas pipes, had lighted a fire in a brazier, round which a party of ragged men and boys were gathered: warming their hands and winking their eyes before the blaze in rapture. The brightness of the shops, where holly sprigs and berries crackled in the heat of the lamps, made pale faces ruddy as they passed. The Lord Mayor, in the Mansion House, gave orders to his fifty cooks and butlers to keep Christmas as a Lord Mayor's household should; and even the little tailor, whom he had fined five shillings on the previous Monday for being drunk and bloodthirsty in the streets, stirred up tomorrow's pudding in his garret, while his lean wife and the baby sailed out to buy beef.

Foggier yet, and colder! Piercing, biting cold. The owner of one scant young nose, gnawed and mumbled by the hungry cold as bones are gnawed by dogs, stooped down at Scrooge's keyhole to regale him with a Christmas carol; but at the first sound of

"God bless you merry gentleman!
May nothing you dismay!"

Scrooge seized the ruler with such energy of action that the singer fled in terror, leaving the keyhole to the fog and frost.

At length the hour of shutting up arrived. With an ill will Scrooge dismounted from his stool, thereby admitting the fact to the clerk, who instantly snuffed his candle out, and put on his hat. "You'll want all day tomorrow, I suppose?" said Scrooge.

"If quite convenient, sir."

"It's not convenient, and it's not fair. If I was to stop your wages for it, you'd think yourself ill-used, I'll be bound?" the clerk smiled faintly. "And yet," said Scrooge, "you don't think me ill-used when I pay a day's wages for no work."

The clerk observed that it was only once a year.

"A poor excuse for picking a man's pocket every twenty-fifth of December!" said Scrooge, buttoning his greatcoat. "But I suppose you must have the whole day. Be here all the earlier next morning."

The clerk promised that he would; and Scrooge walked out with a growl. The office was closed in a twinkling, and the clerk, with the long ends of his white comforter dangling below his waist (for he boasted no greatcoat), went down a slide on Cornhill, at the end of a lane of boys, twenty times, in honor of its being Christmas Eve, and then ran home as hard as he could pelt.

Scrooge took his melancholy dinner in his usual melancholy tavern; and, having beguiled the rest of the evening with his banker's book, went home to bed. He lived in chambers which had once belonged to his deceased partner. They were a gloomy suite of rooms, in an old dreary building far inside a courtyard. Nobody lived in the house but Scrooge, the other rooms being let out as offices. The yard was so dark that even Scrooge, who knew its every stone, was fain to grope with his hands to find the threshold.

Now, it is a fact that there was nothing at all particular about the knocker on the door, except that it was very large. It is also a fact that Scrooge had little of what is called fancy about him. Let it also be borne in mind that he had not bestowed one thought on Marley since his last mention of his seven-years-dead partner that afternoon. And then let any man explain to me, if he can, how it happened that Scrooge, having his key in the door, saw in the knocker, without its undergoing any intermediate process of change—not a knocker, but Marley's face.

Marley's face. It was not in impenetrable shadow, as the other objects in the yard were, but had a dismal light about it. It was not angry, but looked at Scrooge as Marley used to look; with ghostly spectacles turned upon its ghostly forehead. The hair was curiously stirred, as if by hot air; and, though the eyes were wide open, they were perfectly motionless. That, and its livid color, made it horrible; but its horror seemed to be in spite of the face, and beyond its control, rather than a part of its own expression.

As Scrooge looked fixedly at this phenomenon, it was a knocker again.

To say that he was not startled, or that his blood was not conscious of a terrible sensation to which it had been a stranger from infancy, would be untrue. But he turned the key sturdily, walked in, and lighted his candle. He did pause a moment before he shut the door; and he did look cautiously behind it, as if he half expected to see Marley's pigtail sticking out into the hall. But there was nothing there except the screws and nuts that held the knocker on, so he said, "Pooh!" and closed it with a bang.

The sound resounded through the house like thunder. Every room above, every cask in the wine merchant's cellars below, appeared to have a separate peal of echoes of its own. Scrooge was not a man to be frightened by echoes. He fastened the door, and walked up the stairs: slowly, too: trimming his candle as he went.

It was dark; but Scrooge didn't care: darkness is cheap, and he liked it. But, before he shut his heavy door, he walked through his rooms to see that all was right. He had just enough recollection of the face to desire to do that.

Sitting room, bedroom, storage room. All as they should be. Nobody under the table, nobody under the sofa; a small fire in the grate; and a little saucepan of gruel (Scrooge had a cold in his head) upon the hob. Nobody under the bed; nobody in his dressing gown, which was hanging up in a suspicious attitude against the wall. Storage room as usual. Old fireguard, old shoes, two fish baskets, washing stand on three legs, and a poker.

Satisfied, he locked himself in; double-locked himself in, which was not his custom. Then he put on his dressing gown and slippers, and his nightcap, and sat down before the fire to take his gruel.

It was a very low fire indeed. He was obliged to brood over it before he could extract from it the least sensation of warmth. The fireplace had been built by some Dutch merchant long ago, and paved all round with quaint Dutch tiles, illustrating the Scriptures. There were hundreds of figures there to attract his thoughts; and yet that face of Marley, seven years dead, came like the ancient Prophet's rod, and swallowed up the whole. If each smooth tile had been a blank, there would have been a copy of old Marley's head on every one.

"Humbug!" said Scrooge; and walked across the room.

As he sat down again and threw his head back in the chair, his glance happened to rest upon a bell that hung in the room, and communicated, for some purpose now forgotten, with a chamber in the highest story of the building. It was with astonishment and dread that, as he looked, he saw this bell begin to swing. It swung so softly in the outset that it scarcely made a sound; but soon it rang out loudly, and so did every bell in the house.

This might have lasted half a minute, but it seemed an hour. The bells ceased, as they had begun, together. They were succeeded by a clanking noise deep down below, as if someone were dragging a heavy chain over the casks in the wine merchant's cellar.

Then the cellar door flew open with a booming sound, and Scrooge heard the noise louder, coming up the stairs, then coming straight towards his door.

"It's humbug still!" said Scrooge. "I won't believe it."

His color changed though, when, without pause, it came on through the heavy door and passed into the room before his eyes. Upon its coming in, the dying flame leaped up, as though it cried, "I know him! Marley's Ghost!" and fell again.

The same face: the very same. Marley in his pigtail, waistcoat, tights, and boots; the tassels on the latter bristling, like his pigtail, and his coat skirts, and the hair upon his head. The chain he drew was clasped about his middle. It was long, and wound about him like a tail; and it was made (for Scrooge observed it closely) of cashboxes, ledgers and heavy purses wrought in steel. His body was transparent: so that Scrooge, looking through his waistcoat, could see the two buttons on his coat behind.

Though he saw the Phantom standing before him; though he felt the chilling influence of its death-cold eyes, and marked the very texture of the folded kerchief bound about its head and chin, Scrooge fought against his senses.

"How now!" he said, caustic and cold as ever. "What do you want with me?"

"Much!"—Marley's voice; no doubt about it.

"Who are you?"

"In life I was your partner, Jacob Marley."

"Can you—can you sit down?" asked Scrooge, looking doubtfully at the transparent Spirit.

"I can."

"Do it then."

The Ghost sat down on the opposite side of the fireplace. "You don't believe in me," it observed. "Why do you doubt your senses?"

"Because," said Scrooge, "a little thing affects them. A slight disorder of the stomach makes them cheats. You may be an undigested bit of beef, a blot of mustard, a crumb of cheese, a fragment of an underdone potato. There's more of gravy than of grave about you!"

Scrooge was not in the habit of cracking jokes, nor did he feel by any means waggish. The truth is that he was trying to distract his own attention, and keep down his terror; for the Specter's voice disturbed the very marrow in his bones. To sit staring at those fixed eyes in silence would play, he felt, the very deuce with him. There was something awful, too, in its being provided with an infernal atmosphere of its own. Scrooge could not feel it himself, but this was clearly the case; for, though the Ghost sat motionless, its hair, and skirts, and tassels were agitated as by hot vapor from an oven.

"You see this toothpick?" he said, to divert the vision's stony gaze. "I have but to swallow it to be haunted by legions of goblins, all of my own creation. Humbug, I tell you!"

At this the Spirit raised a frightful cry, and shook its chain with a dismal and appalling noise; and how much greater was Scrooge's horror when, the Phantom taking off the bandage round its head as if it were too warm to wear indoors, its lower jaw dropped down upon its breast!

Scrooge fell upon his knees, and clasped his hands. "Mercy!" he said. "Dreadful apparition, why do you trouble me?"

"Man of the worldly mind!" replied the Ghost, "do you believe in me or not?"

"I do," said Scrooge; "I must. But why do spirits walk the earth, and why do they come to me?"

"It is required of every man," the Ghost returned, "that the spirit within him should walk abroad among his fellowmen; and if that spirit goes not forth in life, it is condemned to do so after death. It is doomed to wander through the world—oh, woe is me!—and witness what it cannot share, but might have shared on earth and turned to happiness!" And again the Specter raised a cry, and shook its chain and wrung its shadowy hands.

"You are fettered," said Scrooge, trembling. "Tell me why?"

"I wear the chain I forged in life," replied the Ghost. "I made it link by link; I girded it on of my own free will; of my own free will I wore it. Is its pattern strange to you?" Scrooge trembled more and more. "Or would you know," pursued the Ghost, "the weight and length of the strong coil you bear yourself?"

Scrooge glanced about him on the floor, in the expectation of finding himself surrounded by some fifty or sixty fathoms of iron cable; but he could see nothing. "Jacob!" he implored. "Tell me more. Speak comfort to me, Jacob."

"I have none to give," the Ghost replied. "It comes from other regions, Ebenezer, and is conveyed by other ministers, to other kinds of men. Little more is permitted to me: I cannot rest, I cannot linger. In life my spirit never walked beyond our countinghouse—mark me! Now weary journeys lie before me!"

It was habit with Scrooge, whenever he became thoughtful, to put his hands in his breeches pockets. He did so now, but without lifting up his eyes, or getting off his knees. "You must have got over a great quantity of ground, Jacob," he observed in a businesslike manner, though with humility and deference. "Seven years dead, and traveling all the time?"

The Ghost, on hearing this, set up another cry, and clanked its chain hideously. "No rest, no peace," it cried. "Incessant torture of remorse. Oh! captive, bond, and double-ironed, not to know that no space of regret can make amends for one life's opportunities misused! Yet such was I! Oh, such was I!"

"But you were always a good man of business, Jacob," faltered Scrooge, who now began to apply this to himself.

"Business!" cried the Ghost, wringing his hands again. "Mankind was my business; charity, mercy, benevolence were all my business!" It held up its chain at arm's length and flung it heavily upon the ground again. "At this time of the rolling year I suffer the most. Why did I walk through crowds of fellow beings with my eyes turned down, and never raise them to that blessed Star which led the Wise Men to a poor abode? Were there no poor homes to which its light would have conducted me?"

Scrooge was dismayed and began to quake exceedingly.

"Hear me!" cried the Ghost. "My time is nearly gone."

"I will. But don't he hard upon me, Jacob! Pray!"

"How it is that I appear before you now, I may not tell. I have sat invisible beside you many a day."

It was not an agreeable idea. Scrooge shivered, and wiped the perspiration from his brow.

"I am here," pursued the Ghost, "to warn you that you have yet a chance of escaping my fate. A chance of my procuring, Ebenezer."

"You were always a good friend," said Scrooge. "Thank'ee!"

"You will be haunted," resumed the Ghost, "by Three Spirits."

"Scrooge's countenance fell almost as low as the Ghost's. "Is that the chance you mentioned, Jacob?" he faltered.

"It is."

"I—I think I'd rather not," said Scrooge.

"Without their visits, you cannot hope to shun the path I tread. Expect the first tomorrow when the bell tolls One."

"Couldn't I take 'em all at once, and have it over, Jacob?" hinted Scrooge.

"Expect the second on the next night at the same hour. The third, upon the next night when the last stroke of Twelve has ceased to vibrate. Look to see me no more; and, for your own sake, remember what has passed between us?"

The Specter took its wrapper from the table, and bound it round its head: Scrooge knew this by the smart sound its teeth made when the jaws were brought together by the bandage. He ventured to raise his eyes, and found his supernatural visitor standing before him, with its chain wound over and about its arm.

It now walked backward from him; and, at every step it took, the window raised itself a little, so that, when the Specter reached it, it was wide open. It beckoned Scrooge to approach. Then, when they were within two paces of each other, it had up its hand, warning him to come no nearer.

Scrooge stopped, not so much in obedience as in surprise and fear; for he became sensible of confused noises in the air; sounds of lamentation and regret; wailings inexpressibly sorrowful and self-accusatory.

The Specter joined in the mournful dirge, and floated out upon the bleak, dark night.

Scrooge looked out the window, desperate in his curiosity. The air was filled with phantoms, wandering in restless haste, and moaning as they went. Every one of them wore chains like Marley's Ghost; some few (they might be guilty governments) were linked together. Many had been known to Scrooge in their lives.

He had been quite familiar with one old ghost in a white waistcoat, with a monstrous iron safe attached to its ankle, who cried piteously at being unable to assist a wretched woman with an infant whom it saw below upon a doorstep. The misery with them all was, clearly, that they sought to interfere, for good, in human matters, and had lost the power forever.

Finally, the spirits and their voices faded together into mist.

Scrooge closed the window, and examined his door. It was double-locked, as he had locked it with his own hands, the bolts were undisturbed. He tried to say "Humbug!" but stopped at the first syllable. And being, from the emotion he had undergone, much in need of repose, he went straight to bed without undressing, and fell asleep upon the instant.

THE FIRST SPIRIT

When Scrooge awoke it was so dark that, looking out of bed, he could scarcely distinguish the window from the walls of his chamber. The chimes of a neighboring church struck the four quarters, and he listened for the hour. To his astonishment the heavy bell went on from six to seven, from seven to eight, and regularly up to twelve. Twelve! It was past two when he went to bed. The clock was wrong. An icicle must have got into the works. Twleve!

"I can't have slept through a whole day and into another night," said Scrooge. "It isn't possible that anything has happened to the sun, and this is twelve at noon!"

He scrambled out of bed, and groped his way to the window; but all he could make out was that it was still very foggy, cold and quiet. He went to bed again, and thought and thought, but could make nothing of it. Marley's Ghost bothered him exceedingly and he could not resolve within himself that it was all a dream. Then he remembered that the Ghost had warned him of a visitation when the bell tolled One. He resolved to lie awake until the hour was past; but the quarter was so long that he was more than once convinced he must have sunk into a doze and missed the clock. At length it broke upon his listening ear.

"Ding, dong! Ding, dong! Ding, dong!"

"A quarter to," said Scrooge, counting.

"Ding, dong!"

"The hour itself," said Scrooge triumphantly, "and nothing else!"

He spoke before the hour bell sounded, which it now did with a deep, dull, hollow, melancholy One. Light flashed up in the room upon the instant, and the curtains of his bed were drawn.

The curtains of his bed were drawn aside, I tell you, by a hand; and Scrooge, starting up, found himself face-to-face with the unearthly visitor who drew them: as close to it as I am now to you, and I am standing in the spirit at your elbow.

It was a strange figure—like an old man viewed through some supernatural medium which diminished him to a child's proportions. Its hair was white as if with age; and yet the face had not a wrinkle in it. It wore a white tunic, bound with a sparkling belt, and held a branch of holly in its hand. But the strangest thing was that from the crown of its head there sprang a clear jet of light, by which all this was visible; which was doubtless why it held, under its arm, a great extinguisher for a cap.

As Scrooge looked at it the figure fluctuated in its distinctness; being now a thing with one arm, now with one leg, now with twenty legs, now a pair of legs without a head, now a head without a body; and, in the very wonder of this, it would be itself again; distinct and clear as ever. "Are you the Spirit, sir, whose coming was foretold to me?" asked Scrooge.

"I am!" The voice was soft and low, as if at a distance.

"Who and what are you?" Scrooge demanded.

"I am the Ghost of Christmas Past. Your Past. Your welfare brings me here."

Scrooge expressed himself much obliged, but could not help thinking that a night of unbroken rest would have been more conducive to that end. That Spirit must have heard him thinking, for it said, "Your reclamation, then. Take heed!" It clasped him gently by the arm. "Rise! And walk with me!"

It would have been in vain for Scrooge to plead that the thermometer was below freezing; that he was clad in slippers, dressing gown, and nightcap; and that he had a cold. The grasp, though gentle, was not to be resisted. He rose; but, as the Spirit made towards the window, clasped its robe in supplication. "I am mortal," he remonstrated, "and liable to fall."

"Bear but a touch of my hand there," said the Spirit, laying it upon his heart, "and you shall be upheld in more than this!"

As the words were spoken, they passed through the wall, and stood upon an open country road. The city had vanished and the darkness and mist with it; it was a clear, cold, winter day, with snow upon the ground. "Good Heaven!" said Scrooge as he looked about him. "I was bred in this place. I was a boy here!"

"You recollect the way?" inquired the Spirit.

"Remember it!" cried Scrooge. "I could walk it blindfold."

"Strange to have forgotten it for so many years!" observed the Ghost. "Let us go on."

They walked along the road, Scrooge recognizing every gate and tree, until a little market town appeared in the distance, with its church and winding river. Some shaggy ponies were trotting towards them with boys upon their backs, who called to the other boys in country carts, driven by farmers. All were in great spirits, and shouted to each other, until the broad fields were so full of merry music that the crisp air laughed to hear it.

"These are but shadows of the things that have been," said the Ghost. "They have no consciousness of us."

The travelers came on; Scrooge knew them every one. Why was he rejoiced beyond all bounds to see them? Why did his heart leap up when he heard them give each other merry Christmas as they parted for their several homes? What was merry Christmas to Scrooge? What good had it ever done him?

"The school is not quite deserted," said the Ghost. "A solitary child, neglected by his friends, is left there still."

Scrooge said he knew it. And he sobbed.

They left the highroad by a well-remembered lane and soon approached a mansion of dull red brick, with a cupola on the roof, and a bell hanging in it. Its windows were broken, the gates decayed. Fowls clucked and strutted in the stables; the coach houses and sheds were overrun with grass. Entering the dreary hall, and glancing into the many rooms, they found them poorly furnished, cold, and vast. There was a chill in the place, which associated itself somehow with too much getting up by candlelight and not too much to eat.

They went, the Ghost and Scrooge, to a room at the back of the house. It was a long, bare, melancholy room, made barer still by lines of plain deal benches and desks. At one of these a lonely boy was reading near a feeble fire; and Scrooge sat down, and wept to see his poor forgotten self as he had used to be. Not an echo in the house, not a scuffle from the mice behind the paneling, not a drip from the half-thawed waterspout in the yard behind, not the idle swinging of a door, but fell upon him with softening influence, and gave a freer passage to his tears.

The Spirit pointed to his younger self, intent upon his reading. Suddenly a man in foreign garments, wonderfully real, stood outside the window, with an axe stuck in his belt, and leading by the bridle an ass laden with wood.

"Why, it's Ali Baba!" Scrooge exclaimed in ecstasy. "It's dear old Ali Baba! Yes, yes; one Christmastime, when yonder solitary child was left here all alone, he did come, for the first time, just like that. And there's the Parrot! Green body and yellow tail, with a thing like a lettuce growing out of the top of his head. 'Poor Robin Crusoe' he called him, when he came home again after sailing round the island. Where have you been, Robin? And there goes Friday, running for his life to the little creek! Halloa! Hoop! Hallo!" Then, with a rapidity of transition very foreign to his usual character, he muttered, "Poor boy!" in pity for his former self. He dried his eyes. "I wish—but it's to late now. There was a boy singing a Christmas carol at my door last night. I should like to have given him something."

The Ghost smiled. "Let us see another Christmas!"

Scrooge's former self grew larger at the words, and the room became darker and more dirty. Windows cracked; plaster fell out of the ceiling; and there he was, alone again, when all the other boys had gone home for the jolly holidays.

He was not reading now, but walking up and down despairingly. Scrooge glanced anxiously towards the door.

It opened; and a little girl, much younger than the boy, came darting in, and, putting her arms about his neck and kissing him, addressed him as her "dear, dear brother." "I have come to bring you home!" said the child, clapping her tiny hands. "To bring you home for ever and ever! Father is much kinder than he used to be. He spoke so gently to me one night that I was not afraid to ask once more if you might come home; and he said you should, and sent me in a coach to bring you. You're never to come back here. And we're to be together all the Christmas long, and have the merriest time in the world!"

"You are quite a woman, little fan!" exclaimed the boy.

She laughed, and stood on tiptoe to embrace him. Then she began to drag him, in her childish eagerness, towards the door.

A terrible voice in the hall cried, "Bring down Master Scrooge's box, there!" and in the hall appeared the schoolmaster himself, who glared on Master Scrooge with ferocious condescension, and threw him into a dreadful state of mind by shaking hands with him. He then conveyed him and his sister into the veriest old well of a shivering best parlor that ever was seen, produced a decanter of curiously light wine, and a block of curiously heavy cake, and administered installments of those dainties to the young people. Master Scrooge's trunk being by this time tied on to the top of the chaise, the children bade the schoomaster good-by and drove gaily down the garden sweep, the quick wheels dashing snow from the evergreens like spray.

"Always a delicate creature, whom a breath might have withered," said the Ghost. "But she had a large heart! She died a woman, and had, as I think a child. Your nephew!"

Scrooge seemed uneasy and answered briefly, "Yes."

Although they had but that moment left the school behind them, they were now in the busy thoroughfares of a city, where shadowy carts and coaches battled for the way. It was plain enough from the shops that here too it was Christmastime; but it was evening, and the streets were lighted up. The Ghost stopped at a warehouse door, and asked Scrooge if he knew it.

"Know it!" said Scrooge. "I was apprenticed here!"

They went in. At sight of an old gentleman in a wig, sitting behind such a high desk that, if he had been two inches taller he must have knocked his head against the ceiling, Scrooge cried in great excitement—"Why, it's old Fezziwig! Bless his heart!"

Old Fezziwig laid down his pen and looked up at the clock, which pointed to seven. He rubbed his hands; adjusted his capacious waistcoat; laughed all over himself; and called out in a comfortable, rich, fat, jovial voice—"Yo ho, there! Ebenezer! Dick!" And Scrooge's former self, now a young man, came briskly in with his fellow 'prentice.

"Dick Wilkins, to be sure!" said Scrooge to the Ghost. "Bless me, there he is. He was much attached to me, was Dick."

"Yo ho, my boys!" said Fezziwig. "No more work tonight. Christmas Eve, Dick, Ebenezer. Let's have the shutters up," he cried, clapping his hands, "before a man can say Jack Robinson!"

You wouldn't believe how those two fellows went at it! they charged into the street with the shutters—one, two, three—had 'em up in their places—four, five, six—barred 'em and pinned 'em—seven, eight, nine—and came back before you could have got to twelve, panting like racehorses.

"Hilli-ho!" cried old Fezziwig, skipping down from the high desk with wonderful agility. "Clear away, my lads, and let's have lots of room here! Hilli-ho, Dick! Chirrup, Ebenezer!"

There was nothing they couldn't have cleared away with old Fezziwig looking on. Every movable was packed off; the floor was swept and watered, lamps trimmed, fuel heaped on the fire; and the warehouse was as snug, and warm, and bright a ballroom as you would desire to see upon a winter's night.

In came a fiddler with a music book, and went up to the lofty desk, and made an orchestra of it, and tuned like fifty stomachaches. In came Mrs. Fezziwig, one vast substantial smile. In came the three Miss Fezziwigs, beaming and lovable. In came the six young followers whose hearts they broke. In came all the young men and women employed in the business. In came the housemaid, with her cousin the baker. In came the cook with her brother's particular friend the milkman. In came the boy from over the way, who was suspected of not having board enough from his master; trying to hide himself behind the girl from next door but one, who was proved to have had her ears pulled by her mistress. In they all came, one after another, any how and every how. Away they went, twenty couples at once; hands half round and back again the other way; down the middle and up again; old top couple always turning up in the wrong place; new top couple starting off as soon as they got there; all top couples at last, and not a bottom one to help them! When this result was brought about, old Fezziwig, clapping his hands to stop the dance, cried out, "Well done!" and the fiddler plunged his hot face into a pot of porter. But upon his reappearance, he instantly began again, as if the other fiddler had been carried home, exhausted, on a shutter, and he were a brand-new man resolved to beat him out of sight or perish.

So there were more dances, and there were forfeits, and there was a cake, and negus, and a great piece of Cold Roast, and a great piece of Cold Boiled, mince pies, and plenty of beer. But the great effect of the evening came after the Roast and Boiled, when the fiddler (an artful dog! a man who knew his business!) struck up "Sir Roger de Coverley." Then old Fezziwig stood out to dance with Mrs. Fezziwig. Top couple, too, with a good stiff piece of work cut out for them; four and twenty pair of partners; people who would dance, and had no notion of walking.

But if they had been four times as many, old Fezziwig would have been a match for them; and as to Mrs. Fezziwig, she was worthy to be his partner in every sense of the term. A positive light appeared to issue from Fezziwig's calves. They shone in every part of the dance like moons. And when old Fezziwig and Mrs. Fezziwig had gone all through the dance: advance and retire, hands to your partner, bow and curtsy, thread-the-needle, and back again to your place: Fezziwig "cut"—cut so deftly that he appeared to wink with his legs, and came upon his feet again without a stagger.

When the clock struck eleven, this domestic ball broke up. Mr. and Mrs. Fezziwig took their stations at the door, and, shaking hands with every person, wished him or her a merry Christmas. They then did the same to the two 'prentices; and the lads were left to their beds under the counter.

During the whole of this time Scrooge had acted like a man out of his wits. His heart and soul were in the scene with his former self. He remembered everything, enjoyed everything, and underwent the strangest agitation. It was not until now, when the bright faces of his former self and Dick were turned away, that he remembered the Ghost, and became conscious that it was looking full upon him, while the light upon its head burned very clear.

"A small matter," said the Ghost, "to make these silly folks so full of gratitude."

"Small," echoed Scrooge.

The Spirit signed to him to listen to the two apprentices pouring out their hearts in praise of Fezziwig. "He has spent but a few pounds of your mortal money. Is that so much that he deserves this praise?"

"It isn't that," said Scrooge, unconsciously speaking like his former self. "Spirit, he has the power to make our service light or burdensome. His power lies in words and looks; it is impossible to add and count 'em up. What then? The happiness he gives is quite as great as if it cost a fortune."

He felt the Spirit's glance, and stopped.

"What is the matter?" asked the Ghost.

"Nothing particular," said Scrooge. "I should like to be able to say a word or two to my clerk just now! That's all."

His former self turned down the lamps at this; and Scrooge and the Ghost again stood side by side in the open air.

"My time grows short," observed the Spirit. "Quick!"

Again Scrooge saw himself. He was older now, in the prime of life, and his face had already begun to wear the signs of avarice. There was a greedy, restless motion in the eye, which showed the passion that had taken root. He sat by the side of a fair young girl. In her eyes there were tears, which sparkled in the light of the Ghost of Christmas Past.

"To you, it matters little," she said softly. "Another idol has displaced me. If it can cheer and comfort you in time to come as I would have tried to do, I have no just cause to grieve."

"What idol has displaced you?" he rejoined.

"A golden one."

"This is the evenhanded dealing of the world!" he said. "There is nothing on which it is so hard as poverty; and there is nothing it professes to condemn so severely as the pursuit of wealth!"

"You fear the world too much," she answered gently, "with its sordid reproach. I have seen your aspirations fall off one by one until only the master passion, Gain, engrosses you."

"If I have grown so much wiser, what then? I am not changed towards you." She shook her head. "Am I?"

"Our contact," she said, "was made when we were both poor, and content to be so, until we could improve our fortune by patient industry. When it was made you were another man."

"I was a boy," he said impatiently.

"Your own feeling tells you that you were not what you are," she returned mildly. "Can even I believe that you would now choose a dowerless girl—you who weigh everything by Gain? With a full heart I release you, for the love of him you once were." He was about to speak, but, with her head turned from him, she resumed: "The memory of what is past half makes me hope you will—have pain in this. A very brief time, and you will dismiss it as a dream from which it happened well that you awoke. May you be happy in the life you have chosen."

She left him, and they parted.

"Spirit!" said Scrooge, "show me no more! Why do you torture me?"

"One shadow more!" exclaimed the Ghost.

"No more!" cried Scrooge. "I don't wish to see it."

But the relentless Ghost pinioned him in both his arms, and forced him to observe what happened next.

They were in another place; a room not large or handsome but full of comfort. Near the fire sat a beautiful girl, so like the last that Scrooge believed it was the same, until he saw her, now a comely matron, sitting opposite her daughter. The noise in this room was perfectly tumultuous, for there were more children there than Scrooge in his agitated state could count; and every child there was conducting itself like forty. They were uproarious beyond belief; but no one seemed to care; on the contrary, mother and daughter laughed heartily, and the latter, mingling in the sports, got pillaged by the young brigands ruthlessly.

A knocking at the door was heard, and a boisterous rush ensued to greet the father, laden with Christmas toys and presents. Then the shouting and the struggling, and the onslaught that was made on him! The scaling him, with chairs for ladders, to dive into his pockets, despoil him of parcels, hold on tight by his cravat and hug him round his neck in irrepressible affection! The shouts of wonder and delight with which each package was received! The terrible announcement that the baby had put a doll's frying pan into his mouth, and was suspected of having swallowed a fictitious turkey, glued on a wooden platter! The immense relief of finding this a false alarm! The joy, and gratitude, and ecstasy! They are all indescribable. It is enough that, by degrees, the children and their emotions got out of the parlor and, by one stair at a time, up to the top of the house, where they went to bed, and so subsided.

And now the master of the house, his daughter leaning fondly on him, sat down with her and her mother at his own fireside; and when Scrooge thought that such a creature, graceful and full of promise, might have called him father, and been a springtime in the haggard winter of his life, his sight grew dim indeed.

"Belle," said the husband, turning to his wife with a smile, "I saw an old friend of yours this afternoon. Guess who it was!"

"How can I? Tut, don't I know?" she added in the same breath, laughing as he laughed. "Mr. Scrooge."

"Mr. Scrooge it was. I passed his office window; and he had a candle inside. His partner lies at the point of death, I hear; and there he sat, quite alone in the world, I do believe."

"Spirit!" said Scrooge in a broken voice. "Remove me from this place. I cannot bear it." he turned upon the Ghost and, seeing it look upon him with a face in which in some strange way there were fragments of all the faces it had shown him, wrestled with it. "Take me back. Haunt me no longer!"

In the struggle, if that can be called a struggle in which the Ghost was undistrubed by any effort of its adversary, Scrooge observed that its light was burning high and bright; and dimly connecting that with its influence over him, he seized the extinguisher cap, and pressed it down upon its head.

The Spirit dropped beneath it, so that the extinguisher covered its whole form; but though Scrooge pressed down with all his force, he could not hide the light, which streamed from under it in an unbroken flood upon the ground. He was conscious of being exhausted and, further, of being in his own bedroom. He gave the cap a parting squeeze, in which his hand relaxed; and had barely time to reel to bed before he sank into a heavy sleep.

THE SECOND SPIRIT

A waking in the middle of a prodigiously tough snore, Scrooge had no occasion to be told that the bell was again upon the stroke of One. He felt that he was restored to consciousness in the nick of time to hold a conference with the second messenger dispatched to him through Jacob Marley. But finding that he turned uncomfortably cold when he began to wonder which of his bed curtains this new specter would draw back, he put every one aside with his own hands and, laying down again, established a sharp lookout all round the bed. For he wished to challenge the Spirit on the moment of its appearance, and not to be taken by surprise. He was ready for a good broad field of strange appearances, and nothing between a baby and a rhinoceros would have astonished him very much.

Now, being prepared for anything, he was by no means prepared for nothing; consequently, when the bell struck One, and no shape appeared, he was taken with a violent fit of trembling. A quarter of an hour went by, yet nothing came. All this time he lay upon his bed, the very core and center of a blaze of ruddy light, which streamed upon it when the clock proclaimed the hour; and which, to make out what it meant. At last he began to think that the source of this ghostly light might be in the adjoining room, from whence it seemed to shine. He got up softly and shuffled in his slippers to the door; and the moment his hand was on the lock a voice bade him enter. He obeyed.

It was his own room. But it had undergone a transformation. The walls and the ceiling were so hung with living green that it looked a perfect grove. The crisp leaves of holly, mistletoe, and ivy reflected back the light like so many mirrors; and such a mighty blaze went roaring up the chimney as that dull hearth had never known in Scrooge's time, or Marley's. Heaped up on the floor, to form a kind of throne, were turkeys, geese, game, great joints of meat, long wreaths of sausages, mince pies, plum puddings, barrels of oysters, red-hot chestnuts, cherry-cheeked apples, juicy oranges, and immense cakes. In easy state upon this couch there sat a jolly Giant, glorious to see, who bore a glowing torch, in shape like Plenty's horn, and held it high up, to shed its light on Scrooge as he came peeping round the door.

"Come in!" exclaimed the Ghost. "And know me better, man!"

Scrooge entered timidly and hung his head before this Spirit. He was not the dogged Scrooge he had been; though the Spirit's eyes were clear and kind, he did not like to meet them. "I am the Ghost of Christmas Present," said the Spirit. "Look upon me!"

Scrooge reverently did so. It was clothed in one simple deep-green robe, bordered with fur; and on its head it wore a holly wreath, set here and there with shining icicles. Its dark-brown curls were long and free; as free as its genial face, its open hand, its cheery voice, and its joyful air. Girded round its middle was an antique scabbard; but no sword was in it, and the ancient sheath was eaten up with rust. "You have never seen the like of me before!" exclaimed the Spirit.

"Never," Scrooge made answer to it.

The Ghost of Christmas Present rose.

"Spirit," said Scrooge submissively, "conduct me where you will. I went forth last night on compulsion, but I learned a lesson. Tonight, if you have aught to teach me, let me profit by it."

"Touch my robe!" Scrooge did as he was told, and held it fast.

The room, the fire, the night, all vanished instantly, and they stood in the city streets on Christmas morning, where (for the weather was severe) the people made a rough but pleasant kind of music, scraping the snow from the pavement and from the tops of their houses, whence it was mad delight to the boys to see it come plumping into the road below in little snowstorms.

The house fronts looked black, the windows blacker, contrasting with the white snow upon the roofs, and with the dirtier snow upon the streets, which had been plowed up in deep furrows by the heavy wheels of carts and wagons. The furrows were channels of yellow mud and icy water. The sky was gloomy, and the shortest streets were choked up with a dingy mist.

Yet the people on the housetops were full of glee; calling to one another, and now and then exchanging a snowball—laughing heartily if it went right, and not less heartily if it went wrong.

The poulterers' shops were still open, and the fruiterers' were radiant in their glory. There were great, potbellied baskets of chestnuts, shaped like the waistcoats of jolly old gentlemen, lolling at the doors and tumbling out into the street in their apoplectic opulence, and ruddy, brown-faced Spanish onions. There were blooming pyramids of pears and apples; and bunches of grapes, dangling from hooks so that people's mouths might water gratis as they passed; piles of nuts and apples, all beseeching to be carried home in paper bags and eaten after dinner.

And the grocers nearly closed, with perhaps two shutters down, but through those gaps such glimpses! It was not alone that the spices were so delicious, the candied fruits so caked with molten sugar; but the grocer and his people were so frank and fresh; and the customers were so hurried in the hopeful promise of the day that they tumbled up against each other at the door, clashing their wicker baskets wildly, left their purchases and came running back to fetch them, and committed hundreds of mistakes in the best humor possible.

But soon the steeples called good people all to church, and away they came, flocking through the streets in their best clothes and with their gayest faces. At the same time there emerged from lanes nameless bystreets innumerable people, carrying their dinners to be cooked at bakers' shops. The sight of these poor revelers appeared to interest the Spirit very much, for he stood with Scrooge in a doorway, and, taking off the covers as their bearers passed, sprinkled incense on their dinners from his torch. It was a very uncommon kind of torch, for once or twice, when there were angry words between some dinner-carriers who had jostled each other, he shed a few drops on them from it, and their good humor was restored directly. It was a shame, they said, to quarrel on Christmas Day. And so it was! God love it, so it was!

"Is there a peculiar flavor in what you sprinkle from your torch?" asked Scrooge.

"There is. My own."

"Would it apply to any kind of dinner on this day?"

"To any kindly given. To a poor one most, because it needs it most."

They went on, invisible as before, into the shrubs. Notwithstanding his gigantic size, the Ghost could accommodate himself to any place with ease; and he stood beneath a low roof quite as gracefully as in any lofty hall. Perhaps it was the pleasure the good Spirit had in showing off this power of his, or else it was his sympathy with all poor men, that led him straight to Scrooge's clerk's; for there he went, and took Scrooge with him; and at the door the Spirit smiled, and stopped to bless Bob Cratchit's dwelling with the sprinklings of his torch. Think of that! Bob pocketed on Saturdays but fifteen shillings; and yet the Ghost of Christmas Present blessed his four-room house!

Then up rose Mrs. Crachit, dressed out but poorly in a twice-turned gown, but brave in ribbons, which are cheap, and make a goodly show for sixpence; and she laid the cloth, assisted by Belinda, second of her daughters, also brave in ribbons; while Master Peter Cratchit plunged a fork into the saucepan of potatoes and, getting the corners of his monstrous shirt collar (Bob's private property, conferred upon his son and heir in honour of the day) into his mouth, rejoiced to find himself so gallantly attired. And now two smaller Cratchits, boy and girl, came tearing in, screaming that at the baker's they had smelled the goose, and known it for their own; and basking in luxurious thoughts of sage and onion, these young Cratchits danced about the table, and exalted Master Peter Cratchit to the skies, while he (although his collars nearly choked him) blew the fire until the potatoes, bubbling up, knocked loudly at the saucepan lid to be let out and peeled.

"What has ever got your precious father, then?" said Mrs. Cratchit. "And your brother, Tiny Tim? And Martha warn't as late last Christmas Day by half-an-hour!"

"Here's Martha, mother!" said a girl, appearing as she spoke.

"Why, bless your heart alive, my dear, how late you are!" said Mrs. Cratchit, kissing her a dozen times, and taking off her shawl and bonnet for her.

"We'd a deal of work to finish up last night," replied the girl, "and had to clear away this morning, mother!"

"Well! Never mind so long as you are come. Sit ye down before the fire, my dear, and have a warm, Lord bless ye!"

"No, no! There's father coming!" cried the two young Cratchits, who were everywhere at once. "Hide, Martha, hide!"

So Martha hid herself, and in came little Bob, the father, with at least three feet of comforter hanging down before him, his threadbare clothes darned and brushed to look seasonable, and Tiny Tim upon his shoulder. Alas for Tiny Tim, he bore a little crutch, and had his limbs supported by an iron frame!

"Why, where's our Martha?" cried Bob Cratchit, looking round.

"Not coming," said Mrs. Cratchit.

"Not coming!" said Bob, with a sudden declension in his high spirits; for he had been Tim's blood horse all the way from church, and had come home rampant. "Not coming upon Christmas Day!"

Martha didn't like to see him disappointed, if only in joke; so she came out prematurely from behind the closet door and ran into his arms, while the two young Cratchits hustled Tiny Tim, and bore him off into the wash-house, that he might hear the pudding singing in the copper.

"And how did little Tim behave?" asked Mrs. Cratchit when Bob had hugged his daughter to his heart's content.

"As good as gold," said Bob. "Somehow he gets thoughtful sitting by himself so much he told me, coming home, that he hoped the people saw him in the church, because he was a cripple, and it might be pleasant to them to remember upon Christmas Day, who made lame beggars walk and blind men see." Bob's voice was tremulous when he told them this, and trembled more when he said that Tiny Tim was growing strong and hearty.

His active little crutch was heard upon the floor, and back came Tiny Tim, escorted by his brother and sister to his stool before the fire; and while Bob, turning up his cuffs, compounded some hot mixture with gin and lemons in a jug and put it on the hob to simmer, Master Peter and the two young Cratchits went to fetch the goose, with which they soon returned in high procession.

Such a bustle ensued that you might have thought a goose the rarest of all birds; a feathered phenomenon, to which a black swan was a matter of course, and in truth it was something very like it in that house. Mrs. Cratchit made the gravy hissing hot; Master Peter mashed the potatoes with incredible vigor; Miss Belinda sweetened up the applesauce; Martha dusted the hot plates; Bob took Tiny Tim beside him in a tiny corner at the table; the two young Cratchits set chairs for everybody, and crammed spoons into their mouths, lest they should shriek for goose before their turn came to be helped. At last the dishes were set on, and grace was said. It was succeeded by a breathless pause, as Mrs. Cratchit, looking slowly all along the carving knife, prepared to plunge it in the breast; but when she did, and when the long-expected gush of stuffing issued forth, one murmur of delight arose all around the board, and even Tiny Tim beat on the table with the handle of his knife and feebly cried Hurrah!

There never was such a goose. Bob said he didn't believe there ever was such a goose cooked. Its tenderness and flavor, size and cheapness, were the themes of universal admiration. Eked out by applesauce and mashed potatoes, it was a sufficient dinner for the whole family; indeed, as Mrs. Cratchit said with great delight (surveying one small atom of a bone upon the dish), they hadn't ate it all at last! Yet everyone had had enough, and the youngest Cratchits were steeped in sage and onion to the eyebrows!

Now, Mrs. Cratchit left the room alone—too nervous to bear witnesses—to take the pudding up, and bring it in. Suppose it should not be done enough! Suppose it should break in turning out! Suppose somebody should have stolen it, while they were merry with the goose—a supposition at which the two young Cratchits became livid!

Hallo! A great deal of steam! The pudding was out of the copper. In half a minute Mrs. Cratchit entered—flushed, but smiling proudly—with the pudding, like a speckled cannonball, blazing in ignited brandy, with Christmas holly stuck into the top.

Oh, a wonderful pudding! Bob Cratchit said that he regarded it as the greatest success achieved by Mrs. Cratchit since their marriage. Mrs. Cratchit said that, now the weight was off her mind, she would confess she had her doubts about the quantity of flour. Everybody had something to say about it, but nobody said or thought it was at all a small pudding for so large a family. It would have been flat heresy to do so. Any Cratchit would have blushed to hint at such a thing.

At last the dinner was all done, the cloth was cleared, the hearth swept, and the fire made up. The compound in the jug being tasted, and considered perfect, apples and oranges were put upon the table, and a shovelful of chestnuts on the fire. Then all the Cratchit family drew round the hearth in a half circle; and at Bob Cratchit's elbow stood the family display of glass: two tumblers and a custard cup without a handle. These held the hot stuff from the jug, however, as well as golden goblets would have done; and Bob served it out with beaming looks, while the chestnuts on the fire cracked noisily. Then Bob proposed:

"A Merry Christmas to us all, my dears. God bless us!"

Which all the family re-echoed.

"God bless us every one!" said Tiny Tim, the last of all.

He sat very close to his father's side, upon his little stool. Bob held his withered little hand in his, as if he wished to keep him by his side and dreaded that he might be taken from him.

"Spirit," cried Scrooge, "tell me if Tiny Tim will live."

"I see a vacant seat," replied the Ghost, "in the poor chimney corner, and a crutch without an owner, carefully preserved."

"No, no," said Scrooge. "Oh, say he will be spared!"

"If these shadows remain unaltered by the Future, the child will die. What then? If he be like to die, he had better do it, and decrease the surplus population."

Scrooge hung his head to hear his own words quoted by the Spirit, and was overcome with penitence and grief.

"Man," said the Ghost, "if man you be in heart, forbear that wicked cant until you have discovered what the surplus is, and where it is. Will you decide what men shall live, what men shall die? It may be that, in the sight of Heaven, you are more worthless and less fit to live than millions like this poor man's child!"

Scrooge bent before the rebuke, trembling. But he raised his eyes speedily on hearing his own name.

"Mr. Scrooge!" said Bob. "I'll give you Mr. Scrooge, the Founder of the Feast!"

"The Founder of the Feast, indeed!" cried Mrs. Cratchit, reddening. "I wish I had him here. I'd give him a piece of my mind to feast upon, and I hope he'd have a good appetite for it."

"My dear," said Bob, "the children! Christmas Day!"

"It should be Christmas Day, I am sure," said she, "on which one drinks the health of such an odious, hard, unfeeling man. You know he is, Robert! Nobody knows it better than you, poor fellow!"

"My dear," was Bob's mild answer, "Christmas Day."

"I'll drink his health for your sake and the Day's," said Mrs. Cratchit, "not for his. A merry Christmas and a happy New Year to him! He'll be very merry and very happy, I have no doubt!"

The children drank the toast after her. It was the first of their proceedings which had no heartiness in it. Scrooge was the Ogre of the family. The mention of his name cast a dark shadow on the party, which was not dispelled for a full five minutes.

After it had passed, they were ten times merrier than before, from mere relief. Bob Cratchit told them how he had a situation in his eye for Master Peter, which could bring in full five-and-sixpence weekly. The two young Cratchits laughed tremendously at the idea of Peter's being a man of business; and Peter himself looked thoughtfully at the fire, as if he were deliberating what investments he should favor when he came into the receipt of that bewildering income. Martha, who was apprenticed at a milliner's, then told them how she had seen a countess and a lord some days before, and how the lord "was much about as tall as Peter"; at which Peter pulled up his collar so high that you couldn't have seen his head if you had been there. All this time the chestnuts and the jug went round and round; and by-an-by they had a song, about a lost child in the snow, from Tiny Tim, who sang it very well indeed.

There was nothing of high mark in this. They were not a handsome family; they were not well-dressed; their shoes were far from being waterproof; their clothes were scanty. But they were happy, grateful, pleased with one another, and contented with the time; and when they faded, and looked happier yet in the bright sprinklings of the Spirit's torch at parting, Scrooge had his eye upon them, and especially on Tiny Tim, until the last.

By this time it was getting dark, and snowing heavily; and, as Scrooge and the Spirit went along the streets, the brightness of the roaring fires in the kitchens and parlors was wonderful. If you had judged from the numbers of people on their way to friendly gatherings, you might have thought that no one was at home to give them welcome when they got there, instead of every house expecting company. How the Ghost exulted! How it opened its palm, and poured its mirth on everything within its reach! The very lamplighter, dotting the dusky street with specks of light, laughed out loudly as the Spirit passed, though little kenned the lamplighter that he had any company but Christmas!

And now, without a word of warning, they stood upon a desert moor, where masses of rude stone were cast about, as though it were the burial place of giants. The setting sun had left a streak of fiery red, which glared upon the desolation for an instant, and, frowning lower yet, was lost in the thick gloom of night.

"What place is this?" asked Scrooge.

"A place where miners live, who labor in the bowels of the earth," returned the Spirit. "But they know me. See!"

A light shone from the window of a hut, and, swiftly passing through its wall of mud and stone, they found a cheerful company round the fire: an old, old man and woman, with their children and their children's children, all decked in holiday attire. The old man was singing them a Christmas song; and from time to time they all joined in the chorus.

Now the spirit bade Scrooge hold his robe, and, to Scrooge's horror, sped out to sea above the thundering water. Upon a dismal reef there stood a solitary lighthouse; but even here, two men who watched the light had made a fire that through the loophole in the thick stone wall shed out a ray of brightness on the awful sea. Joining their horny hands over the rough table at which they sat, they wished each other merry Christmas in their can of grog; and the elder of them, face scarred with weather as the figurehead of an old ship might be, struck up a sturdy song that was like a gale in itself.

It was a great surprise to Scrooge, as they moved on again through the lonely darkness, to hear, suddenly, a hearty laugh. It was a much greater surprise to recognize it as his own nephew's, and to find himself in a dry and gleaming room, with the Spirit smiling at the same nephew. "Ha, ha!" laughed Scrooge's nephew. "Ha, ha, ha!" If you should happen to know a man more blessed in a laugh than Scrooge's nephew, all I can say is, I should like to know him too.

It is an evenhanded adjustment of things that, while there is infection in disease and sorrow, there is nothing in the world so irresistibly contagious as laughter and good humor. When Scrooge's nephew laughed, Scrooge's niece, by marriage, laughed as heartily as he. And their assembled friends roared out lustily. "Ha, ha! Ha, ha, ha, ha!"

"He said that Christmas was a humbug, as I live!" cried Scrooge's nephew. "He believed it, too!"

"More shame for him, Fred!" said Scrooge's niece indignantly.

She was exceedingly pretty, with a dimpled, surprised-looking face; a ripe little mouth, that seemed to be kissed—as no doubt it was; and the sunniest pair of eyes you ever saw. Altogether she was what you would call provoking; but satisfactory, too. Oh, perfectly satisfactory!

"He's a comical old fellow," said Scrooge's nephew; "that's the truth; and not so pleasant as he might be. But I am sorry for him."

"I'm sure he is very rich, Fred," hinted Scrooge's niece. "At least you always tell me so."

"What of that, my dear!" said Scrooge's nephew. "His wealth is of no use to him. He don't do any good with it. He don't make himself comfortable with it."

"I have no patience with him," observed Scrooge's niece. Scrooge's niece's sisters, and all the other ladies, expressed the same opinion.

"Oh, I have!" said Scrooge's nephew. "Who suffers by his ill whims? Himself always. Here he won't come and dine with us. What's the consequence? He don't lose much of a dinner."

"Indeed, I think he loses a very good dinner," interrupted Scrooge's niece. Everybody else said the same, and they must have been competent judges, because they had just had dinner; and were clustered round the fire, by lamplight.

"Well! I am glad to hear it," said Scrooge's nephew, "because I haven't any great faith in those young housekeepers. What do you say, Topper?"

The chimes were ringing the three quarters past eleven.

"Forgive me," said Scrooge, looking intently at the Spirit's robe, "but I see something strange, and not belonging to yourself, protruding from your skirts. Is it a foot or a claw?"

"It might be a claw, for the flesh there is upon it," was the Spirit's sorrowful reply. "Look here!"

From the foldings of its robe it brought two children, frightful, hideous, miserable. They knelt down at its feet, and clung upon its garment. They were a boy and girl: ragged, scowling, wolfish, but abject, too, in their humility. Where youth should have filled their features out, a stale and shriveled hand had pinched and twisted them. Where angels might have sat enthroned, devils glared out menacing.

Scrooge started back, appalled. "Spirit! are they yours?"

"They are Man's," said the Spirit, looking down upon them. "And they cling to me, appealing from their fathers. This boy is Ignorance. This girl is Want. Beware them both."

"Have they no refuge or resource?" cried Scrooge.

"Are there no prisons?" said the Spirit, turning on him for the last time with his own words. "Are there no workhouses?"

The bell struck Twelve.

Scrooge looked about him for the Ghost, and saw it not. As the last stroke ceased to vibrate, he remembered the prediction of old Jacob Marley, and, lifting up his eyes, beheld a solemn Phantom, draped and hooded, coming like a mist along the ground towards him.

THE LAST OF THE SPIRITS

The Phantom slowly, gravely, silently approached. When it came near him, Scrooge bent down upon his knee; for in the very air through which this Spirit moved it seemed to scatter gloom and mystery. Tall and stately, it was shrouded in a deep black garment, which left nothing of it visible save one outstretched hand.

"Are you the Ghost of Christmas Yet To Come?" said Scrooge.

The Spirit answered not, but pointed downward with its hand.

"You are about to show me shadows of the things that will happen in the time before us?" Scrooge pursued.

The Spirit seemed in incline its head. That was its only answer.

Although well used to ghostly company by this time, Scrooge feared the silent shape so much that his legs trembled beneath him when he prepared to follow it. The Spirit paused a moment, as if giving him time to recover. But Scrooge was all the worse for this. It thrilled him with a vague, uncertain horror to know that there were ghostly eyes intently fixed upon him, while he could see nothing but a spectral hand and one great heap of black.

"Ghost of the Future!" he exclaimed. "I fear you more than any specter I have seen. But as I hope to live to be another man from what I was, I am prepared to bear your company, and do it with a thankful heart. Will you not speak to me?"

It gave him no reply. The hand pointed before them.

"Lead on!" said Scrooge. "Lead on! The night is waning fast, and it is precious time to me, I know."

The Phantom moved away. Scrooge followed in the shadow of its dress, which bore him up, he thought, and carried him along.

They scarcely seemed to enter the City; but there they were in the heart of it, amongst the merchants, who hurried up and down, and chinked the money in their pockets, and conversed in groups, and looked at their watches, as Scrooge had seen them often.

The Spirit stopped beside one little knot of businessmen.

"No," said a fat man with monstrous chin, "I don't know much about it. I only know he died last night."

"What was the matter with him?" asked another, taking some snuff. "I thought he'd never die."

"God knows," said the first, with a yawn.

"What has he done with his money?" asked a third.

"Left it to his company, perhaps," said the man with the chin. "He hasn't left it to me. That's all I know." This was received with a general laugh. "It's likely to be a very cheap funeral," the man went on; "for, upon my life, I don't know of anybody to go to it. Suppose we make up a party and volunteer?"

"I don't mind going if lunch is provided," observed one gentleman. "But I must be fed if I go."

Another laugh.

"Well," said the first speaker, "I never eat lunch. But I'll go if anybody else will. I'm not at all sure that I wasn't his most particular friend; we used to speak whenever we met. Bye, bye!"

Scrooge knew the men, and looked to the Spirit for an explanation.

The Phantom glided on. Its finger pointed to two persons.

Scrooge knew these men, also. They were men of business: wealthy, and of great importance. He had made a point—strictly in a business point of view—of standing well in their esteem.

"Well!" said one. "Old Scratch has got his own at last, hey?"

"So I am told," returned the second. "Cold, isn't it?"

"Seasonable for Chrismastime. Are you a skater?"

"No. No. Something else to think of. Good morning!"

Not another word.

Scrooge was surprised that the Spirit should attach importance to conversations so trivial; but, sure that they must have some hidden purpose, he resolved to treasure up every word he heard; and especially to observe that the conduct of his future self would give him the clue he missed. He looked about for his own image, however; for he had been revolving in his mind a change of life, and hoped he saw his newborn resolutions carried out in this.

Quiet and dark, beside him stood the Phantom; and when Scrooge roused himself from thought, he fancied that the Unseen Eyes were looking at him keenly. It made him shudder.

They left the busy scene, and went into an obscure part of town, where Scrooge had never penetrated before, although he knew its bad repute. Alleys and archways disgorged their smell and filth upon the foul and narrow streets; the drunken, slipshod people, the wretched shops and houses, reeked with misery and crime.

Among them was a low-browed, beetling shop where refuse of all kinds was bought. Secrets that few would like to scrutinize were hidden there in mountains of rags and sepulchers of bones. Sitting among the wares he dealt in, by a charcoal stove, was a gray-haired rascal, nearly seventy years of age, who had screened himself from the cold by a frowzy curtain of miscellaneous tatters hung upon a line, and smoked his pipe in all the luxury of calm retirement.

A woman with a heavy bundle slunk into the shop. She had scarcely entered when another woman, similarly laden, came in too; and she was closely followed by a man in faded black. Startled at first by the sight of each other, they all three burst into a laugh.

"Charwoman first!" cried she who had entered first. "The laundress second; and here's the undertaker's man. If we haven't all three met here without meaning it!"

"You couldn't have met in a better place," said old Joe, removing his pipe from his mouth. "Come into the parlor. Stop till I shut the door of the shop. Ah! how it skreeks! There ain't such a rusty bit of metal in the place as its own hinges, I believe; and I'm sure there's no such old bones here as mine. Ha! ha! We're all well matched. Come into the parlor."

The parlor was the space behind the screen of rags. The charwoman threw her bundle on the floor, and sat on a stool, looking with bold defiance at the other two. She spoke again. "What odds then! What odds, Mrs. Dilber? Every person has a right to take care of themselves. He always did! And who's the worse for the loss of these things? Not a dead man, I suppose?"

"No, indeed," said Mrs. Dilber, laughing.

"If he'd been natural in his lifetime," pursued the woman, "he'd have had somebody to look after him, instead of lying gasping out his last there, alone by himself."

"It's a judgment on him," said Mrs. Dilber.

"I wish it was a little heavier one," replied the woman, looking at her bundle, "and it would have been if I could have laid my hands on anything else. Open that bundle, old Joe, and let me know the value of it."

But the gallantry of her friends would not allow of this; and the man in faded black produced his plunder first. It was not extensive: a seal or two, a pencil case, a pair of sleeve buttons, and a brooch of no great value. Old Joe chalked the sums he was disposed to give for each upon the wall, and added them into a total. "That's your account," said Joe. "And I wouldn't give another sixpence, if I was to be boiled for not doing it. Who's next?"

Mrs. Dilber was next. Sheets and towels, a little wearing apparel, two silver teaspoons, a pair of sugar tongs. Her account was stated on the wall in the same manner.

"I always give too much to ladies. It's a weakness of mine, and that's the way I ruin myself," said Joe. "If you asked me for another penny, I'd repent of being so liberal, and knock off half a crown."

"And now undo my bundle, Joe," said the first woman.

Joe went down on his knees for the greater convenience of opening it, and, having unfastened a great many knots, dragged out a large heavy roll of some dark stuff. "Bed curtains?" said Joe.

"Ah!" returned the woman, laughing and leaning forward on her crossed arms. "Bed curtains!"

"You don't mean to say you took 'em down, rings and all, with him lying there?" said Joe. "His blankets, too?"

"Why not?" replied the woman. "He isn't likely to take cold without 'em, I daresay. Ah! that shirt is the best he had, and a fine one too. They'd have wasted it, if it hadn't been for me."

"What do you call wasting of it?" asked old Joe.

"Putting it on him to be buried in," replied the woman. "Somebody was fool enough to do it, but I took it off again.

Scrooge listened in horror which could hardly have been greater had they been demons marketing the corpse itself.

"Ha! ha!" laughed the charwoman when old Joe counted out their money. "This is the end of it, you see! He frightened everyone away when he was alive, to profit us when he was dead!"

"Spirit!" said Scrooge, shuddering from head to foot. "I see, I see. The case of this unhappy man might be my own. My life tends that way now. Merciful Heaven, what is this?"

He recoiled in terror, for the scene had changed, and now he almost touched a bare, uncurtained bed on which, beneath a ragged sheet, there lay something covered up. The room was dark, but a pale light fell upon the bed; and on it, plundered and bereft, unwatched, unwept, uncared for, was the body of this man. The Phantom's steady hand pointed to the head. The motion of a finger upon Scrooge's part would have raised the cover and disclosed the face; but he had no more power to withdraw the veil than to dismiss the Specter at his side. He thought, *If this man could be raised up now, would he think of avarice and hard dealing?* Here he lay with not a man, a woman, or a child to say: since he was kind to me in this or that, I will be kind to him. There was a sound of gnawing rats beneath the hearthstone. What they wanted in the room of death, Scrooge did not dare to think. "If there is any person in the town who feels emotion caused by this man's death," said Scrooge, quite agonized, "show that person to me, Spirit, I beseech you!"

The Phantom spread its robe before him like a wing; and, withdrawing it, revealed a room by daylight where a mother and her children were. She was expecting someone, and anxious; for she walked up and down the room, started at every sound, looked out from the window, glanced at the clock.

At length the long-expected knock was here. She hurried to the door, and met her husband; a man whose face, though young, was careworn. There was remarkable expression in it now, a kind of serious delight which, with shame, he struggled to repress.

"We are quite ruined?" she asked.

"No. There is hope yet, Caroline."

"If he relents," she said, "there is! Nothing is past hope, if such a miracle has happened."

"He is past relenting," said her husband. "He is dead."

She was a mild and patient creature, if her face spoke truth; but she was thankful in her soul to hear it, and she said so. She prayed forgiveness the next moment, and was sorry; but the first was the emotion of her heart.

He said, "What that half-drunken woman told me when I tried to see him and obtain a week's delay turns out to have been quite true. He was not only very ill, but dying then."

"To whom will our debt be transferred?"

"I don't know. But before that time we'll be ready with the money; and even though we weren't, it would be bad fortune indeed to find another creditor so merciless. We may sleep tonight with light hearts, Caroline!"

Yes, their hearts were lighter. And the children's faces, clustered round to hear what they so little understood, were brighter for this man's death! The only emotion that the Ghost could show him, caused by the event, was one of pleasure.

"Let me see some tenderness connected with a death," said Scrooge; "or that dark chamber, Spirit, will be forever present to me."

Again, they entered Bob Cratchit's house, and found the mother and the children seated round the fire. Quiet. Very quiet. The mother and her daughters were engaged in sewing. The noisy little Cratchits were still as statues in one corner, and sat looking up at Peter, who had a book before him.

"And he took a child, and set him in the midst of them . . ."

Why did the boy not go on reading? The mother laid her work upon the table, and put her hand up to her face. "The color hurts my eyes," she said. "I wouldn't show weak eyes to your father when he comes home for the world. It must be near his time."

"Past it rather," Peter answered, shutting up his book. "But he has walked a little slower than he used to, these few last evenings."

They were quiet again. At last she said, in a steady voice that only faltered once: "I have know him walk with—I have know him walk with Tiny Tim upon his should very fast indeed."

"And so have I," cried Peter. "Often."

"But he was very light to carry," she resumed, intent again upon her work, "and his father loved him so that it was no trouble. And there is your father at the door!"

She hurried out to meet him; and little Bob in his comforter—he had need of it, poor fellow—came in. His tea was ready for him on the hob, and they all tried who should help him to it most. Then the two young Cratchits got upon his knees, and laid, each child, a little cheek against his face, as if they said, "Don't mind it, father. Don't be grieved!"

Bob was very cheerful with them, looked at the work upon the table, and praised the industry and speed of Mrs. Cratchit and the girls. They would be done long before Sunday, he said.

"Sunday! You went today then, Robert?" said his wife.

"Yes, my dear. I wish you could have gone. It would have done you good to see how green a place it is. But you'll see it often. I promised him I would walk there on a Sunday. My little, little child!" cried Bob. "My little child!"

He broke down all at once. He couldn't help it. If he could have helped it, he and his child would have been farther apart, perhaps, than they were.

He went upstairs into the room above, which was lighted cheerfully, and hung with Christmas. There was a chair set close beside the child, and there were signs of someone having been there lately. Poor Bob sat down in it, and when he had composed himself a little, he kissed the boy's face and was reconciled to what had happened.

He went down again and they talked, the girls and mother working still. Bob told them of the kindness of Mr. Scrooge's nephew, who, meeting him in the street that day, and seeing that he looked a little—"Just a little down, you know." said Bob, inquired what had happened to distress him. "On which," said Bob, "for he is the pleasantest-spoken gentleman you every heard, I told him. 'I am heartily sorry for it, Mr. Cratchit,' he said, 'and heartily sorry for your good wife.' By the bye, how he ever knew that I don't know."

"Knew what, my dear."

"Why, that you were a good wife," replied Bob.

"Everybody knows that," said Peter.

"Very well observed, my boy!" cried Bob. "I hope they do. 'If I can be of service to you in any way,' he said, giving me his card, 'pray come to me.' Now, it wasn't," cried Bob, "for the sake of anything he might be able to do for us, so much as for his kind way, that this was quite delightful. It really seemed as if he had known our Tiny Tim, and felt with us. I shouldn't be surprised—mark what I say!—if he got Peter a better situation.

"And then," cried one of the girls, "Peter will be keeping company with someone, and setting up for himself."

"Get along with you!" retorted Peter, grinning.

"It's just as likely as not," said Bob, "one of these days, though there's plenty of time for that, my dear. But, however we part from one another, I am sure we shall none of us forget poor Tiny Tim, or this first parting that there was among us."

"Never, father!" cried they all.

"And I know, my dears," said Bob, "that when we recollect how patient and mild he was, although he was a little, little child, we shall not quarrel easily among ourselves, and forget soon Tiny Tim in doing it."

"No, never, father!" they all cried again.

"I am very happy," said little Bob, "I am very happy!"

Mrs. Cratchit kissed him, his daughters kissed him, the two young Cratchits kissed him, and Peter and himself shook hands. Spirit of Tiny Tim, thy childish essence was from God!

"Specter," said Scrooge, "something informs me that our parting moment is at hand. I know it, but I know not how. Tell me what man that was whom we saw lying dead?"

The Ghost of Christmas Yet To Come conveyed him, as before, into the resorts of businessmen, but went straight on, until they reached a churchyard. Here, then, the wretched man, whose name he had now to learn, lay underneath the ground. Walled in by houses; overrun by grass and weeds; choked up with too much burying. A worthy place!

The Spirit stood among the graves, and pointed down to One. He advanced towards it trembling.

"Before I draw nearer to that stone," said Scrooge, "answer me one question. Are these shadows of the things that Will be, or are they shadows of the things that May be only?"

The Spirit was immovable as ever.

Scrooge crept towards it, trembling as he went; and, following the finger, read upon the stone of the neglected grave his own name, Ebenezer Scrooge.

"Am I that man upon the bed?" he cried upon his knees.

The finger pointed from the grave to him, and back again.

"No, Spirit!" he cried, tight clutching at its robe, "hear me! I am not the man I was. Why show me this, if I am past all hope?"

For the first time the hand appeared to shake.

"Good Spirit," he pursued, as down he fell before it, "your nature intercedes for me, and pities me. Assure me that I yet may change these shadows you have shown me by an altered life?"

The kind hand trembled.

"I will honor Christmas in my heart, and try to keep it all the year. I will live in the Past, the Present, and the Future. The Spirits of all Three shall strive within me. I will not shut out the lessons that they teach. Oh, tell me I may sponge away the writing on this stone!"

In his agony, he caught the spectral hand. It sought to free itself, but he was strong in his entreaty, and detained it. The Spirit, stronger yet, repulsed him.

Holding up his hands in one last prayer to change his fate, he saw an alteration in the Phantom's hood and dress. It shrunk, collapsed, and dwindled down into a bedpost.

THE END OF IT

Yes! and the bedpost was his own. The bed was his own, the room was his own. Best and happiest of all, the Time before him was his own, to make amends in! "I will live in the Past, Present, and the Future!" Scrooge repeated as he scrambled out of bed. "The Spirits of all Three shall strive within me. O Jacob Marley! Heaven and Christmastime be praised for this! I say it on my knees, old Jacob; on my knees!" He was so fluttered and so glowing with his good intentions that his broken voice would scarcely answer to his call. He had been sobbing violently in his conflict with the Spirit, and his face was wet with tears. "They are not torn down," cried Scrooge, folding one of his bed curtains in his arms. "They are here—I am here—the shadows of the things that would have been may be dispelled. I know they will be!"

His hands were busy with his garments all this time: turning them inside out, putting them on upside down.

"I am light as a feather!" cried Scrooge, laughing and crying in the same breath. "I am as happy as an angel, I am as merry as a schoolboy! I am as giddy as a drunken man. A merry Christmas to everybody! A happy New Year to all! Hallo here! Whoop! Hallo!"

He had frisked into the sitting room, and was now standing there, perfectly winded. "There's the saucepan that the gruel was in! There's the door by which the Ghost of Jacob Marley entered! There's the corner where the Ghost of Christmas Present sat! It's all right, it's all true, it all happened. Ha, ha, ha!"

Really, for a man who had been out of practice for so many years, it was a splendid laugh, a most illustrious laugh. The father of a long, long line of brilliant laughs!

"I don't know what day of the month it is," said Scrooge. "I don't know how long I have been among the Spirits. I don't know anything. Never mind. Hallo! Whoop! Hallo here!"

He was checked in his transports by the churches ringing out the lustiest peals he had ever heard. Clash, clang, hammer; ding, dong, bell! Bell, dong, ding; hammer, clang, clash! Oh, glorious!

Running to the window, he opened it, and put out his head. No fog, no mist; clear, stirring cold for the blood to dance to; golden sunlight; sweet fresh air; merry bells. Oh, glorious! Glorious! "What's today?" cried Scrooge, calling down to a boy in Sunday clothes.

"Eh?" returned the boy in wonder. "Why, Christmas Day."

"It's Christmas Day!" said Scrooge to himself. "I haven't missed it. The Spirits have done it all in one night. They can do anything they like. Of course they can. Hallo, my fine fellow!"

"Hallo!" returned the boy.

"Do you know the poulterer's in the next street but one, at the corner?" Scrooge inquired.

"I should hope I did," replied the lad.

"An intelligent boy!" said Scrooge. "A remarkable boy! Do you know whether they've sold the prize turkey that was hanging up there?—the big one."

"What! the one as big as me?" returned the boy.

"What a delightful boy!" said Scrooge. "Yes, my buck! Go buy it, and tell 'em to bring it here, that I may tell them where to take it. Come back with the man, and I'll give you a shilling. Come back with him in less than five minutes, and I'll give you half a crown!"

The boy was off like a shot. "I'll send it to Bob Cratchit's," whispered Scrooge, rubbing his hands. "He shan't know who sends it. It's twice the size of Tiny Tim."

The hand in which he wrote the address was not steady; but write it he did, somehow, and went down to the street door to wait for the poulterer's man.

As he stood there, the knocker caught his eye. "I shall love it as long as I live!" cried Scrooge. "What an honest expression it has! It's a wonderful knocker!— Here's the turkey. Hallo! How are you! Merry Christmas!"

It was a turkey! He never could have stood upon his legs, that bird. "Why, it's impossible to carry that to Camden Town," said Scrooge. "You must have a cab."

The chuckle with which he said this, and the chuckle with which he paid for the cab, and the chuckle with which he recompensed the boy, were only exceeded by the chuckle with which he sat down breathless in his chair again, and chuckled till he cried.

He dressed himself in his best, and at last got out into the streets. The people were by this time pouring forth, and Scrooge regarded everyone with a delighted smile. He looked so irresistibly pleasant that three or four good-humored fellows said, "A merry Christmas to you!" And Scrooge said often afterwards that, of all the sounds he had ever heard, those were the blithest in his ears.

He had not gone far when he saw the portly gentleman who had walked into his countinghouse the day before, and said, "Scrooge and Marley's, I believe?" It sent a pang across his heart to think how this old gentleman would look upon him when they met; but he knew what path lay straight before him, and he took it.

"My dear sir," said Scrooge, taking the old gentleman by both his hands, "how do you do? I hope you succeeded yesterday. It was very kind of you. A merry Christmas to you, sir!"

"Mr. Scrooge?"

"Yes," said Scrooge. "That is my name. Allow me to ask your pardon. And will you have the goodness—" here Scrooge whispered in his ear.

"Lord bless me!" cried the gentleman, as if his breath were taken away. "My dear Mr. Scrooge, are you serious?"

"If you please," said Scrooge. "Not a farthing less. A great many back payments are included in it, I assure you."

"My dear sir," said the other, shaking hands with him, "I don't know what to say to such munifi—"

"Don't say anything, please," retorted Scrooge. "Come and see me. Will you come and see me?"

"I will!" cried the other. And it was clear he meant it.

Scrooge went to church, and walked about the streets, and watched the people hurrying to and fro, and patted children on the head, and looked down into kitchens, and found that everything could give him pleasure. In the afternoon he turned his steps towards his nephew's house. He passed the door a dozen times before he had the courage to knock. But he made a dash and did it.

"Is your master at home, my dear?" said Scrooge to the girl.

"Yes, sir. He's in the dining room, sir, along with the mistress. I'll show you in, if you please."

"Thank'ee. He knows me," said Scrooge. "I'll go in, my dear."

He turned the doorknob gently, and sidled in. They were looking at the table (which was spread out in great array); for these young housekeepers are always nervous on such points, and like to see that everything is right.

"Fred!" said Scrooge.

Dear heart alive, how his niece by marriage started!

"Why, bless my soul!" cried Fred. "Who's that?"

"It's uncle Scrooge, come to dinner. Will you let me in?"

Let him in! It is a mercy Fred didn't shake his arm off. He was at home in five minutes. His niece looked just the same. So did Topper when he came. So did the plump sister when she came. So did everyone when they came. Wonderful party, wonderful games, wonderful unanimity, won-der-ful happiness!

But he was early at the office next morning. Oh, if he could only be there first, and catch Bob Cratchit coming late! That was the thing he had set his heart upon.

And he did it! The clock struck nine. No Bob. A quarter past. No Bob. He was a full eighteen minutes and a half behind this time. Scrooge sat with his door wide open, that he might see him come into the tank.

His hat was off before he opened the door; his comforter too. He was on his stool in a jiffy, driving away with his pen, as if he were trying to overtake nine o'clock.

"Hallo!" growled Scrooge, in what he hoped was his accustomed voice. "What do you mean by coming at this hour?"

"I am very sorry, sir," said Bob. "I am behind my time."

"You are! Step this way, sir, if you please."

"It's only once a year, sir," pleaded Bob, appearing from the tank. "I was making rather merry yesterday, sir."

"I tell you what, my friend," said Scrooge. "I am not going to stand for this sort of thing any longer. And therefore," he continued, leaping from his stool, and giving Bob such a dig in the waistcoat that he staggered—"I am about to raise your salary!"

Bob trembled. He had a momentary idea of knocking Scrooge down, holding him, and calling for help and a straitjacket.

"A merry Christmas, Bob!" said Scrooge, with an earnestness that could not be mistaken, as he clapped him on the back. "A merrier Christmas, Bob, my good fellow, than I have given you for many a year! I'll raise your salary, and assist your struggling family, and we will discuss your affairs this very afternoon, over a bowl of Christmas punch, Bob! Make up the fires and buy another coal scuttle before you dot another i, Bob Cratchit!"

Scrooge was better than his word. He did it all, and more; and to Tiny Tim, who did not die, he was a second father. He became as good a friend, as good a master, and as good a man as the good old City knew, or any other good old city or town in the good old world. Some people laughed to see the alteration in him, but he little heeded them; for he was wise enough to know that nothing ever happened on this globe for good at which some people did not laugh in the outset. His own heart laughed, and that was quite enough for him.

He had no further intercourse with Spirits; but it was said of him ever afterwards that he knew how to keep Christmas well, if any man alive possessed the knowledge. May that be truly said of us, and all of us! And so, as Tiny Tim observed, God Bless Us, Every One

When Christmas Went Outdoors

GRADY JOHNSON

Thirty-five years ago this Christmas, ten-year-old David Jonathan Sturgeon lay in bed in Denver, doomed to die. To cheer him, his father lit a small Christmas tree in his sickroom.

Young David pointed through the window at an evergreen growing on the front lawn, exclaiming, "Oh, Daddy, please put some lights on that tree, too. It would look wonderful."

His father, David D. Sturgeon, operator of an electrical business, strung colored lights on the evergreen, and David lay there smiling as he watched them sparkle like emeralds and rubies against their ermine mantle of snow.

The tree was the talk of the town. In horse-drawn carriages and chugging automobiles, people came from miles around to drive slowly past the Sturgeon home and admire the tree which Denverites proudly believe was the first lighted living Christmas tree in the land.

The Christmas after next, little David was dead. But neighbors, who had marveled at his tree, lit trees in their own yards and gardens, turning their section of town into a glittering fairyland. House by house, block by block, the idea spread; and through the years, more and more of these dazzling monuments to a dying boy's wish appeared.

Eight years later, in San Francisco, another little boy was sick at Christmastime. Because the lad couldn't see the family tree, Clarence F. "Sandy" Pratt painted some full-size light globes and strung them on a wire around an evergreen on his lawn across the street.

Like Denver's tree, it attracted much attention. And before New Year's Eve, the sick boy was well.

This so impressed Sandy Pratt that he resolved to spend the rest of his life persuading others not only to light living trees but to plant them. He organized the Outdoor Christmas Tree Association of California, and began sending two-year-old redwood seedlings to anyone who would promise to care for them and light them at Christmastime.

Today, in city parks, along highways, on dark and snow-drifted lawns alike, lighted living trees remind millions of the birth of Christ.

Christmas Every Day

William Dean Howells

The little girl came into her papa's study, as she always did Saturday morning before breakfast, and asked for a story. He tried to beg off that morning, for he was very busy, but she would not let him. So he began:

"Well, once there was a little pig—"

She stopped him at the word. She said she had heard little pig stories till she was perfectly sick of them.

"Well, what kind of story shall I tell, then?"

"About Christmas. It's getting to be the season."

"Well!" Her papa roused himself. "Then I'll tell you about the little girl that wanted Christmas every day in the year. How would you like that?"

"First-rate!" said the little girl; and she nestled into a comfortable shape in his lap, ready for listening.

"Very well, then, this little pig—Oh, what are you pounding me for?"

"Because you said little pig instead of little girl."

"I should like to know what's the difference between a little pig and a little girl that wanted Christmas every day!"

"Papa!" said the little girl warningly. At this her papa began to tell the story.

Once there was a little girl who liked Christmas so much that she wanted it to be Christmas every day in the year, and as soon as Thanksgiving was over she began to send postcards to the old Christmas Fairy to ask if she mightn't have it. But the old Fairy never answered, and after a while the little girl found out that the Fairy wouldn't notice anything but real letters sealed outside with a monogram—or your initial, anyway. So, then, she began to send letters, and just the day before Christmas, she got a letter from the Fairy, saying she might have it be Christmas every day for a year, and then they would see about having it longer.

The little girl was excited already, preparing for the old-fashioned, once-a-year Christmas that was coming the next day. So she resolved to keep the Fairy's promise to herself and surprise everybody with it as it kept coming true, but then it slipped out of her mind altogether.

She had a splendid Christmas. She went to bed early, so as to let Santa Claus fill the stockings, and in the morning she was up the first of anybody and found hers all lumpy with packages of candy, and oranges and grapes, and rubber balls, and all kinds of small presents. Then she waited until the rest of the family was up, and she burst into the library to look at the large presents laid out on the library table—books, and boxes of stationery, and dolls, and little stoves, and dozens of handkerchiefs, and inkstands, and skates, and photograph frames, and boxes of watercolors, and dolls' houses—and the big Christmas tree, lighted and standing in the middle.

She had a splendid Christmas all day. She ate so much candy that she did not want any breakfast, and the whole forenoon the presents kept pouring in that had not been delivered the night before, and she went round giving the presents she had got for other people, and came home and ate turkey and cranberry for dinner, and plum pudding and nuts and raisins and oranges, and then went out and coasted, and came in with a stomachache crying, and her papa said he would see if his house was turned into that sort of fool's paradise another year, and they had a light supper, and pretty early everybody went to bed cross.

The little girl slept very heavily and very late, but she was wakened at last by the other children dancing around her bed with their stockings full of presents in their hands. "Christmas! Christmas! Christmas!" they all shouted.

"Nonsense! It was Christmas yesterday," said the little girl, rubbing her eyes sleepily.

Her brothers and sisters just laughed. "We don't know about that. It's Christmas today, anyway. You come into the library and see."

Then all at once it flashed on the little girl that the Fairy was keeping her promise, and her year of Christmases was beginning. She was dreadfully sleepy, but she sprang up and darted into the library. There it was again! Books, and boxes of stationery, and dolls, and so on.

There was the Christmas tree blazing away, and the family picking out their presents, and her father looking perfectly puzzled, and her mother ready to cry. "I'm sure I don't see how I'm to dispose of all these things," said her mother, and her father said it seemed to him they had had something just like it the day before, but he supposed he must have dreamed it. This struck the little girl as the best kind of a joke, and so she ate so much candy she didn't want any breakfast, and went round carrying presents, and had turkey and cranberry for dinner, and then went out and coasted, and came in with a stomachache, crying.

Now, the next day, it was the same thing over again, but everybody getting crosser, and at the end of a week's time so many people had lost their tempers that you could pick up lost tempers anywhere, they perfectly strewed the ground. Even when people tried to recover their tempers they usually got somebody else's, and it made the most dreadful mix.

The little girl began to get frightened, keeping the secret all to herself. She wanted to tell her mother, but she didn't dare to, and she was ashamed to ask the Fairy to take back her gift, it seemed ungrateful and ill-bred. So it went on and on, and it was Christmas. On St. Valentine's Day and Washington's Birthday, just the same as any day, and it didn't skip even the First of April, though everything was counterfeit that day, and that was some little relief.

After a while turkeys got to be awfully scarce, selling for about a thousand dollars apiece. They got to passing off almost anything for turkeys—even half-grown hummingbirds. And cranberries—well they asked a diamond apiece for cranberries. All the woods and orchards were cut down for Christmas trees. After a while they had to make Christmas trees out of rags. But there were plenty of rags, because people got so poor, buying presents for one another, that they couldn't get any new clothes, and they just wore their old ones to tatters. They got so poor that everybody had to go to the poorhouse, except the confectioners, and the storekeepers, and the book-sellers, and they all got so rich and proud that they would hardly wait upon a person when he came to buy. It was perfectly shameful!

After it had gone on about three or four months, the little girl, whenever she came into the room in the morning and saw those great ugly, lumpy stockings dangling at the fireplace, and the disgusting presents around everywhere, used to sit down and burst out crying. In six months she was perfectly exhausted, she couldn't even cry anymore.

And now it was on the Fourth of July! On the Fourth of July, the first boy in the United States woke up and found out that his firecrackers and toy pistol and two-dollar collection of fireworks were nothing but sugar and candy painted up to look like fireworks. Before ten o'clock every boy in the United States discovered that his July Fourth things had turned into Christmas things and was so mad. The Fourth of July orations all turned into Christmas carols, and when anybody tried to read the Declaration of Independence, instead of saying, "When in the course of human events it becomes necessary," he was sure to sing, "God rest you merry gentlemen." It was perfectly awful.

About the beginning of October the little girl took to sitting down on dolls wherever she found them—she hated the sight of them so, and by Thanksgiving she just slammed her presents across the room. By that time people didn't carry presents around nicely anymore. They flung them over the fence or through the window, and, instead of taking great pains to write "For dear Papa," or "Mama " or "Brother," or "Sister," they used to write, "Take it, you horrid old thing!" and then go and bang it against the front door.

Nearly everybody had built barns to hold their presents, but pretty soon the barns overflowed, and then they used to let them lie out in the rain, or anywhere. Sometimes the police used to come and tell them to shovel their presents off the sidewalk or they would arrest them.

Before Thanksgiving came it had leaked out who had caused all these Christmases. The little girl had suffered so much that she had talked about it in her sleep, and after that hardly anybody would play with her, because if it had not been for her greediness it wouldn't have happened. And now, when it came Thanksgiving, and she wanted them to go to church, and have turkey, and show their gratitude, they said that all the turkeys had been eaten for her old Christmas dinners and if she would stop the Christmases, they would see about the gratitude. And the very next day the little girl began sending letters to the Christmas Fairy, and then telegrams, to stop it. But it didn't do any good, and then she got to calling at the Fairy's house, but the girl that came to the door always said, "Not at home," or "Engaged," or something like that, and so it went on till it came to the old once-a-year Christmas Eve. The little girl fell asleep, and when she woke up in the morning—

"She found it was all nothing but a dream," suggested the little girl.

"No indeed!" said her papa. "It was all every bit true!"

"What did she find out, then?'"

"Why, that it wasn't Christmas at last, and wasn't ever going to be, anymore. Now it's time for breakfast."

The little girl held her papa fast around the neck.

"You shan't go if you're going to leave it so!"

"How do you want it left?"

"Christmas once a year."

"All right," said her papa, and he went on again.

Well, with no Christmas ever again, there was the greatest rejoicing all over the country. People met together everywhere and kissed and cried for joy. Carts went around and gathered up all the candy and raisins and nuts, and dumped them into the river, and it made the fish perfectly sick. And the whole United States, as far out as Alaska, was one blaze of bonfires, where the children were burning up their presents of all kinds. They had the greatest time!

The little girl went to thank the old Fairy because she had stopped its being Christmas, and she said she hoped the Fairy would keep her promise and see that Christmas never, never came again. Then the Fairy frowned, and said that now the little girl was behaving just as greedily as ever, and she'd better look out.

This made the little girl think it all over carefully again, and she said she would be willing to have it Christmas about once in a thousand years, and then she said a hundred, and then she said ten, and at last she got down to one. Then the Fairy said that was the good old way that had pleased people ever since Christmas began, and she was agreed. Then the little girl said, "What're your shoes made of?" And the Fairy said, "Leather." And the little girl said, "Bargain's done forever," and skipped off, and hippity-hopped the whole way home, she was so glad.

"How will that do?" asked the papa.

"First-rate!" said the little girl, but she hated to have the story stop, and was rather sober. However, her mama put her head in at the door and asked her papa:

"Are you never coming to breakfast? What have you been telling that child?"

"Oh, just a tale with a moral."

The little girl caught him around the neck again.

"We know! Don't you tell what, Papa! Don't you tell what!"

The Wooden Shoes of Little Wolff

François Coppée

Adapted

Once upon a time—so long ago that the world has forgotten the date—in a city of the North of Europe—the name of which is so hard to pronounce that no one remembers it—there was a little boy, just seven years old, whose name was Wolff. He was an orphan and lived with his aunt, a hard-hearted, avaricious old woman, who never kissed him but once a year, on New Year's Day; and who sighed with regret every time she gave him a bowlful of soup.

The poor little boy was so sweet-tempered that he loved the old woman in spite of her bad treatment, but he could not look without trembling at the wart, decorated with four gray hairs, which grew on the end of her nose.

As Wolff's aunt was known to have a house of her own and a woolen stocking full of gold, she did not dare to send her nephew to the school for the poor. But she wrangled so that the schoolmaster of the rich boys' school was forced to lower his price and admit little Wolff among his pupils. The bad schoolmaster was vexed to have a boy so meanly clad and who paid so little, and he punished little Wolff severely without cause, ridiculed him, and even incited against him his comrades, who were the sons of rich citizens. They made the orphan their drudge and mocked at him so much that the little boy was as miserable as the stones in the street, and hid himself away in corners to cry—when the Christmas season came.

On the Eve of the great Day the schoolmaster was to take all his pupils to the midnight mass, and then to conduct them home again to their parents' houses.

Now as the winter was very severe, and a quantity of snow had fallen within the past few days, the boys came to the place of meeting warmly wrapped up, with fur-lined caps drawn down over their ears, padded jackets, gloves and knitted mittens, and good strong shoes with thick soles. Only little Wolff presented himself shivering in his thin everyday clothes, and wearing on his feet socks and wooden shoes.

His naughty comrades tried to annoy him in every possible way, but the orphan was so busy warming his hands by blowing on them, and was suffering so much from chilblains, that he paid no heed to the taunts of the others. Then the band of boys, marching two by two, started for the parish church.

It was comfortable inside the church, which was brilliant with lighted tapers. And the pupils, made lively by the gentle warmth, the sound of the organ, and the singing of the choir, began to chatter in low tones. They boasted of the midnight treats awaiting them at home. The son of the Mayor had seen, before leaving the house, a monstrous goose larded with truffles so that it looked like a black-spotted leopard. Another boy told of the fir tree waiting for him, on the branches of which hung oranges, sugar-plums, and punchinellos. Then they talked about what the Christ Child would bring them, or what he would leave in their shoes which they would certainly be careful to place before the fire when they went to bed. And the eyes of the little rogues, lively as a crowd of mice, sparkled with delight as they thought of the many gifts they would find on waking—the pink bags of burnt almonds, the bonbons, lead soldiers standing in rows, menageries, and magnificent jumping-jacks, dressed in purple and gold.

Little Wolff, alas! knew well that his miserly old aunt would send him to bed without any supper; but as he had been good and industrious all the year, he trusted that the Christ Child would not forget him, so he meant that night to set his wooden shoes on the hearth.

The midnight mass was ended. The worshipers hurried away, anxious to enjoy the treats awaiting them in their homes. The band of pupils, two by two, following the schoolmaster, passed out of the church.

Now, under the porch, seated on a stone bench, in the shadow of an arched niche, was a child asleep—a little child dressed in a white garment and with bare feet exposed to the cold. He was not a beggar, for his dress was clean and new, and—beside him upon the ground, tied in a cloth, were the tools of a carpenter's apprentice.

Under the light of the stars, his face, with its closed eyes, shone with an expression of divine sweetness, and his soft, curling blond hair seemed to form an aureole of light about his forehead. But his tender feet, blue with the cold on this cruel night of December, were pitiful to see!

The pupils so warmly clad and shod, passed with indifference before the unknown child. Some, the sons of the greatest men in the city, cast looks of scorn on the barefooted one. But little Wolff, coming last out of the church, stopped deeply moved before the beautiful, sleeping child.

"Alas!" said the orphan to himself, "how dreadful! This poor little one goes without stockings in weather so cold! And, what is worse, he has no shoe to leave beside him while he sleeps, so that the Christ Child may place something in it to comfort him in all his misery."

And carried away by his tender heart, little Wolff drew off the wooden shoe from his right foot, placed it before the sleeping child; and as best as he was able, now hopping, now limping, and wetting his sock in the snow, he returned to his aunt.

"You good-for-nothing!" cried the old woman, full of rage as she saw that one of his shoes was gone. "What have you done with your shoe, little beggar?"

Little Wolff did not know how to lie, and, though shivering with terror as he saw the gray hairs on the end of her nose stand upright, he tried, stammering, to tell his adventure.

But the old miser burst into frightful laughter. "Ah! the sweet young master takes off his shoe for a beggar! Ah! master spoils a pair of shoes for a barefoot! This is something new, indeed! Ah! well, since things are so, I will place the shoe that is left in the fireplace, and to-night the Christ Child will put in a rod to whip you when you wake. And to-morrow you shall have nothing to eat but water and dry bread, and we shall see if the next time you will give away your shoe to the first vagabond that comes along."

And saying this the wicked woman gave him a box on each ear, and made him climb to his wretched room in the loft. There the heartbroken little one lay down in the darkness, and, drenching his pillow with tears, fell asleep.

But in the morning, when the old woman, awakened by the cold and shaken by her cough, descended to the kitchen, oh! wonder of wonders! she saw the great fireplace filled with bright toys, magnificent boxes of sugar-plums, riches of all sorts, and in front of all this treasure, the wooden shoe which her nephew had given to the vagabond, standing beside the other shoe which she herself had placed there the night before, intending to put in it a handful of switches.

And as little Wolff, who had come running at the cries of his aunt, stood in speechless delight before all the splendid Christmas gifts, there came great shouts of laughter from the street.

The old woman and the little boy went out to learn what it was all about, and saw the gossips gathered around the public fountain. What could have happened? Oh, a most amusing and extraordinary thing! The children of all the rich men of the city, whose parents wished to surprise them with the most beautiful gifts, had found nothing but switches in their shoes!

Then the old woman and little Wolff remembered with alarm all the riches that were in their own fireplace, but just then they saw the pastor of the parish church arriving with his face full of perplexity.

Above the bench near the church door, in the very spot where the night before a child, dressed in white, with bare feet exposed to the great cold, had rested his sleeping head, the pastor had seen a golden circle wrought into the old stones. Then all the people knew that the beautiful, sleeping child, beside whom had lain the carpenter's tools, was the Christ Child himself, and that he had rewarded the faith and charity of little Wolff.

The Little Loaf

FROM McGuffey's Third Reader

Once, when there was a famine, a rich baker sent for twenty of the poorest children in the town and said to them, "In this basket there is a loaf for each of you. Take it, and come back to me every day till God sends us better times."

The hungry children gathered eagerly about the basket, and quarreled for the bread, because each wished to have the largest loaf. At last they went away without even thanking the good man.

But Gretchen, a poorly dressed little girl, did not quarrel or struggle with the rest, but remained standing modestly a pace away. When the ill-behaved children had left, she took the smallest loaf, which alone was left in the basket, kissed the man's hand, and went home.

The next day the children were ill-behaved as before, and poor, timid Gretchen received a loaf scarcely half the size of the one she got the first day. When she came home, and her mother cut the loaf open, many new, shining pieces of silver fell out of it.

The mother was very much alarmed, and said, "Take the money back to the good man at once, for it must have got in the dough by accident. Go quickly, Gretchen, go quickly!" but when the little girl gave the rich man her mother's message, he said, "No, no, my child, it was no mistake. I had the silver pieces put into the smallest loaf to reward you. Always be contented, peaceable and grateful as you are now. Go home, now and tell your mother that the money is your own."

The Quiet Little Woman

Louisa May Alcott

Patty stood at the window looking thoughtfully down at a group of girls playing in the yard below. All had cropped heads, all wore brown gowns with blue aprons, and all were orphans like herself. Some were pretty and some plain, some rosy and gay, some pale and feeble, but all seemed to be happy and having a good time in spite of many hardships.

More than once, one of the girls nodded and beckoned to Patty, but she shook her head decidedly and continued to stand listlessly watching and thinking to herself with a child's impatient spirit—

Oh, if someone would only come and take me away! I'm so tired of living here, and I don't think I can bear it much longer.

Poor Patty might well wish for a change; she had been in the orphanage ever since she could remember. And though everyone was very kind to her, she was heartily tired of the place and longed to find a home.

At the orphanage, the children were taught and cared for until they were old enough to help themselves, then they were adopted or went to work as servants. Now and then, some forlorn child was claimed by family. And once the relatives of a little girl named Katy proved to be rich and generous people who came for her in a fine carriage, treated all the other girls in honor of the happy day, and from time to time, let Katy visit them with arms full of gifts for her former playmates and friends.

Katy's situation made a great stir in the orphanage, and the children never tired of talking about it and telling it to newcomers as a sort of modern-day fairy tale. For a time, each hoped to be claimed in the same way, and listening to stories of what they would do when their turn came was a favorite amusement.

By and by, Katy ceased to come, and gradually new girls took the places of those who had left. Eventually, Katy's good fortune was forgotten by all but Patty. To her, it remained a splendid possibility, and she comforted her loneliness by dreaming of the day her "folks" would come for her and bear her away to a future of luxury and pleasure, rest and love. But year after year, no one came for Patty, who worked and waited as others were chosen and she was left to the many duties and few pleasures of her dull life.

People who came for pets chose the pretty, little ones; and those who wanted servants took the tall, strong, merry-faced girls, who spoke up brightly and promised to learn to do anything required of them. Patty's pale face, short figure with one shoulder higher than the other, and shy ways limited her opportunities. She was not ill now, but looked so, and was a sober, quiet little woman at the age of thirteen.

The good matron often recommended Patty as a neat, capable, and gentle little person, but no one seemed to want her, and after every failure, her heart grew heavier and her face sadder, for the thought of spending the rest of her life there in the orphanage was unbearable.

No one guessed what a world of hopes and thoughts and feeling lay hidden beneath that blue pinafore, what dreams this solitary child enjoyed, or what a hungry, aspiring young soul lived in her crooked little body.

But God knew, and when the time came, He remembered Patty and sent her the help she so desperately needed. Sometimes when we least expect it, a small cross proves a lovely crown, a seemingly unimportant event becomes a lifelong experience, or a stranger becomes a friend.

It happened so now, for as Patty said aloud with a great sigh, "I don't think I can bear it any longer!" a hand touched her shoulder and a voice said gently—

"Bear what, my child?"

The touch was so light and the voice so kind that Patty answered before she had time to feel shy.

"Living here, ma'am, and never being chosen as the other girls are."

"Tell me all about it, dear. I'm waiting for my sister, and I'd like to hear your troubles," the kindly woman said, sitting down in the window seat and drawing Patty beside her. She was not young or pretty or finely dressed. She was instead a gray-haired woman dressed in plain black, but her eyes were so cheerful and her voice so soothing that Patty felt at ease in a minute and nestled up to her as she shared her little woes in a few simple words.

"You don't know anything about your parents?" asked the lady.

"No, ma'am. I was left here as a baby without even a name pinned to me, and no one has come to find me. But I shouldn't wonder if they did come even now, so I keep ready all the time and work as hard as I can so they won't be ashamed of me, for I guess my folks is respectable," Patty replied, lifting her head with an air of pride that made the lady ask with a smile:

"What makes you think so?"

"Well, I heard the matron tell the lady who chose Nelly Brian that she always thought I came of high folks because I was so different from the others, and my ways was nice, and my feet so small—see if they ain't—and slipping them out of the rough shoes she wore, Patty held up two slender, little feet with the arched insteps that tell of good birth.

Miss Murray—for that was her name—laughed right out loud at the innocent vanity of the poor child, and said heartily, "They are small, and so are your hands in spite of work. Your hair is fine, your eyes are soft and clear, and you are a good child I'm sure, which is best of all."

Pleased and touched by the praise that is so pleasant to us all, yet half ashamed of herself, Patty blushed and smiled, put on her shoes, and said with unusual animation—

"I'm pretty good, I believe, and I know I'd be much better if I could only get out. I do so long to see trees and grass, and sit in the sun, and listen to the birds. I'd work real hard and be happy if I could live in the country."

"What can you do?" asked Miss Murray, stroking Patty's smooth head and looking down into the wistful eyes fixed upon her.

Modestly, but with a flutter of hope in her heart, Patty recited her domestic accomplishments. It was a good list for a thirteen-year-old, for Patty had been working hard for so long that she had become unusually clever at all sorts of housework as well as needlework.

As she ended, she asked timidly, "Did you come for a girl, ma'am?"

"My sister-in-law, Mrs. Murray, did, but she found one she likes and is going to take her on trial." Her answer caused the light to fade from Patty's eyes and the hope to die in her heart.

"Who is it, please?" she asked.

"Lizzie Brown, a tall, nice-looking girl of fourteen."

"You won't like her, I know, for Lizzie is a real—" There Patty stopped short, turned red, and looked down as if ashamed to meet the keen, kind eyes fixed on her.

"A real what?"

"Please, ma'am, don't ask. It was mean of me to say that, and I mustn't go on. Lizzie can't help being good with you, and I am glad she has a chance to go away."

Aunt Jane Murray asked no more questions, but she noted the little glimpse of character, and tried to brighten Patty's mood by talking about something of interest to her.

"Suppose your 'folks,' as you say, never come for you, and you never find your fortune as some girls do, can't you make friends and fortune for yourself?"

"How can I?" questioned Patty, wonderingly.

"By cheerfully taking whatever comes, by being helpful and affectionate to all, and by wasting no time dreaming about what may happen, but bravely making each day a comfort and a pleasure to yourself and others. Can you do that?"

"I can try, ma'am," answered Patty, meekly.

"I wish you would, and when I come again, you can tell me how you're doing. I believe you will succeed, and when you do, you will have found for yourself a fine fortune and confident certainty of your friends. Now I must go. Cheer up, deary, your turn will come one day."

With a kiss that won Patty's heart, Miss Murray went away, casting more than one look of pity at the small figure sobbing in the window seat, with a blue pinafore over her face.

This disappointment was doubly hard for Patty because Lizzie was not a good girl and to her mind, did not deserve such good fortune. Besides, Patty had taken a great fancy to the lady who spoke so kindly to her.

For a week after this, she went about her work with a sad face, and all her daydreams were of living with Miss Jane Murray in the country.

Monday afternoon, as Patty stood sprinkling clothes for ironing, one of the girls burst in, saying all in a breath—

"Patty! Someone has come for you at last, and you are to go right up to the parlor. It's Mrs. Murray. She brought Liz back 'cause she told fibs and was lazy. Liz is as mad as hops, for it is a real nice place with cows and pigs and chickens and children, and the work ain't hard and she wanted to stay. Do hurry, and don't stand staring at me that way."

"It can't be me—no one ever wants me—it's some mistake—" stammered Patty, who was so startled and excited that she did not know what to say or do.

"It's no mistake," the girl insisted. "Mrs. Murray won't have anyone but you, and the matron says you are to come right up. Go along—I'll finish here. I'm so glad you have your chance at last!" and with a good-natured hug, the girl pushed Patty out of the kitchen.

In a few minutes, Patty came flying back in a twitter of delight to report that she was leaving at once and must say good-bye. Everyone was pleased, and when the flurry was over, the carriage drove away with the happiest little girl you have ever seen riding inside, for at last someone did want her. Patty had found a place.

During the first year Patty lived with the Murrays, they found her to be industrious, docile, and faithful—and yet she was not happy and had not found with them all she expected. They were kind to her, providing plenty of food and not too much work. They clothed her comfortably, let her go to church, and did not scold her very often. But no one showed that they loved her, no one praised her efforts, no one seemed to think that she had any hope or wish beyond her daily work; and no one saw in the shy, quiet little maiden a lonely, tenderhearted girl longing for a crumb of the love so freely given to the children of the home.

The Murrays were busy people with a large farm to care for. The master and his oldest son were hard at it all summer. Mrs. Murray was a brisk, smart house-wife who "flew 'round" herself and expected others to do the same. Pretty Ella, the daughter, was about Patty's age and busy with her school, her little pleasures, and all the bright plans young girls love and live for. Two or three small lads rioted about the house making much work and doing very little.

One of these boys was lame, and this fact seemed to establish a sort of friendly understanding between him and Patty. In truth, he was the only one who ever expressed any regard for her. She was very good to him, always ready to help, always patient with his fretfulness, and always quick to understand his sensitive nature.

"She's only a servant, a charity girl who works for her board and wears my old clothes. She's good enough in her place, but of course she can't expect to be like one of us," Ella once said to a young friend—and Patty heard her.

"Only a servant . . ." That was the hard part, and it never occurred to anyone to make it softer, so Patty plodded on, still hoping and dreaming about friends and future.

Had it not been for Aunt Jane, the child might not have gotten on at all. But Miss Murray never forgot her, even though she lived twenty miles away and seldom came to the farm. She wrote once a month and never failed to include a little note to Patty, which she fully expected would be answered.

Patty wrote a neat reply, which was very stiff and short at first. But after a time, she quite poured out her heart to this one friend who sent her encourag-ing words, cheered her with praise now and then, and made her anxious to be all Miss Jane seemed to expect. No one in the house took much notice of this cor-respondence, for Aunt Jane was considered "odd," and Patty posted her replies with the stamps her friend provided. This was Patty's anchor in her little sea of troubles, and she clung to it, hoping for the day when she had earned such a beautiful reward that she would be allowed to go and live with Miss Murray.

Christmas was coming, and the family was filled with great anticipation; for they intended to spend the day at Aunt Jane's and bring her home for dinner and a dance the next day. For a week beforehand, Mrs. Murray flew 'round with more than her accustomed speed, and Patty trotted about from morning till night, lending a hand to all the most disagreeable jobs. Ella did the light, pretty work, and spent much time fussing over her new dress and the gifts she was making for the boys.

When everything was done at last, Mrs. Murray declared that she would drop if she had another thing to do but go to Jane's and rest.

Patty had lived on the hope of going with them, but nothing was said about it. At last, they all trooped gaily away to the station, leaving her to take care of the house and see that the cat did not touch one of the dozen pies carefully stored in the pantry.

Patty kept up bravely until they were gone, then she sat down like Cinderella, and cried and cried until she could cry no more. It certainly did seem as if she were never to have any fun, and no fairy godmother came to help her. The shower of tears did her good, and she went about her work with a meek, patient face that would have touched a heart of stone.

All the morning she worked to finish the odd jobs left for her to do, and in the afternoon, as the only approach to the holiday she dared venture, Patty sat at the parlor window and watched other people go to and fro, intent on merrymaking in which she had no part.

Her only pleasant little task was that of arranging gifts for the small boys. Miss Jane had given her a bit of money now and then, and out of her meager store, the loving child had made presents for the lads—poor ones certainly, but full of goodwill and the desire to win some affection in return.

The family did not return as early as she had expected, which made the evening seem very long. Patty got out her treasure box and, sitting on the warm kitchen hearth, tried to amuse herself while the wind howled outside and the snow fell fast.

When Aunt Jane welcomed the family, her first word, as she emerged from a chaos of small boys' arms and legs, was "Why, where is Patty?"

"At home, of course; where else would she be?" answered Mrs. Murray.

"Here with you. I said 'all come' in my letter; didn't you understand it?"

"Goodness, Jane, you didn't mean to bring her, too, I hope."

"Yes, I did, and I'm quite disappointed. I'd go and get her myself if I had the time."

Miss Jane knit her brows and looked vexed, and Ella laughed at the idea of the servant girl going on holiday with the family.

"It can't be helped now, so we'll say no more and make it up to Patty tomorrow if we can." Aunt Jane smiled her own pleasant smile and kissed the little lads all 'round as if to sweeten her temper as soon as possible.

They had a capital time, and no one observed that Aunty, now and then, directed the conversation to Patty by asking a question about her or picking up on every little hint dropped by the boys concerning her patience and kindness.

At last, Mrs. Murray said, as she sat resting with a cushion at her back, a stool at her feet, and a cup of tea steaming deliciously under her nose, "Afraid to leave her there in charge? Oh, dear, no. I've entire confidence in her, and she is equal to taking care of the house for a week if need be. On the whole, Jane, I consider her a pretty promising girl. She isn't very quick, but she is faithful, steady, and honest as daylight."

"High praise from you, Maria; I hope she knows your good opinion of her."

"No, indeed! It wouldn't do to pamper a girl's pride by praising her. I say, 'Very well, Patty' when I'm satisfied, and that's quite enough."

"Ah, but you wouldn't be satisfied if George only said, 'Very well, Maria' when you had done your very best to please him in some way."

"That's a different thing," began Mrs. Murray, but Miss Jane shook her head, and Ella said, laughing—

"It's no use to try to convince Aunty on that point; she has taken a fancy to Pat and won't see any fault in her. She's a good enough child, but I can't get anything out of her; she is so odd and shy."

"I can! She's first rate and takes care of me better than anyone else," said Harry, the lame boy, with sudden warmth. Patty had quite won his selfish little heart by many services.

"She'll make Mother a nice helper as she grows up, and I consider it a good speculation. In four years, she'll be eighteen, and if she goes on doing so well, I won't begrudge her wages," added Mr. Murray, who sat nearby with a small son on each knee.

"She'd be quite pretty if she were straight and plump and jolly. But she is as sober as a deacon, and when her work is done, she sits in a corner watching us with big eyes as shy and mute as a mouse," said Ned, the big brother, lounging on the sofa.

"A dull, steady-going girl, suited for a servant and no more," concluded Mrs. Murray, setting down her cup as if the subject were closed.

"You are quite mistaken, and I'll prove it!" Aunt Jane announced, jumping up so energetically that the boys laughed and the elders looked annoyed. Pulling out a portfolio, Aunt Jane untied a little bundle of letters, saying impressively—

"Now listen, all of you, and see what has been going on with Patty this year."

Then Miss Jane read the little letters one by one, and it was curious to see how the faces of the listeners first grew attentive, then touched, then self-reproachful, and finally filled with interest and respect and something very like affection for little Patty.

These letters were pathetic, as Aunty read them to listeners who could supply much that the writer generously left unsaid, and the involuntary comments of the hearers proved the truth of Patty's words.

"Does she envy me because I'm pretty and gay and have a good time? I never thought how hard it must be for her to see me have all the fun and she all the work. She's a girl like me, and I might have done more for her than give her my old clothes and let her help me get dressed for parties," said Ella hastily as Aunt Jane laid aside one letter in which poor Patty told of many "good times and she not in 'em."

"Sakes alive! If I'd known the child wanted me to kiss her now and then as I do the rest, I'd have done it in a minute!" said Mrs. Murray, with sudden softness in her sharp eyes as Aunt Jane read this little bit—

"I am grateful, but, oh! I'm so lonely, and it's so hard not to have any mother like the other children. If Mrs. Murray would only kiss me good night sometimes, it would do me more good than pretty clothes or nice food."

"I've been thinking I'd let her go to school ever since I heard her showing Bob how to do his lessons. But Mother didn't think she could spare her," broke in Mr. Murray apologetically.

"If Ella would help a little, I guess I could allow it. Anyway, we might try for a while, since she is so eager to learn," added his wife, anxious not to seem unjust in Jane's eyes.

"Well, Joe laughed at her as much as I did when the boys hunched up their shoulders the way she does," cried conscious stricken Bob, who had just heard a sad little paragraph about her crooked figure and learned that it came from lugging heavy babies at the orphanage.

"I cuffed 'em both for it, and I have always liked Patty," said Harry, in a moral tone, which moved Ned to say—

"You'd be a selfish little rascal if you didn't when she slaves so for you and gets no thanks for it. Now that I know how it tires her poor little back to carry wood and water, I shall do it myself, of course. If she'd only told me, I'd have done it all the time."

And so it went until the letters were done and they knew Patty as she was. Each felt sorry that he or she had not found out before. Aunt Jane freed her mind on the subject, but the others continued to discuss it until quite an enthusiastic state of feeling set in, and Patty was in danger of being killed with kindness.

It is astonishing how generous and clever people are when once awakened to duty, a charity, or a wrong. Now everyone was eager to repair past neglect, and if Aunt Jane had not wisely restrained them, the young folks would have done something absurd.

They laid many nice little plans to surprise Patty, and each privately resolved not only to give her a Christmas gift but also to do the better thing by turning over a new leaf for the new year.

All the way home, they talked over their various projects, and the boys kept bouncing into the seat with Aunt Jane to ask advice about their funny ideas.

"It must have been rather lonesome for the poor little soul all day. I declare, I wish we'd taken her along!" said Mrs. Murray, as they approached the house through the softly falling snow.

"She's got a jolly good fire all ready for us, and that's a mercy, for I'm half frozen," said Harry, hopping up the step.

"Don't you think if I touch up my blue merino, it would fit Patty and make a nice dress along with one of my white aprons?" whispered Ella, as she helped Aunt Jane out of the sleigh.

"I hope the child isn't sick or scared. It's two hours later than I expected to be home," added Mr. Murray, stepping up to peep in at the kitchen window, for no one came to open the door and no light but the blaze of the fire shone out.

"Come softly and look in," he whispered, beckoning to the rest. "It's a pretty little sight even if it is in a kitchen."

Quietly creeping to the two low windows, they all looked in, and no one said a word, for the lonely little figure was both pretty and pathetic when they remembered the letters lately read. Patty lay flat on the old rug, fast asleep with one arm pillowed under her head. In the other arm lay Puss in a cozy bunch, as if she had crept there to be sociable since there was no one else to share Patty's long vigil. A row of slippers, large and small, stood warming on the hearth, two little nightgowns hung over a chair, the teapot stood in a warm nook, and through the open door, they could see the lamp burning brightly in the sitting room, the table ready, and all things in order.

"Faithful little creature! She's thought of every blessed thing, and I'll go right in and wake her with a good kiss!" cried Mrs. Murray, darting for the door.

But Aunt Jane drew her back, begging her not to frighten the child by any sudden, unexpected demonstrations of affection. So they all went softly in—so softly that tired Patty did not wake, even though Puss pricked up her ears and opened her moony eyes with a lazy purr.

"Look here!" whispered Bob, pointing to the poor little gifts half tumbling out of Patty's apron. She had been pinning names on them when she fell asleep, and now her secret was known too soon.

No one laughed at the presents, and with a look of tender pity, Ella covered the few humble treasures in Patty's box. As she laid back, she remembered what she had once called "rubbish," how full her own boxes were with the pretty things girls love, and how easy it would have been to add to Patty's pitiful store.

No one exactly knew how to awaken the sleeper, for she was something more than a servant in their eyes now. Aunt Jane settled the matter by stooping down and taking Patty in her arms. The big eyes opened at once and stared up at the face above. Then a smile so bright, so glad, shone all over the child's face as she clung to Aunt Jane, crying joyously—

"Is it really you? I was so afraid you wouldn't come that I cried myself to sleep."

Never before had any of them seen such love and happiness in Patty's face, heard such a glad, tender sound in her voice, or guessed what an ardent soul dwelt in her quiet body.

She was herself again in a minute, and jumping up, slipped away to see that everything was ready should anyone want supper after the cold drive.

Soon the family went off to bed, and there was not time to let out the secret. Patty was surprised by the kind good nights everyone sent her way, but she thought no more of it than to feel that Miss Jane brought a warmer atmosphere to the home.

Patty's surprise began early the next day, for the first thing she saw upon opening her eyes was a pair of new stockings crammed full of gifts hanging at the foot of her bed and several parcels lying on the table.

What a good time she had opening the delightful bundles. She laughed and cried at the droll things the boys gave and the comfortable and pretty things the elders sent. Such a happy child was she that when she tried to say her prayers, she couldn't find words beautiful enough to express her gratitude for so much kindness!

A new Patty went downstairs that morning—a bright-faced girl with smiles on the mouth that used to be so sad and silent, confidence in the timid eyes, and the magic of the heartiest goodwill to make her step light, her hand skillful, her labor a joy, and service no burden.

They do care for me, after all, and I never will complain again, she thought with a glad flutter at her heart and sudden color in her cheeks as everyone welcomed her with a friendly, "Merry Christmas, Patty!"

It was the merriest Christmas ever, and when the bountiful dinner was spread and Patty stood ready to wait, you can imagine her feelings as Mr. Murray pointed to a seat near Miss Jane and said in a fatherly tone that made his gruff voice sweet—

"Sit down and enjoy it with us, my girl; nobody has more right to it, and we are all one family today."

Patty could not eat much, her heart was so full, but it was a splendid feast to her, and when toasts were drunk she was overwhelmed by the honor Harry did her, for he bounced up and exclaimed: "Now we must drink to 'Our Patty'—long life and good luck to her!"

That really was too much, and she fairly ran away to hide her blushes in the kitchen and work off her excitement washing dishes.

More surprises came that evening. When she went to put on her clean calico smock, she found the pretty blue dress and white apron laid ready on her bed along with a note that read, "With Ella's love."

"It's like a fairy story that keeps getting nicer and nicer since the godmother came," whispered Patty, as she glanced shyly at Aunt Jane.

"Christmas is the time for all sorts of pleasant miracles," answered Aunt Jane, smiling back at her little maiden, who looked so neat and blithe in her new dress and happy face.

Patty thought nothing further in the way of bliss could happen to her that night, but it did when Ned, anxious to atone for his past neglect, pranced up to her as a final dance was forming and said heartily—

"Come, Patty, everyone is to dance this one, even Harry and the cat!" And before she could collect her wits enough to say "No," she was leading off and flying down the middle with the young master, in great style.

That was the crowning honor, for she was a girl with all a girl's innocent hopes, fears, desires, and delights, and it had been rather hard to stand by while all the young neighbors were frolicking together.

When everyone was gone, the tired children asleep, and the elders on their way up to bed, Mrs. Murray suddenly remembered she had not covered the kitchen fire. Aunt Jane said she would do it, and went down so softly that she did not disturb faithful Patty, who had also gone to see that all was safe.

Aunt Jane stopped to watch the little figure standing on the hearth alone, looking into the embers with thoughtful eyes. If Patty could have seen her future there, she would have found a long life spent in glad service to those she loved and who loved her. Not a splendid future, but a useful, happy one—"only a servant" perhaps, yet a good and faithful woman, blessed with the confidence, respect, and affection of those who knew her genuine worth.

As a smile broke over Patty's face, Miss Jane said with an arm round the little blue-gowned figure—

"What are you dreaming and smiling about, deary? The friends that are to come for you someday, with a fine fortune in their pockets?"

"No, Ma'am. I feel as if I've found my folks. I don't want any finer fortune than the love they've given me today. I'm trying to think how I can deserve it, and smiling because it's so beautiful and I'm so happy," answered Patty, looking up at her first friend with full eyes and a glad glance that made her lovely.

The First Christmas Tree

EUGENE FIELD

✴

Once upon a time the forest was in a great commotion. Early in the evening the wise old cedars had shaken their heads ominously and predicted strange things. They had lived in the forest many, many years; but never had they seen such marvelous sights as were to be seen now in the sky, and upon the hills, and in the distant village.

"Pray tell us what you see," pleaded a little vine; "we who are not as tall as you can behold none of these wonderful things. Describe them to us, that we may enjoy them with you."

"I am filled with such amazement," said one of the cedars, "that I can hardly speak. The whole sky seems to be aflame, and the stars appear to be dancing among the clouds; angels walk down from heaven to the earth, and enter the village or talk with the shepherds upon the hills."

The vine listened in mute astonishment. Such things never before had happened. The vine trembled with excitement. Its nearest neighbor was a tiny tree, so small it scarcely ever was noticed; yet it was a very beautiful little tree, and the vines and ferns and mosses and other humble residents of the forest loved it dearly.

"How I should like to see the angels!" sighed the little tree, "and how I should like to see the stars dancing among the clouds! It must be very beautiful."

As the vine and the little tree talked of these things, the cedars watched with increasing interest the wonderful scenes over and beyond the confines of the forest. Presently they thought they heard music, and they were not mistaken, for soon the whole air was full of the sweetest harmonies ever heard upon earth.

"What beautiful music!" cried the little tree. "I wonder whence it comes."

"The angels are singing," said a cedar; "for none but angels could make such sweet music."

"But the stars are singing, too," said another cedar; "yes, and the shepherds on the hill join in the song, and what a strangely glorious song it is!"

The trees listened to the singing, but they did not understand its meaning; it seemed to be an anthem, and it was of a Child who had been born; but further than this they did not understand. The strange and glorious song continued all the night; and all that night the angels walked to and fro, and the shepherd-folk talked with the angels, and the stars danced and caroled in high heaven. And it was nearly morning when the cedars cried out, "They are coming to the forest! The angels are coming to the forest!" And, surely enough, this was true. The vine and the little tree were very terrified, and they begged their older and stronger neighbors to protect them from harm. But the cedars were too busy with their own fears to pay any heed to the faint pleadings of the humble vine and the little tree.

The angels came into the forest, singing the same glorious anthem about the Child, and the stars sang in chorus with them, until every part of the woods rang with echoes of that wondrous song. There was nothing in the appearance of this angel host to inspire fear; they were clad in white, and there were crowns upon their fair heads, and golden harps in their hands; love, hope, charity, compassion, and joy beamed from their beautiful faces, and their presence seemed to fill the forest with a divine peace. The angels came through the forest to where the little tree stood, and gathering around it, they touched it with their hands, and kissed its little branches, and sang even more sweetly than before. And their song was about the Child, the Child, the Child who had been born. Then the stars came down from the skies and danced and hung upon the branches of the tree, and they, too, sang that song—the song of the Child. And all the other trees and the vines and the ferns and the mosses beheld in wonder; nor could they understand why all these things were being done, and why this exceeding honor should be shown the little tree.

When the morning came the angels left the forest—all but one angel, who remained behind and lingered near the little tree. There a cedar asked: "Why do you tarry with us, holy angel?" And the angel answered: "I stay to guard this little tree, for it is sacred, and no harm shall come to it."

The little tree felt quite relieved by this assurance, and it held up its head more confidently than ever before. And how it thrived and grew, and waxed in strength and beauty! The cedars said they never had seen the like. The sun seemed to lavish its choicest rays upon the little tree, heaven dropped its sweetest dew upon it, and the winds never came to the forest that they did not forget their rude manners and linger to kiss the little tree and sing it their prettiest songs. No danger ever menaced it, no harm threatened; for the angel never slept—through the day and through the night the angel watched the little tree and protected it from all evil. Oftentimes the trees talked with the angel; but of course they understood little of what he said, for he spoke always of the Child who was to become the Master; and always when thus he talked, he caressed the little tree, and stroked its branches and leaves, and moistened them with his tears. It all was so very strange that none in the forest could understand.

So the years passed, the angel watching his blooming charge. Sometimes the beasts strayed toward the little tree and threatened to devour its tender foliage; sometimes the woodman came with his axe, intent upon hewing down the straight and comely thing; sometimes the hot, consuming breath of drought swept from the south, and sought to blight the forest and all its verdure: the angel kept them from the little tree. Serene and beautiful it grew, until now it was no longer a little tree, but the pride and glory of the forest.

One day the tree heard someone come through the forest. Hitherto the angel had hastened to its side when men approached; but now the angel strode away and stood under the cedars yonder.

"Dear angel," cried the tree, "can you not hear the footsteps of someone approaching? Why do you leave me?"

"Have no fear," said the angel; "for he who comes is the Master."

The Master came to the tree and beheld it. He placed his hands upon its smooth trunk and branches, and the tree was thrilled with a strange and glorious delight. Then he stooped and kissed the tree, and then he turned and went away.

Many times after that the Master came to the forest, and when he came it always was to where the tree stood. Many times he rested beneath the tree and enjoyed the shade of its foliage, and listened to the music of the wind as it swept through the rustling leaves. Many times he slept there, and the tree watched over him, and the forest was still, and all its voices were hushed. And the angel hovered near like a faithful sentinel.

Ever and anon men came with the Master to the forest, and sat with him in the shade of the tree, and talked with him of matters which the tree never could understand; only it heard that the talk was of love and charity and gentleness, and it saw that the Master was beloved and venerated by the others. It heard them tell of the Master's goodness and humility—how he healed the sick and raised the dead and bestowed inestimable blessings wherever he walked. And the tree loved the Master for his beauty and his goodness; and when he came to the forest it was full of joy, but when he came not it was sad. And the other trees of the forest joined in its happiness and its sorrow, for they, too, loved the Master. And the angel always hovered near.

The Master came one night alone into the forest, and his face was pale with anguish and wet with tears, and he fell upon his knees and prayed. The tree heard him, and all the forest was still, as if it were standing in the presence of death. And when the morning came, lo! the angel had gone.

Then there was a great confusion in the forest. There was sound of rude voices, and a clashing of swords and staves. Strange men appeared, uttering loud oaths and cruel threats, and the tree was filled with terror. It called aloud for the angel, but the angel came not.

"Alas," cried the vine, "they have come to destroy the tree, the pride and glory of the forest!"

The forest was sorely agitated, but it was in vain. The strange men plied their axes with cruel vigor, and the tree was hewn to the ground. Its beautiful branches were cut away and cast aside, and its soft, thick foliage was strewn to the tenderer mercies of the winds.

"They are killing me!" cried the tree; "why is not the angel here to protect me?"

But no one heard the piteous cry—none but the other trees of the forest, and they wept, and the little vine wept too.

Then the cruel men dragged the despoiled and hewn tree from the forest; and the forest saw that beauteous thing no more.

But the night wind that swept down from the City of the Great King that night to ruffle the bosom of distant Galilee, tarried in the forest awhile to say that it had seen that day a cross upraised on Calvary—the tree on which was stretched the body of the dying Master.

✳

Stubby Pringle's Christmas

JACK WARNER SCHAEFER

H igh on the mountainside by the little line cabin in the crisp and clean dusk of evening Stubby Pringle swings into saddle. He has shape of bear in the dimness, bundled thick against cold. Double socks crowd scarred boots. Leather chaps with hair out cover patched corduroy pants. Fleece-lined jacket with wear of winters on it bulges body and heavy gloves blunt fingers. Two gay red bandannas folded together fatten throat under chin. Battered hat is pulled down to sit on ears and in side pocket of jacket are rabbit-skin earmuffs he can put to use if he needs them.

Stubby Pringle swings up into saddle. He looks out and down over worlds of snow and ice and tree and rock. He spreads arms wide and they embrace whole ranges of hills. He stretches tall and hat brushes stars in sky. He is Stubby Pringle, cowhand of the Triple X, and this is his night to howl he is Stubby Pringle, son of the wild jackass, and he is heading for the Christmas dance at the schoolhouse in the valley.

Stubby Pringle swings up and his horse stands like rock. This is the pride of his string, flop-eared ewe-necked cat-hipped strawberry roan that looks like it should have died weeks ago but has iron rods for bones and nitroglycerin for blood and can go from here to doomsday with nothing more than mouthfuls of snow for water and tufts of winter-cured bunch-grass snatched between drifts of food. It stands like rock. It knows the folly of trying to unseat Stubby. It wastes no energy in futile explosions. It knows that twenty-seven miles of hard winter going are foreordained for this evening and twenty-seven more of harder uphill return by morning. It has done this before. It is saving the dynamite under its hide for the destiny of a true cowpony which is to take its rider where he wants to go—and bring him back again.

Stubby Pringle sits his saddle and he grins into cold and distance and future full of festivity. Join me in a look at what can be seen of him despite the bundling and frosty breath vapor that soon will hang icicles on his nose. Those are careless haphazard scrambled features under the low hat brim, about as handsome as a blue boar's snout. Not much fuzz yet on his chin. Why, shucks, is he just a boy? Don't make that mistake, though his twentieth birthday is six weeks away. Don't make the mistake Hutch Handley made last summer when he thought this was young unseasoned stuff and took to ragging Stubby and wound up with ears pinned back and upper lip split and nose mashed flat and the whole of him dumped in a rain barrel. Stubby has been taking care of himself since he was orphaned at thirteen. Stubby has been doing man's work since he was fifteen. Do you think Hardrock Harper of the Triple X, would have anything but an all-around hard-proved hand up here at his farthest winter line camp siding Old Jake Hanlon, toughest hard-bitten old cowman ever to ride range?

Stubby Pringle slips gloved hand under rump to wipe frost off the saddle. No sense letting it melt into patches of corduroy pants. He slaps rightside saddlebag. It contains a burlap bag wrapped around a two-pound box of candy, of fancy chocolates with variegated interiors he acquired two months ago and has kept hidden from Old Jake. He slaps leftside saddlebag. It holds a burlap bag wrapped around a paper parcel that contains a close-folded piece of dress goods and a roll of pink ribbon. Interesting items, yes. They are ammunition for the campaign he has in mind to soften the affections of whichever female of the right vintage among those at the schoolhouse appeals to him most and seems most susceptible.

Stubby Pringle settles himself firmly into the saddle. He is just another of far-scattered poorly-paid patched-clothes cowhands that inhabit these parts and likely marks and smells of his calling have not all been scrubbed away. He knows that. But this is his night to howl. He is Stubby Pringle, true-begotten son of the wildest jackass, and he has been riding line through hell and highwater and winter storms for two months without a break and he has done his share of the work and more than his share because Old Jake is getting along and slowing some and this is his night to stomp floorboards till schoolhouse shakes and kick heels up to lanterns above and whirl a willing female till she is dizzy enough to see past patched clothes to the man inside them. He wriggles toes deep into stirrups and settles himself firmly in the saddle.

"I could of et them choc'lates," says Old Jake from the cabin doorway. "They wasn't hid good," he says. "No good at all."

"An' be beat like a drum," says Stubby. "An' wrung out like a dirty dishrag."

"By who?" says Old Jake. "By a young un like you? Why, I'd of tied you in knots afore you knew what's what iffen you tried it. You're a dang-blatted young fool," he says. "And ding-busted dang-blatted fool. Riding out a night like this iffen it is Chris'mas eve. A don-bonging ding-busted dang-blatted fool," he says. "But iffen I was your age agin, I reckon I'd be doing it too." He cackles like an old rooster. "Squeeze one of 'em for me," he says and he steps back inside and he closes the door.

Stubby Pringle is alone out there in the darkening dusk, alone with flop-eared ewe-necked cat-hipped roan that can go to the last trumpet call under him and with cold of wicked winter wind around him and with twenty-seven miles of snow-dumped distance ahead of him. "Wahoo!" he yells. "Skip to my Loo!" he shouts. "Do-si-do and round about!"

He lifts reins and the roan sighs and lifts feet. At easy warming-up amble they drop over the edge of benchland where the cabin snugs into tall pines and on down the great bleak expanse of mountainside.

Stubby Pringle, spurs a jingle, jogs upslope through crusted snow. The roan, warmed through, moves strong and steady under him. Line cabin and line work are far forgotten things back and back and up and up the mighty mass of mountain. He is Stubby Pringle, rooting tooting hard-working hard-playing cowhand of the Triple X, heading for the Christmas dance at the schoolhouse in the valley.

He tops out on one of the lower ridges. He pulls rein to give the roan a breather. He brushes an icicle off his nose. He leans forward and reaches to brush several more off sidebars of old bit in the bridle. He straightens tall. Far ahead, over top of last and lowest ridge, on into the valley, he can see tiny specks of glowing allure that are schoolhouse windows. Light and gaiety and good liquor and fluttering skirts are there. "Wahoo!" he yells. "Gals an' women an' Grand-mothers!" he shouts. "Raise your skirts and start askipping! I'm acoming!"

He slaps spurs to roan. It leaps like mountain lion, out and down, full into hard gallop downslope, rushing, reckless of crusted drifts and ice-coated bush-branches slapping at them. He is Stubby Pringle, born with spurs on, nursed on tarantula juice, weaned on rawhide, at home in the saddle of a hurricane in shape of horse that can race to outer edge of eternity and back, heading now for high-jinks two months overdue. He is ten feet tall and the horse is gigantic, with wings, iron-boned and dynamite-fueled, soaring in forty-foot leaps down the flank of the whitened wonder of a winter world.

They slow at the bottom. They stop. They look up the rise of the last ridge ahead. The roan paws frozen ground and snorts twin plumes of frosty vapor. Stubby reaches around to pull down fleece-lined jacket that has worked a bit up back. He pats rightside saddlebag. He pats leftside saddlebag. He lifts reins to soar up and over last low ridge.

Hold it, Stubby. What is it? Off to the right.

He listens. He has ears that can catch snitch of mouse chewing on chunk of bacon rind beyond the log wall by his bunk. He hears. Sound of ax striking wood.

What kind of dong-bonging ding-busted dang-blatted fool would be chopping wood on a night like this and on Christmas Eve and with a dance underway at the schoolhouse in the valley? What kind of chopping is this anyway? Uneven in rhythm, feeble in stroke. Trust Stubby Pringle, who has chopped wood enough for cookstove and fireplace to fill a long freight train, to know how an ax should be handled.

There. That does it. That whopping sound can only mean that the blade has hit at an angle and bounced away without biting. Some don-bonged ding-busted dang-blatted fool is going to be cutting off some of his own toes.

He pulls the roan around to the right. He is Stubby Pringle, born to tune of bawling bulls and blatting calves, branded at birth, cowman raised and cowman to the marrow, and no true cowman rides on without stopping to check anything strange on range. Roan chomps on bit, annoyed at interruption. It remembers who is in saddle. It sighs and obeys. They move quietly in dark of night past boles of trees jet black against dim greyness of crusted snow on ground. Light shows faintly ahead. Lantern light through a small oiled-paper window.

Yes. Of course. Just where it has been for eight months now. The Henderson place. Man and woman and small girl and waist-high boy. Homesteaders. Not even fools, homesteaders. Worse than that. Out of their minds altogether. All of them. Out here anyway. Betting the government they can stave off starving for five years in exchange for one hundred sixty acres of land. Land that just might be able to support seven jack-rabbits and two coyotes and nine rattlesnakes and maybe all of four thin steers to a whole section. In a good year. Homesteaders. Always out of almost everything, money and food and tools and smiles and joy of living. Everything. Except maybe hope and stubborn endurance.

Stubby Pringle nudges the reluctant roan along. In patch-light from the window by a tangled pile of dead tree branches he sees a woman. Her face is grey and pinched and tired. An old stocking-cap is pulled down on her head. Ragged man's jacket bumps over long woolsey dress and clogs arms as she tried to swing an ax into a good-sized branch on the ground.

Whopping sound and ax bounces and barely misses an ankle.

"Quit that!" says Stubby, sharp. He swings the roan in close. He looks down at her. She drops ax and backs away, frightened. She is ready to bolt into two-room bark-slab shack. She looks up. She sees that haphazard scrambled features under low hat brim are crinkled in what could be a grin. She relaxes some, hand on door latch.

"Ma'am," says Stubby. "You trying to cripple yourself?" She just stares at him. "Man's work," he says. "Where's your man?"

"Inside," she says; then, quick, "He's sick."

"Bad?" says Stubby.

"Was," she says. "Doctor that was here this morning thinks he'll be all right now. Only he's almighty weak. All wobbly. Sleeps most of the time."

"Sleeps," says Stubby, indignant. "When there's wood to be chopped."

"He's been almighty tired," she says, quick, defensive. "Even afore he was took sick. Wore out." She is rubbing cold hands together, trying to warm them. "He tried," she says, proud. "Only a while ago. Couldn't even get his pants on. Just fell flat on the floor."

Stubby looks down at her. "An' you ain't tired?" he says.

"I ain't got time to be tired," she says. "Not with all I got to do."

Stubby Pringle looks off past dark holes of trees at last row ridgetop that hides valley and schoolhouse. "I reckon I could spare a bit of time," he says. "Likely they ain't much more'n started yet," he says. He looks again at the woman. He sees grey pinched face. He sees cold-shivering under bumpy jacket. "Ma'am," he says. "Get on in there an' warm your gizzard some. I'll just chop you a bit of wood."

Roan stands with dropping reins, ground-tied, disgusted. It shakes head to send icicles tinkling from bit and bridle. Stopped in midst of epic run, wind-eating, mile-gobbling, iron-boned and dynamite-fueled, and for what? For silly chore of chopping.

Fifteen feet away Stubby Pringle chops wood. Moon is rising over last low ridgetop and its light, filtered through trees, shines on leaping blade. He is Stubby Pringle, moonstruck maverick of the Triple X, born with ax in hand, with strength of stroke in muscles, weaned on whetstone, fed on cordwood, raised to fell whole forests. He is ten feet tall and ax is enormous in moonlight and chips fly like stormflakes of snow and blade slices through branches thick as his arm, through logs thick as his thigh.

He leans ax against a stump and he spreads arms wide and he scoops up whole cords at a time and strides to door and kicks it open . . .

Both corners of front room by fireplace are piled full now, floor to ceiling, good wood, stout wood, seasoned wood, wood enough for a whole wicked winter week. Chore done and done right, Stubby looks around him. Fire is burning bright and well-fed, working on warmth. Man lies on big old bed along opposite wall, blanket over, eyes closed, face grey-pale, snoring long and slow. Woman fusses with something at old woodstove. Stubby steps to doorway to backroom. He pulls aside hanging cloth.

Faith in dimness inside he sees two low bunks and in one, under an old quilt, a curly-headed small girl and in the other, under other old quilt, a boy who would be waist-high awake and standing. He sees them still and quiet, sleeping sound. "Cute little devils," he says.

He turns back and the woman is coming toward him, cup of coffee in hand, strong and hot and steaming. Coffee the kind to warm the throat and gizzard of chore-doing hard-chopping cowhand on a cold cold night. He takes the cup and raises it to his lips. Drains it in two gulps. "Thank you, ma'am," he says. "That was right kindly of you." He sets cup on table. "Where's your tree?" he says. "Kids got to have a Christmas tree."

He sees the woman sink down on chair. He hears a sigh come from her. "I ain't had time to cut one," she says.

"I reckon not," says Stubby. "Man's job anyway," he says. "I'll get it for you. Won't take a minute. Then I got to be going."

He strides out. He scoops up ax and strides off, upslope some where small pines climb. He stretches tall and his legs lengthen and he towers huge among trees swinging with ten-foot steps. He is Stubby Pringle, born an expert on Christmas trees, nursed on pine needles, weaned on pine cones, raised with an eye for size and shape and symmetry. These. A beauty. Perfect. Grown for this and for nothing else. Ax blade slices keen and swift. Tree topples. He strides back with tree on shoulder. He rips leather whangs from his saddle and lashes two pieces of wood to tree bottom, crosswise, so tree can stand upright again.

Stubby Pringle strides into shack, carrying tree. He sets it up, center of front-room floor, and it stands straight, trim and straight, perky and proud and pointed. "There you are, ma'am," he says. "Get your things out an' start decorating. I got to be going." He moves toward outer door.

He stops in outer doorway. He hears the sigh behind him. "We got no things," she says. "I was figuring to buy some but sickness took the money."

Stubby Pringle looks off at last low ridgetop hiding valley and schoolhouse. "Reckon I still got a bit of time," he says. "They'll be whooping it mighty late." He turns back, closing door. He sheds hat and gloves and bandannas and jacket. He moves about checking everything in the sparse front room. He asks for things and the woman jumps to get those few of them she has. He tells her what to do and she does. He does plenty himself. With this and with that magic wonders arrive. He is Stubby Pringle, born to poverty and hard work, weaned on nothing, fed on less, raised to make do with least possible and make the most of that. Pinto beans strung on thread brighten tree in firelight and lantern light like strings of store-bought beads. Strips of one bandanna, cut with shears from sewing-box, bob in bows on branch-ends like gay red flowers. Snippets of fleece from jacket-lining sprinkled over tree glisten like fresh fall of snow. Miracles flow from strong blunt fingers through bits of old paper-bags and dabs of flour paste into link chains and twisted small streamers and two jaunty little hats and two smart little boats with sails.

"Got to finish it right," says Stubby Pringle. From strong blunt fingers comes five-pointed star, triple-thickness to make it stiff, twisted bit of old wire to hold it upright. He fastens this to topmost tip of topmost bough. He wraps lone bandanna left around throat and jams battered hat on head and shrugs into now-skimpy-lined jacket. "A right nice little tree," he says. "All you got to do now is get out what you got for the kids and put it under. I really got to be going." He starts toward the door.

He stops in open doorway. He hears the sigh behind him. He knows without looking around the woman has slumped into old rocking chair. "We ain't got anything for them," she says. "Only now this tree. Which I don't mean it isn't a fine grand tree. It's more'n we'd of had 'cept for you."

Stubby Pringle stands in open doorway looking out into cold clean moonlit night. Somehow he knows without turning head two tears are sliding down thin pinched cheeks. "You go on along," she says. "They're good young uns. They know how it is. They ain't expecting a thing."

Stubby Pringle stands in open doorway looking out at last ridgetop that hides valley and schoolhouse. "All the more reason," he says soft to himself. "All the more reason something should be there when they wake." He sighs too. "I'm dong-bonging ding-busted dang-blatted fool," he says. "But I reckon I still got a mite more time. Likely they'll be sashaying around till it's most morning."

Stubby Pringle strides on out, leaving door open. He strides back, closing door with heel behind him. In one hand he has burlap bag wrapped around paper parcel. In other hand he has squarish chunk of good pine wood. He tosses bag-parcel into lap-folds of woman's apron.

"Unwrap it," he says. "There's the makings for a right cute dress for the girl. Needle-and-threader like you can whip it up in no time. I'll just whittle me out a little something for the boy."

Moon is high in cold cold sky. Frosty clouds drift up there with it. Tiny flakes of snow float through upper air. Down below by a two-room shack droops a disgusted cowpony roan, ground-tied, drooping like statue snow-crusted. It is accepting the inescapable destiny of its kind which is to wait for its rider, to conserve deep-bottomed dynamite energy, to be ready to race to the last margin of motion when waiting is done.

Inside the shack fire in fireplace cheerily gobbles wood, good wood, stout wood, seasoned wood, warming two-rooms well. Man lies on bed, turned on side, curled up some, snoring slow and steady. Woman sits in rocking chair, sewing. Her head nods slow and drowsy and her eyelids sag weary but her fingers fly, stitch-stitch-stitch. A dress has shaped under her hands, small and flounced and with little puff-sleeves, fine dress, fancy dress, dress for smiles, and joy of living. She is sewing pink ribbon around collar and down front and into fluffy bow on back.

On a stool nearby sits Stubby Pringle, piece of good pine wood in one hand, knife in other hands, fine knife, splendid knife, all-around-accomplished knife, knife he always has with him, seven-bladed knife with four for cutting down little to big and corkscrew and can opener and screwdriver. Big cutting blade has done its work. Little cutting blade is in use now. He is Stubby Pringle, born with feel for knives in hand, weaned on emery wheel, fed on shavings, raised to whittle his way through the world. Tiny chips fly and shavings flutter. There in his hands, out of good pine wood, something is shaping. A horse. Yes. Flop-eared ewe-necked, stretched out, sniffing wind, snorting into distance. Cat-hips are hunched forward, caught in crouch for forward leap. It is a horse fit to carry a waist-high boy to uttermost edge of eternity and back.

Stubby Pringle carves swift and sure. Little cutting blade makes final little cutting snitches. Yes. Tiny mottlings and markings make no mistaking. It is a strawberry roan. He closes knife and puts it in pocket. He looks up. Dress is finished in woman's lap. But woman's head has dropped down in exhaustion. She sits slumped deep in rocking chair and she too snores slow and steady.

Stubby Pringle stands up. He takes dress and puts it under tree, fine dress, fancy dress, dress waiting now for small girl to wake and wear it with smiles and joy of living. He sets wooden horse beside it, fine horse, proud horse, snorting-into-distance horse, cat-hips crouched, waiting now for waist-high boy to wake and ride it around the world.

Quietly he piles wood on fire and banks ashes around to hold it for morning. Quietly he pulls on hat and wraps bandanna around and shrugs into skimpy-lined jacket. He looks at old rocking chair and tired woman slumped in it. He strides to outer door and out, leaving door open. He strides back, closing door with heel behind. He carries other burlap bag wrapped around box of candy, of fine chocolates, fancy chocolates with variegated interiors. Gently he lays this in lap of woman. Gently he takes big old shawl from wall nail and lays this over her. He stands by big old bed and looks down at snoring man. "Poor devil," he says. "Ain't fair to forget him." He takes knife from pocket, fine knife, seven-bladed knife, and lays this on blanket on bed. He picks up gloves and blows out lantern and swift as sliding moon shadow he is gone.

High high up frosty clouds scuttle across face of moon. Wind whips through topmost tips of tall pines. What is it that hurtles like hurricane far down there on upslope of last low ridge, scattering drifts, smashing through brush, snorting defiance at distance? It is flop-eared ewe-necked cat-hipped roan, iron-boned and dynamite-fueled, ramming full gallop through the dark of night. Firm in saddle is Stubby Pringle, spurs a jingle, toes atingle, out on prowl, ready to howl, heading for the dance at the schoolhouse in the valley. He is ten feet tall, great as a grizzly, and the roan is gigantic, with wings, soaring upward in thirty-foot leaps. They top out and roan rears high, pawing stars out of sky, and drops down, cat-hips hunched for fresh leap out and down.

Hold it, Stubby. Hold hard on reins. Do you see what is happening on out there in the valley?

Tiny lights that are schoolhouse windows are winking out. Tiny dark shapes moving about are horsemen riding off, are wagons pulling away.

Moon is dropping down the sky, haloed in frosty mist. Dark grey clouds dip and swoop and sweep of horizon. Cold winds weave rustling through ice-coated bushes and trees. What is that moving slow and lonesome up snow-covered mountainside? It is a flop-eared ewe-necked cat-hipped roan, just that, nothing more, small cowpony, worn and weary, taking its rider back to clammy bunk in cold line cabin. Slumped in saddle is Stubby Pringle, head down, shoulders sagged. He is just another of far-scattered poorly-paid patched-clothes cowhands who inhabit these parts. Just that. And something more. He is the biggest thing there is in the whole wide roster of the human race. He is a man who has given himself, of what little he has and is, to bring smiles and joy of living to others along the way.

He jogs along, slump-sagged in saddle, thinking of none of this. He is thinking of dances undanced, of floorboards unstomped, of willing women left unwhirled.

He jogs along, half-asleep in saddle, and he is thinking now of bygone

Christmas seasons and of a boy born to poverty and hard work and make-do poring in flicker of firelight over ragged old Christmas picturebook. And suddenly he hears something. The tinkle of sleigh bells.

Sleigh bells?

Yes. I am telling this straight. He and roan are weaving through thick-clumped brush. Winds are sighing high overhead and on up the mountainside and lower down here they are whipping mists and snow flurries all around him. He can see nothing in mystic moving dimness. But he can hear. The tinkle of sleigh bells, faint but clear, ghostly but unmistakable. And suddenly he sees something. Movement off to the left. Swift as wind, glimmers only through brush and mist and whirling snow, but unmistakable again. Antlered heads high, frosty breath streaming, bodies rushing swift and silent, floating in flash of movement past, seeming to leap in air alone needing no touch of ground beneath. Reindeer? Yes. Reindeer strong and silent and fleet out of some far frozen northland marked on no map. Reindeer swooping down and leaping past and rising again and away, strong and effortless and fleeting. And with them, hard on their heels, almost lost in swirling snow mist of their passing, vague and formless but there, something big and bulky with runners like sleigh and flash of white beard whipping in wind and crack of long whip snapping.

Startled roan has seen something too. It stands rigid, head up, staring left and forward. Stubby Pringle, body atingle, stares too. Out of dark of night ahead, deep deep chuckle, jolly and cheery and full of smiles and joy of living. And with it long-drawn words.

We-e-e-l-l-l do-o-o-ne . . . pa-a-a-artner!

Stubby Pringle shakes his head. He brushes an icicle from his nose. "An' I didn't have a single drink," he says. "Only coffee an' can't count that. Reckon I'm getting soft in the head."

But he is cowman through and through, cowman through to the marrow. He can't ride on without stopping to check anything strange on his range. He swings down and leads off to the left. He fumbles in jacket pocket and finds a match. Strikes it. Holds it cupped and bends down. There they are. Unmistakable. Reindeer tracks.

Stubby Pringle stretches up tall. Stubby Pringle swings into saddle. Roan needs no slap of spurs to unleash strength in upward surge, up up up steep mountainside. It knows. There in saddle once more is Stubby Pringle, moonstruck maverick of the Triple X, all-around hard-proved hard-boned cowhand, ten feet tall, needing horse gigantic, with wings, iron-boned and dynamite-fueled, to take him home to little line cabin and some few winks of sleep before another day's hard work . . .

Stubby Pringle slips into cold clammy bunk. He wriggles vigorous to warm blanket under and blanket over.

"Was it worth all that riding?" comes voice of Old Jake Hanlon from other bunk on other wall.

"Why, sure," says Stubby. "I had me a right good time."

All right, now. Say anything you want. I know, you know, any dong-bonged ding-busted dang-blatted fool ought to know, that icicles breaking off branches can sound to drowsy ears something like sleigh bells. That blurry eyes half-asleep can see strange things. That deer and elk make tracks like those of reindeer. That wind sighing and soughing and moaning and maundering down mountains and through piny treetops can sound like someone shaping words. But we could talk and talk and it would mean nothing to Stubby Pringle.

Stubby is wiser than we are. He knows, he will always know, who it was, plump and jolly and belly-bouncing, that spoke to him that night out on wind-whipped winter-worn mountainside.

We-e-e-l-l-l do-o-o-ne . . . pa-a-a-artner!

The Angel and the Shepherds

Lew Wallace

A mile and a half, it may be two miles, southeast of Bethlehem there is a plain separated from the town by an intervening swell of the mountain—

At the side farthest from the town, and close under a bluff, there was an extensive marah, or sheep-cote, ages old. In some long-forgotten foray the building had been unroofed and almost demolished. The inclosure attached to it remained intact, however, and that was of more importance to the shepherds who drove their charges thither than the house itself—

There were six of these men, omitting the watchman, and after a while they assembled in a group near the fire, some sitting and some lying prone—

They rested and talked; and their talk was all about their flocks, a dull theme to the world, and yet a theme which was all the world to them—

While they talked, and before the first watch was over, one by one the shepherds went to sleep, each lying where he had sat.

The night, like most nights of the winter season in the hill country, was clear, crisp, and sparkling with stars. There was no wind. The atmosphere seemed never so pure, the stillness was more than silence; it was a holy hush, a warning that heaven was stooping low to whisper some good thing to the listening earth.

By the gate, hugging his mantle close, the watchman walked; at times he stopped, attracted by a stir among the sleeping herd, or by a jackal's cry off on the mountainside. The midnight was slow in coming to him, but at last it came. His task was done; and now for the dreamless sleep with which labor blesses its wearied children! He moved toward the fire, but paused; a light was breaking around him, soft and white, like the moon's. He waited breathlessly. The light deepened; things before invisible came into view; he saw the whole field, and all it sheltered. A chill sharper than that of the frosty air—a chill of fear—smote him. He looked up; the stars were gone; the light was dropping as from a window in the sky; and as he looked it became a splendor; then, in terror, he cried, "Awake, awake!"

Up he sprang and the dogs, howling, ran away.

The herds rushed together, bewildered.

The men clambered to their feet, weapons in hand.

"What is it?" they asked in one voice.

"See!" cried the watchman, "the sky is on fire!"

Suddenly the light became intolerably bright, and they covered their eyes and dropped upon their knees; then as their souls shrank with fear, they fell upon their faces, blind and fainting, and would have died had not a voice said unto them: "Fear not!"

And they listened.

"Fear not; for behold, I bring you good tidings of great joy, which shall be to all people. For unto you, this day, in the city of David, is born a Saviour, which is Christ the Lord! And this shall be a sign unto you, ye shall find the babe wrapped in swaddling clothes and lying in a manger."

The voice in sweetness and soothing more than human, and low and clear, penetrated all their being and filled them with assurance. They rose upon their knees, and looking worshipfully up, beheld in the center of a great glory the appearance of a man, clad in a robe intensely white; above its shoulders towered the tops of wings shining and folded. A star over its forehead glowed with a steady luster, brilliant as Hesperus. Its hands were stretched toward them in blessing; its face was serene and divinely beautiful.

The herald spoke not again; his good tidings were told; and yet he stayed awhile. Then suddenly the light, of which He seemed the center, turned roseate and began to tremble; and then up, as far as the men could see, there was a flashing of white wings, and a coming and going of radiant forms, and voices as of a whole multitude chanting in unison, "Glory to God in the highest, and on earth, peace, good-will to men!"

Then the shepherds said one to another, "Come let us take a wee ewe lamb from the fold, and go yonder to Bethlehem, and see this thing which has come to pass. The priests and doctors have been a long time looking for the Christ. Now He is born, and the Lord has given us a sign by which to know Him. Let us go and worship Him."

And they followed the light until it came and stood over where the young Child lay. And they went in and found Mary and Joseph and the Child asleep in the sweet-smelling hay. And they worshipped Him, leaving the wee ewe lamb without spot or blemish as their offering; and returned again to their flock on the hillside, believing anew the words of the prophets.

"For unto us a Child is born. Unto us a Son is given. And the government shall be upon His shoulders; and of the increase of His Kingdom there shall be no end. And His name shall be called, 'Wonderful, Counselor, the Mighty God, the Everlasting Father, the Prince of Peace.'"

A Shepherd

HEYWOOD BRAUN

The host of heaven and the angel of the Lord had filled the sky with radiance. Now the glory of God was gone and the shepherds and the sheep stood under dim starlight. The men were shaken by the wonders they had seen and heard and, like the animals, they huddled close.

"Let us now," said the eldest of the shepherds, "go even unto Bethlehem, and see this thing which has come to pass, which the Lord hath made known unto us."

The City of David lay beyond a far, high hill upon the crest of which there danced a star. The men made haste to be away, but as they broke out of the circle there was one called Amos who remained. He dug his crook into the turf and clung to it.

"Come," cried the eldest of the shepherds, but Amos shook his head. They marveled, and one called out, "It is true. It was an angel. You heard the tidings. A Savior is born!"

"I heard," said Amos. "I will abide."

The eldest walked back from the road to the little knoll on which Amos stood.

"You do not understand," the old man told him. "We have a sign from God. An angel commanded us. We go to worship the Savior, who is even now born in Bethlehem. God has made His will manifest."

"It is not in my heart," replied Amos.

And now the eldest of the shepherds was angry.

"With your own eyes," he cried out, "you have seen the host of heaven in these dark hills. And you heard, for it was like the thunder when 'Glory to God in the highest' came ringing to us out of the night."

And again Amos said, "It is not in my heart."

Another shepherd then broke in. "Because the hills still stand and the sky has not fallen, it is not enough for Amos. He must have something louder than the voice of God."

Amos held more tightly to his crook and answered, "I have need of whisper."

They laughed at him and said, "What should this voice say in your ear?"

He was silent and they pressed about him and shouted mockingly, "Tell us now. What says the God of Amos, the little shepherd of a hundred sheep?"

Meekness fell away from him. He took his hands from off the crook and raised them high.

"I too am a god," said Amos in a loud, strange voice, "and to my hundred sheep I am a savior."

And when the din of the angry shepherds about him slackened, Amos pointed to his hundred.

"See my flock," he said. "See the fright of them. The fear of the bright angel and of the voices is still upon them. God is busy in Bethlehem. He has no time for a hundred sheep. They are my sheep. I will abide."

This the others did not take so much amiss, for they saw that there was a terror in all the flocks and they too knew the ways of sheep. And before the shepherds departed on the road to Bethlehem toward the bright star, each talked to Amos and told him what he should do for the care of the several flocks. And yet one or two turned back a moment to taunt Amos, before they reached the dip in the road which led to the City of David. It was said, "We shall see new glories at the throne of God, and you, Amos, you will see sheep."

Amos paid no heed, for he thought to himself, "One shepherd the less will not matter at the throne of God." Nor did he have time to be troubled that he was not to see the Child who was come to save the world. There was much to be done among the flocks and Amos walked between the sheep and made under his tongue a clucking noise, which was a way he had, and to his hundred and to the others it was a sound more fine and friendly than the voice of the bright angel. Presently the animals ceased to tremble and they began to graze as the sun came up over the hill where the star had been.

"For sheep," said Amos to himself, "the angels shine too much. A shepherd is better."

With the morning the others came up the road from Bethlehem, and they told Amos of the manger and of the wise men who had mingled there with shepherds. And they described to him the gifts: gold, frankincense and myrrh. And when they were done they said, "And did you see wonders here in the fields with the sheep?"

Amos told them, "Now my hundred are one hundred and one," and he showed them a lamb which had been born just before the dawn.

"Was there for this a great voice out of heaven?" asked the eldest of the shepherds.

Amos shook his head and smiled, and there was upon his face that which seemed to the shepherds a wonder even in a night of wonders.

Tessa's Surprises

LOUISA MAY ALCOTT

Tessa sat alone by the fire waiting. Her father was expected home soon. The children were fast asleep, all three in the big bed behind the curtain; the wind blew hard outside, and the snow beat on the windowpanes; the room was large, and the fire so small and feeble that it didn't half warm the little bare toes peeping out of the old shoes on the hearth.

Tessa's father was a poor but kind and honest Italian plaster worker. The mother had died not long ago and twelve-year-old Tessa was left to take care of the children. She tried to be wise and motherly and worked for them like any little woman, but it was so hard to keep the small bodies warm and fed and the small souls good and happy that poor Tessa was often at her wit's end. She always waited for her father, no matter how tired she was, so that he might find his supper warm, and a bit of fire and a loving little face to welcome him.

Tessa thought over her troubles at these quiet times and made her plans, because her father left things to her a good deal; and she had no friends but Tommo, the harp boy upstairs, and the lively cricket who lived in the chimney. Tonight her face was very sober and her pretty brown eyes very thoughtful as she stared at the fire and knit her brows as if perplexed. She was not thinking of her old shoes or the empty closet or the boys' ragged clothes just then. No, she had a fine plan in her good little head and was trying to imagine how she could carry it out.

Christmas was coming in a week, and she had her heart set on putting something in the children's stockings, as Mother used to do; for while she had lived things had been comfortable. Now Tessa had not a penny in the world and didn't know how to get one. All the father's earnings had to go for food, fire, and rent.

"I must earn the money; there is no one to give it to me, and I cannot beg. But what can I do, so small and stupid and shy as I am?" Tessa said to herself. "I must find some way to give the little ones a nice Christmas. I must! I must!" And Tessa pulled her long hair as if that would help her think.

But it didn't; and her heart grew heavier and heavier, for it did seem hard that in a great city full of fine things there should be none for poor Nono, Sep, and little Speranza. Just as Tessa's tears began to tumble off her eyelashes onto her brown cheeks, the cricket began to chirp. Of course, he didn't say a word, but before he had piped a dozen shrill notes, an idea popped into Tessa's head—such a truly splendid idea that she clapped her hands and burst out laughing. "I'll do it! I'll do it! If Father will let me," she said to herself, smiling and nodding at the fire.

"Tommo will like to have me go with him and sing while he plays his harp in the streets. I know many songs and may get money if I am not frightened. People throw pennies to other little girls who only play the tambourine. I will sing, yes, I will try; and then, if I do well, the little ones will have a merry Christmas."

So full of her plan was Tessa that she ran upstairs at once and asked Tommo if he would take her with him on the morrow. Her friend was delighted, for he thought Tessa's songs very sweet and was sure she would get money if she tried.

"But see, then, it is cold in the streets; the wind bites, and the snow freezes one's fingers. The day is very long, people are cross, and at night one is ready to die with weariness. Thou art so small, Tessa, I am afraid it will go badly with thee," said Tommo, who was a merry, black-eyed boy of fourteen, with the kindest heart in the world under his old jacket.

"I do not mind cold and wet and cross people, if I can get the pennies," answered Tessa, feeling very brave with such a friend to help her. She thanked Tommo and ran away to get ready, for she felt sure her father would not refuse her anything. She sewed up the holes in her shoes as well as she could, for she had much of that sort of cobbling to do. She mended her only gown and laid ready the old hood and shawl that had been her mother's. Then she washed out little Ranza's frock and put it to dry, because she would not be able to do it the next day. She set the table and got things ready for breakfast, for Tommo went out early and must not be kept waiting for her.

Tessa longed to make the beds and dress the children overnight, she was in such a hurry to have it all in order; but as that could not be, she sat down again and tried over all the songs she knew. She chose six pretty ones; and she sung away with all her heart in a fresh little voice and so sweetly that the children smiled in their sleep and her father's tired face brightened as he entered, for Tessa was his cheery cricket on the hearth. When she had told her plan, Peter Benari shook his head and thought it would never do, but Tessa begged so hard, he consented at last that she should try it for one week and sent her to bed the happiest little girl in New York.

Next morning the sun shone, but the cold wind blew and the snow lay thick in the streets. As soon as her father was gone, Tessa flew about and put everything in order, telling the children she was going out for the day and they were to mind Tommo's mother, who would see about the fire and dinner. The good woman loved Tessa and entered into her plans with all her heart. Nono and Guiseppe, or Sep, as they called him, wondered what she was going away for, and little Ranza cried at being left, but Tessa told them they would know all about it in a week and have a fine time if they were good. So they kissed her all 'round and let her go.

Poor Tessa's heart beat fast as she trudged away with Tommo, who slung his harp over his shoulder and gave her his hand. It was a rather grimy hand, but so kind that Tessa clung to it and kept looking up at the friendly brown face for encouragement.

"We go first to the café where many French and Italians eat breakfast. They like my music and often give me sips of hot coffee, which I like so much. You too shall have the sips, and perhaps the pennies, for these people are greatly kind." Said Tommo, leading her into a large, smoky place, where many people sat at little tables, eating and drinking. "See, now, have no fear. Give them 'Bella Monica'; that is merry and will make them laugh," whispered Tommo, tuning his harp.

For a moment Tessa felt so frightened that she wanted to run away; but she remembered the empty stockings at home and the fine plan, and she resolved not to give it up. One fat old Frenchman nodded to her, and it seemed to help her very much; for she began to sing before she thought. Her voice trembled, and her cheeks grew redder and redder as she went on; but she kept her eyes fixed on her old shoes and so got through without breaking down. The people laughed, for the song was merry, and the fat man smiled and nodded again. This gave her courage to try another, and she sang better and better each time; for Tommo played his best and kept whispering to her, "Yes, we go well; this is fine. They will give money and coffee."

So they did; for when the little concert was over, several men put pennies in the cap Tessa offered, and the fat man took her on his knee and ordered a mug of coffee and some bread and butter for them both. This quite won her heart, and when they left the café, she kissed her hand to the old Frenchman and said to her friend, "How kind they are! I like this very much, and now it is not hard."

But Tommo shook his curly head and answered, soberly: "Yes, I took you there first, for they love music and are of our country, but up among the great houses we shall not always do well. The people there are busy or hard or idle and care nothing for harps and songs. Do not skip and laugh too soon, for the day is long, and we have but twelve pennies yet."

Tessa walked more quietly and rubbed her cold hands, feeling that the world was a very big place and wondering how the children got on at home without their little mother. Till noon they did not earn much, for everyone seemed in a hurry, and the noise of many sleigh bells drowned the music. Slowly they made their way up to the great squares where the big houses were, with fine ladies and pretty children at the windows. Here Tessa sung all her best songs, and Tommo played as fast as his fingers could fly; but it was too cold to have the windows open, so the pretty children could not listen long, and the ladies tossed out a little money and soon went back to their own affairs.

All the afternoon the two friends wandered about, singing and playing and gathering up their small harvest. At dusk they went home—Tessa so hoarse she could hardly speak and so tired she fell asleep over her supper. But she had made half a dollar, for Tommo divided the money fairly, and she felt rich with her share. Other days were very much like this. Sometimes they made more, sometimes less, but Tommo always "went halves"; and Tessa kept on, in spite of cold and weariness. Her plans grew as her earning increased, and now she hoped to get useful things instead of candy and toys alone.

On the day before Christmas, she made herself as tidy as she could, for she hoped to earn a good deal. She tied a bright scarlet handkerchief over the old hood, and the brilliant color set off her brown cheeks and bright eyes, as well as the pretty black braids of her hair. Tommo's mother lent her a pair of boots so big that they turned up at the toes; but there were no holes in them, and Tessa felt quite elegant in whole boots. Her hands were covered with chilblains, for she had no mittens; but she put them under her shawl and scuffled merrily away in her big boots, feeling so glad that the week was over and nearly three dollars safe in her pocket. How gay the streets were that day! How brisk everyone was, and how bright the faces looked as people trotted about with big baskets, holly wreaths, and young evergreens going to blossom into splendid Christmas trees.

"If I could have a tree for the children, I'd never want anything more. But I can't, so I'll fill the socks full and be happy," said Tessa, as she looked wistfully into the gay stores and saw the heavy baskets go by.

"Who knows what may happen if we do well?" returned Tommo, nodding wisely, for he had a plan as well as Tessa and kept chuckling over it as he trudged through the mud. They did not do well, somehow, for everyone seemed so full of their own affairs they could not stop to listen, even to "Bella Monica," but bustled away to spend their money on turkeys, toys, and trees. In the afternoon it began to rain and poor Tessa's heart to fail her. The big boots tired her feet; the cold wind made her hands ache; and the rain spoiled the fine red handkerchief. Even Tommo looked sober and didn't whistle as he walked, for he also was disappointed; and his plan looked rather doubtful—the pennies came in so slowly.

"We'll try one more street, and then go home, thou art so tired, little one. Come, let me wipe thy face and give me thy hand here in my jacket pocket. There it will be as warm as any kitten." Then kind Tommo brushed away the drops that were not all rain from Tessa's cheeks, tucked the poor hand into his ragged pocket, and led her carefully along the slippery streets, for the boots nearly tripped her.

At the first house, an old gentleman flapped his newspaper at them; at the second, a young gentleman and lady were so busy talking that they never turned their heads; and at the third, a servant came out and told them to go away because someone was sick. At the fourth, they were allowed to sing all their songs, but the listeners gave nothing. The next three houses were empty, and the last showed not a single face, as they looked up anxiously. It was so cold, so dark and discouraging that a sob escaped Tessa's lips. As he glanced down at the little red nose and wet figure beside him, Tommo gave his harp an angry thump and said something very fierce in Italian. They were just going to turn away; but they didn't because that angry thump happened to be the best thing they could have done. All of a sudden a little head appeared at the window, as if the sound had brought it; then another and another, till there were five, of all heights and colors, and five eager faces peeped out, smiling and nodding to the two below.

"Sing, Tessa, sing! Quick! Quick! cried Tommo, twanging away with all his might, as he smiled back at the gentlefolk.

How Tessa did tune up at that! She chirped away like a bird, forgetting all about the tears on her cheeks, the ache in her hands, and the heaviness at her heart. The children laughed and clapped their hands, and cried, "More! More! Sing another, little girl! Please, do!" And away they went again, piping and playing, till Tessa's breath was gone and Tommo's stout fingers tingled.

"Mamma says, come to the door. It's too muddy to throw money in the street!" cried out a kindly child's voice, as Tessa held up the old cap with beseeching eyes.

Up the wide stone steps went the street musicians, and the whole flock came running down to give a handful of silver and ask all sorts of questions. Tessa felt so grateful that, without waiting for Tommo, she sang her sweetest little song all alone. It was about a lost lamb, and her heart was in the song; therefore, she sang it well, so well that a pretty young lady came down to listen and stood watching the bright-eyed child, who looked about her as she sang, evidently enjoying the light and warmth of the fine hall and the sight of the lovely children with their gay dresses, shining hair, and dainty little shoes.

"You have a charming voice, child. Who taught you to sing?" asked the young lady kindly.

"My mother. She is dead now, but I do not forget," answered Tessa in her pretty, broken English.

"I wish she could sing at our tree, since Bella is ill," cried one of the children, peeping through the banisters.

"She is not fair enough for the angel and too large to go up in the tree. But she sings sweetly and looks as if she would like to see a tree," said the young lady.

"Oh, so much!" exclaimed Tessa, adding eagerly, "My sister Ranza is small and pretty as a baby angel. She could sit up in the fine tree, and I could sing for her from under the table."

"Sit down and warm yourself, and tell me about Ranza," said the kind elder sister, who liked the confiding little girl in spite of her shabby clothes.

So Tessa sat down and dried her big boots over the furnace and told her story, while Tommo stood modestly in the background and the children listened with faces full of interest.

"O Rose! Let us see the little girl, and if she will do, let us have her; and Tessa can learn our song, and it will be splendid!" cried the biggest boy, who sat astride a chair and stared at the harp with round eyes.

"I'll ask Mamma," said Rose, and away she went into the dining room close by. As the door opened, Tessa saw what looked to her like a grand feast—all silver mugs and flowery plates and oranges and nuts and punch in tall glass pitchers and smoking dishes that smelt so deliciously she could not restrain a little sniff of satisfaction.

"Are you hungry?" asked the boy in a grand tone.

"Yes, sir," meekly answered Tessa.

"I say, Mamma, she wants something to eat. Can I give her an orange?" called the boy, prancing away into the splendid room quite like a prince, Tessa thought.

A plump, motherly lady came out and looked at Tessa, asked a few questions, and then told her to come tomorrow with Ranza, and they would see what could be done. Tessa clapped her hands for joy—she didn't mind the chilblains now—and Tommo played a lively match, he was so pleased.

"Will you come, too, and bring your harp? You shall be paid and shall have something from the tree, likewise," said the lady, who admired what Tessa gratefully told about his kindness.

"Ah, yes; I shall come with much gladness, and play as never in my life before," cried Tommo with a flourish of his old cap.

"Give these to the little girl," added one of the young princesses, flying out of the dining room with cakes and rosy apples for Ranza.

Tessa didn't know what to say; but her eyes were full, and she took the mother's white hand in both her little grimy ones and kissed it many times in her pretty Italian fashion. The lady understood her and stroked her cheek softly, saying to her elder daughter, "We must take care of this good little creature. Freddy, bring me your mittens; these poor hands must be covered. Alice, get your play hood; this handkerchief is all wet. And Maud, bring the old chinchilla tippet."

The children ran, and in a minute there were lovely blue mittens on the red hands, a warm hood over the black braids, and a soft fur 'round the sore throat.

"Ah! So kind, so very kind! I have no way to say thank you; but Ranza shall be for you a heavenly angel, and I will sing my heart out for your tree!" cried Tessa, folding the mittens as if she would say a prayer of thankfulness.

Then they went away, and the pretty children called after them, "Come again, Tessa! Come again, Tommo!" Now the rain didn't seem dismal, the wind cold, or the way long, as they shopped for gifts and hurried home.

The spirit of Christmas, who flies about on Christmas Eve to help the loving fillers of little stockings, smiled very kindly on Tessa as she brooded joyfully over the small store of presents that seemed so magnificent to her. All the goodies were divided evenly into three parts and stowed away in Father's three big socks, which hung against the curtain. With her three dollars, she had bought a pair of white stockings for Ranza. To her she also gave the new hood; to Nono the mittens; and to Sep the tippet.

"Now the dear boys can go out, and my Ranza will be ready for the lady to see in her nice new things," said Tessa, quite sighing with pleasure to see how well the gifts looked pinned up beside the bulging socks, which wouldn't hold them all. The little mother kept nothing for herself but the pleasure of giving everything away, yet, I think, she was both richer and happier than if she had kept them all. Her father laughed as he had not done since the mother died when he saw how comically the old curtain had broken out into boots and hoods, stockings and tippets.

"I wish I had a gold gown and a silver hat for thee, my Tessa, thou art so good. May God bless and keep thee always!" said Peter Benari tenderly, as he held his little daughter close and gave her a good-night kiss.

Tessa felt very rich as she crept under the faded counterpane, feeling as if she had received a lovely gift, and fell happily asleep with chubby Ranza in her arms and the two rough black heads peeping out at the foot of the bed. She dreamed wonderful dreams that night and woke in the morning to find real wonders before her eyes. She got up early, to see if the socks were all right, and there she found the most astonishing sight. Four socks, instead of three, and by the fourth, pinned out quite elegantly, was a little dress, evidently meant for her—a warm, woolen dress, all made and with bright buttons on it. It nearly took her breath away—so did the new boots on the floor and the funny long stocking like a gray sausage, with a wooden doll staring out at the top, as if she said, politely, "A Merry Christmas, Ma'am!"

Tessa screamed and danced in her delight, and up tumbled all the children to scream and dance with her, making a regular carnival on a small scale. Everybody hugged and kissed everybody else, offered sucks of orange, bites of cake, and exchanges of candy. Everyone tried on the new things and pranced about in them like a flock of peacocks. Ranza skipped to and fro airily, dressed in her white socks and the red hood; and the boys promenaded in their little shirts, one with his creaking new shoes and mittens, the other in his cap and fine tippet; and Tessa put her dress straight on, feeling that her father's "gold gown" was not all a joke. In her long stocking she found all sorts of treasures, for Tommo had stuffed it full of unusual things; and his mother had made gingerbread into every imaginable shape from fat pigs to full omnibuses.

What happy little souls they were that morning; and when they were quiet again, how like a fairy tale did Tessa's story sound to them! Ranza was quite ready to be an angel, and the boys promised to be marvellously good if they were only allowed to see the tree at the "palace," as they called the great house.

Little Ranza was accepted with delight by the kind lady and her children, and Tessa learned the song quite easily. The boys were asked to play a part; and after a happy day, the young Italians all returned to be part of the fine Christmas party. Mamma and Miss Rose drilled them all; and when the folding doors flew open, one rapturous "Oh!" arose from the crowd of children gathered at the festival. It was splendid. The great tree glittered with lights and gifts; and on her invisible perch, up among the green boughs, sat the little golden-haired angel, all in white, with downy wings, a shining crown on her head, and the most serene satisfaction in her blue eyes as she stretched her chubby arms to those below and smiled her baby smile at them.

Before anyone could speak, a voice, as fresh and sweet as a lark's, sang a Christmas carol so blithely that everyone stood still to hear and then clapped till the little angel shook on her perch and cried out, "Be 'till, or me'll fall!" How they laughed at that, and what fun they had talking to Ranza, while Miss Rose stripped the tree; for the angel could not resist temptation and amused herself by eating all the bonbons she could reach till she was taken down to dance about like a fairy in a white frock and red shoes. Tessa and her friends had many presents; the boys were perfect as lambs; Tommo played for the little folks to dance; and every one said something friendly to the strangers, so that they did not feel shy in spite of shabby clothes. It was a happy night, and all their lives they remembered it as something too beautiful and bright to be quite true.

Before they went home, the kind woman told Tessa she would be her friend and gave her a motherly kiss. Tessa's heart was warmed, and it seemed to her that a seal had been set upon that promise. It was faithfully kept, because the rich lady had been touched by Tessa's patient struggles and sacrifices. And for many years, thanks to her benevolence, there was no end to Tessa's surprises.

The Nutcracker

BASED ON THE NUTCRACKER AND THE NUTCRACKER BALLET

E. T. A. HOFFMANN AND PETER ILYICH TCHAIKOVSKY

More than one hundred years ago on Christmas Eve, a twelve-year-old girl named Clara Stahlbaum and her younger brother Fritz were having a party at their house. Clara and Fritz peeked through a keyhole into the drawing room.

"What do you see?" Fritz asked.

"Nothing yet," Clara replied. "The grown-ups are just dancing and talking."

A moment later the door swung open and the parlor was flooded with light. "Merry Christmas, children!" Dr. Stahlbaum said. The time had come when they might join the party! The children raced past their father into the drawing room, with Fritz leading the way. Before them stood a Christmas tree at least ten feet tall! Beneath it were sugarplums, bonbons, toy soldiers, miniature swords and cannons, ceramic dolls, silk dresses, wooden horses, picture books, and dozens of other gifts. The children scurried about, discovering treasure after treasure. Everything in the room seemed bright with candles and the fire crackled cheerfully.

Then the front door burst open and out of the winter night stepped a man dressed in black. He held a cape over his face and wore a tall hat. The click of his boots echoed off the marble floor and he entered the room. Slowly and dramatically, he drew aside his cape and the children were relieved to see the smiling face of Godpapa Drosselmeier, a master woodcarver in the village.

"Oh, Godpapa!" cried Clara, "you scared us!" Godpapa Drosselmeier gave her a big hug as he said, "My dear, I've brought you and the other children a surprise." He drew the sides of his cape together to make a great circle and three wooden figures stood on the floor in front of him: a prince, a princess, and a wicked-looking mouse wearing a crown. The figures began to move.

The mouse challenged the prince, they drew their swords, and a fight began. The children shouted encouragement. Finally, the prince defeated the mouse king, and then he kneeled, kissing the princess softly on her outstretched hand. Clara almost felt as if she could feel the kiss on her own hand.

When the wooden figures stopped moving, the guests clapped and cheered. Godpapa Drosselmeier took a bow, then turned to Clara and said, "And now, I have one more surprise. It's a special gift for a very special girl."

Godpapa drew his cape aside, and there stood another wooden figure wearing a handsome military uniform. Its face, though, was not handsome. Brightly painted, it had enormous eyes and a wide, gaping mouth. Still, something about the face filled Clara with tenderness. She picked up the figure and cradled it in her arms. Her eyes shone as she said, "Isn't this lovely?"

"Look closely at the wooden head," Godpapa said.

"His face is very sad," Clara thought, "but I like it."

"What is it?" the other children asked.

"It's a nutcracker," Godpapa answered. Then he took a walnut from his pocket and placed it in the little man's mouth. He closed the mouth and broke the nut.

"Let me do that!" said Fritz. He grabbed the nutcracker and tried to pull it away from his sister. There was a loud crack, and the wooden figure's head broke off.

"He's ruined!" Clara cried, holding her precious gift close and weeping bitterly.

"Now, now, my dear," said Godpapa Drosselmeier, taking the nutcracker from her. He put the wooden figure back together, and the nutcracker was as good as new. And from that moment Clara carried the little nutcracker doll with her everywhere, refusing to let anyone else hold it.

Meanwhile Fritz continued to drill his new toy soldiers with cries of "Bang, bang."

"My soldiers are brave and handsome," he said to Clara, "better than your ugly little doll."

"Take no notice of him," Clara whispered to the nutcracker. "He doesn't mean to be unkind." But the noise in the hot, crowded room made Fritz very excited and he marched up to Clara, snatched the little nutcracker and held it above his head. "Catch it if you can!" he yelled, dancing up and down. Clara tried to grab his arm but naughty Fritz hurled the little wooden doll across the room where it landed near the Christmas tree.

Just then, Clara's mother came to her and said, "It's supper time, Clara. Come and help me." Poor Clara had to leave her new toy where it had fallen.

Much later, the party was over and the children's friends went home, calling "Merry Christmas" to each other as they made their way through the snow to their carriages. Clara and Fritz went to bed and it was not long before everyone in the house was asleep—except for Clara. She could not stop thinking about the nutcracker. Finally, she slipped out of bed, crept downstairs, and opened the drawing-room door. The drawing room was dark, but Clara had no trouble picking out the brightly painted face of the nutcracker beneath the Christmas tree. She went over to her new friend, lay down beside him, and fell into a deep sleep.

Suddenly, there was a noise in the room. Clara awoke and peered into the darkness. Slinking toward her was a mouse as big as a man. He was joined by ten others! They began running about, fighting and biting, and chewing all the presents under the Christmas tree! Then they began to circle around her, drawing closer and closer. When they were near enough to touch her, the clock chimed the first stroke of midnight.

Clara felt the nutcracker next to her beginning to move. Yawning and stretching, he rose to his feet and as the clock continued to strike, he began to grow. By the time the twelfth chime had died, he was a real-life soldier, standing six feet tall!

Clara watched as Nutcracker put one arm around her and, calling to the toy soldiers, the Nutcracker led them into a charge and the mice backed away. Then there was a puff of smoke and out stepped another mouse. Bigger and uglier than the others, he was the evil Mouse King, waving a sword of shining steel. Encouraged by the arrival of their leader, the other mice edged forward once again. The wooden swords of the toy soldiers were powerless against the steel blade of the Mouse King and the Nutcracker had no sword at all. In a flash, Clara tore off her slipper and threw it across the room as hard as she could. It hit the Mouse King and he dropped his sword. The Nutcracker seized it, and with one stroke cut off the King's head. At this, the other mice stopped fighting and scurried away to their holes.

Clara turned, and to her great surprise, the ugly Nutcracker had been transformed into a handsome prince dressed in silver and white. He smiled down at her. "You've saved my life and broken a wicked spell, little Clara," he said. "Now I am free to go back to my country at last."

Then the prince sat Clara down under the Christmas tree and told her of his adventures.

Once upon a time, his story began, a queen quarreled with all the mice in her palace and banished them from her kingdom. As he slunk out of the hall, a wicked old wizard rat turned to the queen and squeaked, "You'll be sorry for this—and so will your daughter." The queen ran to her baby's crib, but too late. The baby's tiny cheeks were thin and hairy and whiskers grew under her pointed nose. She had been turned into a rat!

The grief-stricken queen called all the wisest men in her kingdom together, and they studied their magic books looking for a formula to break the wizard mouse's spell. They finally concluded that a Krakatuk tree must be found, one of its nuts must be picked, and then someone strong enough must be found to crack open the nut and give the kernel to the rat princess. As soon as she ate it, the spell would be broken. And so the wise men searched the kingdom, as did all the queen's subjects. At long last they found a Krakatuk tree nut and a young prince to open it. With a loud crack he split the shell and gave the kernel to the rat princess. She ate it, and instantly became a beautiful young girl again.

"Oh, thank you, thank you," cried the queen. But even as she spoke the prince began to grow smaller and smaller until he turned into a little wooden nutcracker. The wizard mouse squeaked with delight, "You may have your princess back, but you've lost the prince, and one day King Mouse will cut off his head!"

The prince explained to Clara, "And so I became an ugly little nutcracker. One day your godfather found me. He was sure you wouldn't mind my ugly face, and he was right. Thank you for saving my life. I must return to my country now. Would you like to come with me to the Kingdom of Sweets and visit my Sugar Palace?"

Clara was too excited to speak. She nodded yes, her eyes singing. And instantly, the Christmas tree before her began to grow taller and taller until its lights glittered like stars. The walls of the drawing room disappeared and Clara and the prince began to float through the shimmering moonlight in a walnut-shell boat. All around them, snowflake fairies danced to sweet music as they gently guided the boat to the shore of Candyland.

In Candyland, the prince and Clara stepped out of their boat and walked up an avenue laden with toffee apples, glittering sugarplums, and chocolate nuts. They passed cottages made of chocolate bars, with barley-sugar windows. The breeze smelled of honey and strawberry jam.

"It's so delicious!" Clara whispered, her eyes trying to take in all the strange sights. The nutcracker prince laughed as he said, "Just wait until you see my palace!" He pointed toward a mass of glittering towers that were barely visible through the trees.

Then, a beautiful Sugarplum Fairy came toward the Prince and Clara, "My snowflake fairies have told me what you did," she said, "and I want to thank you for saving our prince." She led Clara to a magnificent throne in the palace and said, "Tonight you are Queen Clara!"

With that, the celebration began! Sugar sticks twirled, chocolate drop cymbals clashed, a Chinese teapot and a set of Arabian coffee cups waltzed together, and a troupe of Cossacks leaped across the floor. Spun-sugar roses curtsied gracefully as the Prince invited the Sugarplum Fairy to dance. How the people cheered and clapped!

"Welcome to our prince," they shouted. "Hurrah for Clara! Hurrah for the Nutcracker! Hurrah! Hurrah!"

Clara blinked. Her eyes were dazzled by all the beauty before her.

Suddenly she heard a different voice. "Hurrah! It's Christmas Day!" The voice was that of her brother Fritz, shouting to her as she struggled to open her eyes. The dancers, the Sugarplum Fairy, and the Prince were gone, as was the Sugar Palace.

"It must have been a dream," Clara thought sadly.

Even so, years later . . . on her wedding day . . . Clara was reminded of the sugary towers as she gazed at her wedding cake, and as she looked closely, she was sure she glimpsed a tiny sugarplum fairy dancing.

Mrs. Brownlow's Christmas Party

WILLIS BOYD ALLEN

✳

I t was fine Christmas weather. Several light snowstorms in the early part of December had left the earth fair and white, and the sparkling, cold days that followed were enough to make the most crabbed and morose of mankind cheerful, as with a foretaste of the joyous season at hand. Downtown the sidewalks were crowded with mothers and sisters, buying gifts for their sons, brothers, and husbands.

Among those who were looking forward to the holidays with keen anticipations of pleasure, were Mr. and Mrs. Brownlow, of Elm Street, Boston. They had quietly talked the matter over together, and decided that, as there were three children in the family (not counting themselves, as they might well have done), it would be a delightful and not too expensive luxury to give a little Christmas party.

"You see John," said Mrs. Brownlow, "we've been asked, ourselves, to half a dozen candy-pulls and parties since we've lived here, and it seems nothin' but fair that we should do it once ourselves."

"That's so, Clarissy," replied her husband slowly; "but then—there's so many of us, and my salary's—well, it would cost considerable, little woman, wouldn't it?"

"I'll tell you what!" she exclaimed. "We needn't have a regular grown-up party, but just one for children. We can get a small tree, and a bit of a present for each of the boys and girls, with ice cream and cake, and let it go at that. The whole thing shan't cost ten dollars."

"Good!" said Mr. Brownlow heartily. "I knew you'd get some way out of it. Let's tell Bob and Sue and Polly, so they can have the fun of looking forward to it."

So it was settled and all hands entered into the plan with such a degree of earnestness that one would have thought these people were going to have some grand gift themselves, instead of giving to others, and pinching for a month afterwards, in their own comforts, as they knew they would have to do.

The first real difficulty they met was in deciding whom to invite. John was for asking only the children of their immediate neighbors; but Mrs. Brownlow said it would be kindness, as well as polite, to include those who were better off than themselves.

"I allus think, John," she explained, laying her hand on his shoulder, "that it's just's much despisin' to look down on your rich neighbors—as if all they'd got was money—as on your poor ones. Let's ask 'em all: Deacon Holsum's, the Brights, and the Nortons." The Brights were Mr. Brownlow's employers.

"Anybody else?" queried her husband, with his funny twinkle. "P'raps you'd like to have me ask the governor's family!"

"Now, John, don't you be saucy," she laughed, relieved at having carried her point. "Let's put our heads together, and see who to set down. Susie will write the notes in her nice hand, and Bob can deliver them, to save postage."

"Well, you've said three," counted Mr. Brownlow on his fingers. "Then there's Mrs. Sampson's little girl, and the four Williamses, and"—he enumerated one family after another, till nearly thirty names were on the list.

Once Susie broke in, "Oh, Pa, don't invite that Mary Spenfield; she's awfully stuck-up and cross!"

"Good!" said her father again. "This will be just the thing for her. Let her be coffee and you be sugar, and see how much you can sweeten her that evening."

In the few days that intervened before the twenty-fifth, the whole family was busy enough, Mrs. Brownlow shopping, Susie writing the notes, and the others helping wherever they got a chance. Every evening they spread out upon the sitting-room floor such presents as had been bought during the day. These were not costly, but they were chosen lovingly, and seemed very nice indeed to Mr. Brownlow and the children, who united in praising the discriminating taste of Mrs. B.

The tree seemed at first inclined to be sulky, perhaps at having been decapitated and curtailed; for it leaned backward, licked over the soapbox in which it was set, bumped against Mr. Brownlow, tumbled forward, and in short, behaved itself like a tree which was determined to lie on its precious back all the next day, or perish in the attempt. At length, just as they were beginning to despair of ever getting it firm and straight, it gave a little quiver of its limbs, yielded gracefully to a final push by Bob, and stood upright, as fair and comely a Christmas tree as one would wish to see. Mr. Brownlow crept out backward from under the lower branches, and regarded it with a sigh of content. Such presents as were to be disposed of in this way were not hung upon the branches; then strings of popcorn, bits of wool, and glistening paper, a few red apples, and lastly the candles. When all was finished, which was not before midnight, the family withdrew to their beds, with weary limbs and brains, but with lighthearted anticipation of tomorrow.

"Do you s'pose Mrs. Bright will come with her children, John?" asked Mrs. Brownlow, as she turned out the gas.

"Shouldn't—wonder"—sleepily from the four-poster.

"Did Mr. Bright say anything about the invitation we sent, when he paid you off?"

Silence. More silence. Good Mr. Brownlow was asleep, and Clarissa soon followed him.

Meanwhile the snow, which had been falling fast during the early part of the evening, had ceased, leaving the earth as fair to look upon as the fleece-drifted sky above it. Slowly the heavy banks of cloud rolled away, disclosing star after star, until the moon itself looked down, and sent a soft "Merry Christmas" to mankind. At last came the dawn with a glorious burst of sunlight and church-bells and glad voices, ushering in the gladdest and dearest day of all the year.

The Brownlows were early astir, full of the joyous spirit of the day. There was a clamor of Christmas greetings, and a delighted medley of shouts from the children over the few simple gifts that had been secretly laid aside for them. But the ruling thought in every heart was the party. It was to come off at five o'clock in the afternoon, when it would be just dark enough to light the candles on the tree.

In spite of all the hard work of the preceding days, there was not a moment to spare that afternoon. The house, as the head of the family facetiously remarked, was a perfect hive of B's.

As the appointed hour drew near, their nervousness increased. Nor was the excitement confined to the interior of the house. The tree was placed in the front parlor, close to the window, and by half-past four a dozen ragged children were gathered about the iron fence of the little front yard, gazing open-mouthed and open-eyed at the spectacular wonders within. At a quarter before five Mrs. Brownlow's heart beat hard every time she heard a strange footstep in their quiet street. It was a little odd that none of the guests had arrived; but then, it was fashionable to be late!

Ten minutes more passed. Still no arrivals. It was evident that each was planning not to be the first to get there, and that they would all descend on the house and assault the doorbell at once. Mrs. Brownlow repeatedly smoothed the wrinkles out of her tidy apron, and Mr. Brownlow began to perspire with responsibility.

Meanwhile the crowd outside, recognizing no rigid bonds of etiquette, rapidly increased in numbers. Mr. Brownlow, to pass the time and please the poor little homeless creatures, lighted two of the candles.

The response from the front-yard fence was immediate. A low murmur of delight ran along the line, and several dull-eyed babies were hoisted, in the arms of babies scarcely older than themselves, to behold the rare vision of candles in a tree, just illumining the further splendors glistening here and there among the branches.

The kind man's heart warmed towards them, and he lighted two more candles. The delight of the audience could now hardly be restrained, and the babies, having been temporarily lowered by the aching little arms of their respective nurses, were shot up once more to view the redoubled grandeur.

The whole family had become so much interested in these small outcasts that they had not noticed the flight of time. Now someone glanced suddenly at the clock, and exclaimed, "It's nearly half-past five!"

The Brownlows looked at one another blankly. Poor Mrs. Brownlow's smart ribbons drooped in conscious abasement, while mortification and pride struggled in their wearer's kindly face, over which, after a moment's silence, one large tear slowly rolled, and dropped off.

Mr. Brownlow gave himself a little shake and sat down, as was his wont upon critical occasions. As his absent gaze wandered about the room, so prettily decked for the guests who didn't come, it fell upon a little worn, gilt-edged volume on the table. At that sight, a new thought occurred to him. "Clarissy," he said softly, going over to his wife and putting his arm around her, "Clarissy, seein's the well-off folks haven't accepted, don't you think we'd better invite some of the others in?" And he pointed significantly toward the window.

Mrs. Brownlow stepped to the front door. Nay more, he walked down the short flight of steps, took one little girl by the hand, and said in his pleasant, fatherly way, "Wouldn't you like to go in and look at the tree? Come, Puss" (to the waif at his side), "we'll start first."

With these words he led the way back through the open door, and into the warm, lighted room. The children hung back a little, but seeing that no harm came to the first guest, soon flocked in, each trying to keep behind all the rest, but at the same time shouldering the babies up into view as before.

In the delightful confusion that followed, the good hosts forgot all about the miscarriage of their plans. They completely outdid themselves, in efforts to please their hastily acquired company. Bob spoke a piece, the girls sang duets. Mrs. Brownlow had held every individual baby in her motherly arms before half an hour was over. And as for Mr. Brownlow, it was simply marvelous to see him go among those children, giving them the presents, and initiating their owners into the mysterious impelling forces of monkeys with yellow legs and gymnastic tendencies; filling the boys' pockets with popcorn, blowing horns and tin whistles; now assaulting the tree (it had been lighted throughout, and—bless it—how firm it stood now!) for fresh novelties, now diving into the kitchen and returning in an unspeakably cohesive state of breathlessness and molasses candy—all the while laughing, talking, patting heads, joking, until the kindly Spirit of Christmas Present would have wept and smiled at once, for the pleasure of the sight.

"And now, my young friends," said Mr. Brownlow, raising his voice, "We'll have a little ice cream in the back room. Ladies, first, gentlemen afterward!" So saying, he gallantly stood on one side, with a sweep of his hand, to allow Mrs. Brownlow to precede him. But just as the words left his mouth there came a sharp ring at the door-bell.

"It's a carriage!" gasped Mrs. Brownlow, flying to the front window, and backing precipitately. "Susie, go to that door an' see who 'tis. Land sakes, what mess this parlor's in!" And she gazed with a true housekeeper's dismay at the littered carpet and dripping candles.

"Deacon Holsum and Mrs. Hartwell, Pa!" announced Susie, throwing open the parlor door.

The lady thus mentioned came forward with outstretched hand. Catching a glimpse of Mrs. Brownlow's embarrassed face she exclaimed quickly—

"Isn't this splendid! Father and I were just driving past, and we saw your tree through the window, and couldn't resist dropping in upon you. You won't mind us, will you?"

"Mind—you!" repeated Mrs. Brownlow, in astonishment. "Why of course not—only you are so late—we didn't expect—"

Mrs. Hartwell looked puzzled.

"Pardon me—I don't think I quite understand—"

"The invitation was for five, you know, ma'am."

"But we received no invitation!"

Mr. Brownlow, who had greeted the deacon heartily and then listened with amazement to this conversation, now turned upon Bob, with a signally futile attempt at a withering glance.

Bob looked puzzled as the rest, for a moment. Then his face fell, and he flushed to the roots of his hair.

"I—I—must have—forgot—" he stammered.

"Forgotten what?"

"The invitations—they're in my desk now!" Bob said in an utterly despairing tone.

"You poor dear!" Mrs. Hartwell cried, kissing her hostess, who stood speechless, not knowing whether to laugh or cry, "so that's why noboby came! But who has cluttered—who has been having such a good time here, then?"

Mr. Brownlow silently led the last two arrivals to the door of the next room, and pointed in. It was now the kind deacon's turn to be touched.

"Into the highways!" he murmured, as he looked upon the unwashed, hungry little circle about the table.

"I s'pose," said Mr. Brownlow doubtfully, "they'd like to have you sit down with 'em, just's if they were folks—if you didn't mind?"

Mind! I wish you could have seen the rich furs and overcoat come off and go down on the floor in a heap, before Polly could catch them!

When they were all seated, Mr. Brownlow looked over to the deacon, and he asked a blessing on the little ones gathered there. "Thy servants, the masters of this house, have suffered them to come unto them," he said in his prayer. "Wilt Thou take them into Thine arms, O Father of lights, and bless them!"

A momentary hush followed, and then the fun began again. Sweetly and swiftly kind words flew back and forth across the table, each one carrying its own golden thread and weaving the hearts of poor and rich into the one fine fabric of brotherhood and humanity they were meant to form.

Outside, the snow began to fall once more, each crystaled flake whispering softly as it touched the earth that Christmas night, "Peace—peace!"

✳

The Ox and the Ass at the Manger

Jules Supervielle

T he ass, led by Joseph, bore the Virgin along the road to Bethlehem. She weighed little, being full of nothing but the future within her.

The ox followed, by himself.

On reaching the city, the travelers made their way into a deserted stable, and Joseph at once set to work.

"These men really are astonishing," thought the ox, "the things they manage to do with their hands and arms! Those objects are certainly much more useful than our hoofs and pasterns. And there's no one like our master when it comes to odd jobs and fixing things, straightening what's twisted and twisting what's straight, and doing all that has to be done without repining or getting down-hearted."

Joseph went out and soon returned carrying some straw on his back, wonderful straw, so crisp and glowing that it seemed to herald a miracle.

"What are they preparing there?" said the ass to himself. "It looks like a little bed for a child."

"We may have need of you tonight," said the Virgin to the ox and the ass. The beasts stared at each other for a long time in an effort to understand, and then lay down to sleep.

Soon they were awakened by a voice which, light though it was, had just carried across the whole of heaven. The ox got to his feet, found that there was a naked child asleep in the manger, and methodically warmed him with his breath, all over. The Virgin thanked him with a smiling look. Winged beings came and went, pretending not to see the walls they passed through so easily.

Joseph returned with some swaddling clothes lent him by a neighbor. "It's marvelous," he said in his carpenter's voice, rather loud for such an occasion, "it's midnight, and yet it's day. And there are three suns instead of one. But they're trying to join together."

At dawn the ox got up, taking care where he put his hoofs for fear of waking the child, crushing a heavenly flower, or hurting an angel. How marvelously difficult everything had become!

Neighbors came to see Jesus and the Virgin. They were poor people who had nothing to offer but their beaming faces. After them came others bringing nuts, or a flageolet. The ox and the ass moved aside a little to let them pass, and wondered what impression they themselves would make on the child, who had not yet seen them. He had only just awakened.

"We aren't monsters," said the ass.

"No, but you see we might frighten him with our faces, which aren't at all like his own or his parents'."

"The manger and the stable and its beamed roof haven't got a face like his either, but he isn't afraid of them."

But the ox was not convinced. He thought of his horns and ruminated: "It really is very upsetting not to be able to draw near those you love best without looking threatening. I always have to take care not to hurt anyone, and yet it isn't in my nature to attack people or things without good cause. I'm neither mischievous nor spiteful. But wherever I go, immediately my horns are there with me. I wake up with them, and even when I'm dropping with sleep and shuffle off in a daze, those two hard, pointed things are there and never forget me. I even feel them on the fringe of my dreams in the middle of the night."

A great fear seized the ox and he thought how near he had drawn to the child to warm him. What if he had accidentally gored him! "You oughtn't to go too close to the little one," said the ass, who had guessed his companion's thought. "You mustn't even dream of it, you'd hurt him. Besides, you don't keep your slaver in very well, you might let a drop of it fall on him, and that wouldn't be clean. Thinking of that, why do you slobber like that when you're happy? Keep it to yourself, there's no need to show it to everyone."

(Silence on the part of the ox.)

"For my part, I'm going to offer him my two ears. They twitch, you know, and move in all directions, they haven't any bones and they're soft to touch. They frighten and comfort at the same time. They're just the thing to amuse a child, and at his age they're instructive too."

"Yes, I do know, I've never said the contrary. I'm not a fool."

But since the ass looked really too self-satisfied, the ox added: "But don't you go and bray in his face, or you'd kill him."

"Country bumpkin!" said the ass.

The ass stood on the left of the manger, the ox on the right. These were the positions they occupied at the moment of the Nativity, and the ox, who favored a certain formality, set great store by them. There they remained for hours together, motionless and respectful, as though they were posing for some invisible painter.

Eager for sleep again, the child closed his eyes. Just on the further side of sleep, a shining angel awaited him, to teach him, or perhaps to ask him something. The angel came out of Jesus' dream and appeared, a living presence, in the stable. After bowing to the newly born, he painted a very pure halo round his head, another for the Virgin, and a third for Joseph. Then off he went in a dazzle of wings and feathers, ever as freshly white and rustling as the whiteness of the tides.

"There's no halo for us," the ox noticed. "The angel's sure to have reasons why not. We're too lowly, the ass and I. Besides, what have we done to deserve such a radiance?"

"You've certainly done nothing, but you forget that I carried the Virgin."

The ox thought to himself: "The Virgin's so beautiful and so fragile, how did she manage to hide this lovely babe?" But perhaps he was thinking aloud, for the ass answered: "There are some things you can't understand."

"Why do you always say that I don't understand? I've had a fuller life than you. I've worked in the mountains, on the plains, and by the sea."

"That isn't the point," said the ass, and went on: "It's not only the halo. I feel sure, ox, that you haven't noticed that all about the child there floats a sort of marvelous dust, or rather it's something better than dust."

"It's much more delicate," said the ox, "it's like a light, a golden mist given off by his little body."

"Yes, but you say that to make people think you'd seen it."

"And hadn't I seen it?"

The ox led the ass to a corner of the stable where, in token of worship, the ruminant had placed a small branch delicately surrounded with wisps of straw, which gave a very good idea of the rays emanating from the divine flesh. It was the first chapel. The ox had brought the straw in from outside. He dared not touch the straw of the manger; he had a superstitious fear of that, because it was good to eat.

The ox and the ass went off to graze until nightfall. Although stones generally take such a long time to understand anything, there were already a good many in the fields which knew. They even came across a pebble which, by a slight change of shape and color, showed them that it was in the secret.

There were meadow flowers, too, which knew and had to be spared. It was quite a business to graze in the fields without committing sacrilege. And to the ox, eating seemed more and more unnecessary. His happiness was food enough.

Before he drank, too, he would ask himself: "And what about this water, does it know?" When in doubt, he preferred not to drink, and would go a little further to some muddy water which was obviously still quite in the dark. Sometimes the only way he could tell was by an infinite sweetness in his throat at the moment when he was swallowing the water. "Too late," the ox would think, "I ought not to have drunk it."

He hardly dared breathe, so sacred and aware did the air seem to him. He was afraid of inhaling an angel.

The ox was ashamed at not always feeling himself as clean as he would have liked. "Well then, I must just be cleaner than before, that's all. It only needs a little more care, and paying attention where I put my feet."

The ass was quite unperturbed.

The sun shone into the stable and the two beasts competed for the honor of shading the child. "I daresay a little sun wouldn't do any harm either," thought the ox, "but the ass is sure to say again that I know nothing about it."

The child went on sleeping and sometimes, in his sleep, he would ponder and frown.

One day, while the Virgin was at the door, answering the thousands of questions put by future Christians, the ass, with his muzzle, delicately turned the child on his side. On going back to her son, Mary had a great fright, as she kept looking for the child's face where she had left it. When she realized what had happened, she gave the ass to understand that it was advisable not to touch the child. The ox showed his agreement by a silence of exceptional quality. He knew how to put rhythm, and shades of meaning, and punctuation, into his dumbness. On cold days you could easily follow the trend of his thoughts by the length of the column of steam that escaped from his nostrils. In that way you could learn a great deal.

The ox thought he had no right to render any but indirect services to the child, such as attracting to himself the flies in the stable (every morning he went and rubbed his back against a hive of wild bees), or squashing insects against the wall. The ass kept a lookout for noises from outside, and when he thought something was suspicious, he barred the entrance. Then the ox would immediately place himself behind the ass, to form a block. Then both of them made themselves as heavy as possible: while the danger lasted, their heads and bellies were full of lead. But their eyes shone, more watchful than ever.

The ox was dumbfounded to see that, when the Virgin drew near to the manger, she had the gift of making the child smile. And in spite of his beard, Joseph managed it also without too much difficulty, either by his mere presence or by playing on the flageolet. The ox would have liked to play something too. After all, one only had to blow.

"I don't want to say anything against the master, but I don't think he would have been able to warm the Child Jesus with his breath. And as for the flute, all I need is to be alone with the little one, and then he no longer frightens me. He becomes once more a creature who needs protection. And after all, an ox is aware of his strength."

When they were grazing together in the fields, the ox often used to leave the ass.

"Where are you going?"

"I'll be back in a moment."

"But where are you going?" insisted the ass.

"I'm going to see if he needs anything. You never know."

"For goodness' sake leave him alone!"

But the ox went. In the stable there was a kind of round window—such as was later to be called, for that very reason, a bull's eye—through which the ox looked in from outside.

One day he noticed neither Mary nor Joseph was there. He found the flageolet on a bench, within reach of his muzzle, neither too far away from the child, nor too near to him.

"What shall I be able to play him?" thought the ox, who dared not approach the ear of Jesus except through this musical go-between. "A song of the plow, the war cry of the brave little bull, or the enchanted heifer?"

Oxen often pretend to be ruminating when in their inmost hearts they are singing. The ox blew delicately into the flute and it is not at all certain that an angel did not help him to obtain such pure sounds. The child, on his bed, raised his head and shoulders a little, so as to see. For all that, the flutist was not satisfied with the result. But at least he felt sure that no one outside had heard him. He was mistaken. Then he made off in haste, for fear lest someone, and especially the ass, should come in and catch him too near the little flute.

One day the Virgin said to the ox: "Come and look at my child. You warmed him so well when he was still quite naked; why do you never go near him now?"

Emboldened, the ox placed himself quite close to Jesus who, to put him entirely at ease, seized his muzzle with both hands. The ox held his breath, which had become unnecessary. Jesus smiled. The joy of the ox was a silent joy. It had taken the exact shape of his body and filled it right up to the tips of its horns.

The child looked at the ass and the ox in turn, the ass a little too sure of himself, and the ox who felt himself extraordinarily opaque beside that face so delicately illuminated from within, as though one should see, through thin curtains, a lamp passing from one room to another in a very tiny, distant dwelling.

Seeing the ox look so gloomy, the child began to crow with laughter. The animal did not quite understand this laughter, in the future to be more reserved, or even to go away? Then the child laughed again, and his laugh seemed to the ox so luminous, and so filial, that he knew he had been right to stay.

The Virgin and her son often gazed at each other quite close to, and one couldn't tell which was the prouder of the other. "It seems to me that there should be universal rejoicing," thought the ox. "Never has there been seen a purer mother or a more beautiful child. But every now and then how grave they both look!"

The ox and the ass were preparing to return to the stable when the ox, after looking carefully about for fear of making some mistake, said:

"Do look at that star moving across the sky. It's so beautiful it warms my heart."

"Leave your heart out of it, it has nothing to do with the great events we've been witnessing lately."

"You can say what you like, but in my opinion that star is coming in our direction. See how low it is in the sky. It looks as though it's making for our stable. And below it there are three personages covered with precious stones."

The beasts reached the threshold of the stable.

"Well, ox, what is going to happen, according to you?"

"You expect too much of me, ass. I'm content to see what is happening, and that's already a good deal."

"I have my own idea."

"Now then, make way," Joseph said to them, opening the door. "Don't you see you're blocking the entrance and preventing these personages from coming in?"

The beasts moved aside to let the Magi pass. There were three of them, one of whom, completely black, represented Africa. At first the ox kept a discreet but watchful eye on him. He wanted to be sure the Negro had none but good intentions toward the new-born. But when the black man, who must have been a little shortsighted, bent down to see Jesus close to, his face, polished and lustrous as a mirror, reflected the image of the child with so much deference, so great a self-forgetfulness, that the heart of the ox was pierced with sweetness because of it.

"It's somebody very distinguished," he thought. "The two others would never have been able to do that." After a few moments he added: "He is indeed the best of the three." The ox had just surprised the white kings at the moment when they were very carefully stowing away in their luggage a wisp of straw, which they had just stolen from the manger. The black king had not wanted to take anything.

The kings slept side by side on an improvised bed lent by some neighbors. "How odd to keep your crown on for sleeping!" thought the ox. "A hard thing like that must be much more uncomfortable than horns. And it must be difficult to get to sleep with all those shining jewels on one's head."

They slept soberly, like statues stretched out on tombs. And their star shone above the manger.

Just before dawn all three got up at the same time, with identical movements. In a dream they had just seen the same angel who advised them to leave at once and not to go back to the jealous Herod to tell him that they had seen the Child Jesus.

They went out, leaving the star shining above the manger so that everyone should know that that was the place.

THE OX'S PRAYER

"Celestial Child, please don't judge me by my dazed obtuse air. May I not one day cease to look like a little lump of rock rolling along?

"As for these horns, I must explain that they are more an ornament than anything else; I'll even admit to you that I've never made use of them.

"Jesus, shed a little of your light on all these imperfections, these confusions that are in me. Teach me a little of your delicacy, you whose tiny feet and hands are attached with such minute care to your body. Can you tell me, little sir, why one day it was enough for me to turn my head to see the whole of you? How I thank you for having been allowed to kneel down before you, marvelous Child, and to live on familiar terms in this way with stars and angels! Sometimes I wonder if you may not have been misinformed, and if I am really the one who ought to be here. Perhaps you haven't noticed that I have a great scar on my back and that some of the hair has been rubbed off my coat on the sides, which is rather unpleasant. Even without going outside my own family, they might have chosen to come here my brother or my cousins who are much better looking than I. Wouldn't the lion or the eagle have been a more suitable choice?"

"Be quiet," said the ass, "Why do you keep sighing like that, don't you see you're preventing him sleeping, with all those ruminations of yours?"

"He's right," said the ox to himself, "one ought to know when it's time to be silent, even if one is conscious of a happiness so great that one doesn't know where to put it."

But the ass was praying too!

"Draught asses and pack asses, our path in life is going to be beautiful, and our foals will wait in cheerful pastures to see what happens next. Thanks to you, my little man, stones will remain in their proper places at the side of the road and we shan't have them falling on top of us. And another thing. Why should there still be hills and even mountains in our way? Wouldn't it suit everyone better to have flat country everywhere? And why does the ox, who is stronger than I, never carry anyone on his back? And why are my ears so long, and I've no hair on my tail, and my shoes are so small, and my chest is narrow, and my voice has the color of bad weather? But perhaps these things haven't yet been finally settled?"

During the nights which followed, it was the task now of one star and now of another to be on guard; and sometimes of whole constellations. In order to hide the secret of the sky, a cloud always occupied the place where the absent stars ought to have been, and it was marvelous to see the Infinitely Remote making themselves quite tiny so as to take up their positions over the crib, and keeping their excess of heat and light, and their immensity, for themselves alone, giving off only enough to warm and light the stable, and not to frighten the child. In those first nights of Christianity, the Virgin, Joseph, the Child, the Ox, and the Ass were extraordinarily themselves. During the daytime this likeness to themselves was less noticeable, being scattered about among the visitors; but after sunset it became miraculously concentrated and reliable.

Many animals approached the ox and the ass to ask if they could make the acquaintance of the Child Jesus. And one fine day a horse, known for his friendly disposition and his speed, was chosen by the ox, with Joseph's agreement, to summon the very next day all those who wanted to come.

The ass and the ox wondered whether they ought to let the wild beasts enter, and also the dromedaries, camels, and elephants, all of them animals whose humps and trunks and surplus of flesh and bone render them somewhat suspect.

There was the same doubt about such frightful insects as the scorpions, tarantulas, great trap-door spiders, and vipers who, both male and female, secrete poison in their glands night and day, and even at dawn, when all things are pure.

The Virgin did not hesitate. "You can let them all come in. My child is as safe in his crib as he would be in the topmost heights of heaven."

"And one by one!" added Joseph, in an almost military tone. "I don't want to have two animals at a time passing through the door, or we shan't know where we are."

The poisonous animals were allowed in first, since everyone felt that one owed them this compensation. Particularly noticeable was the fact of the serpents, who avoided looking at the Virgin, gliding by as far away from her person as possible. And they departed with as much calmness and dignity as if they had been doves or watchdogs.

There were also some animals so small that it was difficult to know if they were there or still waiting outside. These atoms were allowed a whole hour in which to present themselves and make the tour of the crib. When the time was up, although Joseph felt from a slight pricking of his skin that they had not all gone, he ordered the next animals to appear.

The dogs could not help showing their surprise that they had not been allowed to live in the stable like the ox and the ass. Everyone stroked them by way of an answer where upon they retired full of visible gratitude.

When it was evident from his smell that the lion was approaching, in spite of everything the ox and the ass were not easy in their minds, and the less so because that smell passed right through the incense and myrrh and other perfumes which the three kings had liberally diffused, without even taking any notice of them.

The ox appreciated the generous motives which inspired the confidence of the Virgin and Joseph; but to put such a delicate flame as a child beside a beast whose breath might extinguish it with a single puff . . .!

The anxiety of the ox and the ass was the greater because, as they clearly saw, it was only fitting that they should be totally paralyzed before the lion. They could no more think of attacking him than of thunder or lightning. And the ox, weakened by fasting, felt airy rather than pugnacious.

The lion entered with his mane, which only the wind of the desert had ever combed, and his melancholy eyes which said: "I am the lion, I can't help it, I am only the king of beasts." You could see that his chief concern was to take up as little room as possible in the stable, which was not easy, to breathe without upsetting anything around him, and to forget his retractile claws and the very powerful muscles that moved his jaws. He advanced with lowered lids, hiding his admirable teeth like a shameful disease, and with such a modest bearing that it was quite obvious he belonged to the family of lions who were one day to refuse to devour Saint Blandine. The Virgin took pity and tried to reassure him with a smile like those she kept for her child. The lion gazed straight in front of him, as though to say in a tone still more desperate than a moment ago:

"What have I done that I should be so big and strong? You know well that I've never eaten except when hunger and fresh air compelled me. And you know, too, that I had to consider the cubs. All of us have tried, more or less, to be herbivorous. But grass doesn't suite us; we can't digest it."

Then, in the midst of a great silence which embarrassed everyone, he bent his huge head, like an explosion of hair and fur, and laid it sadly on the hard earth, while the tuft at the end of his tail seemed as overcome as his head.

When it was the tiger's turn, he flattened himself out on the ground until, by sternly humbling himself, he became a veritable bedside mat at the foot of the crib. Then in a moment, with incredible exactitude and elasticity, he reconstituted himself and went out without a word.

The giraffe showed his feet for a moment in the embrasure of the door, and it was unanimously agreed that "that counted" as if he had walked all round the crib.

It was the same with the elephant; all he did was to kneel before the threshold and swing his trunk with a kind of censing movement which was greatly appreciated by all.

A tremendously woolly sheep clamored to be shorn on the spot. They thanked her but did not take her fleece.

The mother kangaroo was desperately eager to give Jesus one of her young, pleading that she really longed to make the present, that it was no sacrifice for her, and that she had other little kangaroos at home. But Joseph took a different view and she had to take her child away.

The ostrich was more fortunate; she took advantage of a moment of inattention to lay her egg in a corner and quietly depart, leaving this souvenir which no one noticed till the next morning. The ass discovered it. He had never seen anything so big or so hard in the way of an egg, and thought it was a miracle. Joseph did his best to undeceive him; he made an omelette of it.

The fish, not having been able to put in an appearance because of their wretched breathing when out of water, had delegated a sea gull to represent them.

The birds departed leaving their songs, the pigeons their love, the monkeys their tricks, the cats their gaze, and the turtledoves their throaty sweetness.

The animals who have not yet been discovered would have liked to present themselves too, those who await a name in the bosom of the earth or the sea, in depths so great that for them it is always night, without stars or moon or change of seasons.

One could feel, beating in the air, the souls of those who had not been able to come, or were late, and of others who, living at the end of the world, had nevertheless set out on insect feet so small that they could only have gone a yard in an hour, and whose life so short that they could never hope to cover more than half a yard—and even that only with a good deal of luck.

There were some miracles: the tortoise hurried, the iguana slackened his pace, the hippopotamus was graceful in his genuflections, and the parrots kept silence.

A little before sunset, something happened which upset everyone. Exhausted from having superintended the procession all day, without a bite to eat, in an absent-minded moment Joseph squashed a poisonous spider with his foot, forgetting that it had come to pay its respects to the Child. And the saint looked so upset that everyone felt distressed for quite a long time.

Certain animals who might have been expected to show more discretion lingered in the stable: the ox had to drive out the ferret, the squirrel, and the badger, who did not want to leave.

A few moths remained, taking advantage of the fact that they were the same color as the beams of the roof to spend the whole night above the crib. But the first sunbeam next day revealed them and, since Joseph did not wish to favor anyone, he turned them out immediately.

Some flies, who were also asked to leave, conveyed by their reluctance to depart that they had always been there, and Joseph did not know what to say to them.

The supernatural apparitions among which the ox lived often took his breath away. Having got into the habit of holding it, as Eastern ascetics do, like them he became a visionary; and although much less at ease among great than among humble things, he experienced genuine ecstasies. But he was governed by a scruple which would not let him imagine angels or saints. He saw them only when they really were in the neighborhood.

"Poor me!" thought the ox, scared by these apparitions, which seemed to him suspect. "Poor me, who am only a beast of burden, or maybe even the devil. Why have I got horns like him, when I've never done evil? And what if I were nothing but a sorcerer?"

Joseph did not fail to notice the anxieties of the ox, who was growing visibly thinner. "Go and eat out of doors!" he cried. "You stay here glued to us all day, soon you'll be nothing but skin and bones."

The ass and the ox went out.

"It's true you're thin," said the ass. "Your bones have become so sharp that you'll have horns sticking out all over your body."

"Don't talk to me of horns!"

And the ox said to himself: "He's quite right, of course, one must live. Go on, then, eat that lovely tuft of green! And what about that other one? What's the matter with you, are you wondering if it's poisonous? No, I'm not hungry. All the same, how beautiful that child is! And those splendid figures who come and go, breathing through their ever-beating wings, all those celestial great ones who find their way into our simple stable without ever getting dirty. Come now, eat, ox, don't trouble your head with all that. And another thing, you mustn't always wake up when happiness tugs at your ears in the middle of the night. And don't stay so long on one knee near the crib that it hurts you. Your hide is all worn away at the knee joint; a bit more and flies will be at it."

One night it was the turn of the Taurus, the constellation of the Bull to stand guard above the manger, against a stretch of black sky. The red eye of Aldebaran, blazing and magnificent, shone quite close, and the taurine flanks and horns were adorned with huge precious stones. The ox was proud to see the Child so well guarded. Everyone was sleeping peacefully, the ass with his ears trustingly lowered. But the ox, although fortified by the supernatural presence of that constellation which was both a relation and a friend, felt weak all over. He thought of his sacrifices for the Child, of his useless vigils, of the paltry protection he had offered.

"Has the constellation of the Bull seen me?" he wondered. "Does that big starry eye, shining enough to frighten you, know that I'm here? Those stars are so high and far off that one doesn't even know which way they're looking."

Suddenly Joseph, who had been tossing on his bed for the past few moments, got up, raising his arms to heaven. Though as a rule so restrained in words and gestures, he now wakened everyone, even the Child.

"I've seen the Lord in a dream. We must leave without delay. It's because of Herod, he wants to get hold of Jesus."

The Virgin took her son in her arms as though the king of the Jews were already at the door, with a butcher's knife in his hand.

The ass got to his feet.

"And what about him?" said Joseph to the Virgin, pointing to the ox.

"I'm afraid he's too weak to come with us."

The ox wanted to show that it wasn't so. He made a terrific effort to rise, but never had he felt himself so tethered to the ground. Desperate for help, he looked up at the constellation of the Bull, on which alone he now relied for strength to leave. But the celestial bovine, still in profile to the ox, his eye red and blazing as ever, gave no sign.

"It's several days now since he ate anything," said the Virgin to Joseph.

"Oh, I know very well they're going to leave me here," thought the ox. "It was too good to last. Besides, I should only have been a bony, laggard apparition on the road. All my ribs are tired of my skin and the only thing they want now is to lie down and rest under the open sky.

The ass went up to the ox and rubbed his muzzle against that of the ruminant, to let him know that the Virgin had just recommended him to a neighbor, and that he would lack nothing after their departure. But the ox, his lids half-closed, seemed utterly crushed.

The Virgin stroked him and said: "But we're not going on a journey, of course we aren't. It was only to frighten you!"

"Why of course, we're coming back immediately," added Joseph, "one doesn't set out on a far journey in the middle of the night like this."

"It's a very beautiful night," went on the Virgin, "and we're going to take advantage of it to give the Child some air; he's a bit palish these last days."

"That's absolutely true," said the holy man.

It was a pious lie. The ox knew it and, not wanting to embarrass the travelers in their preparations, he pretended to fall into a deep sleep. That was his way of lying.

"He's fallen asleep," said the Virgin. "Let's put the straw of the crib quite near to him, so that he'll lack nothing when he wakes. And let's leave the flageolet within reach of his breath," she went on in a low voice, "He's very fond of playing it when he's alone."

They got ready to leave. The stable door creaked. "I ought to have oiled it," thought Joseph, who was afraid of wakening the ox. But the ox went on pretending to be asleep. They closed the door carefully.

While the ass of the manger was gradually turning into the ass of the flight into Egypt, the ox remained with his eyes fixed on that straw where a short while before the Infant Jesus lay. Well he knew that he would never touch it, any more than he would touch the flageolet.

The constellation of the Bull regained the zenith with a bound, and with a single toss of his horns settled back in the sky in the pace which he would never leave again.

When the neighbor came in, a little after dawn, the ox had ceased to ruminate.

Christmas Day in the Morning

PEARL S. BUCK

He woke suddenly and completely. It was four o'clock, the hour at which his father had always called him to get up and help with the milking. Strange how the habits of his youth clung to him still! That was fifty years ago, and his father had been dead for thirty, yet he waked at four o'clock every morning. Over the years, he had trained himself to turn over and go to sleep, but this morning it was Christmas.

Why did he feel so awake tonight? He slipped back in time, as he did so easily nowadays. He was fifteen years old and still on his father's farm. He loved his father. He had not known it until one day a few days before Christmas, when he had overheard his father talking to his mother.

"Mary, I hate to wake Rob in the mornings. He's growing so fast and he needs his sleep. If you could see how hard he's sleeping when I go into wake him up! I wish I could manage alone."

"Well, you can't Adam." His mother's voice was brisk, "Besides, he isn't a child anymore. It's time he took his turn."

"Yes," his father said slowly. "But I sure do hate to wake him."

When he heard his father's words, something in him spoke: His father loved him! He had never thought of that before, simply taking for granted the tie of their blood. Neither his father nor his mother talked about loving their children—they had no time for such things. There was always so much to do on the farm.

Now that he knew his father loved him, there would be no loitering in the mornings and having to be called again. He always got up immediately after that. He stumbled blindly in his sleep and pulled on his clothes with his eyes shut, but he got up.

And then on the night before Christmas, that year when he was fifteen, he lay for a few minutes thinking about the next day. They were poor, and most of the excitement about Christmas was in the turkey they had raised themselves and the mince pies his mother had made. His sisters sewed presents for everyone and his mother and father always bought him something he needed, like a warm jacket, but usually something more too, such as a book. And he saved and bought them each something, too.

He wished, that Christmas when he was fifteen, he had a better present for his father. As usual he had gone to the ten-cent store and bought a tie. It had seemed nice enough until he lay thinking the night before Christmas. As he gazed out of his attic window, the stars were bright.

"Dad," he had once asked when he was a little boy, "What is a stable?"

"It's just a barn," his father had replied, "like ours."

Then Jesus had been born in a barn, and to a barn the shepherds had come.

The thought struck him like a silver dagger. Why couldn't he give his father a special gift too, out there in the barn? He could get up early, earlier than four o'clock, and he could creep into the barn and do all the milking before his father even got out of bed. He'd do it all alone, milk the cows and clean up, and then when his father went in to start the milking he'd see it all was done. And he would know who had done it. He laughed to himself as he looked at the stars. It was what he would do! He musn't sleep too sound and forget to get up early.

He must have waked twenty times, scratching a match each time to look at his old watch—midnight, half past one, then two o'clock.

At a quarter to three he got up and put on his clothes. He crept downstairs, careful to avoid the creaky boards, and let himself out. The cows looked at him, sleepy and surprised. It was early for them too.

He had never milked all alone before, but it seemed almost easy. He kept thinking about his father's surprise. His father would come in to get him, saying that he would get things started while Rob was getting dressed. He'd go to the barn, open the door, and then he'd go get the two big empty milk cans waiting to be filled. But they wouldn't be waiting or empty, they'd be standing in the milk house, filled.

"What on earth!" he could hear his father exclaiming.

He smiled and milked steadily, two strong streams rushing into the pail frothing and fragrant.

The task went more easily than he had ever known it to go before. For once, milking was not a chore. It was something else, a gift to his father who loved him. He finished, the two milk cans were full, and he covered them and closed the milk house door carefully, making sure to close the latch.

Back in his room he had only a minute to pull off his clothes in the darkness and jump into bed, for he heard his father up and moving around. He put the covers over his head to silence his quick breathing. The door opened.

"Rob," his father called. "We have to get up, son, even if it is Christmas."

"Aw-right," he said sleepily.

His father closed the door and he lay still, laughing to himself. In just a few minutes his father would know. His dancing heart was ready to jump from his body.

The minutes were endless—ten, fifteen, he did not know how many, it seemed like hours—and he heard his father's footsteps again. When his father opened the door he lay perfectly still.

"Rob!"

"Yes, Dad?"

His father was laughing, a strange sobbing sort of laugh.

"Thought you'd fool me, did you?" His father was standing by his bed, feeling for him, pulling away the covers.

"Merry Christmas, Dad!"

He found his father and clutched him in a great hug. He felt his father's arms wrap around him. It was dark and they could not see each other's faces.

"Son, I thank you. Nobody ever did a nicer thing . . ."

"Oh, Dad, I want you to know—I do want to be good!" The words broke from him of their own will. He did not know what to say. His heart was bursting with love.

He got up and pulled on his clothes again and they went down to the Christmas tree. Oh, what a Christmas, and how his heart had nearly burst again with shyness and pride as his father told his mother and sister about how he, Rob, had got up all by himself and finished all the milking.

"The best Christmas gift I ever had, and I'll remember it, son, every year on Christmas morning, so long as I live."

They had both remembered it every year, and now that his father was dead, he remembered it alone: that blessed Christmas dawn when, alone with the cows in the barn he had made his first gift of true love.

This Christmas he wanted to write a card to his wife and tell her how much he loved her. It had been a long time since he had really told her, although he loved her in a very special way, much more than he ever had when they were young. He had been fortunate that she had loved him. Ah, that was the true joy of life, the ability to love. Love was still alive in him, it still was.

It occurred to him suddenly that it was alive because long ago it had been born in him when he knew his father loved him. That was it: Love alone could awaken love. And he could give the gift again and again. This morning, this blessed Christmas morning, he would give it to his beloved wife. He would write it down in a letter for her to read and keep forever. He went to his desk and began to write: My dearest love . . .

Such a happy, happy, Christmas!

Christmas in the Heart

RACHEL FIELD

Years ago and years ago two little girls trudged up a long hill in the twilight of late December. They carried a basket between them, and one was I, and one was Helga Swanson. The smell of warm coffeecake and braided cinnamon bread and little brown twists like deer horns comes back to me now from that remembered basket. Sweeter than all the perfumes of Arabia that fragrance reached our half-frozen noses, yet we never lifted the folded napkin, for we took our responsibility hard. Helga's mother and grandmother had spent the better part of three days over that Christmas baking, and we had been chosen to deliver it and help trim the tree at the Lutheran Home on the hill above the Fallen Leaf Lake.

"We must hurry," Helga said. "They've lighted the parlors already."

I could hardly see Helga's face for the darkness, but I felt a warm, vigorous presence beside me in her tightly buttoned coat and knitted tam that half covered her fair braids. I would be seven in another month and she had been eight last March when we had moved from the state of Maine to Minnesota. It had seemed strange and a little frightening to me then to hear so many people speaking to one another in words I couldn't understand. Helga, herself, could drop into Swedish if it seemed worth her while to join in such conversations.

"It's nothing. I'll teach you," she had promised. But her enthusiasm had waned after a few attempts. So Helga became my interpreter as well as my most intimate friend. Without her I should never have known the old men and women in the red brick house who were our hosts that night. I should never have seen Pastor Hanson bending over the melodeon or heard old Christine Berglund tell about the star.

"Merry Christmas!" we called even before the door was thrown open and the spiciness of cooking food came out to us as from the gates of heaven.

There were sixteen of us, counting Helga and me, round that table with its white cloth, and its soup tureen at one end and round yellow cheese at the other. We all stood at our places while Pastor Hanson said a blessing in Swedish.

"There is a church in every man's heart," I remember, he said in English at the end of his prayer, "but let us be sure that it is always God who preaches the sermon."

The smell from those bowls of pea soup stays with me yet! Golden and smooth and rich to the last spoonful, we ate it with slices of fresh rye bread and home-churned butter. Pastor Hanson, himself, sliced the cheese with a knife that shaved it into one yellow curl after another. Cinnamon and coffee and hot bread and molasses mingled in one delicious scent as dishes and cups and plates passed from hand to hand.

At last we gathered in the parlor and another scuttle of coal went into the big stove. The time had come for decorating the tree, and everyone took a hand in it except old Mrs. Berglund, who stayed in a wheelchair because of her rheumatism. But even she gave advice about where more strings of popcorn were needed and if the candles were placed where they would show best among the green branches. Mr. Johnson had made birds out of pine cones, and there were cranberries in long strings as red as the popcorn was white. There were hearts and crescents of tinfoil and balls made out of bright bits of worsted. But there was no star anywhere, and I wondered about that, for no Christmas tree could be complete without a star to light its tip. But I need not have been troubled about that, as it turned out.

Pastor Hanson went over to the melodeon against the wall and began to play a Christmas carol. When we had finished, someone went over and whispered to old Mrs. Berglund in her wheelchair. From under the shawl she took out a small box that she held fast in her hands, which were thin and crooked as apple twigs. It was very still in the room for a moment, the kind of stillness that makes you know something exceedingly important is going to happen.

"Well, Pastor Hanson," she said, and held out the little box, "I did not think God would spare me for another year, but here I am, and here is the Christmas star."

"You must tell the children," he said. "It is right that they should hear before we hang it on the tree."

"Yust like tonight it vas," Christine Berglund began, and I felt grateful that she was telling it so for my sake, even though her j's and y's and v's and w's had a way of changing places as she said them, "I vere eleven year old then and sick in my heart because Christmas is coming and I am so far from my mother and brothers and sisters—"

I could see that big country estate as she told us about it—the stone walls and courtyard, the park with its thick woods; the tiled floors and great fireplaces;

the heavy, carved furniture, the enormous beds that would have held her whole family of brothers and sisters. She was young to be sent away into service, and everything and everyone in that house was old, from the mistress to the servants who had tended her for many years.

Pastor Lange came once each month to hold service in the stone chapel, because his parish church was too far away for the servants to attend. Pastor Lange was a very kind old man, and Christine did not feel so lonely on the days when he came. He always spent the night there and, though the mistress of the house never went into the chapel, after the service was over she sent for him and they ate supper together and talked before the fire until bedtime. Christine knew this because once she was sent with a tray from the kitchen to set before them.

"God bless you, my child," Pastor Lange had said. "May you rest well."

But the old lady had kept her lips shut in a thin line and she would not let her eyes rest on her young serving maid. It was the next morning that Pastor Lange answered Christine's questions. Their mistress had hardened her heart against every living thing because years ago she had lost her only child, a daughter as good as she was gay and beautiful. When death had taken her child the mother had turned as cold and gray as a boulder. She had ordered the girl's room closed and the birds let out of their cages. She had had a cloth hung over her portrait and every reminder of her presence taken from each nook and corner. Worst of all, she had summoned Pastor Lange and told him that she would live if she must, but he need never look for her in the family pew again. God had forsaken her, and Sunday and Easter and Christmas would be for her as any other days.

And she had kept her vow, though Pastor Lange had never ceased to pray that a miracle might turn her bitterness into faith once more.

"And did it?" Helga and I interrupted in our impatience.

But the story could not be hurried.

"Christmas it is the vorst," old Christine went on, "for in that big house there is not one cake baked or one bit of green hung on any door. At home ve are poor, but ve put out grain for the birds and have our candles to light and our songs to sing."

Each night she cried as the holiday grew near. She thought of her mother and brothers and sisters all together in a house that was small but savory with holiday cooking. She thought also of the little church on Christmas Eve, with its lighted windows, and the graves outside, each with a torch set there to burn through the long hours till Christmas morning. It was right, her mother had told her, that even the dead should join with the living on that Holy Night. And there was nothing that Christine could do, a half-grown girl in that house of silence and old, old people, to show that Christmas was in her heart.

But once she had noticed near the chapel some tilted gravestones and among them one not so cold and gray as the others. Lichens covered the letters cut upon it. She was afraid to scrape away the moss to read the name, but there could be no harm, she thought, in putting a branch of green upon it. Perhaps she might even take her own candle out there to burn and say a prayer and sing a carol. The thought of that made her feel less lonely. She hummed a Christmas hymn as she went back to her work, and it was as she crossed the courtyard that something bright caught her eye in a crack between two flagstones. She bent to pick it up and there, half hidden by moss, was a pin, star-shaped and shining and giving out jets of color as she turned it in the sun.

"Like the Star of Bethlehem," she thought, and her heart beat fast under the apron she wore, for surely it seemed like a sign to comfort her.

She pinned it where no one would see it under her dress, and all day she felt it close to her heart as she went about her duties. That night she slept with it beneath her pillow, and she thought of the Wise Men of old who had seen that other star in the East and followed it to Bethlehem.

Next day she slipped out and stopped by the gravestones. On the smallest stone she set a green branch of fir with cones. It stood straight and fine—almost, Christine Berglund told us, like the Christmas tree we had just trimmed.

"That night is Christmas Eve," she went on, "and I think there can be no harm if I go out after it is dark and light my candle and set the star there to keep watch till it is morning."

But, as the afternoon passed and twilight came, Christine did not feel so happy. The hidden star pricked her with its points, almost as if it were her own conscience telling her that stars were not meant to be hidden, that what we pick up is not ours merely for the finding. She tried to tell herself that it would be different if she had found her treasure in the house, not out there between the stones of the courtyard.

So darkness fell and it was Christmas Eve. Some of the old servants remembered and spoke of other times when there had been laughter and festivity in those rooms, and the chapel bell ringing to call them to midnight service. Christine sat quiet until she could slip away to her little room. It was chill there in the darkness because she dared not waste her candle.

At last the fires were banked and the house grew silent. Then Christine put on her cloak and crept down the stairs. She let herself into the courtyard, where nothing stirred but the shadows of trees beyond the walls. The moon was high above the stone turrets. She and it seemed to be the only things which moved in that world of winter quiet. She passed the chapel where no bells pealed from the dark belfry. There were the old tilted gravestones and the one with the bit of green to mark it. Her fingers shook as she set her candle on the headstone and tried to light it. Twice it went out before the small flame shone clear. Her hands still trembled as she took out the star and pinned it among the green needles.

"And then I get down on my knees and first I say 'Our Father.' Then I make another one that is mine, so God shall know that I do not forget the night of our Saviour's birth. It is hard for me to find the words for my prayer and my teeth are chattering like little hammers, so I don't hear someone come tap-tapping on the stones—"

"Oh!" Helga and I drew sharp breaths. "Who was it?"

But old Christine must tell the story her own way.

"There I am on my knees," she repeated, "praying to God, and my candle is still burning. Yes, that is how she found me."

We dared not interrupt her again, but our eyes never left her face.

"'Mistress,' I said," she went on, "'forgive me.' But she don't answer me; she yust stand there and turn it in her hands, and she act like she is seeing a ghost."

They must have stood so a long time. The candle burned out on the headstone before the old mistress took Christine back to the house. She did not speak until they reached the great hall, though tears ran down her cheeks at each step they took. Her hands reached for the bell rope and the house echoed to her frantic ringing. Christine could hear the servants hurrying to and fro upstairs in answer to the summons.

"I think she send for them because I have done a bad thing," old Christine told us, "so I stand and shiver there and don't know what is going to happen to me. And then they come down, all so sleepy they forget to make their curtsies. And Mistress point to me, and I cry so I don't see her face anymore. But she say to them, 'Go; make a fire in the blocker room. Spread linen and blankets on the bed and warm it, and bring food, that this child may eat and be comforted.' I think I don't hear her right, but take me there, and I see the fire lighted and the bed vaiting, so I don't try to think anymore. I yust lie down with flowers spread over me, and I sleep and sleep. And there is no one to come and shake me at sunrise to help in the kitchen. I vake, and it is Christmas morning and bells are ringing so sweet I think I dream them from home. But they are ringing in the chapel. Then the maids come and bring me a beautiful dress that smells of cloves and lavender. And they dress me in it, and I ask them the meaning of all this; but they yust smile and say, 'Pastor Lange, he vill tell you.'"

And, sure enough, Pastor Lange and the old mistress came from the chapel. He had driven since sunrise in the carriage she had sent to bring him there.

"You shall see for yourself, Pastor," the old coachman had said, "that the day of miracles is not past."

So Christine went down to meet them in the dress that was heavy with gold embroidery and slippers so soft she seemed to be walking on snow. These rooms were no longer gray and gloomy but warm with leaping fires. The covers were gone from the portrait of a laughing girl no older than she. Her dress was the same that Christine wore, and the star showed plainly on the painted folds. Christine marveled at each change she saw about her, most of all at her mistress's face, which was still sad, but no longer set like stone.

Then Pastor Lange put his hands on Christine's head and blessed her in God's name. But to the old woman he said, "Blessed are they that mourn, for they shall be comforted."

And Christine sat between them at dinner, and felt strange that she should now be served who had so lately carried in the dishes.

"And after dinner is over Pastor Lange he tells me that it is indeed a miracle God has worked through me to bring faith to our mistress. I don't understand how that can be, for it was not right that I keep the pin and tell no one. But Pastor Lange does not know how to explain that to me. So he says, 'Christine, it must have been that God vas in your heart to do this thing.' 'No, Pastor,' I tell him the truth; 'it was Christmas in my heart.' And Pastor Lange he don't scold me, he yust say maybe that is the same thing."

Old Christine was growing tired. Her voice had dwindled to a thin thread of sound by the time she had answered our questions . . . Yes, the pin had belonged to her mistress's daughter. She had lost it one winter day and grown so chill hunting for it in the courtyard that she had fallen ill and died. It was her gravestone by the chapel that Christine had chosen to light and decorate with green. So great had been that mother's grief that it was more than thirty years since she had spoken her daughter's name or let anything be a reminder. But Christine's candle shining on Christmas Eve had been like a sign sent from her dead child by a living one on that most happy night of the year.

So Christine no longer served as a maid in that great house. She lived as the old woman's daughter, and in winter the rooms were warm and bright with fires and laughter, and in summer sweet with flowers and the singing of birds.

"And see, here is the star to hang on the tree."

"The same one? The very same?"

"Yes, the same. It goes with me always since that night."

We touched the five shining points with wonder in our finger tips before Christine's old fingers lifted it from the bed of cotton.

"Real diamonds and not one missing," she said proudly as she handed it to Captain Christiansen, because he was tall enough to set it on the topmost tip.

"But I never think it vould come all the vay to America. I never think I come all that vay myself."

We watched it send out little jets of brightness when the candles were lighted below and all the old faces shining in the loveliest of light. We sang another carol all together, and then it was time to go home with Helga's father, who had come for us.

"Good night." Their voices follow us to the door. "God Jul! Merry Christmas!"

"Merry Christmas!" Helga and I called back before we turned to follow her father's lantern into the wintry dark.

The Birds' Christmas Carol

KATE DOUGLAS WIGGIN

1. A LITTLE SNOW BIRD

It was very early Christmas morning, and in the stillness of the dawn, with the soft snow falling on the housetops, a little child was born in the Bird household. They had intended to name the baby Lucy, if it were a girl; but they had not expected her on Christmas morning and a real Christmas baby was not to be lightly named.

Mr. Bird said that he had assisted in naming the three boys—Donald, Paul, and Hugh—and that he should leave the naming of the girl entirely to Mrs. Bird. Donald Junior wanted his sister called "Dorothy," and Paul chose "Luella." But Uncle Jack said that the first girl should always be named for her mother, no matter how hideous the name happened to be.

Grandma said that she would prefer not to take any part of the discussion, and then everybody suddenly remembered that Mrs. Bird had thought of naming the baby Lucy, for Grandma herself—so naturally no one expected Grandma to suggest another name.

Hugh, who until then had been "the baby," sat in one corner and said nothing. There was a newer baby now, and the "first girl," too,—and it made him actually green with jealousy.

But it was too important a matter to be settled until Mamma had been consulted.

Meanwhile Mrs. Bird lay in her room, sleepy and happy with her sweet baby girl by her side. Nurse was downstairs in the kitchen, and the room was dim and quiet. There was a cheerful open fire in the grate; but though the shutters were closed, the side windows that looked out on the church next door were a little open.

Suddenly a sound of music poured out into the bright air and drifted into the chamber. It was the boy choir singing Christmas anthems. Higher and higher rose the clear, fresh voices, full of hope and cheer, as children's voices always are. Fuller and fuller grew the burst of melody as one glad strain fell upon another in joyful harmony:

> "Carol, brothers, carol,
> Carol joyfully,

Carol the good tidings,
Carol merrily!
And pray a gladsome Christmas
For all your fellow-men:
Carol, brothers, carol,
Christmas Day again."

One verse followed another, always with the same glad refrain:
"And pray a gladsome Christmas
For all your fellow men:
Carol, brothers, Carol,
Christmas Day again."

Mrs. Bird thought, as the music floated in upon her gentle sleep, that she had slipped into heaven with her new baby, and that the angels were bidding them welcome. But the tiny bundle by her side stirred a little, and though it was scarcely more than the ruffling of a feather, she awoke.

She opened her eyes and drew the baby closer. She looked like a rose dipped in milk, Mrs. Bird thought, like a pink cherub, with its halo of pale yellow hair, finer than floss silk.

"Carol, brothers, carol
Carol joyfully,
Carol the good tidings,
Carol merrily!"

The voices were brimming over with joy.

"Why, my baby," whispered Mrs. Bird in soft surprise, "I had forgotten what day it was. You are a little Christmas child, and we will name you 'Carol'—mother's Christmas Carol!"

"What!" said Mr. Bird, coming in softly and closing the door behind him.

"Why, Donald, don't you think 'Carol' is a sweet name for a Christmas baby?"

"I think it is a charming name, dear heart, and sounds just like you, and I hope that, being a girl, this baby has some chance of being as lovely as her mother"—at this speech from the baby's papa, Mrs. Bird blushed with happiness.

And so Carol came by her name.

Uncle Jack declared laughingly that it was very strange if a whole family of

Birds could not be indulged in a single Carol; and Grandma, who adored the child, thought the name much more appropriate than Lucy.

Perhaps because she was born in holiday time, Carol was a very happy baby. Of course, she was too tiny to understand the joy of Christmas-tide, but people say there is everything in a good beginning; and she may have breathed in unconsciously the fragrance of evergreens and holiday dinners, while the peals of sleigh bells and the laughter of happy children may have fallen upon her baby ears and wakened in them a glad surprise at the merry world she had come to live in.

Her cheeks and lips were as red as holly berries; her hair was for all the world the color of a Christmas candle flame; her eyes were bright as stars; her laugh like the chime of Christmas bells, and her tiny hands forever out-stretched in giving.

Such a generous little creature! A spoonful of bread and milk had always to be taken by Mamma or Nurse before Carol could enjoy her supper; whatever bit of cake or sweet found its way into her pretty fingers was straightway broken in half to be shared with Donald, Paul, or Hugh; and when they made believe nibble the morsel, she would clap her hands and crow with delight.

"Why does she do it?" asked Donald thoughtfully. "None of us boys ever did."

"I hardly know," said Mamma, catching her darling to her heart, "except that she is a little Christmas child, and so she has a tiny share of the blessedest birthday the world ever knew!"

2. DROOPING WINGS

It was December, ten years later.

Carol had seen nine Christmas trees lighted on her birthdays, one after another; nine times she had helped in the holiday festivities of the household, and for five years, certainly, she had hidden presents for Mamma and Papa in their own bureau drawers.

For five years she had heard "Twas the night before Christmas," and hung up a scarlet stocking many sizes too large for her, and pinned a sprig of holly on her little white nightgown, to show Santa Claus that she was "truly" a Christmas child, and dreamed of fur-coated saints and toy-packs and reindeer, and wished everybody a "Merry Christmas" before it was light in the morning, and lent every one of her new toys to the neighbors' children before noon, and eaten turkey and plum pudding, and gone to bed at night in a trance of happiness at the day's pleasures.

Donald was away at college now. Paul and Hugh were great manly fellows, taller than their mother. Papa Bird had gray hairs in his whiskers; and Grand-ma, God bless her, had been four Christmases in heaven.

But there was a reason why Christmas in the Birds' Nest was not as merry now as it used to be. The little child that had once brought such an added joy to Christmas Day, now lay, month after month, a patient, helpless invalid, in the room where she was born.

Carol had never been very strong in body, and it was with a pang of terror that her mother and father noticed her beginning to limp slightly, soon after she was five years old. She also complained often of weariness and would nestle close to her mother saying she "would rather not go out to play, please."

The illness was slight at first, and hope was always stirring in Mrs. Bird's heart. "Carol will feel stronger in the summertime," she would say. Or "Carol will be better when she has spent a year in the country"; or "She will outgrow it"; or "We will try a new physician."

But slowly it became plain even to Mrs. Bird that no physician on earth could make Carol strong again; and that no "summertime" nor "country air," unless it was the everlasting summertime in a heavenly country, could bring the little girl back to health.

The cheeks and lips that were once red as holly berries faded to faint pink; the star-like eyes grew softer, for they often gleamed through tears; and the gay child-laugh, that had been like a chime of Christmas bells, gave place to a smile so lovely, so touching, so tender and patient, that it filled every corner of the house with a gentle radiance.

The love they all felt for her could do nothing. And when we have said that we have said all, for it is stronger than anything else in the world. Mr. and Mrs. Bird were talking it over one evening, when all the children were asleep. A famous physician had visited them that day, and told them that some time, it might be in one year, it might be in more, Carol would slip quietly off forever.

"It is no use to close our eyes to it any longer," said Mr. Bird, as he paced up and down the library floor. "Carol will never be well again. It seems as if I could not bear it when I think of that loveliest child doomed to lie there day af-ter day, and, what is more, to suffer pain that we are helpless to keep away from her. Merry Christmas, indeed! It gets to be the saddest day in the year to me!"

And poor Mr. Bird sank into a chair by the table, and buried his face in his hands to keep his wife from seeing the tears that would come in spite of all his efforts.

"But, Donald, dear," said sweet Mrs. Bird, with a trembling voice, "Christmas Day may not be so merry with us as it used, but it is very happy, and that is better, and very blessed, and that is better yet. I suffer chiefly for Carol's sake, but I have almost given up being sorrowful for my own. I am too happy in the child, and I see too clearly what she has done for us and the other children. Donald and Paul and Hugh were three strong, willful, boisterous boys. But now you seldom see such tenderness, devotion, thought for others, and self-denial in boys of their years. A quarrel or a hot word is almost unknown in this house, and why? Because Carol would hear it, and it would distress her, she is so full of love and goodness. What's more, the boys study as hard as they can. Why? Partly, at least, because they like to teach Carol, and amuse her by telling her what they read. Everyone loves to be in Carol's room, because there they can forget their own troubles. And as for me, Donald, I am a better woman every day for Carol's sake. I have to be her strength, her hope; and she, my own little child, is my example!"

"I was wrong, dear heart," said Mr. Bird more cheerfully; "we will try not to sorrow, but to rejoice instead, that we have an 'angel of the house' like Carol"

"And as for her future," Mrs. Bird went on, "I think we need not be overanxious. I feel as if she did not belong altogether to us, but that when she has done what God sent her for, He will take her back to Himself—and it may not be very long!" Here it was poor Mrs. Bird's turn to break down, and Mr. Bird's turn to comfort her.

3. BIRD'S NEST

Carol herself knew nothing of her mother's tears and her father's anxieties. They hid their feelings, knowing their sadness would distress her. So she lived on peacefully in the room where she was born.

But you never would have known that room. You see, Mr. Bird had a great deal of money. And though he felt sometimes as if he wanted to throw it all in the ocean, since it could not buy a strong body for his little girl, still he was glad that he could use his money to make the place Carol lived in as beautiful as it could be.

The room had been extended by building a large addition that hung out over the garden below. It was a kind of sun porch, and it was so filled with windows that it might have been a greenhouse. The ones on the side were even nearer the little church next door than they used to be. Those in front looked out on the beautiful harbor. And although those in the back commanded a view of nothing more than a little alley, nevertheless they were pleasantest of all to Carol, for the Ruggles family lived in the alley, and the nine Ruggles children were a source of endless interest to Carol.

The window shutters could all be opened and Carol could take a real sun bath in this lovely glass house, or they could all be closed when her head ached or her eyes were tired. The carpet was a soft gray, with clusters of green bay and holly leaves. The furniture was painted white, and on each piece an artist had painted snow scenes and ringing bells and singing carols.

Donald had made a polished shelf and screwed it on the outside of the footboard of the bed, and the boys always kept this full of blooming plants, which they changed from time to time. The headboard, too, had a bracket on either side, where there were pots of maidenhair ferns.

In the windows were golden cages in which lovebirds and canaries sang. They, poor caged things, could hop as far from their wooden perches as Carol could venture from her little white bed.

On one side of the room was a bookcase filled with hundreds—yes, I mean it—with hundreds of books; books with gay-colored pictures, books without; books with black and white outline sketches, books with none at all; books with verses, books with stories; books that made children laugh, and some, only a few, that made them cry; books with words of one syllable for tiny boys and girls, and books with words of fearful length to puzzle wise ones.

This was Carol's "circulating library." Every Saturday she chose ten books, jotting their names down in a little diary; into these she slipped cards that said:

"Please keep this book two weeks and read it.
With love, Carol Bird."

Then Mrs. Bird stepped into her carriage and took the ten books to the Children's Hospital, and brought home ten others that she had left there the fortnight before.

These books were a source of great happiness; for some of the hospital children that were old enough to print or write, and were strong enough to do it, wrote Carol sweet little letters about the books, and she answered them, and they grew to be friends. (You do not always have to see people to love them.)

There was a shoulder-high wood ledge about the room, and on top of this, in a narrow gilt framework, ran a row of illuminated pictures, illustrating fairy tales, all in dull blue and gold and scarlet and silver. From the door to the closet there was the story of "The Fair One with Golden Locks"; from closet to bookcase, ran "Puss in Boots"; and on the other side of the room were "Hop o' My Thumb," "The Sleeping Beauty," and "Cinderella."

Then there was a great closet full of beautiful things to wear, but they were all dressing gowns and slippers and shawls; and there were drawers full of toys and games, but they were such as you could play with on your lap. There were no skates nor balls, nor bean bags, nor tennis rackets; but, after all, other children needed these more than Carol Bird, for she was always happy and contented, whatever she had or whatever she lacked; and on her eighth Christmas after the room had been made so lovely for her, she always called herself, in fun, a "bird of paradise."

On these particular December days she was happier than usual, for Uncle Jack was coming from Europe to spend the holidays. Dear, funny, jolly, loving, wise Uncle Jack, who came every two or three years, and brought so much joy with him that the world looked as black as a thundercloud for a week after he went away again.

The mail had brought this letter:

London, November 28th,—

Wish you merry Christmas, you dearest birdlings in America! Preen your feathers, and stretch the Birds' Nest a little, if you please, and let Uncle Jack in for the holidays. I am coming with such a trunk full of treasures that you'll have to borrow the stockings of a giant and giantess; I am coming to squeeze a certain little lady bird until she cries for mercy; I am coming to see if I can find a boy to take care of a little black pony that I bought lately. It's the strangest thing I ever knew; I've hunted all over Europe, and can't find a boy to suit me! I'll tell you why. I've set my heart on finding one with a dimple in his chin, because this pony particularly likes dimples! ["Hurrah!" cried Hugh. "I'll never be ashamed of my dimple again."]

Please drop a note to the clerk of the weather, and have a good, rousing snowstorm—say on the twenty-second. None of your meek, gentle nonsensical, shilly-shallying snowstorms; not the sort where the flakes float lazily down from the sky as if they didn't care whether they ever got here or not and then melt away as soon as they touch the earth, but a regular, businesslike, whizzing, whirring, blurring, cutting snowstorm, warranted to freeze and stay on!

I should like rather a LARGE Christmas tree. We can cut a hole in the roof if the tree chances to be too high for the room.

Tell Bridget to begin to fatten a turkey, and tell her that the pudding must be unusually huge and darkly, deeply, lugubriously blue in color. It must be stuck so full of plums that the pudding itself will ooze out into the pan and not be brought on to the table at all. I expect to be there by the twentieth to manage these things myself, but give you these instructions in case I should be delayed.

And Carol must plead for the snowstorm—the "clerk of the weather" may pay some attention to her as she is a Christmas child. And she must look up the boy with the dimple for me—she's likelier to find him than I am, this minute. She must advise about the turkey, and Bridget must bring the pudding to her bedside and let her drop every separate plum into it and stir it once for luck, or I'll not eat a single slice—for Carol is the dearest part of Christmas to Uncle Jack, and he'll have none of it without her. She is better than all the turkeys and puddings and apples and spareribs and wreaths and garlands and mistletoe and stockings and chimneys and sleigh bells in the world. She is the very sweetest Christmas Carol that was ever written, said, sung, or chanted, and I am coming, as fast as ships and railway trains can carry me, to tell her so.

Carol's joy knew no bounds. Mr. and Mrs. Bird laughed and kissed each other in delight, and when the boys heard it they whooped for joy, until the Ruggles family, whose back yard joined their garden, gathered at the gate and wondered what was up in the big house.

4. "BIRDS OF A FEATHER FLOCK TOGETHER"

Uncle Jack really did come on the twentieth. He was not detained by business, nor did he get left behind nor snowed up, as frequently happens in stories, and in real life, too. The snowstorm came also; and the turkey. Donald came, too,—Donald, with a line of down upon his upper lip, and stores of knowledge in his handsome head, and stories! You couldn't turn over a page without reminding Donald of something that happened "at college." One or the other was always at Carol's bedside, for they fancied her paler than she used to be, and they could not bear her out of sight. It was Uncle Jack, though, who sat beside her in the winter twilights. The room was quiet, and almost dark, save for the snowlight outside and the flickering flame of the fire, that danced over the "Sleeping Beauty's" face and touched the golden locks with ruddier glory. Carol's hand, all too thin and white these days, lay close clasped in Uncle Jack's, and they talked together quietly of many, many things.

"I want to tell you all about my plans for Christmas this year, Uncle Jack," said Carol, on the first evening of his visit, "because it will be the loveliest one I ever had. The boys laugh at me for caring so much about it; but it isn't altogether because it is Christmas nor because it is my birthday. Long, long ago, when I first began to be ill, I used to think, the first thing when I waked on Christmas morning, 'Today is Christ's birthday—and mine!' And so I do not quite feel about Christmas as other girls do. Mamma says she supposes that ever so many other children have been born on that day. I often wonder where they are, Uncle Jack, and whether it is a dear thought to them, too, or whether I am so much in bed, and so often alone, that it means more to me. Oh, I do hope that none of them are poor, or cold, or hungry; and I wish, I wish they were all as happy as I, because they are really my brothers and sisters. Now, Uncle Jack dear, I am going to try and make somebody happy every single Christmas that I live and this year it is to be the 'Ruggleses in the rear.'"

"That large and interesting brood of children in the little house at the end of the black garden?"

"Yes; isn't it nice to see so many together? And, Uncle Jack, why do the big families always live in the small houses, and the small families in the big houses? We ought to call them the Ruggles children, of course; but Donald began talking of them as the 'Ruggleses in the rear,' and Papa and Mama took it up, and now we cannot seem to help it.

"When they first moved in, I used to sit in my window and watch them play in their back yard; they are so strong, and jolly, and good-natured—and then, one day, I had a terrible headache, and Donald asked them if they would please not scream so loud, and they explained that they were having a game of circus, but that they would change and play 'Deaf and Dumb Asylum' all the afternoon."

Uncle Jack smiled, "An obliging family, to be sure."

"Yes, we all thought it very kind, and I smiled at them from the window when I was well enough to be up again. Now, Sarah Maud comes to her door when the children come home from school, and if Mamma nods her head, 'Yes,' that means 'Carol is very well,' and then you ought to hear the little Ruggleses yell—I believe they try to see how much noise they can make; but if Mamma shakes her head they always play at quiet games. Then, one day, Cary, my pet canary, flew out of her cage, and Peter Ruggles caught her and brought her back, and he came up here in my room so that I could thank him."

"Is Peter the oldest?"

"No. Sarah Maud is the oldest—she helps do the washing; and Peter is the next. He is a delivery boy."

"And which is the pretty little red-haired boy."

"That's Kitty."

"And the fat youngster?"

"Baby Larry."

"And that—most-freckled one?"

"Now, don't laugh—that's Peoria."

"Carol, you are joking."

"No, really, Uncle dear. She was born in Peoria; that's all."

"And is the next boy Oshkosh?"

"No," laughed Carol. "The others are Susan, and Clement, and Eily, and Carnelius. They all look pretty much alike except that some have more freckles than the others."

"How did you ever learn all their names?"

"Well, I have what I call 'window school.' It is too cold now; but in warm weather I am wheeled out on my balcony, and the Ruggleses climb up and walk along the garden fence, and sit on the roof of our carriage-house. That brings them quite near, and I read to them and tell them stories. On Thanksgiving Day they came up for a few minutes—it was quite warm at eleven o'clock—and we told each other what we had to be thankful for. But they gave such queer answers that I couldn't understand them very well. Susan was thankful for trunks of all things in the world Cornelius, for the horse-car; Kitty, for pork steak; and Clem, who is very quiet, brightened up when I came to him, and said he was thankful for his lame puppy. Wasn't that strange."

"It might teach some of us a lesson, mightn't it, little girl?"

"That's what Mamma said. Now I'm going to give this whole Christmas to the Ruggleses. And, Uncle Jack, I earned part of the money myself."

"You, my bird! How?"

"Well, you see, it could not be my own, own Christmas if Papa gave me all the money, and I decided that I should do something on my very own; and so I talked with Mamma. Of course she thought of something lovely—she always does. Mamma's head is just brimming over with lovely thoughts—all I have to do is ask, and out pops the very one I want. This thought was to let her write down, just as I told her, a description of how a child lived in her own room for three years, and what she did to amuse herself; and we sent it to a magazine and got twenty-five dollars for it. Just think!"

"Well, well," cried Uncle Jack, "my little girl a real author! And what are you going to do with this wonderful 'own' money of yours?"

"I shall give the nine Ruggleses a grand Christmas dinner here in this very room—that will be Papa's contribution—and afterwards a beautiful Christmas tree, fairly blooming with presents—that will be my part; for I have another way of adding to my twenty-five dollars, so that I can buy everything I like. I should like it very much if you would sit at the head of the table, Uncle Jack, for nobody could ever be frightened of you. Mamma is going to help us, but Papa and the boys are going to eat together downstairs for fear of making the little Ruggleses shy; and after we've had a merry time with the tree and presents, we can open my window and all listen to the music at the church if it comes before the children go. I have written a letter to the organist, and asked him if I might have the two songs I like best. Will you see if it is all right?"

> Birds' Nest, December 21st,—
> Dear Mr. Wilkie,
> I am the little girl who lives next door to the church, and, as I seldom go out, the music on practice days and Sundays is one of my greatest pleasures.
> I want to know if you can have "Carol, Brothers, Carol," on Christmas night, and if the boy who sings "My Own Country" so beautifully may please sing that too. I think it is the loveliest thing in the world, but it always makes me cry; doesn't it you?
> If it isn't too much trouble, I hope they can sing them both quite early, as after ten o'clock I may be asleep.
> Yours respectfully,
> Carol Bird
>
> P.S.—The reason I like "Carol, Brothers, Carol," is because the choirboys sang it eleven years ago, the morning I was born, and put it into Mamma's head to call me Carol. She didn't remember then that my other name would be Bird, because she was half asleep, and could only think of one thing at a time. Donald says if I had been born on the Fourth of July they would have named me "Independence," or if on the twenty-second of February, "Georgina," or even "Cherry" like

Cherry in "Martin Chuzzlewit"; but I like my own name and birthday best.

Yours truly,

Carol Bird

Uncle Jack thought the letter quite right, and did not even smile at her telling the organist so many family items.

The days flew by as they always fly in holiday time, and it was Christmas Day before anybody knew it. The family festival was quiet and very pleasant, but almost overshadowed by the grander preparations for the next day. Carol and her pretty German nurse, Elfrida, had ransacked books, and introduced so many plans, and plays, and customs, and merry-makings from Germany, and Holland, and England, and a dozen other countries, that you would scarcely have known how or where you were keeping Christmas.

Elfrida had scattered handfuls of seed over the snow in the garden, that the wild birds might have a comfortable breakfast the next morning, and had stuffed bundles of dry grasses in the fireplaces, so that the reindeer of Santa Claus could refresh themselves after their long gallops across country. This was really done only for fun, but it pleased Carol.

And when, after dinner, the whole family had gone to church to see the Christmas decorations, Carol limped out on her crutches, and with Elfrida's help, placed all the family shoes in a row in the upper hall. That was to keep the dear ones from quarreling all through the year. There were Papa's heavy shoes; Mamma's pretty slippers next; then Uncle Jack's, Donald's, Paul's, and Hugh's. And at the end of the line her own white woolly slippers. Last, and sweetest of all, like the little children in Austria, she put a lighted candle in her window to guide the dear Christ child, lest He should stumble in the dark night as He passed up the deserted street. That done, she dropped into the bed, a rather tired, but happy Christmas fairy.

5. SOME OTHER BIRDS ARE TAUGHT TO FLY

Before the earliest Ruggles could wake and toot his five-cent tin horn, Mrs. Ruggles was up and stirring about the house, for it was a gala day in the family. Were not all her nine children invited to a dinner party at the Birds' great house? She had been preparing for this grand occasion ever since the receipt of the invitation, which now was in an old photograph frame and hanging under the looking-glass in the most prominent place in the kitchen, where any visitor would see it.

Birds' Nest, December 17th, —

Dear Mrs. Ruggles,

I am going to have a dinner party on Christmas Day, and would like to have all your children come. I want everyone, please, from Sarah Maud to Baby Larry. Mamma says dinner will be at half past five, and the Christmas tree at seven; so you may expect them home at nine o'clock. Wishing you a Merry Christmas and a Happy New Year, I am yours truly,

Carol Bird

Breakfast at the Ruggles' was on the table promptly at seven o'clock, and there was very little of it, too. But it was an excellent day for short rations, though Mrs. Ruggles heaved a sigh as she reflected that the boys, with their Indian-rubber stomachs, would be just fine as hungry the day after as if they had never had gone to a dinner party at all.

As soon as the scanty meal was over, she announced the plan of action: "Now Susan, you and Kitty wash up the dishes, so I can get to cutting Larry's new suit! I'm not satisfied with his clothes, and I thought in the night of a way to make him a dress out of my old red plaid shawl—kind of Scotch style, you know, with the fringe at the bottom.

"Eily, you go find the comb and take the snarls out of the fringe. You little boys clear out from under foot! Clem, you and Con hop into bed with Larry while I wash your underclothes; 't won't take long to dry 'em—Yes, I know it's bothersome, but you can't go into society without taking some trouble, and anyhow I couldn't get round to 'em last night—Sarah Maud, I think 't would be perfectly handsome if you ripped them brass buttons off your uncle's policeman's coat and sewed 'em in a row up the front of your green skirt. Susan, you must iron out your and Kitty's aprons; and there, I come mighty near forgetting Peory's stockings! I counted the whole lot last night when I was washing 'em, and there ain't but nineteen anyhow you fix 'em, and no nine pairs mates nohow; and I'm not going to have my children wear odd stockings to a company dinner fetched up as I was!—Eily, you run out and ask Mrs. Cullen to lend me a pair of stockings for Peory, and tell her if she will, Peory'll give Jim half her candy when she gets home. Won't you, Peory?"

Peoria set up a deafening howl at the idea of this projected bargain—a howl so rebellious that her mother started in her direction with flashing eye and uplifted hand; but Mrs. Ruggles let it fall suddenly, saying, "No, I vow I won't hit you Christmas Day, if you drive me crazy. But speak up smart, now, and say whether you'd rather give Jim Cullen half your candy or go bare-legged to the party?"

The matter being put so plainly, Peoria still sniffling, dried her tears, and chose the lesser evil, Clem having hastened the decision by an affectionate wink, that meant he'd go halves with her on his candy.

"That's a lady!" cried her mother. "Now, you want ones that aren't doing anything, play all you want to before noontime, and after you get through eating at twelve o'clock me and Sarah Maud's going to give you sech a washing and combing and dressing as you never had before and never will again likely, and then I'm going to set you down and give you two solid hour's training in manners; and 't won't be no fooling neither."

"All we've got to do's go eat!" grumbled Peter.

"Well, that's enough," responded his mother, "there's more'n one way of eating, let me tell you, and you've got a heap to learn about it, Peter Ruggles. Land sakes, I wish you children could see the way I was fetched up to eat. I never took a meal in the kitchen before I married Ruggles; but you can't keep up that style with nine young ones'n' your Pa always off to sea."

The big Ruggleses worked so well, and the little Ruggleses kept from "under foot" so successfully, that by one o'clock nine outfits were carefully laid out on the beds.

"Now, Sarah Maud," said Mrs. Ruggles, her face shining with excitement, "we can begin. I've got a boiler and a kettle and a pot of hot water. Peter, you go into the back bedroom, and I'll take Susan, Kitty, Peory, and Cornelius; and Sarah Maud, you take Clem and Eily and Larry, one at a time. Scrub 'em and rinse 'em, or at any rate get as far as you can with 'em, and then I'll finish 'em while you do yourself."

Sarah Maud couldn't have scrubbed with any more decision and force if she had been doing floors, and the little Ruggleses bore it bravely, not from natural heroism, but for the joy that was set before them. And when the clock struck four they were all clothed, and most of them in their right minds, ready for those last touches that always take the most time.

Kitty's red hair was curled in thirty-four ringlets, Sarah Maud's was braided in one pig-tail, and Susan's, Eily's, and Peroia's, in two braids apiece. Then, exciting moment, came linen collars for some and neckties and bows for others—a magnificent green glass pin was sewed into Peter's purple necktie—and Eureka! the Ruggleses were dressed.

A row of seats was then formed directly through the middle of the kitchen. There were not quite chairs enough for ten, since the family had rarely wanted to sit down all at once, somebody's always being out, or in bed, but the wood-box and the coal-hod finished out the line nicely. The children took their places according to age, Sarah Maud at the head and Larry on a board laid across the coal-hod, and Mrs. Ruggles seated herself in front, surveying them proudly as she wiped the sweat of honest toil from her brow.

"Well," she exclaimed, "if I do say so as I shouldn't, I never have seen a cleaner, more stylish mess of children in my life! I do wish Ruggles could look at you for a minute!—Larry Ruggles, how many times have I got to tell you not to keep pulling at your sash? Haven't I told you if it comes untied your top and bottom will part company in the middle, and then where'll you be?—Now look me in the eye, all of you! I've often told you what kind of a family the McGrills were. I've got reason to be proud, goodness knows! Your uncle is on the police force of New York City; you can take up the paper most any day and see his name printed out—James McGrill—and I can't have my children fetched up common, like some folks'; when they go out they've got to have clothes, and learn to act decent! Now I want to see how you're going to behave when you get there tonight. Let's start in at the beginning and act out the whole business. Pile into the bedroom, there, every last one of you and show me how you're going to go into the parlor. This'll be the parlor, and I'll be Mrs. Bird."

The youngsters hustled into the room in high glee, and Mrs. Ruggles drew herself up in the chair with a haughty expression that was not at all like modest Mrs. Bird.

In the small bedroom there was such a clatter that you would have thought a herd of wild cattle had broken loose. The door opened, and they straggled in, all the little ones giggling, with Sarah Maud at the head, looking as if she had been caught in the act of stealing sheep; while Larry, being last in line, seemed to think the door a sort of gate to heaven which would be shut in his face if he didn't get there in time; accordingly he struggled ahead of his elders and disgraced himself by tumbling in head foremost.

Mrs. Ruggles looked severe. "There, I knew you'd do it some such fool way! Now go in there and try it over again, every last one of you, and if Larry can't come in on two legs he can stay home—d' you hear?"

The matter began to assume a graver aspect. The little Ruggleses stopped giggling and backed into the bedroom, issuing presently with lock step, Indian file, a scared and hunted expression on every face.

"No, no, no!" cried Mrs. Ruggles, in despair. "That's worse yet; you look for all the world like a gang of pris'ners! There isn't any style to that. Spread out more, can't you, and act kind of careless like—nobody's goin' ter kill you!" The third time brought deserved success, and the pupils took their seats in the row. "Now, you know," said Mrs. Ruggles impressively, "there aren't enough decent hats to go round, and if there were I don't know as I'd let you wear 'em, for the boys would never think to take 'em off when they got inside—but anyhow, there aren't enough good ones. Now, look me in the eye. You needn't wear any hats, none of you, and when you get into the parlor, and they ask you to lay off your hats, Sarah Maud must speak up and say it was such a pleasant evening and such a short walk that you left your hats at home to save trouble. Now, can you remember?"

All the little Ruggleses shouted, "Yes, ma'am!" in chorus.

"What have you got to do with it?" demanded their mother; "did I tell you to say it? Wasn't I talkin' to Sarah Maud?"

The little Ruggleses hung their heads. "Yes, ma'am," they piped, more feebly.

"Now get up, all of you, and try it. Speak up, Sarah Maud."

Sarah Maud's tongue clove to the roof of her mouth.

"Quick!"

"Ma thought—it was—such a pleasant hat that we'd—we'd better leave our short walk to home," recited Sarah Maud, in an agony of mental effort.

This was too much for the boys. An earthquake of suppressed giggles swept all along the line.

"Oh, whatever shall I do with you?" moaned the unhappy mother; "I s'pose I've got to teach it to you!"—which she did, word for word, until Sarah Maud thought she could stand on her head and say it backward.

"Now Cornelius, what are you going to say to make yourself good company?"

"Me? Dunno!" said Cornelius, turning pale.

"Well, you ain't going to sit there like a bump on a log without saying a word to pay for your vittles, are you? Ask Mrs. Bird how she's feelin' this evening, or if Mr. Bird's having a busy season, or how this kind of weather agrees with him, or somethin' like that—Now we'll make believe we've got to the dinner—that won't be so hard, 'cause you'll have something to do—t's awful bothersome to stand round and act stylish. If they have napkins, Sarah Maud down to Peory may put 'em in their laps, and the rest of you can tuck 'em in your necks. Don't eat with your fingers—don't grab no vittles off one another's plates; don't reach out for nothing, but wait till you're asked, and if you never get asked don't get up and grab it . . . Don't spill nothing on the tablecloth, or like as not Mrs. Bird'll send you away from the table—and I hope she will if you do!

"Now we'll try a few things to see how they'll go! Mr. Clement, do you eat cranberry sauce?"

"Bet your life!" cried Clem, who in the excitement of the moment had not taken in the idea exactly and had mistaken this for an ordinary bosom-of-the-family question.

"Clement McGrill Ruggles, do you mean to tell me that you'd say that at a dinner party? I'll give you one more chance. Mr. Clement, will you take some of the cranberry?"

"Yes, Ma'am, thank you kindly, if you happen to have any handy."

"Very good, indeed! But they won't give you two tries tonight, you just remember that!—Miss Peory, do you speak for white or dark meat?"

"I'm not partic'lar—anything that nobody else wants, will suit me," answered Peory with her best air.

"First rate! Nobody could speak more genteel than that. Miss Kitty, will you have hard or soft sauce with your pudding?"

"Hard or soft? Oh! A little of both, if you please, and I'm much obliged," said Kitty, bowing with decided ease and grace; at which all the other Ruggleses pointed the finger of shame at her, and Peter grunted expressively, that their meaning might not be mistaken.

"You just stop your grunting, Peter Ruggles; that wasn't greedy, that was all right. I wish I could get it into your heads that it ain't so much what you say, as the way you say it. Eily, you and Larry are too little to train, so you just look at the rest, and do's they do, and the Lord have mercy on you and help you to act decent! Now, is there anything more you'd like to practice?"

"If you tell me one more thing, I can't set up and eat," said Peter, gloomily; "I'm so cram full of manners now I'm ready to bust, without no dinner at all."

"Me too," chimed in Cornelius.

"Well, I'm sorry for you both," rejoined Mrs. Ruggles, sarcastically; "if the amount of manners you've got on hand now troubles you, you're dreadful easy hurt! Now, Sarah Maud, after dinner, you must get up and say, 'I guess we'd better be going'; and if they say, 'Oh, no, sit a while longer,' you can sit; but if they don't say anything, you've got to get up and go . . . Now have you got that into your head?"

"Well," answered Sarah Maud, mournfully, "seems as if this whole dinner party set right square on top of me! Maybe I could manage my own manners, but to manage nine mannerses is worse'n staying to home!"

"Oh, don't fret," said her mother, good-naturedly, "I guess you'll get along. I wouldn't mind if folks would only say, 'Oh, children will be children'; but they won't. They'll say, 'Land o' goodness, who fetched them children up?' Now it's quarter past five, and you can go now. Remember about the hats, don't all talk ter once, and Susan, lend your handkerchief to Peory. Peter, don't keep wiggling yer tiepin. Cornelius, hold your head up straight—Sarah Maud, don't take your eyes off Larry, and Larry you keep hold of Sarah Maud and do just as she says—and whatever you do, all of you never forget for one second that your mother was a McGrill."

The children went out of the back door quietly, and were presently lost to sight, Sarah Maud slipping and stumbling along absent-mindedly, as she recited rapidly under her breath, "Itwassuchapleasantevenin'n'suchasshortwalk, thatwethoughtwe'dleaveourhatstohome."

Peter rang the doorbell, and presently a servant admitted them, and, whispering something in Sarah's ear, drew her downstairs into the kitchen. The other Ruggleses stood in horror-stricken groups as the door closed behind their commanding officer; but there was no time for reflection, for a voice from above was heard, saying, "Come right upstairs, please!"

Accordingly they walked upstairs, and Elfrida, the nurse, ushered them into a room more splendid than anything they had ever seen. But, oh woe! Where was Sarah Maud? And was it Fate that Mrs. Bird should say, at once, "Did you lay your hats in the hall?" Peter felt himself elected by circumstance the head of the family, and, casting one imploring look at tongue-tied Susan, standing next to him, said huskily, "It was so very pleasant—that—that—" "That we hadn't good hats enough to go round," put in little Susan bravely, to help him out, and then froze with horror that the ill-fated words had slipped off her tongue.

However, Mrs. Bird said, pleasantly, "Of course you wouldn't wear hats such a short distance—I forgot when I asked. Now will you come right in to Miss Carol's room? She is so anxious to see you."

Just then Sarah Maud came up the backstairs, so radiant with joy from her secret interview with a clear conscience, and Carol gave them a joyful welcome. "But where is Baby Larry?" she cried. "Didn't he come?"

"Larry! Larry!" Good gracious, where was Larry? They were all sure that he had come in with them, for Susan said she remembered scolding him for tripping over the doormat. Uncle Jack laughed. "Are you sure there were nine of you?" he asked, jokingly.

"I think so, sir," said Peoria, timidly, "but anyhow, there was Larry," and she showed signs of weeping.

"Oh, well, cheer up!" cried Uncle Jack. "I guess he's not lost—only mislaid. I'll go and find him before you can say Jack Robinson."

"I'll go, too, if you please sir," said Sarah Maud, "for it was my place to mind him, an' if he's lost I can't relish my vittles!"

The other Ruggleses stood rooted to the floor. If this was a dinner party, why were such things ever spoken of as festive occasions?

Sarah Maud went out through the hall, calling, "Larry! Larry!" and without any interval of suspense a little voice piped up from below, "Here I be!"

The truth was that Larry, being deserted by his natural guardian, dropped behind the rest, and wriggled into the hat tree to wait for her, having no notion of walking unprotected into the jaws of a dinner party. Finding that she did not come, he tried to crawl from his refuge and call somebody, when—dark and dreadful ending to a tragic day—he found that he was too much intertwined with umbrellas and canes to move a single step. He was afraid to yell, but the sound of Sarah Maud's familiar voice, some seconds later, carried him upstairs, and soon had him in breathless fits of laughter, while Carol so made the other Ruggleses forget themselves that they were presently talking like accomplished diners-out.

Carol's bed had been moved into the farthest corner of the room, and she was propped up on it, dressed in a wonderful soft white robe. Her golden hair fell in fluffy curls over her white forehead and neck, her cheeks flushed delicately, her eyes beamed with joy, and the children told their mother afterward that she looked as beautiful as the angels in the picture books.

There was a great bustle behind a huge screen in another part of the room, and at half past five this was taken away, and the Christmas dinner table stood revealed. What a wonderful sight it was to the poor little Ruggles children. It blazed with tall, colored candles, it gleamed with glass and silver, it blushed with flowers, it groaned with good things to eat; so it was not strange that the Ruggleses, forgetting that their mother was a McGrill, shrieked in admiration of the fairy spectacle. But Larry's behavior was the most disgraceful, for he went at once to a high chair, climbed up like a squirrel, gave a look at the turkey, clapped his hands in ecstasy, rested his fat arms on the table, and cried with joy, "I beat the hull lot o' yer!" Carol laughed until she cried, giving orders, meanwhile—"Uncle Jack, please sit at the head, Sarah Maud at the foot, and that will leave four on each side; Mamma is going to help Elfrida, so that the children need not look after each other, but just have a good time."

A sprig of holly lay by each plate, and nothing would do but each little Ruggles must leave his seat and have it pinned on by Carol, and as each course was served, one of them pleaded to take something to her. There was hurrying to and fro, I can assure you, for it is quite a difficult matter to serve a Christmas dinner on the third floor of a great city house; but if it had been necessary to carry every dish up a rope ladder the servants would gladly have done so—both for Carol's sake, and the joy and gusto with which the Ruggles children ate up the food. There were turkey and chicken, with delicious gravy and stuffing, and there were half a dozen vegetables, with cranberry jelly, and celery, and pickles; and as for the elegant way these delicacies were served, the Ruggleses never forgot it as long as they lived.

Peter nudged Kitty, who sat next to him, and said, "Look, every feller's got his own partic'lar butter; I s'pose that's to show you can eat that and no more. No, it ain't either, for that pig of a Peory's just gettin' another helping!"

"Yes," whispered Kitty, "and the napkins are marked with big red letters! I wonder if that's so nobody'll nip 'em; an' oh, Peter, look at the pictures sticking right on the dishes! Did you ever?"

"The plums is all took out o'my cramb'ry sauce an' it's friz to a stuff jell" whispered Peoria, in wild excitement.

"Hi-yah! I got a wishbone!" sang Larry, regardless of Sarah Maud's frown. She asked to have his seat changed, giving as excuse that he generally sat beside her, and would "feel strange"; the true reason was that she desired to kick him gently, under the table, whenever he passed beyond what might be termed "the McGrill line."

"I declare to goodness," murmured Susan, on the other side, "there's so much to look at I can't scarcely eat anything!"

"Bet your life I can!" said Peter, who had kept one servant busily employed ever since he sat down; for, luckily, no one was asked by Uncle Jack whether he would have a second helping, but the dishes were quietly passed under their noses, and not a single Ruggles refused anything that was offered.

Then, when Carol and Uncle Jack perceived that more turkey was a physical impossibility, the dessert was brought in—a dessert that would have frightened a strong man after such a dinner as had preceded it! Not so the Ruggleses!

There were plum-pudding, mince pie, and ice cream; and there were nuts, and raisins, and oranges. Kitty chose ice cream, explaining that she knew it "by sight, though she hadn't never tasted any"; but all the rest took the entire variety, without any regard to consequences.

"My dear child," whispered Uncle Jack, as he took Carol an orange, "there is no doubt about the necessity of this feast, but I do advise you after this to have them twice a year, or quarterly perhaps, for the way these children eat is positively dangerous; I assure you I tremble for that terrible Peoria. I'm going to run races with her after dinner."

"Never mind," laughed Carol; "let them have enough for once; it does my heart good to see them, and they shall come oftener next year."

The feast being over, the Ruggleses lay back in their chairs languidly, like little gorged boa constrictors, and the table was cleared in a trice. Then a door was opened into the next room, and there, in a corner facing Carol's bed, which had been wheeled as close as possible, stood the brilliantly lighted Christmas tree, glittering with gilded walnuts and tiny silver balloons, and wreathed with snowy chains of popcorn. The presents had been bought mostly with Carol's story-money, and were selected after long consultations with Mrs. Bird. Each girl had a blue knitted hood and each boy a red crocheted comforter, all made by Mamma, Carol, and Elfrida. Then every girl had a pretty plaid dress of a different color, and every boy a warm coat of the right size.

Here the useful presents stopped, and they were quite enough; but Carol had pleaded to give them something "for fun." "I know they need the clothes," she had said, when they were talking over the matter just after Thanksgiving, "but they don't care much for them, after all. Now, Papa, won't you please give me the money you would spend on presents for me, so that I can buy presents for the Ruggleses?"

"You can have both," said Mr. Bird, promptly; "is there any need of my little girl's going without her own Christmas, I should like to know? Spend all the money you like."

"But that isn't the thing," objected Carol, nestling to her father. "The presents wouldn't really be from me, then, and haven't I almost everything already? I'm the happiest girl in the world this year, with Uncle Jack and Donald at home. Why won't you let me do it? You never look half as happy when you are getting your presents as when you are giving us ours. Now, Papa, submit, or I shall have to be very firm and disagreeable with you!"

"Very well, your Highness, I surrender. But a bronze figure of Santa Claus, and in the little round belly that shakes when he laughs like a bowl of jelly, is a wonderful clock—oh, you would never give it up if you could see it!"

"Nonsense," laughed Carol. "As I never have to get up to breakfast, nor go to bed, nor catch trains, I think my old clock will do very well! Now, Mamma, what were you going to give me?"

"Oh, I hadn't decided. A few more books, and a gold thimble, and a smelling bottle, and a music box, perhaps."

"Poor Carol," laughed the child, merrily, "she can afford to give up these lovely things, for there will still be left Uncle Jack, and Donald, and Paul, and Hugh, and Uncle Bob, and Aunt Elsie, and a dozen other people to fill her Christmas stocking!"

So Carol had her way, as she generally did, and Sarah Maud had a set of Louisa May Alcott's books, and Peter a modest silver watch, Cornelius a tool chest, Clement a dog house for his lame puppy, Larry a magnificent Noah's ark, and each of the younger girls a beautiful doll.

You can well believe that everybody was very merry! All the family, from Mr. Bird down to the cook, said that they had never seen so much happiness in the space of three hours! But it had to end, as all things do. The candles flickered and went out, the tree was left alone with its gilded ornaments. Mrs. Bird had Elfrida led the children downstairs at half past eight, thinking Carol looked tired.

"Now, my darling, you have done quite enough for one day," said Mrs. Bird, getting Carol into her nightgown. "If you were to feel worse tomorrow that would be a sad ending to such a charming evening."

"Oh, wasn't it a lovely, lovely time?" sighed Carol. "From first to last, everything was just right. I shall never forget Larry's face when he looked at the turkey; nor Peter's when he saw his watch; nor that sweet, sweet Kitty's smile when she kissed her dolly; nor the tears in poor, Sarah Maud's eyes when she thanked me for her books; nor—"

"But we mustn't talk any longer about it tonight," said Mrs. Bird, anxiously. "You are too tired, dear."

"I am not so very tired, Mamma. I have felt well all day; not a bit of pain anywhere. Perhaps this has done me good."

"Perhaps," Mrs. Bird smiled. "It was a merry time. Now, may I close the door and leave you alone, dear? Papa and I will steal in softly by and by to see if you are all right; but I think you need to be very quiet."

"Oh, I'm willing to stay alone; but I am not sleepy yet, and I am going to hear the music, you know."

"Yes, I have opened the window a little, and put the screen in front of it, so that you won't feel the draft."

"Can I have the shutters open? And won't you turn my bed a little, please? This morning I woke ever so early, and one bright, beautiful star shone in that eastern window. I never noticed it before, and I thought of the Star in the East, that guided the wise men to the place where the baby Jesus was. Good night, Mamma. Such a happy, happy day!"

"Good-night, my precious Christmas Carol—mother's blessed Christmas child."

"Bend your head a minute, mother dear," whispered Carol, calling her mother back. "Mamma, dear, I do think that we have kept Christ's birthday this time just as He would like it. Don't you?"

"I am sure of it," said Mrs. Bird, softly. The Ruggleses had finished a last romp in the library with Paul and Hugh, and Uncle Jack had taken them home and stayed awhile to chat with Mrs. Ruggles, who opened the door for them, her face all aglow with excitement and delight. When Kitty and Clem showed her the oranges and nuts that they had kept for her, she astonished them by saying that at six o'clock Mrs. Bird had sent her in the finest dinner she had ever seen in her life; and not only that, but a piece of dress-goods that must have cost a dollar a yard if it cost a cent.

As Uncle Jack went down the rickety steps he looked back into the window for a last glimpse of the family, as the children gathered about their mother, showing their beautiful presents again and again—and then upward to a window in the great house yonder. "A little child shall lead them," he thought. "Well, if—if anything ever happens to Carol, I will take the Ruggleses under my wing."

"Softly, Uncle Jack," whispered the boys, as he walked into the library a while later. "We are listening to the music in the church. The choir has sung 'Carol, Brothers, Carol,' and now we think the organist is beginning to play 'My Own Country' for Carol."

"I hope she hears it," said Mrs. Bird; "But they are very late tonight, and I dare not speak to her lest she should be asleep. It is almost ten o'clock."

The boy soprano, clad in white surplice, stood in the organ loft. The light shone full upon his crown of fair hair, and his pale face, with its serious blue eyes, looked paler than usual. Perhaps it was something in the tender thrill of the voice, or in the sweet words, but there were tears in many eyes, both in the church and in the great house next door.

"I am far from my home,
I am weary after a while
For the longed-for home-bringin',
An' my Father's welcome smiles;
An' I'll ne'er be full content,
Until my eyes do see
The golden gates o' heaven
In my own country.

"Like a bear to its mother,
A wee birdie to its nest,
I want to be held now,
Unto my Father's breast;
For He gathers in His arms
Helpless, worthless lambs like me,
An' carries them Himself
To His own country."

There were tears in many eyes, but not in Carol's. The loving heart had quietly ceased to beat, and the "wee birdie" in the great house had flown to its "home nest."

So sad an ending to a happy day! Perhaps—to those who were left; and yet Carol's mother even in the freshness of her grief, was glad that her darling had slipped away on the loveliest day of her life, out of its glad content, into everlasting peace.

The Thieves Who Couldn't Help Sneezing

Thomas Hardy

Many years ago, when oak trees now past their prime were about as large as an elderly gentleman's walking stick, there lived in Wessex a yeoman's son, whose name was Hubert. He was about fourteen years of age, and was as remarkable for his candor and lightness of heart as for his physical courage, of which he was a little vain.

One cold Christmas Eve his father sent him on an important errand to a small town several miles from home. He traveled on horseback, and was detained by the business till a late hour of the evening. At last, however, it was completed; he returned to the inn, the horse was saddled, and he started on his way. His journey homeward lay through the Vale of Blackmore, a fertile but somewhat lonely district, with heavy clay roads and crooked lanes. In those days, too, a great part of it was thickly wooded.

It must have been about nine o'clock when, riding along amid the overhanging trees upon his stout-legged nag, Jerry, and singing a Christmas carol at the top of his lungs, Hubert fancied that he heard a strange noise among the boughs. This brought to his mind that the spot he was traversing bore an evil name. Men had been waylaid there. He looked at Jerry, and wished the horse had been of any other color than light gray; for the docile animal's form was visible even here in the dense shade. "What do I care?" he said aloud, after a few minutes of reflection. "Jerry's legs are too nimble to allow any highwayman to come near me."

"Ha! ha! Indeed," was said in a deep voice; and the next moment a man darted from the thicket on his right hand, another man from the thicket on his left hand, and another from a tree trunk a few yards ahead. Hubert's bridle was seized, he was pulled from his horse, and although he struck out with all his might, as a brave boy would naturally do, he was overpowered. His arms were tied behind him, his legs bound tightly together, and he was thrown into the ditch. The robbers, whose faces he could now dimly perceive to be artificially blackened, at once departed, leading off the horse.

As soon as Hubert had a little recovered himself, he found that by great exertion he was able to extricate his legs from the cord; but, in spite of every endeavor, his arms remained bound as fast as before. All, therefore, that he could do was to rise to his feet and proceed on his way with his arms behind him, and trust to chance for getting them unfastened. He knew that it would be impossible to reach home on foot that night, and in such a condition; but he walked on. Owing to the confusion which this attack caused in his brain, he lost his way, and would have been inclined to lie down and rest till morning among the dead leaves had he not known the danger of sleeping without covers in a frost so severe. So he wandered further onwards, his arms aching for the loss of poor Jerry, who never had been known to kick, or bite, or show a single vicious habit. He was not a little glad when he discerned through the trees a distant light. Towards this he made his way, and presently found himself in front of a large mansion with flaking wings, gables, and towers, the battlements and chimneys showing their shape against the stars.

All was silent; but the door stood wide open, it being from the door that the light shone which had attracted him. On entering he found himself in a vast apartment arranged as a dining-hall, and brilliantly illuminated. The walls were covered with a great deal of dark paneling, formed into molded panels, carvings, closet doors, and the usual fittings of a house of that kind. But what drew his attention most was the large table in the midst of the hall, upon which was spread a sumptuous supper, as yet untouched. Chairs were placed around, and it appeared as if something had occurred to interrupt the meal just at the time when all were ready to begin.

Even had Hubert been so inclined, he could not have eaten in his helpless state, unless by dipping his mouth into the dishes, like a pig or cow. He wished first to obtain assistance; and was about to penetrate further into the house for that purpose when he heard hasty footsteps in the porch and the words, "Be quick!" uttered in the deep voice which he heard when he was dragged from the horse. There was only just time for him to dart under the table before three men entered the dining hall. Peeping from beneath the hanging edges of the table-cloth, he perceived that their faces, too, were blackened, which at once removed any remaining doubts he may have felt that these were the same thieves.

"No, then," said the first—the man with the deep voice—"Let us hide ourselves. They will be back again in a minute. That was a good trick to get them out of the house—eh?"

"Yes. You well imitated the cries of a man in distress," said the second.

"Excellently," said the third.

"But they will soon find out that it was a false alarm. Come, where shall we hide? It must be some place we can stay in for two or three hours, till all are in bed and asleep. Ah! I have it. Come this way! I have learnt that the further closet is not opened once in a twelve-month; it will serve our purpose exactly."

The speaker advanced into the corridor which led from the hall. Creeping a little further forward. Hubert could discern that the closet stood at the end, facing the dining-hall. The thieves entered it, and closed the door. Hardly breathing, Hubert glided forward, to learn a little more of the intention, if possible; and coming close, he could hear the robbers whispering about the different rooms where the jewels, silver plates, and other valuables of the house were kept, which they plainly meant to steal.

They had not been long in hiding when a gay chattering of ladies and gentlemen was audible outside on the terrace. Hubert felt that it would not do to be caught prowling about the house, unless he wished to be taken for a robber himself; and he slipped softly back to the hall, out at the door, and stood in a dark corner of the porch, where he could see everything without being seen himself. In a moment or two a whole troop of people came gliding past him and into the house. There were an elderly gentleman and a lady, eight or nine young ladies, as many young men, besides half-a-dozen men-servants and maids. The mansion had apparently been quite emptied of its occupants.

"Now, children and young people, we will resume our meal," said the old gentleman. "What the noise could have been I cannot understand. I never felt so certain in my life that there was a person being murdered outside my door."

The ladies began saying how frightened they had been, and how they had expected an adventure, and how it had ended in nothing after all.

"Wait a while," Hubert said to himself. "You'll have adventure enough by-an-by, ladies."

It appeared that the young men and women were married sons and daughters of the old couple, who had come that day to spend Christmas with their parents.

The door was then closed, Hubert being left outside on the porch. He thought this a proper moment for asking their assistance; and, since he was unable to knock with is hands, began boldly to kick the door.

"Hullo! What disturbance are you making here?" said a footman who opened it; and seizing Hubert by the shoulder, he pulled him into the dining-hall. "Here's a strange boy I have found making a noise in the porch, Sir Simon."

Everybody turned.

"Bring him forward," said Sir Simon, the old gentleman before mentioned. "What were doing there my boy?"

"Why his arms are tied!" said one of the ladies.

"Poor fellow!" said another.

Hubert at once began to explain that he had been waylaid on his journey home, robbed of his horse, and mercilessly left in this condition by the thieves.

"Only to think of it!" exclaimed Sir Simon.

"That's a likely story," said one of the gentlemen guests, incredulously.

"Doubtful, hey?" asked Sir Simon.

"Perhaps he's a robber himself," suggested a lady.

"There is a curiously wild wicked look about him, certainly, now that I examine him closely," said the old mother.

Hubert blushed with shame; and instead of continuing his story, and relating that robbers were concealed in the house, he doggedly held his tongue, and half resolved to let them find out their danger of themselves.

"Well, untie him," said Sir Simon. "Come, since it is Christmas Eve, we'll treat him well. Here, my lad; sit down in that empty seat at the bottom of the table, and make as good a meal as you can. When you have had your fill we will listen to more particulars of your story."

The feast then proceeded; and Hubert, now at liberty, was not at all sorry to join in. The more they ate and drank the merrier did the company become. All went as noisily and as happily as a Christmas gathering in old times possibly could do.

Hubert, in spite of his hurt feelings at their doubts of his honesty, could not help but being warmed both in mind by the good cheer, the scene and the example of hilarity set by his neighbors. At last he laughed as heartily at their stories and repartees as the Baronet, Sir Simon, himself. When the meal was almost over one of the sons said to Hubert, "Well, my boy, how are you? Can you take a pinch of snuff?" He held out one of the snuff boxes which were becoming common among young and old throughout the country.

"Thank you," said Hubert, accepting a pinch.

"Tell the ladies who you are, what you are made of, and what you can do," the young man continued, slapping Hubert upon the back.

"Certainly," said our hero, drawing himself up, and thinking it best to put a bold face on the matter. "I am a travelling magician."

"Indeed!"

"What shall we hear next?"

"I can conjure up a tempest in a cupboard," Hubert replied.

"Ha-ha!" said the old Baronet, pleasantly rubbing his hands. "We must see this performance. Girls, don't go away: here's something to be seen."

"Not dangerous, I hope?" said the old lady.

Hubert rose from the table. "Hand me your snuff box, please," he said to the young man who had offered it to him. "And now," he continued, "without the least noise, follow me. If any of you speak the spell will be broken."

They promised obedience. He entered the corridor, and, taking off his shoes, went on tiptoe to the closet door. The guests advanced in a silent group at a little distance behind him. Hubert next placed a stool in front of the door, and, by standing upon it was tall enough to reach the top. He then, just as noiselessly, poured all the snuff from the box along the upper edge of the door, and, with a few short puffs of breath, blew the snuff through the open space above the door into the interior of the closet. He held his finger to his lips to the assembly, warning them to be silent.

"Dear me, what's that?" said the old lady, after a minute or two had elapsed.

A suppressed sneeze had come from inside the closet.

Hubert pressed his finger against his lips again.

"How very singular," whispered Sir Simon, "This is most interesting."

Hubert took advantage of the moment to gently slide the bolt of the closet door into place. "More snuff," he said, calmly.

"More snuff," said Sir Simon. Two or three gentlemen passed their boxes, not quite so well suppressed as the first was heard: then another, which seemed to say that it would not be suppressed under any circumstance whatever. At length there arose a perfect storm of sneezes.

"Excellent, excellent conjuring for one so young!" said Sir Simon. "I am much interested in this trick of throwing the voice—called ventriloquism, I believe."

"More snuff," said Hubert.

"More snuff," said Sir Simon. Sir Simon's man brought a large jar of the best scented.

Hubert once more charged the upper crack of the closet, and blew the snuff unto the interior, as before. Again he charged the closet, emptying the whole contents of the jar. The tumult of sneezes became really extraordinary to hear—there was no stopping them. It was like wind, rain, and sea battling in a hurricane.

"I believe there are men inside, and that it is no trick at all!" exclaimed Sir Simon, the truth flashing on him.

"There are," said Hubert. "They are come to rob your house this Christmas Eve; and they are the same who stole my horse."

The sneezes changed to spasmodic groans. One of the thieves, hearing Hubert's voice, cried, "Oh! mercy! mercy! let us out of this closet!"

"Where's my horse?" called out Hubert.

"Tied to the tree in the hollow behind Shorts store. Mercy! mercy! let us out, or we shall die of suffocation!"

All the Christmas guests now perceived that this was no longer sport, but serious business. Guns and cudgels were procured; all the men-servants were called in, and arranged in position outside the closet. At a signal Hubert withdrew the bolt, and stood on the defensive. But the three robbers, far from attacking them, were found crouching in the corner, gasping for breath. They made no resistance; and, being pinioned, were placed in an outhouse till the morning.

Hubert now gave the remainder of his story to the assembled company, and was profusely thanked for the services he had rendered. Sir Simon pressed him to stay overnight, and accept the use of the best bedroom the house afforded, which had been occupied by Queen Elizabeth and King Charles successively when on their visits to this part of the country. But Hubert declined, being anxious to find his horse Jerry.

Several of the guests accompanied Hubert to the spot behind the store, alluded to by the thieves, and there the horse stood, uninjured, and quite unconcerned. At sight of Hubert he neighed joyfully; and nothing could exceed Hubert's gladness at finding him. He mounted, wished his friends "Happy Christmas!" and cantered off, reaching home safely about four o'clock in the morning.

A Christmas Dream and How It Came True

Louisa May Alcott

I'm so tired of Christmas I wish there never would be another one!" exclaimed a discontented-looking little girl, as she sat idly watching her mother arrange a pile of gifts two days before they were to be given.

"Why, Effie, what a dreadful thing to say! You are as bold as old Scrooge; and I'm afraid something will happen to you, as it did to him, if you don't care for dear Christmas," answered Mamma, almost dropping the silver horn she was filling with delicious candies."

"Who was Scrooge? What happened to him?" asked Effie, with a glimmer of interest in her listless face, as she picked out the sourest lemon-drop she could find; for nothing sweet suited her just then.

"He was one of Dickens's best people, and you can read the charming story someday. He hated Christmas until a strange dream showed him how dear and beautiful it was, and made a better man of him."

"I shall read it; for I like dreams, and have a great many curious ones myself. But they don't keep me from being tired of Christmas," said Effie, poking discontentedly among the sweeties for something worth eating.

"Why are you tired of what should be the happiest time of the year?" asked Mamma, anxiously.

"Perhaps I shouldn't be if I had something new. But it is always the same, and there isn't any more surprise about it. I always find heaps of goodies in my stocking. Don't like some of them, and soon get tired of those I do like. We always have a great dinner, and I eat too much, and feel ill the next day. Then there is a Christmas tree somewhere, with a doll on top, or a stupid old Santa Claus, and children dancing and screaming over bonbons and toys that break, and shiny things that are of no use. Really, Mamma, I've had so many Christmases all alike that I don't think I can bear another one." And Effie laid herself flat on the sofa, as if the mere idea was too much for her.

Her mother laughed at her despair, but was sorry to see her little girl so discontented, when she had everything to make her happy, and had known but ten Christmas days.

"Suppose we don't give you any presents at all—how would that suit you?" asked Mamma, anxious to please her spoiled child.

"I should like one large and splendid one, and one dear little one, to remember some very nice person by," said Effie, who was a fanciful little body, full of old whims and notions, which her friends loved to gratify, regardless of time, trouble, or money; for she was the last of three little girls, and very dear to all the family.

"Well, my darling, I will see what I can do to please you, and not say a word until all is ready. If I could only get a new idea to start with!" And Mamma went on tying up her pretty bundles with a thoughtful face, while Effie strolled to the window to watch the rain that kept her in-doors and made her dismal.

"Seems to me poor children have better times than rich ones. I can't go out, and there is a girl about my age splashing along, without any maid to fuss about rubbers and cloaks and umbrellas and colds. I wish I was a beggar-girl."

"Would you like to be hungry, cold, and ragged, to beg all day, and sleep on an ash-heap at night?" asked Mamma, wondering what would come next.

"Cinderella did, and had a nice time in the end. This girl out here has a basket of scraps on her arms, and a big old shawl all round her, and doesn't seem to care a bit, though the water runs out of the toes of her boots. She goes paddling along, laughing at the rain, and eating a cold potato as if it tasted nicer than the chicken and ice-cream I had for dinner. Yes, I do think poor children are happier than rich ones."

"So do I, sometimes. At the Orphan Asylum today I saw two dozen merry little souls who have no parents, no home, and no hope of Christmas beyond a stick of candy or a cake. I wish you had been there to see how happy there were, playing with the old toys some richer children had sent them."

"You may give them all mine; I'm so tired of them I never want to see them again," said Effie, turning from the window to the pretty baby-house full of everything a child's heart could desire.

"I will, and let you begin again with something you will not tire of, if I can only find it." And Mamma knit her brows trying to discover some grand surprise for this child who didn't care for Christmas.

Nothing more was said then; and wandering off to the library, Effie found "A Christmas Carol," and, curling herself up in the sofa corner, read it all before tea. Some of it she did not understand; but she laughed and cried over many parts of the charming story, and felt better without knowing why.

All the evening she thought of poor Tiny Tim, Mrs. Cratchit with the pudding, and the stout old gentleman who danced so gayly that "his legs twinkled in the air." Presently bed-time arrived.

"Come now, and toast your feet," said Effie's nurse, "while I do your pretty hair and tell stories."

"I'll have a fairy tale tonight, a very interesting one," commanded Effie, as she put on her blue silk wrapper and little fur-lined slippers to sit before the fire and have her long curls brushed.

So Nursey told her best tales; and when at last the child lay down under her lace curtains, her head was full of a curious jumble of Christmas elves, poor children, snow-storms, sugar-plums, and surprises. So it is no wonder that she dreamed all night; and this was the dream, which she never quite forgot.

She found herself sitting on a stone, in the middle of a great field, all alone. The snow was falling fast, a bitter wind whistled by, and night was coming on. She felt hungry, cold, and tired, and did not know where to go nor what to do.

"I wanted to be a beggar-girl, and now I am one; but I don't like it, and wish somebody would come and take care of me. I don't know who I am, and I think I must be lost," thought Effie, with the curious interest one takes in one's self in dreams.

But the more she thought about it, the more bewildered she felt. Faster fell the snow, colder blew the wind, darker grew the night; and poor Effie made up her mind that she was quite forgotten and left to freeze alone. The tears were chilled on her cheeks, her feet felt like icicles, and her heart died within her, so hungry, frightened, and forlorn was she. Laying her head on her knees, she gave herself up for lost, and sat there with the great flakes turning her to a little white mound, when suddenly the sound of music reached her, and starting up, she looked and listened with all her eyes and ears.

Far away a dim light shone, and a voice was heard singing. She tried to run toward the welcome glimmer, but could not stir, and stood like a small statue of expectation while the light drew nearer, and the sweet words of the song grew clearer.

"From our happy home
Through the world we roam
One week in all the year,
Making winter spring
With the joy we bring
For Christmas-tide is here.

"Now the eastern star
Shines from afar

To light the poorest home;
Hearts warmer grow,
Gifts freely flow,
For Christmas-tide has come.

"Now gay trees rise
Before young eyes,
Abloom with tempting cheer;
Blithe voices sing.
And blithe bells ring,
For Christmas-tide is here.

"Oh, happy chime,
Oh, blessed time,
That draws us all so near!

"Welcome, dear day,"
All creatures say,
"For Christmas-tide is here."

A child's voice sang, a child's hand carried the little candle; and in the circle of soft light it shed, Effie saw a pretty child coming to her through the night and snow. A rosy, smiling creature, wrapped in white fur, with a wreath of green and scarlet holly on its shining hair, the magic candle in one hand, and the other outstretched as if to shower gifts and warmly press all other hands.

Effie forgot to speak as this bright vision came nearer, leaving no trace of footsteps in the snow, only lighting the way with its little candle, and filling the air with the music of its song.

"Dear child, you are lost, and I have come to find you," said the stranger, taking Effie's cold hands in his, with a smile like sunshine, while every holly berry glowed like a little fire.

"Do you know me?" asked Effie, feeling no fear, but a great gladness, at his coming.

"I know all children, and go to find them; for this is my holiday, and I gather them from all parts of the world to be merry with me once a year."

"Are you an angel?" asked Effie, looking for the wings.

"No; I am a Christmas spirit, and live with my mates in a pleasant place, getting ready for our holiday, when we are let out to roam about the world, helping to make this a happy time for all who will let us in. Will you come and see how we work?"

"I will go anywhere with you. Don't leave me again," cried Effie, gladly.

"First I will make you comfortable. That is what we love to do. You are cold; and you shall be warm; hungry, and I will feed you; sorrowful, and I will make you gay."

With a wave of his candle all three miracles were wrought—for the snow flakes turned to a white fur cloak and hood on Effie's head and shoulders; a bowl of hot soup came sailing to her lips, and vanished when she had eagerly drunk the last drop; and suddenly the dismal field changed to a new world so full of wonders that all her troubles were forgotten in a minute.

Bells were ringing so merrily that it was hard to keep from dancing. Green garlands hung on the walls, and every tree was a Christmas tree full of toys, and blazing with candles that never went out.

In one place many little spirits sewed like mad on warm clothes, turning off work faster than any sewing-machine ever invented, and great piles were made ready to be sent to poor people. Other busy creatures packed money into purses, and wrote checks which they sent flying away on the wind—a lovely kind of snow-storm to fall into a world below full of poverty.

Older and graver spirits were looking over piles of little books, in which the records of the past year were kept, telling how different people had sent it, and what sort of gifts they deserved. Some got peace, some disappointment, some remorse and sorrow, some great joy and hope. The rich had generous thoughts sent them; the poor, gratitude and contentment. Children had more love and duty to parents; and parents renewed patience, wisdom, and satisfaction for and in their children. No one was forgotten.

"Please tell me what splendid place this?" asked Effie, as soon as she could collect her wits after the first look at all these astonishing things.

"This is the Christmas world; and here we work all the year round, never tired of getting ready for the happy day. See, these are the saints just setting off, for some have far to go, and the children must not be disappointed."

As he spoke the spirit pointed to four gates, out of which four great sleighs were just driving, laden with toys, while a jolly old Santa Claus sat in the middle of each, drawing on his mittens and tucking up his wraps for a long cold drive.

"Why, I thought there was only one Santa Claus, and even he was a humbug," cried Effie, astonished at the sight.

"Never give up your faith in the sweet old stories, even after you come to see that they are only the pleasant shadow of a lovely truth."

Just then the sleighs went off with a great jingling of bells and pattering of reindeer hoofs, while all the spirits gave a cheer that was heard in the lower world, where people said, "Hear the stars sing."

"I never will say there isn't any Santa Claus again. Now, show me more."

"You will like to see this place, I think, and may learn something here perhaps."

The spirit smiled as he led the way to a little door, through which Effie peeped into the world of dolls. Baby-houses were in full blast, with dolls of all sorts going on like live people. Waxen ladies sat in their parlors elegantly dressed; some dolls cooked in the kitchens; nurses walked out with the bits of dollies; and the streets were full of tin soldiers marching, wooden horses prancing, express wagons rumbling; and little men hurrying to and fro. Shops were there, and tiny people buying legs of mutton, pounds of tea, mites of clothes, and everything dolls use or wear or want.

But presently she saw that in some ways the dolls improved upon the manners and customs of human beings, and she watched eagerly to learn why they did these things. A fine Paris doll driving in her carriage took up another doll who was hobbling along with a basket of clean clothes, and carried her to her journey's end, as if it were the proper thing to do. Another interesting china lady took off her comfortable red cloak and put it round a poor wooden creature done up in a paper shift, and so badly painted that its face would have sent some babies into fits.

"Seems to me I once knew a rich girl who didn't give her things to poor girls. I wish I could remember who she was, and tell her to be as kind as that china doll," said Effie, much touched at the sweet way the pretty creature wrapped up the poor fright, and then ran off in her little gray gown to buy a shiny fowl stuck on a wooden platter for her invalid mother's dinner.

A little bell rang as she looked, and away scampered the children into the red-and-green school-house with the roof that lifted up, so one could see how nicely they sat at their desks with mites of books, or drew on the inch-square blackboards with crumbs of chalk.

"They know their lessons very well, and are as still as mice. We make a great racket at our school, and get bad marks every day. I shall tell the girls they had better mind what they do, or their dolls will be better scholars than they are," said Effie, much impressed, as she peeped in and saw no rod in the hand of the little mistress, who looked up and shook her head at the intruder, as if begging her to go away before the order of the school was disturbed.

Effie retired at once, but could not resist one look in the window of a fine mansion, where the family were at dinner, the children behaved so well at table and never grumbled a bit when their mamma said they could not have any more fruit.

"Now, show me something else," she said, as they came again to the low door that led out of Doll-land.

"You have seen how we prepare for Christmas; let me show you where we love best to send our good and happy gifts," answered the spirit, giving her his hand again.

"I know. I've seen ever so many," began Effie, thinking of her own Christmases.

"No, you have never seen what I will show you. Come away, and remember what you see tonight."

Like a flash that bright world vanished, and Effie found herself in a part of the city she had never seen before. It was far away from the gayer places, where every store was brilliant with lights and full of pretty things, and every house wore a festival air, while people hurried to and fro with merry greetings. It was down among the dingy streets where the poor lived, and where there was no making ready for Christmas.

Hungry women looked in at shabby shops, longing to buy meat and bread, but empty pockets forbad. Tipsy men drank up their wages in the bar-rooms; and in many cold dark chambers little children huddled under the thick blankets, trying to forget their misery in sleep.

No nice dinners filled the air with savory smells, no gay trees dropped toys and bonbons into eager hands, no little stockings hung in rows beside the chimney-piece ready to be filled, no happy sounds of music, gay voices, and dancing feet were heard; and there were no signs of Christmas anywhere.

"Don't they have any in this place?" asked Effie, shivering, as she held fast the spirit's hand, following where he led her.

"We come to bring it. Let me show you our best workers." And the spirit pointed to some sweet-faced men and women who came stealing into the poor houses, working such beautiful miracles that Effie could only stand and watch.

Some slipped money into the empty pockets, and sent the happy mothers to buy all the comforts they needed; others led the drunken men out of temptation and took them home to find safer pleasures there. Fires were kindled on cold hearths, tables spread as if by magic, and warm clothes wrapped round shivering limbs. Flowers suddenly bloomed in the chambers of the sick; old people found themselves remembered; sad hearts were consoled by a tender word, and wicked ones softened by the story of Him who forgave all sin.

But the sweetest work was for the children; and Effie held her breath to watch these human fairies hang up and fill the little stockings without which a child's Christmas is not perfect, putting in things that once she would have thought very humble presents, but which now seemed beautiful and precious because these poor babies had nothing.

"That is so beautiful! I wish I could make merry Christmases as these good people do, and be loved and thanked as they are," said Effie, softly, as she watched the busy men and women do their work and steal away without thinking of any reward but their own satisfaction.

"You can if you will. I have shown you the way. Try it, and see how happy your holiday will be hereafter."

As he spoke, the spirit seemed to put his arms about her, and vanished with a kiss.

"Oh, stay and show me more!" cried Effie, trying to hold him fast.

"Darling, wake up, and tell me why you are smiling in your sleep," said a voice in her ear; and opening her eyes, there was Mamma bending over her, and morning sunshine streaming into the room.

"Are they all gone? Did you hear the bells? Wasn't it splendid?" she asked, rubbing her eyes, and looking about her for the pretty child who was so real and sweet.

"You have been dreaming at a great rate—talking in your sleep, laughing, and clapping your hands as if you were cheering someone. Tell me what was so splendid," said Mamma, smoothing the tumbled hair and lifting up the sleepy head.

Then, while she was being dressed, Effie told her dream, and Nursey thought it very wonderful; but Mamma smiled to see how curiously things the child had thought, read, heard, and seen through the day were mixed up in her sleep.

"The spirit said I could work lovely miracles if I tried; but I don't know how to begin, for I have no magic candle to make feasts appear, and light up groves of Christmas trees, as he did," said Effie, sorrowfully.

"Yes you have. We will do it! And clapping her hands, Mamma suddenly began to dance all over the room as if she had lost her wits.

"How? How? You must tell me, Mamma," cried Effie, dancing after her, and ready to believe anything possible when she remembered the adventures of the past night.

"I've got it! I've got it!—the new idea. A splendid one, if I can only carry it out!" And Mamma waltzed the little girl round till her curls flew wildly in the air, while Nursey laughed as if she would die.

"Tell me! Tell me!" shrieked Effie.

"No, no; it is a surprise—a grand surprise for Christmas day!" sung Mamma, evidently charmed with her happy thought. "Now, come to breakfast; for we must work like bees if we want to play spirits tomorrow. You and Nursey will go out shopping, and get heaps of things, while I arrange matters behind the scenes."

They were running downstairs as Mamma spoke, and Effie called out breathlessly—

"It won't be a surprise; for I know you are going to ask some poor children here, and have a tree or something. It won't be like my dream; for they had ever so many trees, and more children than we can find anywhere."

"There will be no tree, no party, no dinner, in this house at all, and no presents for you. Won't that be a surprise?" And Mamma laughed at Effie's bewildered face.

"Do it. I shall like it, I think; and I won't ask any questions, so it will all burst upon me when the time comes," she said; and she ate her breakfast thoughtfully, for this really would be a new sort of Christmas.

All that morning Effie trotted after Nursey in and out of shops, buying dozens of barking dogs, woolly lambs, and squeaking birds; tiny tea-sets, gay picture-books, mittens and hoods, dolls and candy. Parcel after parcel was sent home; but when Effie returned she saw no trace of them, though she peeped everywhere. Nursey chuckled, but wouldn't give a hint, and went out again in the afternoon with a long list of more things to buy; while Effie wandered forlornly about the house, missing the usual merry stir that went before Christmas dinner and the evening of fun.

As for Mamma, she was quite invisible all day, and came in at night so tired that she could only lie on the sofa to rest, smiling as if some very pleasant thought made her happy in spite of weariness.

"Is the surprise going on all right?" asked Effie, anxiously; for it seemed an immense time to wait till another evening came.

"Beautifully! Better than I expected; for several of my good friends are helping, or I couldn't have done as I wish. I know you will like it, dear, and long remember this new way of making Christmas merry."

Mamma gave her a very tender kiss, and Effie went to bed.

The next day was a very strange one; for when she woke there was no stocking to examine, no pile of gifts under her napkin, no one said, "Merry Christmas!" to her, and the dinner was just as usual to her. Mamma vanished again, and Nursey kept wiping her eyes and saying: "The dear things! It's the prettiest idea I ever heard of. No one but your blessed ma could have done it."

"Do stop, Nursey, or I shall go crazy because I don't know the secret!" cried Effie, more than once; and she kept her eye on the clock, for at seven in the evening the surprise was to come off.

The longed-for hour arrived at last, and the child was too excited to ask questions when Nursey put on her cloak and hood, led her to the carriage, and they drove away, leaving their house the one dark and silent one in the row.

"I feel like the girls in the fairy tales who are led off to strange places and see fine things," said Effie, in whisper, as they jingled through the gay streets.

"Ah, my deary, it is like a fairy tale, I do assure you, and you will see finer things than most children will tonight. Steady, now, and do just as I tell you, and don't say one word whatever you see," answered Nursey, quite quivering with excitement as she patted a large box in her lap, and nodded and laughed with twinkling eyes.

They drove into a dark yard, and Effie was led through a back door to a little room, where Nursey coolly proceeded to take off not only Effie's cloak and hood but her dress and shoes also. Effie stared and bit her lips, but kept still until out of the box came a little white fur coat and boots, a wreath of holly leaves and berries, and a candle with a frill of gold paper round it. A long "Oh!" escaped her then; and when she was dressed and saw herself in the glass, she started back, exclaiming, "Why, Nursey, I look like the spirit in my dream!"

"So you do; and that's the part you are to play, my pretty! Now whist, while I blind your eyes and put you in your place."

"Shall I be afraid?" whispered Effie, full of wonder; for as they went out she heard the sound of many voices, the tramp of many feet, and, in spite of the bandage, was sure a great light shone upon her when she stopped.

"You needn't be; I shall stand close by, and your ma will be here."

After the handkerchief was tied about her eyes, Nursey led Effie up some steps, and placed her on a high platform, where something like leaves touched her head, and the soft snap of lamps seemed to fill the air.

Music began as soon as Nursey clapped her hands, the voices outside sounded nearer, and the tramp was evidently coming up the stairs.

"Now, my precious, look and see how you and your dear ma have made a merry Christmas for them that needed it!"

Off went the bandage; and for a minute Effie really did think she was asleep again, for she actually stood in "a grove of Christmas trees," all gay and shining as in her vision. Twelve on a side, in two rows down the room, stood the little pines, each on its low table; and behind Effie a taller one rose to the roof, hung with wreaths of popcorn, apples, oranges, horns of candy, and cakes of all sorts, from sugary hearts to gingerbread Jumbos. On the smaller trees she saw many of her own discarded toys and those Nursey bought, as well as heaps that seemed to have rained down straight from that delightful Christmas country where she felt as if she was again.

"How splendid! Who is it for? What is that noise? Where is Mamma?" cried Effie, pale with pleasure and surprise, as she stood looking down the brilliant little street from her high place.

Before Nursey could answer, the doors at the lower end flew open, and in marched twenty-four little blue-gowned orphan girls, singing sweetly, until amazement changed the song to cries of joy and wonder as the shining spectacle appeared. While they stood staring with round eyes at the wilderness of pretty things about them, Mamma stepped up beside Effie, and holding her hand fast to give her courage, told the story of the dream in a few simple words, ending in this way:

"So my little girl wanted to be a Christmas spirit too, and make this a happy day for those who had not as many pleasures and comforts as she has. She likes surprises, and we planned this for you all. She shall play the good fairy, and give each of you something from this tree, after which everyone will find her own name on a small tree, and can go to enjoy it in her own way. March by, my dears, and let us fill your hands."

Nobody told them to do it, but all the hands were clapped heartily before a single child stirred; then one by one they came to look up wonderingly at the pretty giver of the feast as she leaned down to offer them great yellow oranges, red apples, bunches of grapes, bonbons, and cakes, till all were gone, and a double row of smiling faces turned toward her as the children filed back to their places in the orderly way they had been taught.

Then each was led to her own tree by the good ladies who had helped Mamma with all their hearts; and the happy hubbub that arose would have satisfied even Santa Claus himself—shrieks of joy, dances of delight, laughter and tears (for some tender little things could not bear so much pleasure at once, and sobbed with mouths full of candy and hands full of toys). How they ran to show one another the new treasures! How they peeped and tasted, pulled and pinched, until the air was full of queer noises, the floor covered with papers, and the little trees left bare of all but candles!

"I don't think heaven can be any gooder than this," sighed one small girl, as she looked about her in a blissful maze, holding her full apron with one hand, while she luxuriously carried sugar-plums to her mouth with the other.

"Is that a truly angel up there?" asked another, fascinated by the little white figure with the wreath on its shining hair, who in some mysterious way had been the cause of all this merry-making.

"I wish I dared to go and kiss her for this splendid party," said a lame child, leaning on her crutch, as she stood near the steps, wondering how it seemed to sit in a mother's lap, as Effie was doing, while she watched the happy scene before her.

Effie heard her, and remembering Tiny Tim, ran down and put her arms about the pale child, kissing the wistful face, as she said sweetly, "You may; but Mamma deserves the thanks. She did it all; I only dreamed about it."

Lame Katy felt as if "a truly angel" was embracing her, and could only stammer out her thanks, and touch her soft dress, until she stood in a crowd of blue gowns laughing as they held up their gifts for her to see and admire.

Mamma leaned down and whispered one word to the older girls; and suddenly they all took hands to dance round Effie, singing as they skipped.

It was a pretty sight, and the ladies found it hard to break up the happy revel; but it was late for small people, and too much fun is a mistake. So the girls fell into line, and marched before Effie and Mamma again, to say good-night with such grateful little faces that the eyes of those who looked grew dim with tears. Mamma kissed every one; and many a hungry childish heart felt as if the touch of those tender lips was their best gift. Effie shook so many small hands that her own tingled; and when Katy came she pressed a small doll into Effie's hand, whispering, "You didn't have a single present, and we had lots. Do keep that; it's the prettiest thing I got."

"I will," answered Effie, and held it fast until the last smiling face was gone, the surprise all over, and she safe in her own bed, too tired and happy for anything but sleep.

"Mamma, it was a beautiful surprise, and I thank you so much! I don't see how you ever did it; but I like it best of all the Christmases I ever had, and mean to make one every year. I had my splendid big present, and here is the little one to keep for love of poor Katy; so even that part of my wish came true."

And Effie fell asleep with a happy smile on her lips, her one humble gift still in her hand, and a new love for Christmas in her heart that never changed through a long life spent in doing good.

Christmas

HARRIET BEECHER STOWE

"Oh, dear! Christmas is coming in a fortnight, and I have got to think up presents for everybody!" said young Ellen Stuart, as she leaned languidly back in her chair. "Dear me, it's so tedious! Everybody has got everything that can be thought of."

"No, no," said her confidential adviser, Miss Lester, in a soothing tone. "You have means of buying everything you can fancy; and when every shop and store is glittering with all manner of splendors, you cannot surely be at a loss."

"Well, now, just listen. To begin with, there's Mamma. What can I get for her? I have thought of ever so many things. She has three card cases, four gold thimbles, two or three gold chains, two writing desks of different patterns; and then as to rings, brooches, boxes, and all other things, I should think she might be sick of the sight of them. I am sure I am," said she, languidly gazing on her white and jeweled fingers.

This view of the case seemed rather puzzling to the adviser, and there was silence for a few minutes, when Ellen, yawning, resumed:

"And then there's cousins Jane and Mary; I suppose they will be coming down on me with a whole load of presents; and Mrs. B. will send me something—she did last year; and then there's cousins William and Tom—I must get them something; and I would like to do it well enough, if I only knew what to get."

"Well," said Eleanor's aunt, who had been sitting quietly rattling her knitting needles during this speech, "it's a pity that you had not such a subject to practice on as I was when I was a girl. Presents did not fly about in those days as they do now. I remember, when I was ten years old, my father gave me a most marvelously ugly sugar dog for a Christmas gift, and I was perfectly delighted with it, the very idea of a present was so new to us."

"Dear aunt, how delighted I should be if I had any such fresh, unsophisticated body to get presents for! But to get and get for people that have more than they know what to do with now; to add pictures, books, and gilding when the centre tables are loaded with them now, and rings and jewels when they are a perfect drug! I wish myself that I were not sick, and sated, and tired with having everything in the world given me."

"Well, Eleanor," said her aunt, "if you really do want unsophisticated subjects to practice on, I can put you in the way of it. I can show you more than one family to whom you might seem to be a very good fairy, and where such gifts as you could give with all ease would seem like a magic dream."

"Why, that would really be worth while, aunt."

"Look over in that back alley," said her aunt. "You see those buildings?"

"That miserable row of shanties? Yes."

"Well, I have several acquaintances there who have never been tired of Christmas gifts or gifts of any other kind. I assure you, you could make quite a sensation over there."

"Well, who is there? Let us know."

"Do you remember Owen, that used to make your shoes?"

"Yes, I remember Owen something about him."

"Well, he has fallen into consumption, and cannot work any more; and he, and his wife, and three little children live in one of the rooms."

"How do they get along?"

"His wife takes in sewing sometimes, and sometimes goes out washing. Poor Owen! I was over there yesterday; he looks thin and wasted, and his wife was saying that he was parched with constant fever, and had very little appetite. She had, with great self-denial, and by restricting herself almost of necessary food, got him two or three oranges; and the poor fellow seemed so eager after them."

"Poor fellow!" said Eleanor, involuntarily.

"Now," said her aunt, "suppose Owen's wife should get up on Christmas morning and find at the door a couple of dozen of oranges, and some of those nice white grapes, such as you had at your party last week; don't you think it would make a sensation?"

"Why, yes, I think very likely it might; but who else, aunt? You spoke of a great many."

"Well, on the lower floor there is a neat little room, that is always kept perfectly trim and tidy; it belongs to a young couple who have nothing beyond the husband's day wages to live on. They are, nevertheless, as cheerful and chipper as a couple of wrens; and she is up and down half a dozen times a day, to help poor Mrs. Owen. She has a baby of her own about five months old, and of course does all the cooking, washing, and ironing for herself and husband; and yet, when Mrs. Owen goes out to wash, she takes her baby, and keeps it whole days for her."

"I'm sure she deserves that the good fairies should smile on her," said Eleanor; "one baby exhausts my stock of virtues very rapidly."

"But you ought to see her baby," said Aunt E.; "so plump, so rosy, and good-natured, and always as clean as a lily. This baby is a sort of household shrine; nothing is too sacred or too good for it; and I believe the little thrifty woman feels only one temptation to be extravagant, and that is to get some ornaments to adorn this little divinity."

"Why, did she ever tell you so?"

"No; but one day, when I was coming down stairs, the door of the room was partly open, and I saw a peddler there with open box. John, the husband, was standing with a little purple cap on his hand, which he was regarding mystified, admiring air, as if he didn't quite comprehend it, and trim little Mary gazing at it with longing eyes."

"'I think we might get it,' said John."

"'Oh, no,' said she, regretfully; 'yet I wish we could, it's so pretty!'"

"Say no more, aunt. I see the good fairy must pop a cap into the window on Christmas morning. Indeed, it shall be done. How they will wonder where it came from, and talk about it for months to come!"

"Well, then," continued her aunt, "in the next street to ours there is a miserable building, that looks as if it were just going to topple over; and away up in the third story, old women. They are both nearly on to ninety. I was in there day before yesterday. One of them is constantly confined to her bed with rheumatism; the other, weak and feeble, with failing sight and trembling hands, totters about, her only helper; and they are entirely dependent on charity."

"Can't they do anything? Can't they knit?" said Eleanor.

"You are young and strong, Eleanor, and have quick eyes, and nimble fingers; how long would it take you to knit a pair of stockings?"

"I?" said Eleanor. "What an idea! I never tried, but I think I could get a pair done in a week, perhaps."

"And if somebody gave you twenty-five cents for them, and out of this you had to get food, and pay room rent, and buy coal for your fire, and oil for your lamp—"

"Stop, aunt, for pity's sake!"

"Well, I will stop; but they can't; they must pay so much every month for that miserable shell to live in, or be turned into the street. The meal and flour that some kind person sends goes off for them just as it does for others, and they must get more or starve; and coal is now scarce and high priced."

"O aunt, I'm quite convinced, I'm sure; don't run me down and annihilate me with all these terrible realities. What shall I do to play good fairy to these old women?"

"If you give me full power, Eleanor, I will put up a basket to be sent to them that will give them something to remember all winter."

"Oh, certainly I will. Let me see if I can't think of something myself."

"Well, Eleanor, suppose, then, some fifty or sixty years hence, if you were old, and your father, and mother, and aunts, and uncles, now so thick around you, lay cold and silent in so many graves—you have somehow got away off to a strange city, where you were never known—you live in a miserable garret, where snow blows at night through the cracks, and the fire is very apt to go out in the cold cracked stove—you sit crouching over the dying embers the evening before Christmas—nobody to speak to you, nobody to care for you, except another poor old soul who lies moaning in bed. Now, what would you like to have sent you?"

"O aunt, what a dismal picture!"

"And yet, Ella, all poor, forsaken old women are made of young girls, who expected it in their youth as little as you do, perhaps."

"Say no more, aunt. I'll buy—let me see—a comfortable warm shawl for each of these poor women; and I'll send them—oh, some tea—nothing goes down with old women like tea; and I'll make John wheel some coal over to them; and, aunt, it would not be a very bad thought to send them a new stove. I remember, the other day, when mamma was pricing stoves, I saw some such nice ones for two or three dollars."

"For a new hand, Ella, you work up the idea very well," said her aunt.

"But how much ought I to give, for any one case, to these women, say?"

"How much did you give last year for nay single Christmas present?"

"Why, six or seven dollars for some; those elegant souvenirs were seven dollars; that ring I gave Mrs. B. was twenty."

"And do you suppose Mrs. B. was any happier for it?"

"Not, really, I don't think she cared much about it; but I had to give her something, because she had sent me something the year before, and I did not want to send a paltry present to one in her circumstances."

"Then, Ella, give the same to any poor, distressed, suffering creature who really needs it, and see in how many forms of good such a sum will appear. That one hard, cold, glittering ring, that now cheers nobody, and means nothing, that you give because you must, and she takes because she must, might, if broken up into smaller sums, send real warm and heartfelt gladness through a cold and cheerless dwelling, through many an aching heart."

"You are getting to be an orator, aunt; but don't you approve of Christmas presents, among friends and equals?"

"Yes, indeed," said her aunt, fondly stroking her head. "I have had some Christmas presents that did me a world of good—a little bookmark, for instance, that a certain niece of mine worked for me, with wonderful secrecy, three years ago, when she was not a young lady with a Christmas purse full of money—that bookmark was a true Christmas present; and my young couple across the way are plotting a profound surprise to each other on Christmas morning. John has contrived, by an hour of extra work every night, to lay by enough to get Mary a new calico dress; and she, poor soul, has bargained away the only thing in the jewelry line she ever possessed, to be laid out on a new hat for him.

"I know, too, a washerwoman who has a poor lame boy—a patient, gentle little fellow—who has lain quietly for weeks and months in his little crib, and his mother is going to give him a splendid Christmas present."

"What is it, pray?"

"A whole orange! Don't laugh. She will pay ten whole cents for it; for it shall be none of your common oranges, but a picked one of the very best going! She has put by the money, a cent at a time, for a whole month; and nobody knows which will be happiest in it, Willie or his mother. These are such Christmas presents as I like to think of—gifts coming of love, and tending to produce love; these are the appropriate gifts of the day."

"But don't you think that it's right for those who have money to give expensive presents, supposing always, as you say, they are given from real affection."

"Sometimes, undoubtedly. The Saviour did not condemn her who broken an alabaster box of ointment—very precious—simply as a proof of love, even although the suggestion was made, 'This might have been sold for three hundred pence, and given to the poor.' I have thought he would regard with sympathy the fond efforts which human love sometimes makes to express itself by gifts, the rarest and most costly. How I rejoiced with all my heart, when Charles Elton gave his poor mother that splendid Chinese shawl and gold watch! Because I knew they came from the very fullness of his heart to a mother that he could not do too much for—a mother that has done and suffered everything for him. In some such cases, when resources are ample, a costly gift seems to have a graceful appropriateness; but I cannot approve of it if it exhausts all the means of doing for the poor; it is better, then, to give a simple offering, and to do something for those who really need it."

Eleanor looked thoughtful; her aunt laid down her knitting, and said, in a tone of gentle seriousness, "Whose birth does Christmas commemorate, Ella?"

"Our Saviour's, certainly, aunt."

"Yes," said her aunt. "And when and how was he born? In a stable! Laid in a manger; thus born, that in all ages he might be known as the brother and friend of the poor. And surely, it seems but appropriate to commemorate his birthday by a special remembrance of the lowly, the poor, the outcast, and distressed; and if Christ should come back to our city on a Christmas day, where should we think it most appropriate to his character to find him? Would he be carrying splendid gifts to splendid dwellings, or would he be gliding about in the cheerless haunts of the desolate, the poor, the forsaken, and the sorrowful?"

And here the conversation ended.

"What sort of Christmas presents is Ella buying?" said Cousin Tom, as the servant handed in a portentous-looking package, which had just been rung in at the door."

"Let's open it," said saucy Will. "Upon my word, two great gray blanket shawls! These must be for you and me, Tom! And what's this? A great bolt of cotton flannel and gray yarn stockings!"

The door bell rang again, and the servant brought in another bulky parcel, and deposited it on the marble-topped centre table.

"What's here?" said Will, cutting the cord. "Whew! A perfect nest of packages! Oolong tea! oranges! grapes! white sugar! Bless me, Ella must be going to housekeeping!"

"Or going crazy!" said Tom; "and on my word," said he, looking out the window, "there's a drayman ringing at our door, with a stove, with a teakettle set in the top of it!"

"Ella's cook stove, of course," said Will; and just at this moment the young lady entered, with her purse hanging gracefully over her hand.

"No, boys, you are too bad!" she exclaimed, as each of the mischievous youngsters was gravely marching up and down, attired in a gray shawl.

"Didn't you get them for us? We thought you did," said both.

"Ella, I want some of that cotton flannel, to make me a pair of pantaloons," said Tom.

"I say, Ella," said Will, "when are you going to housekeeping? Your cooking stove is standing down in the street; 'pon my word, John is loading some coal on the dray with it."

"Ella, isn't that going to be sent to my office?" said Tom; "do you know I do so languish for a new stove with a teakettle in the top, to heat a fellow's shaving-water!"

Just then, another ring at the door, and the grinning servant handed in a small brown paper parcel for Miss Ella. Tom made a dive at it, and tearing off the brown paper, discovered a jaunty little purple velvet cap, with silver tassels.

"My cap, as I live!" said he; "only I shall have to wear it on my thumb, instead of my head—too small entirely," said he, shaking his head gravely.

"Come, you saucy boys," said Aunt E., entering briskly. "What are you teasing Ella for?"

"Why, do you see this lot of things, aunt! What in the world is Ella going to do with them?"

"Oh, I know!"

"You know! Then I can guess, aunt, it is some of your charitable works. You are going to make a juvenile Lady Bountiful of El, eh?"

Ella, who had colored to the roots of her hair at the exposé of her very unfashionable Christmas preparations, now took heart, and bestowed a very gentle and salutary little cuff on the saucy head that still wore the purple cap, and then hastened to gather up her various purchases.

"Laugh, away," said she, gayly; "and a good many others will laugh, too, over these things. I got them to make people laugh—people that are not in the habit of laughing!"

"Well, well, I see into it," said Will; "and I tell you I think right well of the idea, too. There are worlds of money wasted, at this time of year, in getting things that nobody wants, and nobody cares for after they are got; and I am glad, for my part, that you are going to get up a variety in this line; in fact, I should like to give you one of these stray leaves to help on," said he, dropping a ten dollar note into her paper. "I like to encourage girls to think of something besides breastpins and sugar candy."

But our story spins on too long. If anybody wants to see the results of Ella's first attempts at good fairyism, they can call at the doors of two or three old buildings on Christmas morning, and they shall hear all about it.

Joseph's Letter Home

Dr. Ralph F. Wilson

Dear Mom,

We're still in Bethlehem—Mary and I and little Jesus.

There were lots of things I couldn't talk to you about last summer. You wouldn't have believed me then, but maybe I can tell you now. I hope you can understand.

You know, Mom, I've always loved Mary. You and Dad used to tease me about her when she was still a girl. She and her brothers used to play on our street. Our families got together for supper. But the hardest day of my life came scarcely a year ago when I was twenty and she only fifteen. You remember that day, don't you?

The trouble started after we were betrothed and signed the marriage agreement at our engagement. That same spring Mary had left abruptly to visit her old cousin Elizabeth in Judea. She was gone three whole months. After she got back, people started wondering out loud if she were pregnant.

It was cloudy the day when I finally confronted her with the gossip.

"Mary," I asked at last, "are you going to have a baby?"

Her clear brown eyes met mine. She nodded.

I didn't know what to say. "Who?" I finally stammered.

Mom, Mary and I had never acted improperly—even after we were betrothed.

Mary looked down. "Joseph," she said. "There's no way I can explain. You couldn't understand. But I want you to know I've never cared for anyone but you." She got up, gently took my hands in hers, kissed each of them as if it were the last time she would ever do that again, and then turned toward home. She must have been dying inside.

I know I was.

The rest of the day I stumbled through my chores. It's a wonder I didn't hurt myself in the woodshop. At first I was angry and pounded out my frustrations on the doorframe I was making. My thoughts whirled so fast I could hardly keep my mind on my work. At last I decided just to end the marriage contract with a quiet divorce. I loved her too much to make a public scene.

I couldn't talk to you. Or anyone, for that matter. I went to bed early and tried to sleep. Her words came to me over and over. "I've never cared for anyone but you—I've never cared for anyone but you—" How I wished I could believe her!

I don't know when I finally fell asleep. Mom, I had a dream from God. An angel of the Lord came to me. His words pulsated through my mind so intensely I can remember them as if it were yesterday.

"Joseph, son of David," he thundered, "do not fear to take Mary home as your wife, because what is conceived in her is from the Holy Spirit."

I couldn't believe my ears, Mom. This was the answer! The angel continued, "She will give birth to a son, and you are to give Him the name Jesus, because He will save His people from their sins."

The angel gripped my shoulders with his huge hands. For a long moment his gaze pierced deep within me. Just as he turned to go, I think I saw a smile on his shining face.

I sat bolt upright in bed. No sleep after that! I tossed about for a while, going over the words in my mind. Then I got up and dressed quietly so I wouldn't wake you.

I must have walked for miles beneath the moonless sky. Stars pricked the blackness like a thousand tiny pinpoints. A warm breeze blew on my face.

I sang to the Lord, Mom. Yes, me, singing, if you can imagine that. I couldn't contain my joy. I told Him that I would take Mary and care for her. I told Him I would watch over her—and the child—no matter what anyone said.

I got back just as the sun kissed the hilltops. I don't know if you still recall that morning, Mom. I can see it in my mind's eye as if it were yesterday. You were feeding the chickens, surprised to see me out. Remember?

"Sit down," I said to you. "I've got to tell you something." I took your arm and helped you find a seat on the big rock out back. "Mom," I said, "I'm going to bring Mary home as my wife. Can you help make a place for her things?"

You were silent a long time. "You do know what they're saying, don't you, son?" you said at last, your eyes glistening.

"Yes, Mom, I know."

Your voice started to rise. "If your father were still alive, he'd have some words, I'll tell you. Going about like that before you are married. Disgracing the family and all. You . . . you and Mary ought to be ashamed of yourselves!"

You'd never have believed me if I'd tried to explain, so I didn't. Unless the angel had spoken to you, you'd have laughed me to scorn.

"Mom, this is the right thing to do," I said.

And then I started talking to you as if I were the head of the house. "When she comes I don't want one word to her about it," I sputtered. "She's your daughter-in-law, you'll respect her. She'll need your help if she's to bear the neighbors' wagging tongues!"

I'm sorry, Mom. You didn't deserve that. You started to get up in a huff.

"Mom," I murmured, "I need you." You took my hand and got to your feet, but the fire was gone from your eyes.

"You can count on me, Joseph," you told me with a long hug. And you meant it. I never heard another word. No bride could hope for a better mother-in-law than you those next few months.

Mom, after I left you I went up the road to Mary's house and knocked. Her mother glared at me as she opened the door. Loudly, harshly she called into the house, "It's Joseph!" almost spitting out my name as she said it.

My little Mary came out cringing, as if she expected me to give her the back of my hand, I suppose. Her eyes were red and puffy. I can just imagine what her parents had said.

We walked a few steps from the house. She looked so young and afraid. "Pack your things, Mary," I told her gently. "I'm taking you home to be my wife."

"Joseph!" She hugged me as tight as she could. Mom, I didn't realize she was so strong.

I told her what I'd been planning. "We'll go to Rabbi Ben-Ezer's house this week and have him perform the ceremony."

I know it was awfully sudden, Mom, but I figured the sooner we got married the better it would be for her, and me, and the baby.

"Mary, even if our friends don't come, at least you and I can pledge our love before God." I paused. "I think my mom will be there. And maybe your friend Rebecca would come if her dad will let her. How about your parents?"

I could feel Mary's tiny frame shuddering as she sobbed quietly.

"Mary," I said. I could feel myself speaking more boldly. "No matter what anyone says about you, I'm proud you're going to be my wife. I'm going to take good care of you. I've promised God that."

She looked up.

I lowered my voice. "I had a dream last night, Mary. I saw an angel. I know."

The anguish that had gripped her face vanished. She was radiant as we turned away from the house and began to walk up the hill together.

Just then her mother ran out into the yard. "Wait," she called. She must have been listening from behind the door. Tears were streaming down her cheeks.

"I'll get your father," she called, almost giddy with emotion. "We," she cried as she gathered up her skirts. "We," she shouted as she began to run to find her husband. "We . . . are going to have a wedding!"

That's how it was, Mom. Thanks for being there for us. I'll write again soon.

Love, Joseph